From Randy Johnson to Dallas Braden

No-hitters Beyond the Box Score
Volume I

Written by
Kevin Hurd

Edited by
Bruce Hurd

From Randy Johnson to Dallas Braden
No-hitters Beyond the Box Score
Volume I

Copyright © 2024 Kevin Hurd

All rights reserved. No part of this publication may be reproduced, distributed, or transmitted in any form or by any means, including photocopying, recording, or other electronic or mechanical methods, without the prior written permission of the publisher, except in the case of brief quotations embodied in critical reviews and certain other noncommercial uses permitted by copyright law. For permission requests, write to the author at the address below.

ISBN: 979-8-9902594-0-9 (E-book)
ISBN: 979-8-9902594-1-6 (Paperback)
ISBN: 979-8-9902594-2-3 (Hardcover)

Library of Congress Control Number: 2024918733

Cover design by Cherie Fox at www.cheriefox.com

Printed in the United States of America

Kevin Hurd
P.O.Box 1272
Aledo, TX 76008

For more information on this book, the author, and book-related programs and events, please contact me at kevinhurd@sbcglobal.net

To my parents, Ann and Walt Hurd,
who were always there when I needed them

And to my lovely wife Doris, and my two beautiful daughters
Christine and Catherine, who have supported me throughout my life

Table of Contents

Acknowledgements ix
Introduction xi
Chapter 1: Jim Maloney: A Very Long No-Hitter 1
    Table 1-1. Individual No-hitters with Eight or More Baserunners 3
    Table 1-2. Extra Inning Individual No-Hitters 5
    Table 1-3. Pitchers With the Most One-Hitters 8
    Table 1-4. Reds Highest Game Scores 11
    Table 1-5. Reds Highest Game Scores of 10 innings or less 13
    Table 1-6. Best Pitchers Born in Cuba 17
    Jim Maloney Interview 21
    Johnny Edwards Interview 23
Chapter 2: Juan Nieves: Milwaukee's First No-Hitter 26
    Table 2-1. Brewer Defensive Gems during Nieves No-Hitter 28
    Table 2-2. Milwaukee Brewers Longest Winning Streaks 30
    Table 2-3. Longest Winning Streaks to Start a Season 32
    Table 2-4. Milwaukee Brewers Longest Losing Streaks 34
    Table 2-5. Longest Consecutive Game Hitting Streaks (1900-2021) 36
    Table 2-6. Brewers Highest Game Scores 38
    Juan Nieves Interview 42
    Bill Schroeder Interview 45
Chapter 3: Dave Stieb: Fifth Time's a Charm 52
    Table 3-1. Dave Stieb's No-Hitter Attempts Broken Up in the Ninth Inning .. 55
    Table 3-2. A World Series Championship and an Olympic Gold Medal ... 56
    Table 3-3. Best Pitchers of the 1980s 58
    Table 3-4. Blue Jays Highest Game Scores 59
    Dave Stieb Interview excerpts 62
    Pat Borders Interview 69

Chapter 4: Randy Johnson: A Perfect 40-year-old 73
    Table 4-1. Oldest Perfect Game Pitchers 75
    Table 4-2. Highest Negative Win Differential Between No-Hitter Teams . . . 77
    Table 4-3. Winningest Pitchers on the Worst Teams in Baseball. 79
    Table 4-4. Top Ten Pitchers with Two or More No-hitters 81
    Table 4-5. Best Pitchers of the 2000s (2000-2009). 83
    Table 4-6. Mariners Highest Game Scores 85
    Randy Johnson Interview. 88
    Robby Hammock Interview 94
Chapter 5: Ed Halicki: Ho-Ho Throws a No-No 99
    Table 5-1. San Francisco Giants Season Records from 1972-1981 101
    Table 5-2. Giants Highest Game Scores 105
    Table 5-3. Giants Highest Game Scores of 10 innings or less. 107
    Table 5-4. Tallest Players in Major League History 111
    Table 5-5. Best Pitchers Born in the Dominican Republic 112
    Ed Halicki Interview 117
Chapter 6: Andy Hawkins: No-hitter Taken Away. 123
    Table 6-1. No-hitters Lost in Games Ended
        After Eight and a Half Innings. 125
    Table 6-2. New York Yankees Sub-.500 Seasons 130
    Table 6-3. Yankees Highest Game Scores. 131
    Table 6-4. Yankees Highest Game Scores of 10 innings or less 134
    Table 6-5. Best Pitchers of the 1990s 137
    Table 6-6. Best Pitchers Born in Panama 138
    Andy Hawkins Interview 141
Chapter 7: Bud Smith: Putting on a Show. 145
    Table 7-1. Youngest Pitchers to Throw a No-Hitter 147
    Table 7-2. Fewest Wins after Pitching a No-Hitter 148
    Table 7-3. Teams No-hit Twice in the Same Season 152
    Table 7-4. Longest Active Franchise No-hit Droughts 154
    Bud Smith interview excerpts. 156
Chapter 8: Dallas Braden: Mother's Day Perfection 167
    Table 8-1. Game Scores for Perfect Games. 171
    Table 8-2. Longest Team Streaks Without Being No-Hit 174
    Table 8-3. Perfect Game Pitcher-Catcher JAWS rankings. 177

Table 8-4. Youngest Perfect Game Pitchers 180
Dallas Braden Interview. 181
Chapter 9: Harvey Haddix: 12 Perfect Innings 187
Table 9-1. No-hitters Broken Up After the Ninth Inning. 190
Table 9-2. Pirates Highest Game Scores. 193
Table 9-3. Pirates Highest Game Scores of 10 Innings or Less. 196
Table 9-4. Best Pitchers of the 1950s 200
Chapter 10: Nolan Ryan: Best for Last 203
Table 10-1. Oldest Pitchers to Throw a No-hitter 205
Table 10-2. Nolan Ryan's Seven No-hitters 206
Table 10-3. Longest Time Between First and Last No-hitters 207
Table 10-4. Pitchers with No-hitters for Two or More Teams 208
Table 10-5. Senators and Rangers Highest Game Scores 210
Table 10-6. Colt .45s and Astros Highest Game Scores 213
Chapter 11: Max Scherzer: Best No-Hitter of All Time?. 220
Table 11-1. Major League Baseball's Highest Nine-Inning Game Scores . . . 222
Table 11-2. Highest Game Scores Ever Recorded. 225
Table 11-3. Expos and Nationals Highest Game Scores 226
Table 11-4. Best Pitchers of the 2010s 229
Table 11-5. Pitchers with Fewest Games Between No-hitters 230
Table 11-6. Best Pitchers Born in Nicaragua 232
Chapter 12: Hideo Nomo: Rocky Mountain High 234
Table 12-1. Top Nine-Inning No-Hitters by Composite
  Batting Average (BAc). 237
Table 12-2. Dodgers Highest Game Scores. 239
Table 12-3. Dodgers Highest Game Scores of 10 innings or less 243
Table 12-4. Best Pitchers Born in Japan. 248
Table 12-5. Best Pitchers Born in Mexico 250
Table 12-6. Best Pitchers Born in South Korea. 253
Conclusion 257
Appendix I: Career Ranking of All No-hit Pitchers. 261
About the Author 275

Acknowledgements

This two-volume set is the result of an entire team of dedicated people who put in countless hours helping me compile information, research, and write this book. Specifically, the three who helped me the most were:

My brother (fellow Air Force aviator and coach for first-time authors) Bruce Hurd, who provided detailed content editing and publishing expertise so my book would be informative, insightful, and entertaining.

My friend and teammate on the KKUP Klones recreational league softball team Kevin McCaffrey, who conducted in-depth interviews of Hall of Famer Randy Johnson, multi-season All-Star Dave Stieb, rookie sensation Bud Smith, and renowned Milwaukee Brewers broadcaster – and no-hit catcher – Bill Schroeder

My friend from grade school and junior high school Rob Adams, who inspired me to write this book and conducted an in-depth interview of perfect game pitcher and highly talented Oakland A's broadcaster Dallas Braden. Rob came up with the idea for me to write about no-hit games. Without his initial push, this book wouldn't have happened.

With eternal gratitude to all the pitchers and catchers who graciously provided their time and permission to be interviewed for this book. I cannot thank you enough (listed in order of appearance): Jim Maloney, Johnny Edwards, Juan Nieves, Bill Schroeder, Dave Stieb, Pat Borders, Randy Johnson, Robby Hammock, Ed Halicki, Andy Hawkins, Bud Smith, Dallas Braden, Buck Rodgers, Don Werner, Mike Heath, Ron Karkovice, Terry Steinbach, Eli Whiteside, Miguel Montero, and Koyie Hill.

I would also like to extend my sincere gratitude to numerous organizations and websites that provided detailed and authoritative information on these players, teams, and games referenced and analyzed in this book: baseball-reference.com, stathead.com, the Society for Advanced Baseball Research (SABR), nonohitters.com, and the Baseball Almanac. This book would not have been possible without your generous contributions.

Introduction

I let out something between a yell and a scream as I saw all kinds of bad things happening. It was déjà vu at the worst possible moment. My wife and oldest daughter came running into the room, thinking I'd had a heart attack. I hadn't. As a typically subdued husband and father, what shocked them was simply the exasperation and deep-seated fear of a long-suffering Giants fan coming out.

There were two outs in the bottom of the ninth inning in the seventh and deciding game of the 2014 World Series between my beloved San Francisco Giants and the American League Champion Kansas City Royals. The Giants were leading 3-2 and Kansas City left fielder Alex Gordon was at the plate with a count of no balls and one strike. Giants ace Madison Bumgarner – who was finishing a legendary World Series performance – was on the mound.

The Giants just needed to retire Gordon and the championship was theirs. It was one of the most exciting World Series finishes in history. Gordon hit a line drive to left field on the next pitch. As the ball went past left fielder Juan Perez and skipped by center fielder Gregor Blanco, I felt like I was watching a train wreck unfold right in front of my eyes.

The two fielders fumbled around with the ball. I envisioned a complete collapse as Gordon raced around the bases, threatening to tie the game in one debacle of a play. Even though the Giants had recently won two championships, they also had a long history of collapsing at the worst possible moment. I could barely watch what was unfolding in front of my eyes.

I have been a baseball fan since August 1965 when I was eight years old. I lived in Los Altos, a suburb of San Francisco, and my Giants were doing well. They were in an exciting pennant race with the "evil" Los Angeles Dodgers. Of course, as I've grown older, I realize Dodger fans may be misguided, but they're not "evil." To borrow a line from that great philosopher Mitt Romney, "(Dodger fans) are people too."

I was such a fanatic that when an extremely violent incident occurred between Giants pitcher Juan Marichal and Dodgers catcher John Roseboro mid-game on August 22 – Marichal viciously hit Roseboro on the head with his bat – I thought Baseball Commissioner Ford Frick was being really unfair by suspending Marichal for eight days. This would equate to the All-Star pitcher missing two starts in the midst of a heated pennant race. Of course, if I had been a Dodgers fan, I would have insisted that Marichal at least have a "fair trial." This would have meant having a firing squad walking into the courtroom before the verdict was rendered, handing a blindfold and cigarette to Marichal, proceeding to the "Execution Yard," and then finishing the entire process within five minutes of the already decided verdict. I was a fanatic.

From 1965-1969 I played Little League baseball. I was in the "Midget League" (yes, that was its actual name) from 1965-1966 where I went from being a bad player at the beginning to an All-Star in my second year. I was in the "Majors" from ages 10-12. I wasn't much of a hitter, but I was a good outfielder, which was a huge asset in Little League. I could actually catch the ball with regularity!

I bring this up because the first two years I played in the Majors against a pitcher (let's call him Harvey) on one of the other teams. Harvey was athletically coordinated well beyond his years and totally dominated all of us. We played 15 games a season and no pitcher could throw more than one game per week. This meant Harvey would pitch 7-8 games a year and they were all no-hitters! He did the same thing the next year.

In another game during my 12-year-old year, one of our pitchers was heavily congratulated after we won. I asked what was going on. I found out he had thrown a no-hitter. Nobody had talked about it in our dugout. That's when I first realized the superstition of not talking to a pitcher as he's throwing a no-hitter goes all the way down to the Little League level.

From 1965-1983, I followed baseball very closely. After graduating from California Polytechnic State University in San Luis Obispo (commonly referred to as "Cal Poly"), I went to Air Force Officer Training School in 1984 and was commissioned as a second lieutenant. I then went to flight school and became a navigator in the RC-135 Rivet Joint, a large aircraft used primarily for strategic reconnaissance during the Cold War. After I left active duty in 1992 as a captain, I joined the Air Force Reserve as a full-time technician where I performed the same job as I did on active duty, minus all the moving around.

As I was promoted, I assumed more responsibility, including developing and disseminating war plans and performing other staff duties. I also was called upon to deploy and fly in support of the 1990-1991 Gulf War and the 1998-1999 Kosovo War. I retired from the Air Force in 2014 at the rank of lieutenant colonel. After the Air Force, I was employed in support of security operations at the U.S. Western Currency Facility (WCF) in Fort Worth until just recently. The WCF is one of two facilities in the United States that prints paper money. The WCF is the only facility that prints $100 bills.

While I was in the Air Force, I was deployed frequently and flew long missions. I also got married and began raising a family. This meant I didn't follow baseball nearly as closely as when I was ages 8-26 and had time to do that sort of thing. Even so, I did follow the 1989 World Series, although it sucked, with the Oakland A's crushing my beloved Giants in four straight games. Much worse, the Loma Prieta earthquake devastated the Bay Area – it even happened on national TV right as the third game was about to begin. My parents and one of my brothers and my sister still lived in the South Bay. None of them were hurt, thankfully.

The result was that I didn't pay too much attention to baseball until Barry Bonds was chasing Mark McGwire's home run record in 2001, and the Giants made it to the 2002 World Series. The team did much better this time, even though they lost to the Anaheim Angels in a heart-breaking seven-game series. From that point, I was far more engaged in following baseball and was rewarded (so to speak) when the Giants won three World Series championships from 2010-2014.

Besides being energized by the Giants' success during that golden period of the early 2010s, I also became fascinated by no-hitters. For those who aren't familiar, a no-hitter is considered the pinnacle of pitching success. For nine innings or more, a pitcher retires an opposing team's batters without allowing any of them to reach base by getting a hit. It's a rare accomplishment that places a pitcher in an elite group of major league professionals who have achieved that status.

From the beginning of the modern era of baseball in 1900 until 2021 there have only been 261 no-hitters, equating to slightly more than two per season. There have even been seasons that had zero no-hitters. Of course, a small subset of no-hitters represents the epitome of pitching perfection: the perfect game. A perfect game is one in which a pitcher retires 27 hitters in a row, with none of them reaching base. From 1900 to 2021, only 21 perfect games were thrown.

In 2014, both San Francisco's Tim Lincecum and Los Angeles's Clayton Kershaw threw no-hitters. This piqued my interest. That season, I was fascinated to hear that legendary Dodger announcer Vin Scully had personally covered 21 no-hitters, an extraordinarily high number of all no-hitters ever pitched. I also discovered the incredible baseball website baseball-reference.com, which allowed me to do independent research. I was hooked. I spent days researching different aspects of baseball, with a particular focus on no-hitters.

Ever since I've been a baseball fan, I have been fascinated with no-hit games. Part of it is that there really isn't really an equivalent in the other major team sports in North America: football, basketball, and hockey. To begin with, throwing a no-hitter is a rare occurrence. With only 261 no-hitters thrown between 1900-2021, simple math indicates that averages out to slightly more than two no-hitters each year; although there were only 16 major league baseball teams when the American League began in 1901; whereas now there are 30. As a result, there are more no-hitters in recent years because there are nearly twice as many games played.

A comparable performance in other team sports roughly equates to a quarterback throwing five touchdown passes in a game, a basketball player scoring 50 points in a game, or a hockey player scoring three goals in a game. Like a no-hitter, these are all rare and extremely impressive accomplishments. The difference is that in each of the other sports, these peak performances are almost always accomplished by star players. For example, more than 80% of the NBA players who scored 50 points or more in a game were members of the NBA Hall of Fame or were All-Stars. In football, more than 19% of the quarterbacks who have had five-touchdown games were Hall of Famers and an additional 62% were selected to be in the Pro Bowl. Understandably, it is the stars of the game who achieve such lofty goals.

Yet, in baseball, the pinnacle of a pitcher's performance – throwing a no-hitter – is accomplished by pitchers within a wide range of career achievements. Pitchers who are journeymen or replacement-level players accomplish almost half of no-hitters. Sometimes, it is especially astounding because a pitcher with a struggling team can achieve greatness by throwing a no-hitter against a far superior squad. It is the magic of knowing that any player, in any game, against any given team, can be nearly perfect as they have their time in the spotlight.

This is part of the magic of baseball to me. Unlike other sports, it is not just the great players who can reach the pinnacle of achievement. The pitcher who is thrilled just to be part of a major league team – even if for a little while – can do this, as well. And behind each game is a thrilling story full of excitement and hard work in pursuit of a lofty goal. I am excited and honored to be able to tell their stories.

This book is about the pitchers and catchers who participated in what is often recalled as the most memorable game of their professional careers. Their stories are far more than a statistical analysis, although statistics help tell their stories, and this book is loaded with insightful analysis. Their stories are best told by them. What led up to their crowning achievement? What was working for them that day, and what wasn't? What do they remember most? And what have they been doing since their remarkable achievement?

As part of my years-long research for this book, I reached out to all living pitchers and catchers who threw or caught a no-hitter. I asked each of them for an interview that would help me answer these questions about them. Twenty of them were gracious enough to allow me or one of my colleagues (Kevin McCaffrey and Rob Adams) to interview them. The players' generous and revealing insights were fascinating and deeply appreciated. The players who granted interviews ranged from Hall of Famers (Randy Johnson) and perennial All-Stars (Jim Maloney and Dave Stieb) to journeyman pitchers like Bud Smith of the St. Louis Cardinals, a player who was out of Major League baseball less than a year after his no-hitter as a 21-year-old rookie. They all have wonderful, magnificent stories to tell.

While the focus of this book is rightfully on the players involved in these remarkable no-hitters and the stories associated with those games, a myriad of questions arose as I dug into the research and analysis behind these events. One important question I asked myself surrounded the big question of "which no-hitter was the greatest game ever pitched?" This is not a simple question to answer, yet I believe I've narrowed it down to five prominent candidates:

- Was it Max Scherzer, who struck out 17 batters as he threw a no-hitter against the playoff-bound Mets in 2015?
- Was it Hideo Nomo, who shut down one of the greatest-hitting teams of all-time – the 1996 Colorado Rockies – in their notoriously hitter-friendly stadium in Denver?

- Was it 40-year-old Randy Johnson, who threw a perfect game for a truly terrible Arizona team in 2004 against the Atlanta Braves, one of that era's baseball dynasties?
- Was it Harvey Haddix, who threw a perfect game for 12 innings in 1959 against the defending two-time National League Champion Milwaukee Braves, only to lose in the 13th inning?
- Was it Sandy Koufax, who threw his fourth no-hitter in four years, a perfect game in 1965 against a Cubs lineup that featured three future Hall of Famers?

Each of these five candidates is discussed in this book, with separate chapters featuring in-depth discussion on the first four games mentioned.

Other questions arose as I dug into each of these games. What are the best games each team has pitched over the years? Who are the oldest and youngest players to participate in a no-hitter? Who are the most accomplished no-hit pitchers and catchers, and who are the least accomplished? Who's the best Japanese (or Dominican or Cuban or …) pitcher to play in the Major Leagues? Who are the best pitchers of the 1980s (or 1950s or 2010s or …). These questions and many more are researched and presented within the chapters of this book.

Of course, there is a balance between telling the fascinating story of these games and presenting so much statistical analysis that the reader's eyes glaze over. While I know I can't be everything to everyone, my goal throughout this book is to keep the casual fan engaged by telling a compelling story. Yet, at the same time, I strive to provide the avid baseball fan with a wealth of information, analysis, and food for thought that won't be found elsewhere. I hope I have accomplished both.

Also, I want to describe the structure of the book. As I neared the end, it became clear that I had to either publish an enormous book that would be more than twice the size of a lengthy novel, or I could divide it up into two volumes. I chose the latter. While there is in-depth analysis and compelling storytelling throughout both volumes, Volume I contains all the pitcher interviews and any catcher interviews associated with those pitchers. I've also analyzed some additional no-hitters to answer the question of which game could be considered the greatest.

Volume II contains game stories associated with all the remaining catcher interviews and analysis of some of the more remarkable no-hitters. Volume II also addresses the subject of which is the most unlikely no-hitter and other topics. Because the cutoff date for our statistical analysis was the 2021 season, I added a chapter in Volume II that talks about the no-hitters thrown in the 2022 and 2023 seasons and what we learned from them.

Each chapter and table within a chapter is designed as a stand-alone story. The reader doesn't need to have read previous chapters to be able to enjoy and understand chapters and statistical tables near the end of the book. They are all self-contained so that readers can jump to whatever topic interests them without being concerned about not having been exposed to background material that is presented earlier. As a baseball fan, I fully understand the attraction of being able to simply enjoy those areas of interest that relate to my favorite players and teams without having to sort through other background information.

I have made every attempt to structure my information tables using the same basic rules throughout the book. Each table has a paragraph describing the methodology used in constructing the table and a legend that defines terms within the table. Table entries that are "ties" are identified as such and are typically listed with the game that occurred earliest ahead of ones that came afterward.

Finally, I want to acknowledge an article that provided unintentional inspiration to me at a time when this book was only a vague idea in the back of my mind. It was written by award-winning sportswriter Jim Murray, of the Los Angeles Times. I was living in Southern California at the time and the premise of the article was that pitchers who threw no-hitters didn't deserve the recognition they received because most no-hit pitchers weren't very good to begin with. To Murray, throwing a no-hitter was all a matter of luck.

I was incensed. I felt he was completely off base with his flip analysis, and I decided to research this on my own. That was the start of my wonderful educational journey that has ended here, with my two-volume analysis focused on the fascinating world of no-hit baseball. I hope you enjoy reading it as much as I enjoyed putting it together.

Chapter 1

Jim Maloney:
A Very Long No-Hitter

August 19, 1965
Jim Maloney throws a 10-inning no-hitter with
10 walks, 12 strikeouts, and 187 pitches

"It was unbelievable. He walked 10 batters and every time I looked up it seemed like there was a man in scoring position. He was so wild, I had to do everything just to block the ball. He threw 187 pitches. He was worn out after the game, and I was right there with him."
Cincinnati catcher Johnny Edwards describing Jim Maloney's no-hit efforts (Interview with Gregory Wolf, "August 19, 1965: Reds' Jim Maloney tosses 10-inning no-hitter — with 187 pitches, 10 walks, and 12 strikeouts," *SABR.org*, March 7, 2017).

"I think this was the biggest game of my career. I knew I had the no-hitter going all the way."
Jim Maloney describing his in-game confidence ("Reds' Ace Fans 12 in 1-to-0 Victory," *New York Times*, August 20, 1965).

"When trouble loomed — and there was plenty — he called on his resourcefulness to wriggle free."
Sportswriter Bill Ford describing Maloney's achievement ("000 000 000 0," *Cincinnati Enquirer*, August 20, 1965).

"I may have thrown 187 pitches, but I made them count when I had to. Actually, I consider myself darn lucky to be in the big leagues at all. I was terrible in the minors and never thought I would make it until manager Jim Turner straightened me out in 1960 at Nashville."

Jim Maloney talking about his performance immediately following the game ("Cubs Go Hitless On 187 Pitches," *The (Toledo, Ohio) Blade*, August 20, 1965).

"I didn't feel any different, but Jim was wilder than a March hare. (Laughs) I do remember being anxious during the game because Chicago constantly had men on base, and they were on third base a couple times. I didn't want the ball to get past and have a run score and Jim lose a no-hitter."

Johnny Edwards remembering how he felt (Interview with the author, March 2, 2022).

It had been a trying day for Jim Maloney. Nine innings had passed and the talented hitters of the Chicago Cubs, including Hall of Famers Billy Williams, Ernie Banks, and Ron Santo, hadn't scored a single run off him. Not that they didn't have lots of opportunities. Through the first nine innings of the game, Maloney allowed ten baserunners due to nine walks and a hit batsman.

In the third inning, Maloney walked the bases loaded before getting Billy Williams to ground out to second. In the fourth inning, Maloney walked two batters before getting Chicago shortstop Don Kessinger to strike out to end the inning. In the eighth inning, Maloney fanned Ernie Banks for the third out, stranding runners on first and third. In the ninth, Maloney loaded the bases again by plunking Ron Santo, walking catcher Ed Bailey, and issuing a free pass to pitcher Larry Jackson for the second time. Leadoff hitter Don Landrum then popped out to shortstop to end the inning. Through nine innings, Maloney had allowed 10 baserunners, with the go-ahead runner stranded on third base in three of those frames. This included the bottom of the ninth inning in a scoreless game where a Chicago run would have instantly won it for the Cubs.

The Reds would break the 0-0 tie in the top of the 10th when their number eight hitter, slick-fielding shortstop Leo Cardenas, punched a one-out solo home run that was curving foul and hit the screen on the pole just above the fence in left field. The Reds wouldn't score again that inning, so it was left to Jim Maloney to retire the Cubs in the bottom of the 10th for the win. Maloney would start the inning by walking his tenth batter of the day, Chicago outfielder Doug Clemens. After getting Billy Williams to fly out to left field, Ernie Banks would ground into a 6-4-3 double play to end the game and complete Maloney's ten-inning shutout.

There are several remarkable things about this game. One of the most impressive was that Maloney threw a complete game, 10-inning, no-hit shutout while allowing 11 batters to reach base. For the game, the Cubs achieved an on-base percentage of .282 which was only 10% less than the major league average of .311 in 1965. For a no-hitter, it's mind-blowing that such a high percentage of batters reached base without the benefit of a hit, never mind that they didn't score a run. This game places Maloney at the top of the list for the most baserunners allowed in a single-pitcher no-hitter, as shown in the table below.

Table 1-1. Individual No-hitters with Eight or More Baserunners

Rank	Baserunners	Pitcher	Team	Date (Score)	Opponent
1	11 (10 BBs, 1 HBP)	Jim Maloney	Cincinnati Reds	8/19/1965 (1) Cin 1-0 (10 inn)	Chicago Cubs
2 (tie)	10 (9 BBs, 1 HBP)	A.J. Burnett	Florida Marlins	5/12/2001 Fla 3-0	San Diego Padres
2 (tie)	10 (8 BBs, 1 HBP, 1 E)	Edwin Jackson	Arizona D-backs	6/25/2010 Ari 1-0	Tampa Bay Rays
4	9 (8 BBs, 1 HBP)	Dock Ellis	Pittsburgh Pirates	6/12/1970 (1) Pit 2-0	San Diego Padres
5 (tie)	8 (7 BBs, 1 HBP)	Ed Lafitte	Brooklyn Tip-Tops	9/19/1914 (1) Bro 6-2	Kansas City Packers
5 (tie)	8 (8 BBs)	Johnny Vander Meer	Cincinnati Reds	6/15/1938 Cin 6-0	Brooklyn Dodgers
5 (tie)	8 (8 BBs)	Cliff Chambers	Pittsburgh Pirates	6/5/1951 (2) Pit 3-0	Boston Braves
5 (tie)	8 (6 BBs, 2 Es)	Jim Palmer	Baltimore Orioles	8/13/1969 Bal 8-0	Oakland Athletics

Rank	Base-runners	Pitcher	Team	Date (Score)	Opponent
5 (tie)	8 (7 BBs, 1 E)	Bill Stoneman	Montreal Expos	10/2/1972 (1) Mon 7-0	New York Mets
5 (tie)	8 (8 BBs)	Nolan Ryan	California Angels	9/28/1974 Cal 4-0	Minnesota Twins

METHODOLOGY: This table displays the individual (not multi-pitcher) no-hitters with the most baserunners allowed from 1900-2021. Games are ranked by the most runners allowed in descending order.

LEGEND: Dates are shown as month/day/year (for example, June 12, 2018, is shown as 6/12/2018). inn = innings; BBs = bases on balls (or walks); HBP = hit by pitch; E(s) = Error(s). (1) or (2) = first or second game of a doubleheader.

NOTE 1: Ed Lafitte's no-hitter against the Kansas City Packers was a Federal League game. The Federal League was an eight-team major league that played in 1914 and 1915.

NOTE 2: In the first game of a doubleheader on April 30, 1967, against Detroit, Baltimore's Steve Barber (8.2 innings) and Stu Miller (0.1 inning) threw a combined no-hitter where the Tigers had 14 baserunners – the most ever in a no-hit game. Barber allowed 10 walks, hit two batters, and committed an error that allowed a Detroit batter to reach first. Stu Miller got the final out of the ninth inning, but not before Detroit scored its second run on a fielder's choice error. Detroit went on to win the game 2-1.

NOTE 3: Blue Moon Odom of the Chicago White Sox combined with Francisco Barrios to throw a combined no-hitter on July 28, 1976, against the Oakland Athletics. Chicago won the game 2-1, but the two pitchers allowed 11 baserunners in the process. Odom walked nine batters in five innings of work, while Barrios walked two in his four innings to finish the game.

NOTE 4: Zach Davies and three other Cubs pitchers allowed eight Dodgers to reach base during their June 24, 2021, multi-pitcher no-hitter. Davies walked five batters over six innings while relievers Ryan Tepera, Andrew Chafin, and Craig Kimbrel each threw one hitless inning and walked one batter apiece. The Cubs won the game 4-0.

NOTE 5: Maloney's ten baserunners through nine innings places him in a tie with A.J. Burnett and Edwin Jackson at the end of regulation play in a no-hit game.

NOTE 6: Johnny Vander Meer's no-hitter on June 15, 1938, was his second no-hitter in consecutive starts. He no-hit the Boston Braves just four days before on June 11.

NOTE 7: Dock Ellis' no-hitter on June 12, 1970, was immortalized in the well-received 2014 film "No No: A Dockumentary." He was on LSD at the time he threw the no-hitter.

Maloney would also join an exclusive group of three pitchers who threw complete game no-hitters of more than nine innings, as shown below.

Table 1-2. Extra Inning Individual No-Hitters

Base Runners	Pitcher	Team	Date (Score)	Opponent
1 (1 HBP)	Hooks Wiltse	New York Giants	7/4/1908 NY 1-0 (10 inn)	Philadelphia Phillies
2 (2 BBs)	Fred Toney	Cincinnati Reds	5/2/1917 Cin 1-0 (10 inn)	Chicago Cubs
11 (10 BB, 1 HBP)	Jim Maloney	Cincinnati Reds	5/19/1965 Cin 1-0 (10 inn)	Chicago Cubs

METHODOLOGY: This table includes the three multi-inning no-hitters thrown by an individual pitcher from 1900-2021. The games are listed chronologically.

LEGEND: Dates are shown as month/day/year (for example, June 12, 2018, is shown as 6/12/2018). BB(s) = base(s) on balls; HBP = hit by pitch; inn = innings.

NOTE: Pittsburgh's Francisco Cordova threw nine innings of shutout, no-hit ball against the Houston Astros on July 12, 1997. Unfortunately for the Pirates, Pittsburgh didn't score a run, so the game went into extra innings. Pirate reliever Ricardo Rincon threw a hitless top of the 10th inning, and the Pirates won 3-0 in the bottom of the inning when pinch-hitter Mark Smith hit a three-run walk off home run.

Both earlier games in Table 1-2 are extraordinary in their own right. Hooks Wiltse threw what is arguably one of the best-pitched games of all-time. He had a perfect game going with two outs in the top of the ninth inning of a scoreless game. With two strikes on the batter (Philadelphia pitcher George McQuillan), Wiltse threw what appeared to be the third strike. Instead, umpire Cy Rigler called it a ball and McQuillan's at bat continued. The next day even the highly partisan Philadelphia

Inquirer admitted that McQuillan had been "fanned." McQuillan had even turned to walk towards the dugout after the pitch, confirming that even he thought he struck out.

On the next pitch, Wiltse hit McQuillan on the shoulder, allowing the first Philadelphia runner to reach base. The next batter grounded out to second for the third out to end the inning. Despite getting their leadoff hitter on, the Giants failed to score in the bottom of the inning, so the game went into the 10th as a 0-0 tie.

Wiltse retired the Phillies in order in the top of that inning. In the bottom of the frame, New York scraped together a run on two singles and an error for a walk-off win for Wiltse and the Giants. Wiltse had recorded baseball's first walk-off no-hit victory and he remains the only pitcher dating back to the beginning of the twentieth century to throw an extra-inning no-hitter without walking a batter.

The other non-Maloney no-hitter in the 10-inning table represents an extraordinary effort by both starting pitchers. Fred Toney, also of the Cincinnati Reds, threw a 10-inning no-hitter against the Chicago Cubs on May 2, 1917, allowing only two walks to Cy Williams for the Cubs' only baserunners. The opposing pitcher, Chicago's Hippo Vaughn, matched Toney frame for frame, throwing his own nine-inning no-hitter and giving up only two walks while striking out 10 to Toney's five.

This is the only instance of two nine-inning no-hit games being pitched in the same contest. At the end of regulation baseball, there were 54 outs recorded and only four total baserunners, all of whom had reached on walks. In the top of the 10th, the Giants finally got on the scoreboard. New York right fielder Jim Thorpe – he of Olympic and football fame – singled off Vaughn to knock in the first run of the game and give New York a 1-0 lead. The leadoff hitter that inning, shortstop Larry Kopf, had reached base on a sharply hit single through the left side of the infield, ending Vaughn's no-hit bid.

Jim Maloney's no-hitter wasn't as dominating as either Wiltse's or Toney's, or even Vaughn's effort. Maloney's game was full of walks and a hit batsman. Yet, at the end of his game, Maloney found himself in elite company as one of only three pitchers to ever throw an extra-inning, complete game no-hitter.

To some degree, this game was making up for Maloney's effort just two months before when he threw 10 innings of no-hit ball against the New York Mets. Through the first ten innings of play, he had struck out 17 batters while allowing only one walk, and that was to the Mets' dangerous cleanup hitter Ed Kranepool in the top of the second. Unfortunately, despite Maloney's herculean effort, Cincinnati was unable to score.

In a Reds lineup that included Pete Rose, Vada Pinson, Frank Robinson, and many other solid hitters, the Reds were not able to plate one runner. This was despite having 10 batters who reached base on singles, walks, and a hit batsman. Even though he eventually lost the game in the 11th inning, this effort from Maloney was more dominating than his 1965 no-hitter in almost every respect, as he recorded a phenomenal Game Score of 106.

The statistic Game Score (GSc) measures a pitcher's performance in any given game started and is based on the number of innings pitched, strikeouts, hits allowed, runs allowed, and walks allowed by a pitcher. I will be using GSc frequently throughout this book to compare pitching performances. Introduced by baseball writer/statistician Bill James in the 1980s, Game Score is almost always between 0-100. Except for extreme outliers, it usually falls between 40-70.

The game's outcome was determined in the top of the 11th, when New York right fielder Johnny Lewis led off the inning with a home run to deep center field. The Mets now led 1-0, and Maloney's no-hitter was gone. Maloney retired the next batter on a strikeout and, after giving up a single, he got Mets catcher Jesse Gonder to ground into a double play. Unhappily for Maloney and the rest of the Reds, Cincinnati was unable to tie the score in the bottom of the inning, leaving Frank Robinson stranded on first when the game ended in a 1-0 Mets victory.

Within a period of a little more than two months, Jim Maloney had thrown ten-innings of no-hit ball in two separate games. Ironically, in the first, better-pitched game, he gave up a hit and a run in the 11th inning in a 1-0 game his team lost. The year of those two games, 1965, was one of Jim Maloney's best seasons as a pitcher. He went 20-9 with an ERA of 2.54 and earned a berth on the National League All-Star team. It wasn't a fluke, either. In the six seasons from 1963-1968, Maloney accumulated 105 wins as he established himself as an ace on some excellent Cincinnati teams.

Maloney would throw a second no-hitter on April 30, 1969, when he blanked the Houston Astros 10-0. In that game, Maloney struck out 13 hitters while walking five. Amazingly, pitcher Don Wilson of the Astros threw a no-hitter against the Reds the very next day, beating Cincinnati 4-0. It was Wilson's second career no-hitter, and it was only the second time ever that two teams threw no-hitters against each other on consecutive days. The other occasion was the year prior when Gaylord Perry of the San Francisco Giants and Ray Washburn of the St. Louis Cardinals threw consecutive no-hitters at Candlestick Park in September of 1968. Johnny Edwards,

Maloney's catcher for his 1965 no-hitter, also caught Washburn's no-hitter in 1968, the only season Edwards played for the Cardinals.

Maloney also had a string of one-hitters from 1963-1969. A one-hitter, of course, is as close as a pitcher can get to a no-hitter without achieving that goal. Maloney's five one-hitters places him in a tie for fourth place on the list of all-time leaders for most one-hitters since 1920 (depicted in the table below).

Table 1-3. Pitchers With the Most One-Hitters

Rank	One-Hitters	Name	Team (Number of One-Hitters with that Team)	Season(s)
1 (tie)	12	Bob Feller	Cleveland Indians (12)	1938-1955
1 (tie)	12	Nolan Ryan	New York Mets (1) California Angels (6) Houston Astros (2) Texas Rangers (3)	1970 1972-1979 1982-1983 1989-1990
3	6	Steve Carlton	St Louis Cardinals (1) Philadelphia Phillies (5)	1968 1972-1980
4 (tie)	5	Bobo Newsom	St Louis Browns (2) Washington Senators (2) Brooklyn Dodgers (1)	1934 & 1938 1936 & 1942 1943
4 (tie)	5	Jim Maloney	Cincinnati Reds (5)	1963-1969
4 (tie)	5	Jim Palmer	Baltimore Orioles (5)	1967-1982
4 (tie)	5	Tom Seaver	New York Mets (5)	1967-1977
4 (tie)	5	Don Sutton	Los Angeles Dodgers (5)	1969-1977
4 (tie)	5	Bert Blyleven	Minnesota Twins (3) Texas Rangers (1) Cleveland Indians (1)	1973-1974 1976 1984
4 (tie)	5	Dave Stieb	Toronto Blue Jays (5)	1988-1989

METHODOLOGY: This table includes pitchers who threw five or more one-hitters from 1920-2021. Pitchers are listed in rank order of the number of one-hitters they threw during their careers. In the case of ties, pitchers are listed in chronological order of when they threw their first one-hitter.

LEGEND: One-hitters = the total number of one-hitters the pitcher has thrown. Season(s) = the season(s) in which the pitcher threw the one-hitter(s) for the team listed. It is not intended to show all the years that pitcher was on the team.

NOTE 1: Nolan Ryan had four more one-hit performances of eight innings or more, including a 1986 game against the Expos where he threw nine and one-third innings of one-hit ball. Those four games were not complete games, though, and technically don't count as one-hitters.

NOTE 2: Don Sutton also one-hit the Montreal Expos for the first 10 innings of a 13-inning game in 1972. This was not a complete game, so it doesn't officially count as a one-hitter.

NOTE 3: Dave Stieb threw one-hitters in consecutive starts against the Cleveland Indians and Baltimore Orioles to close out the 1988 season. Both games were nine-inning shutouts.

Jim Maloney is in great company here. Of all the pitchers in the table above, only Bobo Newsom, Dave Stieb, and Maloney are not in the Hall of Fame. Bobo Newsom had a long and distinguished career over 20 seasons stretching from 1929 to 1953, including four American League All-Star team selections and two World Series appearances with the Detroit Tigers (1940) and New York Yankees (1947). While Newsom did get as much as 9.4% on the Hall of Fame ballot (in 1969), there doesn't seem to be much movement in the Veterans Committee to get him elected.

With a career record of 211-222 and nearly as many walks (1,732) as strikeouts (2,082), Newsom hasn't been viewed as being worthy of selection, even though he compiled a Wins Above Replacement (WAR) value of 47.8 and Jaffe Wins Above Replacement Score (JAWS) of 42.1.

Because I will be using WAR and JAWS throughout the book, bear with me as I describe what they represent. WAR measures a player's value in all facets of the game by deciphering how many more wins he's worth than a replacement-level player in his same position. JAWS is a sabermetric baseball statistic developed to evaluate the strength of a player's career and merit for induction into the Baseball

Hall of Fame. It is created by averaging a player's career WAR with their 7-year peak WAR (WAR7).

Dave Stieb, arguably, has a stronger case than Newsom for election to the Hall of Fame. He was one of the very best pitchers in the 1980s, earning seven All-Star team selections. Stieb also has WAR and JAWS values comparable to renowned Hall of Fame pitchers Whitey Ford, Jim Kaat, Sandy Koufax, Bob Lemon, Jack Morris, and Catfish Hunter. Unfortunately, Stieb became eligible for the Hall of Fame in 2004, a time when counting stats were still considered benchmarks for election consideration. For example, Stieb had "just" 176 wins and 1,669 strikeouts. With the more advanced metrics available today, Stieb may be considered favorably by the Veterans Committee in future elections. Stieb is already a member of the Canadian Baseball Hall of Fame.

Unlike the other two non-HoF pitchers listed on the one-hitters table, Jim Maloney doesn't have a strong Hall of Fame case despite being one of the very best pitchers in the 1960s. With only 134 career wins and a single All-Star selection, he garnered just two votes on the two HOF ballots on which he competed.

Because the typical baseball fan is laser-focused on their favorite team's performance, I created tables for all 30 franchises identifying the team's top 10 Game Scores from 1900 to 2021. I included these tables in the appropriate chapters that focus on a pitcher from that team. For those franchises that aren't included within any no-hitter chapters, there is a summary chapter near the end of Volume II that includes the top Game Score tables for those teams.

Because the prevailing pitching philosophy during the first part of the Twentieth Century was to let a pitcher finish out a game no matter how long it went, I also created a team's "Top 10" table that only included pitching performances of ten innings or less. In this way, comparing pitchers' performances from games within typical innings limits is easier. I established the 10-inning limit to include all no-hit games (the longest is ten innings).

Expansion teams established beginning in 1961 only have one table, as they typically only have a few extra-inning performances included. All of the tables include both regular season and postseason games. The table below, for instance, represents the highest Game Scores achieved by a Cincinnati Reds pitcher.

Table 1-4. Reds Highest Game Scores

Rank	Pitcher	Date Score	Opponent	GSc	IP, Hits, Runs, ERs, Walks, Strikeouts
1	Johnny Vander Meer	9/11/1946 0-0 Tie (19 inn)	Brooklyn Dodgers	115	15.0 IP, 7 Hits, 0 Runs, 0 ERs, 2 BBs, 14 Ks
2	Rube Benton	6/11/1915 Cin 1-0 (15 inn)	Brooklyn Dodgers	109	15.0 IP, 8 Hits, 0 Runs, 0 ERs, 6 BBs, 14 Ks
3 (tie)	Fred Toney	5/31/1916 Cin 5-2 (16 inn)	Pittsburgh Pirates	106	16.0 IP, 8 Hits, 2 Runs, 2 ERs, 2 BBs, 10 Ks
3 (tie)	Jim Maloney	6/14/1965 NY 1-0 (11 inn)	New York Mets	106	11.0 IP, 2 Hits, 1 Run, 1 ER, 1 BB, 18 Ks
5	Jack Rowan	6/15/1910 3-3 Tie (16 inn)	Philadelphia Phillies	105- 111	16.0 IP, 5 Hits, 3 Runs, ? ERs, 4 BBs, 9 Ks
6 (tie)	Hod Eller	7/25/1918 (1) Cin 4-2 (13 inn)	Boston Braves	103	13.0 IP, 4 Hits, 2 Runs, 0 ERs, 3 BBs, 11 Ks
6 (tie)	Sammy Ellis	6/29/1965 (1) Pit 2-1 (16 inn)	Pittsburgh Pirates	103	14.0 IP, 4 Hits, 1 Run, 1 ER, 7 BBs, 10 Ks
8 (tie)	Red Lucas	7/16/1933 (1) Cin 1-0 (15 inn)	New York Giants	102	15.0 IP, 9 Hits, 0 Runs, 0 ERs, 1 BB, 4 Ks
8 (tie)	Jim Maloney	9/30/1964 Pit 1-0 (16 inn)	Pittsburgh Pirates	102	11.0 IP, 3 Hits, 0 Runs, 0 ERs, 2 BBs, 13 Ks
10 (tie)	Bob Ewing	9/11/1906 0-0 tie (15 inn)	Pittsburgh Pirates	101	15.0 IP, 8 Hits, 0 Runs, 0 ERs, 4 BBs, 4 Ks
10 (tie)	Eppa Rixey	7/8/1924 (2) Cin 2-1 (16 inn)	Philadelphia Phillies	101	16.0 IP, 8 Hits, 1 Run, 1 ER, 4 BBs, 3 Ks
10 (tie)	Ray Starr	6/18/1943 Cin 1-0 (14 inn)	Pittsburgh Pirates	101	14.0 IP, 5 Hits, 0 Runs, 0 ERs, 3 BBs, 2 Ks

METHODOLOGY: This table lists the highest Game Scores of Cincinnati Reds pitchers from 1900-2021. Games are ranked by Game Score (GSc) and consider all franchise regular season and postseason games. Table 1-5 below limits the eligible games to those pitching performances that were 10 innings or less. Game Score (GSc) measures a pitcher's performance in any given game started. Introduced by baseball writer/statistician Bill James in the 1980s, Game Score is presented as a figure between 0-100 — except for extreme outliers — and usually falls between 40-70.

LEGEND: Dates are shown as month/day/year (for example, June 12, 2018, is shown as 6/12/2018). IP = innings pitched. One-third of an inning pitched has 0.1 added and two-thirds of an inning pitched has 0.2 added (for example, 9 1/3 innings pitched is displayed as 9.1); BB(s) = base(s) on balls; K(s) = strikeout(s); ER(s) = earned run(s); inn = innings (associated with the length of extra-inning games); and (1) or (2) = first or second game of a doubleheader. GSc = Game Score.

NOTE 1: The highest postseason Game Score by a Reds pitcher was an 89 achieved by Hod Eller in Game 5 of the 1919 World Series. Eller blanked the Chicago White Sox 5-0 on three hits. This was during the infamous 1919 "Black Sox" World Series wherein some members of the White Sox allegedly threw the series after being paid off by gambling interests. This episode was immortalized in the book and movie *Eight Men Out*. The next highest postseason Game Score was an 87, thrown by Trevor Bauer in the 2020 National League Wild Card game against the Atlanta Braves. Bauer pitched 7.2 innings of shutout ball, yet Atlanta emerged victorious when they pushed across a run in the bottom of the 13th inning and won 1-0.

NOTE 2: Jack Rowan's 16-inning effort in 1910 that resulted in a 3-3 tie against the Phillies does not have a Game Score associated with it. At that time, there was no differentiation between an earned run or an unearned run. Because Cincinnati made three errors during the game, it's possible, though unlikely, that all three runs were unearned since they were scored in three separate innings. Even so, the possible range of Game Scores Rowan could have earned for that game range from 105 (if all three runs were earned) to 111 (if all three runs were unearned). This places him anywhere from fifth place to second place on the Reds all-time list.

Johnny Vander Meer has the highest Game Score achieved by a Cincinnati pitcher (115) and is tied with Homer Bailey for the highest Game Score in a nine-inning game (96). Vander Meer, along with Jim Maloney and Bailey, also holds the Cincinnati record for the most no-hitters with two apiece. Even though he lost, Maloney's 11-inning game in 1965 can arguably be called one of the best pitched games in Cincinnati history. Throwing no-hit ball for 10 innings, Maloney recorded 18 strikeouts, more than any Reds pitcher has ever accomplished in a single game. Along with that, Maloney is the only pitcher listed twice in Table 1-4, with his second game being another high strikeout, low walk 11-inning effort.

Demonstrating his excellence with the Reds, Maloney also ranks highly in games where a pitcher threw 10 innings or less. The chart below shows the highest Reds Game Scores since 1900, and incorporates all no-hitters, including Maloney's 10-inning effort and Fred Toney's 10-inning no-hitter from 1917. Maloney is the only pitcher listed three times among the top 14 games.

Table 1-5. Reds Highest Game Scores of 10 innings or less

Rank	Pitcher	Date Score	Opponent	GSc	IP, Hits, Runs, ERs, Walks, Strikeouts
1 (tie)	Dolf Luque	6/5/1925 Cin 1-0 (10 inn)	Boston Braves	96	10.0 IP, 3 Hits, 0 Runs, 0 ERs, 0 BBs, 10 Ks
1 (tie)	Johnny Vander Meer	6/6/1941 Cin 7-0	Phi Phillies	96	9.0 IP, 1 Hit, 0 Runs, 0 ERs, 1 BB, 12 Ks
1 (tie)	Homer Bailey	9/28/2012 Cin 1-0	Pittsburgh Pirates	96	9.0 IP, 0 Hits, 0 Runs, 0 ERs, 1 BB, 10 Ks
4 (tie)	Orval Overall	7/17/1905 Cin 1-0 (10 inn)	Phi Phillies	95	10.0 IP, 1 Hit, 0 Runs, 0 ERs, 3 BBs, 8 Ks
4 (tie)	Jim Maloney	7/23/1963 Cin 1-0	Chicago Cubs	95	9.0 IP, 1 Hit, 0 Runs, 0 ERs, 3 BBs, 13 Ks
4 (tie)	Jim Maloney	4/30/1969 Cin 10-0	Houston Astros	95	9.0 IP, 0 Hits, 0 Runs, 0 ERs, 5 BBs, 13 Ks
4 (tie)	Mario Soto	6/27/1982 Atl 2-0 (14 inn)	Atlanta Braves	95	10.0 IP, 3 Hits, 0 Runs, 0 ERs, 1 BB, 10 Ks
4 (tie)	Homer Bailey	7/2/2013 Cin 3-0	SF Giants	95	9.0 IP, 0 Hits, 0 Runs, 0 ERs, 1 BB, 9 Ks
9 (tie)	Johnny Vander Meer	9/6/1941 Cin 2-0	St. Louis Cardinals	94	9.0 IP, 2 Hits, 0 Runs, 0 ERs, 3 BBs, 14 Ks
9 (tie)	Joe Nuxhall	7/24/1965 (2) Cin 2-0	Houston Astros	94	9.0 IP, 1 Hit, 0 Runs, 0 ERs, 2 BBs, 11 Ks
9 (tie)	Jim Maloney	8/19/1965 (1) Cin 1-0 (10 inn)	Chicago Cubs	94	10.0 IP, 0 Hits, 0 Runs, 0 ERs, 10 BBs, 12 Ks

Rank	Pitcher	Date Score	Opponent	GSc	IP, Hits, Runs, ERs, Walks, Strikeouts
9 (tie)	Bruce Berenyi	6/7/1981 Cin 2-0	Montreal Expos	94	9.0 IP, 1 Hit, 0 Runs, 0 ERs, 1 BB, 10 Ks
9 (tie)	Tom Browning	9/16/1988 Cin 1-0	LA Dodgers	94	9.0 IP, 0 Hits, 0 Runs, 0 ERs, 0 BBs, 7 Ks
9 (tie)	Wade Miley	5/7/2021 Cin 3-0	Cleveland Indians	94	9.0 IP, 0 Hits, 0 Runs, 0 ERs, 1 BB, 8 Ks
15 (tie)	Noodles Hahn	7/12/1900 Cin 4-0	Phi Phillies	93	9.0 IP, 0 Hits, 0 Runs, 0 ERs, 2 BBs, 8 Ks
15 (tie)	Fred Toney	5/2/1917 Cin 1-0 (10 inn)	Chicago Cubs	93	10.0 IP, 0 Hits, 0 Runs, 0 ERs, 2 BBs, 3 Ks
25 (tie)	Hod Eller	5/11/1919 Cin 6-0	St. Louis Cardinals	92	9.0 IP, 0 Hits, 0 Runs, 0 ERs, 3 BBs, 8 Ks
71 (tie)	Johnny Vander Meer	6/11/1938 Cin 3-0	Boston Braves	88	9.0 IP, 0 Hits, 0 Runs, 0 ERs, 3 BBs, 4 Ks
92 (tie)	Clyde Shoun	5/15/1944 Cin 1-0	Boston Braves	87	9.0 IP, 0 Hits, 0 Runs, 0 ERs, 1 BB, 1 K
92 (tie)	Tom Seaver	6/16/1978 Cin 4-0	St. Louis Cardinals	87	9.0 IP, 0 Hits, 0 Runs, 0 ERs, 3 BBs, 3 Ks
129 (tie)	Johnny Vander Meer	6/15/1938 Cin 6-0	Brooklyn Dodgers	86	9.0 IP, 0 Hits, 0 Runs, 0 ERs, 8 BBs, 7 Ks
129 (tie)	Ewell Blackwell	6/18/1947 Cin 6-0	Boston Braves	86	9.0 IP, 0 Hits, 0 Runs, 0 ERs, 4 BBs, 3 Ks
247 (tie)	George Culver	7/29/1968 (2) Cin 6-1	Phi Phillies	84	9.0 IP, 0 Hits, 1 Run, 0 ERs, 5 BBs, 4 Ks
583 (tie)	Jake Weimer	8/24/1906 (2) Cin 1-0 (7 inn)	Brooklyn Superbas	80	7.0 IP, 0 Hits, 0 Runs, 0 ERs, 1 BB, 4 Ks

METHODOLOGY: This table lists the highest Game Scores of 10 innings or less for Cincinnati Reds pitchers from 1900-2021. Games are ranked by Game Score (GSc) and consider all franchise regular season and postseason games. For comparison purposes, all 15 no-hitters from 1900-2021 are included in this table. The table includes all pitching performances of 10 innings or less because of the desire to incorporate the three no-hitters that went 10 innings -- two of which were thrown by Cincinnati pitchers. Game Score (GSc) measures a pitcher's performance in any given game started. Introduced by baseball writer/statistician Bill James in the 1980s, Game Score is presented as a figure between 0-100 -- except for extreme outliers -- and usually falls between 40-70.

LEGEND: Dates are shown as month/day/year (for example, June 12, 2018, is shown as 6/12/2018). IP = innings pitched; BB(s) = base(s) on balls (or walk(s)); K(s) = strikeout(s); ER(s) = earned run(s); inn = inning. (1) or (2) = first or second game of a doubleheader. *Tom Browning's perfect game against the eventual 1988 World Champion Dodgers is italicized. It is the first and only perfect game in Cincinnati Reds history.*

NOTE 1: Cincinnati pitcher Johnny Vander Meer is famous as the only pitcher to throw no-hitters on two consecutive starts. He threw those games as a 23-year-old rookie in June 1938 and his astounding accomplishment has been rightfully celebrated. As impressive as those were, Vander Meer threw seven games that had higher Game Scores than his best no-hitter (88), including four nine-inning efforts. In addition to having the highest Cincinnati Game Score ever (115), he is tied with Homer Bailey for the best nine-inning Game Score (96). In Vander Meer's 1941 game, he only allowed one baserunner on an infield single with one out in the second inning.

NOTE 2: Homer Bailey deserves special mention as he threw two no-hitters for the Reds within a year, including his extraordinary 10-strikeout, one-walk performance in 2012 against the Pirates that put him at the top of this table with Johnny Vander Meer. While his lone walk in that game occurred in the seventh inning, an error earlier in the game ruled out a perfect game before that was a consideration. In 2013, he had a perfect game going until Gregor Blanco of the Giants walked on a 3-2 count to lead off the seventh inning.

NOTE 3: Fred Toney's 10-inning no-hitter on May 2, 1917, earned him a Game Score of 93. If it had ended after nine innings, he would have had a Game Score of 86, with 0 hits, 0 runs, 2 walks, and 1 strikeout. Jim Maloney's 10-inning no-hitter earned a Game Score of 94. If it had ended after nine innings, he would have had a Game Score of 90, with 0 hits, 0 runs, 9 walks, and 12 strikeouts.

NOTE 4: Bruce Berenyi's 1981 no-hit attempt was broken up when Andre Dawson hit a grounder through the infield between the first and second basemen with two outs in the fourth inning. That was the only hit of the game, as he faced just 28 batters that day, one over the absolute minimum.

NOTE 5: George Culver's no-hitter in 1968 is the lowest ranking in terms of Game Score of all Cincinnati Reds no-hitters thrown since 1900. It was also the only no-hitter in which the other team scored, as the Phillies notched a run in the bottom of the second inning to take a 1-0 lead. Philadelphia scored an unearned run when Dick Allen reached second base to lead off the inning on two errors by two different players. He advanced on a groundout and scored on a sacrifice fly. Cincinnati hitters answered with six runs over the next two innings to put the game out of reach.

NOTE 6: While not counted as a no-hitter under the current rule that requires a pitcher to throw at least nine innings, Jake Weimer threw seven innings of no-hit ball against the Brooklyn Superbas in the second game of a 1906 doubleheader. The two teams agreed ahead of time that they would only play seven innings during the day's final game, to allow the Superbas enough time to catch a train to St. Louis. Weimer only allowed two baserunners during the match, as he hit Brooklyn's leadoff batter in the first inning and then allowed a two-out walk in the third inning. The Reds won the game in the bottom of the seventh when light-hitting Homer Smoot hit a ball in the gap between the left and center fielders. Smoot's triple scored Hans Lobert from first base to give Cincinnati a 1-0 walk-off win.

Standing atop the highest-ranked Game Scores by a Reds pitcher in a game of 10 innings or less is one name that is known by only a few modern fans outside the Cincinnati area: Dolf Luque. Luque was a fixture in the Reds starting rotation from 1918 to 1929. In addition to throwing his 10-inning, three-hit shutout against the Braves in 1925, Luque led the Major Leagues with 27 wins and a 1.93 ERA in his extraordinary 1923 season. With a 10.9 WAR that year, Luque was more than two points higher than his next closest competitor, Hall of Famer Frankie Frisch of the New York Giants. He also helped lead the 1919 Reds and the 1933 Giants to World Series victories. His 4.1 innings of shutout ball in the decisive, 10-inning Game 5 of the 1933 series led to Luque setting the record for the oldest pitcher to win a World Series game – he was 43 at the time.

Luque was also one of the greatest Cuban pitchers ever to throw in the Major Leagues. Eclipsed only by the legendary Luis Tiant in terms of career WAR achieved, Luque blazed a trail for Latin pitchers who came afterward. Luque was popular in the U.S. and had a huge following in his native Cuba. It's also important to recognize that most other Latino pitchers weren't allowed to pitch in the majors at that time because they were black, whereas Luque was white. The Top 10 Cuban pitchers are listed below.

Table 1-6. Best Pitchers Born in Cuba

Rank	Pitcher (Home)	Team	Season(s)	Career IP	WAR (per 200 IP)	Wins (per season)
1	Luis Tiant (Marianao)	Cle Indians Min Twins Bos Red Sox NY Yankees Pit Pirates Cal Angels	1964-1969 1970 1971-1978 1979-1980 1981 1982	3,486.1	65.6 (3.76)	229 (12.1)
2	Dolf Luque (La Habana)	Bos Braves Cin Reds Bro Robins NY Giants	1914-1915 1918-1929 1930-1931 1932-1935	3,220.1	43.8 (2.72)	194 (9.7)
3	Camilo Pascual (La Habana)	Was Senators Min Twins Was Senators Cin Reds LA Dodgers Cle Indians	1954-1960 1961-1966 1967-1969 1969 1970 1971	2,930.2	37.5 (2.56)	174 (9.7)
4	Mike Cuellar (Las Villas)	Cin Reds StL Cardinals Hou Astros Bal Orioles Cal Angels	1959 1964 1965-1968 1969-1976 1977	2,808.0	29.2 (2.10)	185 (12.3)
5	Livan Hernandez (Villa Clara)	Fla Marlins SF Giants Mon Expos Was Nationals Ari D-backs Min Twins Col Rockies NY Mets Was Nationals Atl Braves Mil Brewers	1996-1999 1999-2002 2003-2004 2005-2006 2006-2007 2008 2008 2009 2009-2011 2012 2012	3,189.0	24.8 (1.56)	178 (10.5)
6	Orlando Hernandez (Villa Clara)	NY Yankees Chi W. Sox Ari D-backs NY Mets	1998-2004 2005 2006 2006-2007	1,314.2	23.1 (3.51)	90 (10.0)

Rank	Pitcher (Home)	Team	Season(s)	Career IP	WAR (per 200 IP)	Wins (per season)
7	Pedro Ramos (Pinar del Rio)	Was Senators Min Twins Cle Indians NY Yankees Phi Phillies Pit Pirates Cin Reds Was Senators	1955-1960 1961 1962-1964 1964-1966 1967 1969 1969 1970	2,355.2	22.4 (1.90)	117 (7.8)
8	Aroldis Chapman (Holguin)	Cin Reds NY Yankees Chi Cubs NY Yankees	2010-2015 2016 2016 2017-2021	603.2	19.2 (6.36)	40 Wins (3.3) 306 Saves (25.5)
9	Jose Contreras (Las Martinas)	NY Yankees Chi W. Sox Col Rockies Phi Phillies Pit Pirates	2003-2004 2004-2009 2009 2010-2012 2013	1,173.0	13.5 (2.30)	78 (7.1)
10	Orlando Pena (Victoria de las Tunas)	Cin Reds KC Athletics Det Tigers Cle Indians Pit Pirates Bal Orioles StL Cardinals Cal Angels	1958-1960 1962-1965 1965-1967 1967 1970 1971-1973 1973-1974 1974-1975	1,202.0	13.3 (2.21)	56 Wins (4.0) 40 Saves (2.9)

METHODOLOGY: To qualify for inclusion in this table, pitchers had to be of Cuban heritage and born in Cuba. Pitchers are ranked from 1-10 based upon their career Wins Above Replacement (WAR) between 1900-2021. WAR measures a player's value in all facets of the game by deciphering how many more wins he's worth than a replacement-level player at his same position.

LEGEND: Home = the place a pitcher was born in Cuba. Team and season(s) are the teams a pitcher played for and the season(s) they were with each team listed in chronological order. Career IP = career innings pitched. Career WAR = the pitcher's accumulated WAR over his career. Career Wins = the number of wins each pitcher accumulated over his career. Because pitchers had different career lengths, I included two rate measures (WAR per 200 innings pitched and wins per season).

Multiple pitchers missed entire seasons for various reasons. Therefore, those missed seasons don't count as part of the wins per season calculation. Specifically, Dolf Luque missed the 1916-1917 seasons after playing briefly in 1914-1915; Mike Cuellar rejoined the majors in 1964 after a four-year break from 1960-1963; Orlando Hernandez did not play in the majors in 2003; and Pedro Ramos did not play in the majors in 1968. Because Aroldis Chapman has been used exclusively as a reliever, his career saves and save rate per season are included as well. Pedro Ramos has split his time between being a starter and reliever, so his saves are included too. Aroldis Chapman is active beyond 2021.

NOTE 1: Luis Tiant is arguably the most accomplished pitcher on this list, having been named to the American League All-Star team three times, becoming a 20-game winner four times, and leading the league in ERA in 1968 and 1972. While there was no such thing as an All-Star game when Dolf Luque was in his prime, other pitchers on this list have been named to their league's All-Star team – some of them multiple times: Camilo Pascual (1959-1962 and 1964), Livan Hernandez (2004-2005), Mike Cuellar (1967, 1970, 1971, and 1974, along with being the AL Cy Young Award winner in 1969), Pedro Ramos (1959), Aroldis Chapman (2012-2015, 2018, 2019, and 2021), and Jose Contreras (2006). None of the Cuban pitchers listed have thrown a no-hitter.

NOTE 2: Most of the pitchers in this table have helped their teams achieve postseason success. Luis Tiant was instrumental in Minnesota capturing the AL West Division title in 1970. He also pitched heroically in the 1975 World Series for the AL Champion Red Sox, winning two games as Boston lost that epic seven-game series to the Cincinnati Reds. Dolf Luque, as mentioned previously, was an important part of two World Series champions. Camilo Pascual was integral to the 1965 Minnesota Twins finally breaking the five-time champion Yankees' hold on the American League title.

NOTE 3: Livan Hernandez had perhaps the most postseason heroics of all, being named the MVP for both the 1997 ALCS and 1997 World Series as the Marlins won the World Series Championship in only their fifth year of existence. Hernandez was also on the 2002 NL-pennant-winning Giants. Mike Cuellar was key to the Orioles' success in their 1970 World Series Championship. He was also a member of the World Champion 1964 Cardinals and AL Champion Orioles of 1969 and 1971. Orlando Hernandez was part of the Yankees three-peat World Champion teams of

1998-2000 and the Chicago White Sox 2005 Championship team – the first team title since 1917. Late-season acquisition Aroldis Chapman helped the Cubs win their title in 2016, the team's first in over 100 years (1908). Jose Contreras was also a member of the 2005 World Champion White Sox. Prior to that, he helped the Yankees to the AL title in 2003.

NOTE 4: The Cuban team has fared well in the World Baseball Classic, making it to the finals in the inaugural 2006 games, where they lost to Japan 10-6. For the next three tournaments (2009, 2013, and 2017), the team did not advance beyond Pool play. In 2023, Cuba won their Pool, and advanced to the quarterfinals, where they beat Australia 4-3. The Cuban team lost to the United States in the 2023 semifinal but have gained an automatic berth for the 2026 tournament. Aroldis Chapman was a member of the 2009 Cuban national team prior to his becoming a Major League pitcher.

Jim Maloney was born in Fresno, California and played baseball at Fresno High School and American Legion ball in the summer. He was also an excellent basketball and football player at Fresno High. Signed by the Reds in 1959, he played in their farm system briefly before being called up in 1960. In 1961, Maloney was part of Cincinnati's National League pennant-winning team. After retirement he did some coaching and managing in the Giants organization at Fresno. He also sold cars at his father's dealership and was the former director of the City of Fresno Alcoholism and Drug Abuse Council.

John Edwards, Maloney's batterymate that day, was an excellent player in his own right. Born in Columbus, Ohio and signed by Cincinnati in 1959, he was an All-Star selection for the Reds each year from 1963-1965. Edwards played 14 seasons, mostly for the Reds and the Houston Astros. Even though he was a solid hitter, Edwards was especially known for his outstanding fielding and excellent pitcher handling, winning the Gold Glove Award in both 1963 and 1964. During his playing days, he also worked as a research engineer in Cincinnati. In 1970, he started working at Cameron Ironworks in Houston. He worked for several more companies after that and retired in 2002.

Interviews with Jim Maloney and Johnny Edwards are below. I invite you to enjoy both.

Jim Maloney Interview
Conducted by Kevin Hurd on March 10, 2022

Kevin Hurd (KH): Would you consider yourself to be the best pitcher on your Little League, Babe Ruth League, high school, or college teams?

Jim Maloney (JM): No, I wasn't because through college I mostly played shortstop and the outfield. I only pitched about 20 innings at Fresno City College, and I was scouted as a shortstop in 1958.

KH: Did you feel any different (good or bad) on the day of your no-hitter?

JM: I felt the same as I always did. I went into every game with the goal of throwing a perfect game. If I walked or hit somebody or somebody got on an error, then I was shooting for a no-hitter. If I allowed one hit, I'd want to throw a one-hitter. If I allowed one run, that's all they were going to get. I went into every game feeling I could throw a no-hitter.

KH: What pitches were working best for you that day?

JM: Well, I was very wild that day. Everything I threw moved around a lot. Virtually everything I threw was either a fastball or curve. I may have thrown 3-4 changeups, and no sliders. My changeup was very mediocre that day.

KH: When you played in Little League, did you have any "outlier" players who either always hit home runs or always threw no-hitters?

JM: We had some good players, but nobody like that.

KH: What was the best defensive play, the closest you came to losing the no-hitter?

JM: Most of the outs were regular outs. I don't remember any diving catches.

KH: In your career, which batters did you have the hardest time getting out?

JM: That would be two great left-handed power hitters of my era: Willie McCovey and Willie Stargell.

KH: Do you remember shaking off your catcher's signs much during the game?

JM: I don't think I shook him off once. We were on the same wavelength, we roomed on the road.

KH: Do you have any memorabilia or souvenirs (a baseball, plaque, uniform, glove, or anything like that) from the game in your house?

JM: My no-hit glove is in Cooperstown, the Reds sent me a Hall of Fame plaque, and there are other memorabilia at the Cincinnati Reds Museum at the ballpark.

KH: Any coaches/managers in the minors who helped you more than others to get you into MLB?

JM: Jim Turner. He was my manager in 1960 at Nashville. He helped me a lot with my curveball and changing speeds. Johnny Van Der Meer was my manager at Topeka in 1959 and he was good, also.

KH: Which manager(s) that you played for in MLB did you like playing for the most?

JM: That would be Fred Hutchinson (1961-1964), Dick Sisler (1964-1965) and Dave Bristol (1966-1969).

KH: Do you think the number of pitches you threw that day (187) led to you getting a sore arm?

JM: No, it didn't. There really was no tracking of pitch counts back then. The pitching coach would track how you were doing. Wilder than normal, getting hit harder, things like that, and they went by that rather than a straight pinch count.

KH: Had you requested John Edwards to catch before the game?

JM: No, the manager pretty much always made the decision. Plus, John Edwards was the starting catcher and caught most of the games.

KH: Do you still stay in contact with John Edwards?

JM: Yes, I still contact him via phone every once in a while.

KH: Did your team give you a bonus for your no-hitter?

JM: Yes, I believe it was $1,000. Then again, this happened 57 years ago, but I do think it was $1,000. When I threw a no-hitter against Houston in April 1969, I didn't get a bonus for that one.

KH: During the game, when did you think *"I've got a real shot at a no-hitter?"* Was it the fifth inning, sixth inning, seventh inning, or later?

JM: Going back to how I was feeling during the game, I always thought I had a shot at a no-hitter until the other team got their first hit. I have talked to other pitchers who said the best game they ever pitched was on a day they felt really bad during warm-ups and that the best warm-ups they had happened on a day they got knocked out in the first inning. So, who knows?

KH: Were you able to get a follow-on job in baseball after your playing days were over? MLB, minors, college, high school, or the media?

JM: I did some coaching and managing in the Giants organization at Fresno.

KH: What non-baseball-related jobs did you have after retiring as a player?

JM: I sold used cars at my dad's dealership, and I was also president for the City of Fresno's Alcoholism and Drug Abuse Council. I did that for several years.

KH: If you were able to get a job in baseball, do you think having thrown a no-hitter helped you get the job?

JM: No.

KH: Do you have any kids or grandkids who have pursued or will pursue baseball as a career? Did you encourage them to do so?

JM: I have a grandson who was in the minors for three years in the Colorado Rockies organization. He quit after three years to do something else.

KH: Was the no-hitter the highlight of your career? If not, what was?

JM: I had a lot of highlights. I don't know if any one of them would be on top. Amongst my highlights are my two no-hitters, my first start, playing for the pennant-winning 1961 Reds, my 1963 season (he went 23-7), and my 1965 season (he went 20-9). I had a lot of goals also and accomplished many of them. I did want to get 200 wins but fell short (with 134 wins) due to injuries.

KH: Have you been to the section of the Hall of Fame that focuses on no-hitters?

JM: No.

KH: Have you spent time at autograph shows or at spring training in Florida or Arizona signing autographs?

JM: I've done a few in Cincinnati and one in San Francisco. They don't have autograph shows here in Fresno, but, like I said, I did one in San Francisco.

KH: Anything you'd like to add regarding your no-hitter?

JM: No

KH: Anything you'd like to add regarding your career?

JM: I pitched against a lot of great players. I'm glad I came along when I did.

Johnny Edwards Interview
Conducted by Kevin Hurd on March 2, 2022

Kevin Hurd (KH): Would you consider yourself to be the best catcher on your Little League, junior high, high school, or American Legion teams?

Johnny Edwards (JE): Well, at that time there was no Little League, but yes, I was the starting catcher on all the other teams. I was a catcher from the start. (Laughs)

KH: Did you feel any different, either good or bad, on the day of Jim Maloney's no-hitter?

JE: I didn't feel any different, but Jim was wilder than a March hare. (Laughs) I do remember being anxious during the game because Chicago constantly had men on base, and they were on third base a couple times. I didn't want the ball to get past and have a run score and Jim lose a no-hitter.

KH: What pitches were working best for Jim that day?

JE: He had a super fastball that was riding up, and a good curve. I don't believe he threw any sliders, and he threw a few changeups. If there had been a radar gun at the stadium, it probably would have shown him throwing over 100 miles an hour.

KH: What was the best defensive play or the closest you came to losing the no-hitter?

JE: I don't remember there being any great defensive plays that day.

KH: Did your pitcher shake off your signs much during the game?

JE: Yes, he did. My feeling was that the pitcher was in charge. I wasn't that demanding. Jim and I were good together. We were roommates on the road.

KH: Do you have any memorabilia or souvenirs (a baseball, plaque, uniform, glove, or anything like that) from the game in your house?

JE: I do have a lot of memorabilia in my house, but none from the game.

KH: You were in the minor leagues from 1959-1961. The managers you played for were Dave Bristol, Jim Turner, and Cot Deal. Who did you like playing for the most and who did you learn the most from?

JE: Definitely Jim Turner. Cot Deal was a lot like Jim, but I only played for him for two months. Dave Bristol was kind of fiery. (Laughs) There were several games he got thrown out of and I would take over as manager because I was a little older than the rest of the guys on the team and I'd been to college.

KH: You were in the majors from 1961-1974. The managers you played for were Fred Hutchinson, Dick Sisler, Don Heffner, Dave Bristol, Harry Walker, Leo Durocher, and Preston Gomez. Which one of the above individuals did you like playing for the most?

JE: Without a doubt Fred Hutchinson. He was great. He knew how to manage individuals.

KH: Jim threw 187 pitches that day. Do you think that the number of pitches he threw that day led to him getting a sore arm?

JE: No, there were no repercussions from that game.

KH: Did Jim request you as his catcher for that game?

JE: The manager decided that. I was the starting catcher for the majority of our games.

KH: Do you still stay in contact with Jim Maloney?

JE: Yes, mostly through telephone.

KH: Did your team give you a bonus for catching the no-hit game?

JE: No. (Laughs) I will say that when I caught Ray Washburn's no-hitter (note: that was on September 18, 1968, with the Cardinals) he gave me a set of beer mugs.

KH: During the game, when did you think *"Jim's got a real shot at a no-hitter?"*

JE: Around the fifth or sixth inning.

KH: Were you able to get a follow-on job in baseball after your playing days were over? In the majors, minors, college, high school, or the media?

JE: No.

KH: What other kind of work did you do?

JE: During the off seasons when I played, I worked as a research engineer in Cincinnati. In 1970 I started working at Cameron Ironworks in Houston. I worked for several more companies and retired in 2002.

KH: Who emphasized going into engineering? Both your parents?

JE: My dad died when I was young. My mom really emphasized to my brother and myself to get an education.

KH: Do you have kids or grandkids who have pursued or will pursue baseball as a career? Did you encourage them to do so?

JE: I have a son who played at Rice in the early 1980s and then played two years in the minors.

KH: Was the no-hitter the highlight of your career? If not, what was?

JE: Being a rookie and playing in the 1961 World Series was the highlight. I enjoyed catching Jim's no-hitter and Ray Washburn's 1968 no-hitter.

KH: Have you been to the section of the baseball Hall of Fame that focuses on no-hitters?

JE: I've played in the Hall of Fame game. I don't think I went inside.

KH: Have you spent time signing autographs in Las Vegas, or in Florida or Arizona during spring training?

JE: I did a couple of autograph shows in Cincinnati and one in St. Louis. I also get four to five autograph requests every week.

KH: Do you have last thoughts on the no-hitter?

JE: Jim Maloney was very wild. (Laughs)

KH: Last thoughts on your career?

JE: I was a good defensive catcher, and I could handle a pitching staff well.

Chapter 2

Juan Nieves:
Milwaukee's First No-Hitter

April 15, 1987
Rising star Juan Nieves throws a no-hitter for the red-hot Brewers

"Games like this can make a grown man cry. That's the greatest game I've ever been associated with."
Milwaukee manager Tom Trebelhorn talking about how he felt after the conclusion of the game ("Brewers Nieves Hurls No-Hitter," *New York Times*, April 16, 1987).

"I had a mediocre fastball, and my slider was awful. I just went after them in the final three innings and my slider finally showed up."
Milwaukee pitcher Juan Nieves describing his pitching repertoire during this game ("Brewers Nieves Hurls No-Hitter," *New York Times*, April 16, 1987).

"It was slicing away from me, but I didn't have time to think about it. I ran as far as I could. It's exciting, but Paciorek's catch meant just as much."
Milwaukee center fielder Robin Yount describing his game-ending catch ("Nieves No-Hitter Stops Orioles 7-0," *Washington Post*, April 16, 1987).

"There was a lot of body language and all that on the bench, but no one said anything. It's certainly a great achievement, but so is the next 12

years he pitches in the big leagues. There's just no words to describe it. The whole season has been like this."

Milwaukee manager Tom Trebelhorn describing his young pitcher's potential as the Brewers just won their ninth straight game to start the 1987 season on a no-hitter ("Nieves No-Hitter Stops Orioles 7-0," *Washington Post*, April 16, 1987).

"Once you get by the sixth inning, I think people started thinking about (the no-hitter). Leave him alone at the end of the dugout, nobody talking to him, he's all by himself — no coaches, no nothin'. He's kinda like in the isolation booth. He was there all by himself, but it really hit home (at) the start of the ninth inning."

Milwaukee catcher Bill Schroeder, answering the question as to when he thought about Nieves getting a no-hitter (Interview, April 29, 2021).

When 22-year-old Milwaukee Brewer starter Juan Nieves hurled the first no-hitter ever thrown by a Puerto Rican pitcher, it was considered extraordinary for many reasons. No-hitters are always incredible, distinctive events, and this one generated a lot of excitement. It was not completely unexpected, though. Nieves was already in his second season as part of the Brewers' rotation, and he was rapidly becoming known as a talented, dependable arm behind ace Teddy Higuera.

Milwaukee had already won its first eight games of the season and Nieves had won his first start, an 11-8 slugfest against the Texas Rangers. He was seen as a key piece of a franchise in its 19th year of existence that had been to the World Series just five years earlier in 1982, losing in seven games to the St Louis Cardinals. Things were looking up for the Brewers and Juan Nieves, and the expectation was that both the team and their young pitcher would have much more success.

Unfortunately for Milwaukee, things didn't turn out as well as they would have liked. The Brewers have yet to make it back to the World Series, although they've gone to the National League Championship Series (NLCS) in 2011 (losing to St Louis in six games) and 2018 (losing to Los Angeles in seven games). Their 25-year postseason drought between the team's 1982 World Series loss and their 2008 appearance in the National League Division Series (NLDS) against the

Philadelphia Phillies was particularly frustrating. It still stands as the third longest playoff drought for any team since the start of the expanded postseason era in 1969. The Brewers are behind only the Montreal/Washington franchise (30 seasons without a postseason appearance from 1982-2011) and the Kansas City Royals (28 seasons from 1986-2013).

Nieves' no-hitter was also remarkable because it was the first one ever for the franchise. While early expansion teams such as the Angels, Senators, Colt .45s, Expos, and Royals all had no-hitters recorded by this time, the Mets, Padres, and 1977 newcomers Blue Jays and Mariners were still without one. The Brewers' no-hit drought, consequently, wasn't seen as anything unusual at the time. Thirty-four seasons later, however, the Brewers stand tied for the fewest single-pitcher no-hitters with the Blue Jays, Rockies, Rays, Mets, and Padres – they all have just one. Moreover, the other five teams have all thrown a no-hitter since Juan Nieves threw his in 1987. Milwaukee did throw a combined no-hitter in September 2021 with Corbin Burnes pitching eight innings and Josh Hader closing it out in a 3-0 win over the Cleveland Indians.

Baseball, of course, is a team sport. This can be especially true when a pitcher records a no-hitter. Often, one or two plays are particularly important to preserving the no-hitter. This game stands out for that reason. There was an exceptional number of hit-saving plays that day, highlighted by Robin Yount's diving catch in center field to end the game.

Table 2-1. Brewer Defensive Gems during Nieves No-Hitter

Inning and Outs	Score	Runners and Count	Oriole Hitter	Brewer Fielder	Outcome
2nd Inn No outs	0-0	No runners 2-1 count	Eddie Murray	LF Jim Paciorek	Full extension diving catch of short fly ball
4th Inn No outs	1-0	No runners 3-1 count	Cal Ripken, Jr.	3B Paul Molitor	Snagged a hard-hit line drive to third base
5th Inn Two outs	1-0	Man on 1st 0-0 count	Floyd Rayford	3B Paul Molitor	Again, caught a hard-hit line drive to third
7th Inn No outs	3-0	Man on 1st 2-2 count	Fred Lynn	SS Dale Sveum	Bullet grounder turned into 6-4-3 double play
9th Inn Two outs	7-0	Man on 1st 0-0 count	Eddie Murray	CF Robin Yount	Diving catch of drive to deep right-center

METHODOLOGY: This table lists the most difficult defensive plays made by Milwaukee fielders during Juan Nieves' no-hitter. These specific plays were identified from post-game stories and interviews and correlated with game data provided by baseball-reference.com. The plays are listed in chronological order.

LEGEND: Inn = inning. For example, "7th Inn" indicates the play took place in the 7th inning. Positions are identified as LF = left fielder, 3B = third baseman, SS = shortstop, and CF = center fielder. The phrase "Man on 1st" indicates there was a runner on first base at the time the play was made. The count in balls and strikes to the batter involved was abbreviated 0-0, 1-0, etc. For example, a count of three balls and one strike to the batter was displayed as a "3-1 count." A "6-4-3" double play refers to a double play that went from the shortstop (6) to the second baseman (4) to the first baseman (3). The numbers refer to the scorer's identification of the position a player was playing at the time.

As shown in the table, five plays made the difference between simply a well-pitched game and a no-hit performance by Nieves. In the second inning, Jim Paciorek made a diving catch of Eddie Murray's short flyball in left field. Paul Molitor stabbed two line drives at third base in the fourth and fifth Innings. Dale Sveum made a great play in the seventh on a very hard-hit grounder to shortstop, turning it into a double play. Finally, Robin Yount dove to catch an Eddie Murray line drive to deep right-center field to end the game.

These plays were critical to preserving the no-hitter, of course. They were also important for the Brewers to capture their ninth consecutive win to start the 1987 season. The contest was a pitchers' duel for the first six innings. After second-year shortstop Dale Sveum hit a solo home run just inside the left field line in the fourth inning, the Brewers held onto their precarious 1-0 lead until the seventh. At that point, the team added two more runs when Hall-of-Famer Paul Molitor hit a two-run double off Baltimore starter Mike Flanagan, scoring Paciorek from third and catcher Bill Schroeder all the way from first base. Veteran first baseman Greg Brock then blasted a three-run home run off Baltimore reliever Dave Schmidt, giving Milwaukee a commanding 6-0 advantage over the hometown Orioles. Milwaukee concluded its scoring in the ninth when #3 hitter Glenn Braggs hit a solo home run to make it a 7-0 game.

The team Baltimore fielded that day was particularly imposing, as they had some outstanding hitters in the starting lineup. The number three, four, and five hitters were two Hall of Famers (Cal "Iron Man" Ripken, Jr. and Eddie Murray) and a perennial All-Star and former American League MVP (Fred Lynn). These three powerful batters were ably surrounded by other talented hitters in Ken Gerhart, Rick Burleson, Ray Knight, and Lee Lacy. While the Orioles would limp their way to a disappointing 95-loss season, their record was not due to a lack of hitting skill. Nieves had his work cut out for him.

Young Juan Nieves pitched well on that cold, windy, and rainy night in a game that had a delayed start due to the weather conditions. He struck out seven batters, while getting 10 Oriole hitters to fly out, three to pop out, four to ground out, and three to line out. He walked five during the effort, while throwing a whole lot of pitches. His pitch count was at 53 by the end of the third inning and he had thrown 98 pitches at the end of the sixth inning in a 1-0 game. Milwaukee manager Tom Trebelhorn would surely have been warming a reliever up in the bullpen if this hadn't been a no-hit effort. Nieves became more efficient during his last three innings, yet still required a healthy 128 pitches to complete his no-hitter.

The 1987 Milwaukee Brewers were record setters in numerous ways, earning them the nickname "Team Streak" by the end of the season. The team started the season with a 13-game winning streak, including Nieves's no-hit gem. Nieves also won his previous start on April 10 and started the final winning game on April 20, though he didn't get the decision. This 13-game winning streak is the longest in Brewers' history.

As displayed in Table 2-2 – a compilation of the team's longest winning streaks – putting together a 10 or more-game winning streak didn't ensure success. While four of the seven teams listed earned more than 90 wins, only one of them – the 2021 squad – made it to the postseason. That team eventually lost the NLDS to the World Champion Atlanta Braves. Two of the seven teams shown even finished below .500, with the 2003 team ending up in last place in the NL Central with 94 losses.

Table 2-2. Milwaukee Brewers Longest Winning Streaks

Rank	Streak	Start Date	End Date	W-L Record at End	Season Record	Division Finish
1	13 Games	4/6/1987	4/20/1987	13-0 (1.000)	91-71 (.562 pct)	3rd of 7 AL East (7.0 GB)
2	11 Games	6/22/2021	7/3/2021	51-33 (.607 pct)	95-67 (.586 pct)	1st of 5 NL Central (+5.0)

Rank	Streak	Start Date	End Date	W-L Record at End	Season Record	Division Finish
3 (tie)	10 Games	6/8/1973	6/18/1973	34-27 (.557 pct)	74-88 (.457 pct)	5th of 6 AL East (23.0 GB)
3 (tie)	10 Games	6/9/1978	6/17/1978	36-26 (.581 pct)	93-69 (.574 pct)	3rd of 7 AL East (6.5 GB)
3 (tie)	10 Games	7/11/1979	7/22/1979	59-38 (.608 pct)	95-66 (.590 pct)	2nd of 7 AL East (8.0 GB)
3 (tie)	10 Games	4/30/1988	5/9/1988	18-11 (.621 pct)	87-75 (.537 pct)	T-3rd of 7 AL East (2.0 GB)
3 (tie)	10 Games	8/19/2003	8/28/2003	58-75 (.436 pct)	68-94 (.420 pct)	6th of 6 NL Central (20.0 GB)

METHODOLOGY: The longest winning streaks for this franchise are ranked in order from the highest to the lowest throughout the team's history (1969-2021). All the winning streaks listed occurred when the team played in Milwaukee.

LEGEND: Dates are shown as month/day/year (for example, June 12, 2018, is shown as 6/12/2018). "W-L Record at End" indicates the team's win-loss record at the conclusion of the winning streak. pct = winning percentage (with 1.000 being 100%). Season Record = the team's final record that season. Division Finish = the team's place in the standings at the end of the season followed by the number of teams in the division. For example, "3rd of 7" shows that the team finished in third place in a seven-team division. T-3rd indicates the team was tied for third place in its division. GB = games behind the first-place team (a "+" sign indicates the team was in first place, followed by the number of games it was ahead of the next closest team).

NOTE 1: The 1987 Milwaukee streak in this table reflects only those games played in 1987. The Brewers won their final three games of 1986, so the team won 16 games straight when those contests are included.

NOTE 2: The 2021 Brewers lost their NLDS contest against the Atlanta Braves three games to one.

Milwaukee's 13-game streak is also tied with the 1982 Atlanta Braves for the longest winning streak to start a season. The list in Table 2-3 includes several division or league champions, including the World Champion 1955 Brooklyn Dodgers. The 1966 Cleveland Indians, though, faded after their red-hot start and ended the season with a .500 record, 17 games behind the American League Champion Baltimore Orioles.

Table 2-3. Longest Winning Streaks to Start a Season

Rank	Winning Streak	Team	Season	Season Record	Season Finish
1 (tie)	13 games	Atlanta Braves	1982	89-73 (.549 pct)	1st of 6 NL West (+1.0)
1 (tie)	13 games	Milwaukee Brewers	1987	91-71 (.562 pct)	3rd of 7 AL East (7.0 GB)
3	11 games	Oakland Athletics	1981	64-45 (.587 pct)	1st of 7 AL West (+5.0)
4 (tie)	10 games	Brooklyn Dodgers	1955	98-55 (.641 pct)	1st of 8 NL (+13.5)
4 (tie)	10 games	Pittsburgh Pirates	1962	93-68 (.578 pct)	4th of 10 NL (8.0 GB)
4 (tie)	10 games	Cleveland Indians	1966	81-81 (.500 pct)	5th of 10 AL (17.0 GB)

METHODOLOGY: This table ranks the six longest team winning streaks to start a baseball season from 1900-2021. In case of a tie, team streaks are listed in chronological order.

LEGEND: pct = winning percentage (with 1.000 being 100%). GB = games behind the first-place team (a "+" sign indicates the team was in first place, followed by the number of games it was ahead of the next closest team). A team's finish in its division is indicated by the team's place in the standings followed by the number of teams in the division. For example, "3rd of 7" shows that the team finished in third place in a seven-team division. Showing just "AL" or "NL" without a division identified indicates that this occurred when there were no divisions in the American or National League, as this was the league structure up through the 1968 season.

NOTE 1: The 1982 Atlanta Braves were swept in the NLCS by the St. Louis Cardinals in three games.

NOTE 2: Because of a mid-season players strike in the 1981 season, Oakland's season record and season finish reflect game totals for the entire year. Oakland won the American League West in the first half of season with a record of 37-23, finishing one and a half games ahead of the Texas Rangers. The Athletics finished in second place in the second half of season with a record of 27-22, placing them one game behind the Royals. Because of the split season, both the National and American Leagues introduced the division series between the division winners in each half of the season. The division series would become permanent with the advent of the wild card in 1995. In the American League Division Series (ALDS) for the West Division, Oakland swept Kansas City three games to none. In turn, the Athletics were swept by the New York Yankees in three games in the American League Championship Series (ALCS).

NOTE 3: The 1955 Brooklyn Dodgers beat the New York Yankees in the World Series, four games to three.

The 1987 Brewers could also go from red hot to ice cold in short order. After winning their first 13 games, the Brewers then went 7-3 over the next 10 contests. At that point, they had an incredible 20-3 record, a full five games in front of the second-place Yankees and the season was still in its infancy. While no one expected them to continue that scorching pace, they looked like favorites for the division title, if not the world championship. It was then the team went ice cold, losing their next 12 games in a row. At the time, this losing streak was the franchise's longest in the 19 seasons it had been in existence. Even now, after the 2021 season, this streak remains tied for the second most losses in a row, behind only a 14-game losing streak the 1994 team put together in May of that year.

Table 2-4. Milwaukee Brewers Longest Losing Streaks

Rank	Streak (Home)	Start Date	End Date	W-L Record at End	Season Record	Season Finish
1	14 (Mil)	5/11/1994	5/25/1994	17-28 (.378 pct)	53-62 (.461 pct)	5th of 5 AL Central (14.0 GB)
2 (tie)	12 (Mil)	5/3/1987	5/19/1987	20-15 (.571 pct)	91-71 (.562 pct)	3rd of 7 AL East (7.0 GB)
2 (tie)	12 (Mil)	8/18/2004	8/30/2004	55-74 (.426 pct)	67-94 (.416 pct)	6th of 6 NL Central (37.5 GB)
4	11 (Mil)	7/14/2001	7/24/2001	43-56 (.434 pct)	68-94 (.420 pct)	4th of 6 NL Central (25.0 GB)
5 (tie)	10 (Sea)	8/15/1969	8/24/1969	48-76 (.387 pct)	64-98 (.395 pct)	6th of 6 AL West (33.0 GB)
5 (tie)	10 (Mil)	9/9/1983	9/19/1983	79-71 (.527 pct)	87-75 (.537 pct)	5th of 7 AL East (11.0 GB)
5 (tie)	10 (Mil)	7/29/1984	8/7/1984	47-66 (.416 pct)	67-94 (.416 pct)	7th of 7 AL East (36.5 GB)
5 (tie)	10 (Mil)	8/25/2006	9/3/2006	62-75 (.453 pct)	75-87 (.463 pct)	4th of 6 NL Central (8.5 GB)

METHODOLOGY: The longest losing streaks for this franchise are ranked from the longest to the shortest. In case of a tie, the team streaks are listed in chronological order.

LEGEND: Dates are shown as month/day/year (for example, June 12, 2018, is shown as 6/12/2018). "W-L Record at End" indicates the team's win-loss record at the conclusion of the winning streak. pct = winning percentage (with 1.000 being 100%). Season Record = the team's final record that season. Division Finish = the team's place in the standings followed by the number of teams in the division. For example, "5th of 5" shows that the team finished in fifth place in a five-team division. GB = games behind the first-place team. Home = the city the franchise called home (Mil = Milwaukee and Sea = Seattle). Specifically, the team played in Seattle as the Pilots in 1969 and in Milwaukee as the Brewers from 1970 on.

The Milwaukee Brewers franchise has been on the move regularly throughout the years. They started as the Seattle Pilots as part of the newly established American League West in 1969. While remaining in the AL West, the franchise moved to Milwaukee and became the Brewers in 1970. In 1972, the Brewers switched to the AL East when the Washington Senators became the Texas Rangers and moved to the AL West. The Brewers stayed in the AL East for the next 22 years. They then moved prior to the 1994 season to the brand-new AL Central when both leagues switched from a two-division format to a three-division structure. In 1998, the Brewers became the first team to ever switch leagues as they joined the National League Central Division when the Arizona Diamondbacks were established. This was an effort to ensure both the National League (16 teams) and American League (14 teams) had an even number of teams. This was due to a desire to ensure teams could always play against other teams in their league outside of the small midseason window when interleague games were played.

It's easy to see that the 1987 Brewers would have been in the thick of that season's AL East race if they hadn't dropped a dozen in a row in early May. As it turned out, the Brewers were still very competitive even after losing those 12 games. When the streak ended, the team was in third place in the division, three games behind the Yankees. They couldn't make up that ground as the season progressed, however. In the highly competitive AL East, 91 wins only got them third place behind the powerful 98-win Detroit Tigers. If the Brewers were in the 1987 AL West, Milwaukee's 91 wins would have been good enough to crown them division champions.

Juan Nieves did his best during this dismal time, though. In the last game before the losing streak began, Nieves was the winning pitcher in a 6-4 victory over the Mariners. His next two games were losses, but the second one was a 4-3 defeat to the Royals where Nieves handed over the game to the bullpen with a 3-2 lead in the sixth inning. Nieves was the pitcher who broke the losing streak, as well, throwing eight innings of one-run ball against the Chicago White Sox on May 20 to finally win a game.

While most of the teams on the list above were mired in depressing seasons, there are two additional squads who would have been competitive for division titles if not for their 10-game stumbles. The 1983 team, which included many of the 1987 players, finished the season with 87 wins, only 11 games behind the AL East Champion Baltimore Orioles. Additionally, the 2006 Brewers, while winning only 75 games, were just eight and a half games behind the NL Central Champion St. Louis Cardinals, who won the division with a meager 83 victories. Interestingly, both the 1983 Orioles and 2006 Cardinals would go on to win their league titles and become world champions.

Individual Brewers racked up impressive streaks as well. Paul Molitor put together the fifth-longest hitting streak in post-1900 major league history. From July 16 to August 25, Molitor hit safely in 39 consecutive games, putting him just behind hitting greats Joe DiMaggio, Pete Rose, George Sisler, and Ty Cobb. During his 39-game hitting tear, Molitor compiled 68 hits, including 17 doubles, three triples, and seven home runs for a very impressive On-base Plus Slugging Percentage (OPS) of 1.178. The Brewers did well during his streak, too, going nine games over .500 with a record of 24-15. Molitor was on deck in what would have been his 40th straight game when Milwaukee pinch-hitter Rick Manning rapped a one-out single to score pinch-runner Mike Felder from second base in the bottom of the 10th, thereby winning the game for the Brewers. For comparison, a table with the longest hitting streaks in major league history is included below.

Table 2-5. Longest Consecutive Game Hitting Streaks (1900-2021)

Rank	Streak	Player	Team	Start Date	End Date
1	56 Games	Joe DiMaggio	New York Yankees	5/15/1941	7/16/1941
2	44 Games	Pete Rose	Cincinnati Reds	6/14/1978	7/31/1978
3	41 Games	George Sisler	St. Louis Browns	7/27/1922	9/17/1922
4	40 Games	Ty Cobb	Detroit Tigers	5/15/1911	7/2/1911
5	39 Games	Paul Molitor	Milwaukee Brewers	7/16/1987	8/25/1987
6	38 Games	Jimmy Rollins	Philadelphia Phillies	8/23/2005	4/5/2006
7	37 Games	Tommy Holmes	Boston Braves	6/6/1945	7/8/1945

Rank	Streak	Player	Team	Start Date	End Date
8 (tie)	35 Games	Ty Cobb	Detroit Tigers	5/31/1917	7/5/1917
8 (tie)	35 Games	George Sisler	St. Louis Browns	9/27/1924	5/19/1925
8 (tie)	35 Games	Luis Castillo	Florida Marlins	5/8/2002	6/21/2002
8 (tie)	35 Games	Chase Utley	Philadelphia Phillies	6/23/2006	8/3/2006

METHODOLOGY: This table lists the longest hitting streaks for any player since 1900. In the case of a tie, the streaks are listed in chronological order.

LEGEND: Start Date = the game the player got his first hit to begin his streak. End Date is the day the player got his last hit of the streak.

NOTE: All streaks occurred within the same season, except for Hall of Famer George Sisler's 35-game streak in 1924-1925 and Jimmy Rollins' 38-game streak in 2005-2006. "Wee Willie" Keeler of the National League's Baltimore Orioles had a 44-game hitting streak in 1897 and is recognized as the record holder prior to Joe DiMaggio. Joe DiMaggio shattered Keeler's 44-year-old record when he compiled a 56-game streak in 1941. George Sisler set the modern (post-1900) high water mark of hitting safely in 41 consecutive games in 1922. Sisler is the only player who is listed twice in this table.

In addition to the team's impressive winning and losing streaks and Molitor's hitting streaks, starting pitcher Teddy Higuera set a team record by throwing 32 consecutive scoreless innings from August 26 to September 11. His streak encompassed three shutout games, including one 10-inning contest. During this period late in the season, All-Star Teddy Higuera's ERA dropped from 4.42 to 3.79. Higuera won 18 games in 1987 and set the Brewers' season record for strikeouts when he racked up 240 of them.

Table 2-6. Brewers Highest Game Scores

Rank	Pitcher	Date Score	Opponent	GSc	IP, Hits, Runs, ERs, Walks, Strikeouts
1	Corbin Burnes	9/11/2021 Mil 3-0	Cleveland Indians	95	8.0 IP, 0 Hits, 0 Runs, 0 ERs, 1 BB, 14 Ks
2 (tie)	Jim Colborn	9/27/1974 Bal 1-0 (17 inn)	Baltimore Orioles	94	13.0 IP, 8 Hits, 0 Runs, 0 ERs, 6 BBs, 9 Ks
2 (tie)	Teddy Higuera	8/26/1987 Mil 1-0 (10 inn)	Cleveland Indians	94	10.0 IP, 3 Hits, 0 Runs, 0 ERs, 2 BBs, 10 Ks
2 (tie)	Ben Sheets	5/16/2004 Mil 4-1	Atlanta Braves	94	9.0 IP, 3 Hits, 1 Run, 1 ER, 1 BB, 18 Ks
5	C.C. Sabathia	8/31/2008 Mil 7-0	Pittsburgh Pirates	93	9.0 IP, 1 Hit, 0 Runs, 0 ERs, 3 BBs, 11 Ks
6 (tie)	Marty Pattin (Sea)	4/29/1969 Sea 1-0	California Angels	92	9.0 IP, 2 Hits, 0 Runs, 0 ERs, 2 BBs, 11 Ks
6 (tie)	Teddy Higuera	9/1/1987 Mil 2-0	Kansas City Royals	92	9.0 IP, 1 Hit, 0 Runs, 0 ERs, 2 BBs, 9 Ks
8 (tie)	Bill Wegman	7/7/1986 Cal 3-1 (16 inn)	California Angels	91	11.0 IP, 4 Hits, 0 Runs, 0 ERs, 2 BBs, 4 Ks
8 (tie)	Steve Woodard	7/28/1997 (1) Mil 1-0	Toronto Blue Jays	91	8.0 IP, 1 Hit, 0 Runs, 0 ERs, 1 BB, 12 Ks
10 (tie)	Teddy Higuera	7/20/1988 KC 4-0 (13 inn)	Kansas City Royals	90	9.0 IP, 3 Hits, 0 Runs, 0 ERs, 1 BB, 10 Ks
10 (tie)	Ben Sheets	6/8/2004 Mil 1-0 (17 inn)	Anaheim Angels	90	9.0 IP, 1 Hit, 0 Runs, 0 ERs, 0 BBs, 5 Ks
10 (tie)	Matt Garza	7/5/2014 Mil 1-0	Cincinnati Reds	90	9.0 IP, 2 Hits, 0 Runs, 0 ERs, 2 BBs, 9 Ks
13 (tie)	Juan Nieves	4/15/1987 Mil 7-0	Baltimore Orioles	89	9.0 IP, 0 Hits, 0 Runs, 0 ERs, 5 BBs, 7 Ks

METHODOLOGY: This table includes the highest Game Scores thrown by a pitcher from the Seattle Pilots/Milwaukee Brewers franchise from 1969-2021. Games are ranked by Game Score (GSc) and consider all franchise regular season and postseason games. Game Score measures a pitcher's performance in any given game started. Introduced by baseball writer/statistician Bill James in the 1980s, Game

Score is presented as a figure between 0-100 — except for extreme outliers — and usually falls between 40-70. Both Milwaukee no-hitters are included in this table.

LEGEND: Dates are shown as month/day/year (for example, June 12, 2018, is shown as 6/12/2018). IP = innings pitched; BB(s) = base(s) on balls (or walk(s)); K(s) = strikeout(s); ER(s) = earned run(s); inn = innings and indicates how many innings the game lasted; and (1) = first game of a doubleheader. (Sea) indicates the team was the Seattle Pilots when the game was played. The team played in Seattle as the Pilots in 1969 and in Milwaukee as the Brewers from 1970 on. This table

NOTE 1: The team's second no-hitter was not a single-pitcher game. That game registered the highest Game Score of any Milwaukee pitcher when Corbin Burnes threw the first eight innings of no-hit ball and recorded 14 strikeouts. Josh Hader finished the game by retiring three Cleveland batters in order, including two strikeouts. The only Indian baserunner for the entire game was on a five-pitch walk issued by Burnes to Cleveland's Myles Straw leading off the top of the seventh.

NOTE 2: The highest postseason Game Score was an 83 by Mike Caldwell in Game 1 of the 1982 World Series against St. Louis. Caldwell threw a three-hit shutout en route to a 10-0 victory over the Cardinals. Caldwell was dominant, as he only allowed four baserunners, and no Cardinal ever made it past second base. The thrilling World Series went the full seven games, with St. Louis coming out on top. Caldwell started two games during the series and won both.

NOTE 3: Ben Sheets' 18 strikeouts in his 2004 game is the most ever in a single game by a Milwaukee pitcher. It is also tied for 12th place for most strikeouts by any major league pitcher in a nine-inning game. The next closest Brewer pitcher to Sheets is Corbin Burnes with 15 in an August 2021 game thrown one month prior to his multi-pitcher no-hitter.

NOTE 4: The only hit given up by C.C. Sabathia in his 2008 one-hitter was a leadoff single in the fifth inning on a groundball that he fielded off the mound. Bill Schroeder, in his interview at the end of this chapter, insists that Sabathia bobbled the ball, and the play should have been ruled an error.

NOTE 5: Marty Pattin's 1969 game took place during the team's inaugural month as the expansion Seattle Pilots. Pattin had a no-hitter going until California's Tom Satriano hit a two-out single in the top of the eighth inning. While the 26-year-old Pattin would become an accomplished pitcher in time – even earning an American League All-Star berth as a member of the 1971 Brewers – his 1969 season was mostly forgettable apart from this very impressive game. He finished the season with a 7-12 record and a 5.62 ERA.

NOTE 6: Teddy Higuera gave up two walks in the fifth inning during his 1987 one-hitter against the Royals. He had a no-hitter going until there were two outs in the eighth inning. At that point Royals shortstop Ross Jones hit a triple down the left field line. Jones was a late season call-up for Kansas City, accumulating 145 at bats over three seasons. Higuera's 92 Game Score was the second best of his career. His best Game Score (94) had been achieved in a 10-inning, three-hit shutout win against the Indians in his previous start six games earlier.

NOTE 7: Facing the Toronto Blue Jays and the mighty Roger Clemens in his 1997 rookie debut, Steve Woodard threw 119 pitches over eight shutout innings. The only hit the Blue Jays got for the entire game was a leadoff double by Otis Nixon in the first inning. Milwaukee closer Mike Fetters came in to pitch the ninth to close out the game for a 1-0 Brewer victory and Woodard's first major league win.

NOTE 8: The only hit given up in Ben Sheets' nine-inning effort against Anaheim in 2004 was a two-out single by Vladimir Guerrero with two outs in the seventh inning. At the end of nine innings, the game was tied 0-0 and headed into extra innings as the relievers for both teams took over. The scoreless game ended when Brewer Danny Kolb shut down the Angels in the bottom of the 17th after Milwaukee's Scott Podsednik doubled to deep right field scoring Craig Counsell from first base with two outs in the top of the inning. While the longest game in franchise history is a 25-inning marathon in 1984 between the Brewers and the White Sox (Bill Schroeder played in that game and discusses it in his interview at the end of this chapter, too), this game is tied for the team's longest scoreless game, going a full 16 innings before either team crossed the plate with a run. The other 16-inning scoreless streak was the Brewers-Orioles game on September 27, 1974. That contest ended in a 1-0 Baltimore walk-off win in the bottom of the 17th, too. This game is also included in Table 2-6, as Jim Colborn's 13 shutout innings earned him a game score of 94, tying him with Ben Sheets and Teddy Higuera for second place on the list of highest franchise Game Scores.

Growing up in Puerto Rico, Juan Nieves did not start pitching until he was 14. Fortunately, his life changed when he got a prep-school scholarship at Avon Old Farms school in Connecticut. It was during his prep career that he took up baseball and excelled. He dominated the other teams with a 19-1 record and 1.05 ERA, striking out 288 batters in 196 innings. Nieves signed as an undrafted free agent by

Milwaukee in July 1983 (Puerto Rican players were not subject to the draft until 1989). Nieves rose through the Milwaukee farm system and debuted early in the 1986 season. His debut year was impressive, as he went 11-12 with 116 strikeouts in 184 innings pitched.

At the time he threw his no-hitter, Nieves was one of the youngest players to have accomplished this feat, and it looked like the sky was the limit for this talented young hurler. Despite his promising start to the season, Nieves would struggle with inconsistency throughout 1987, although he did manage to rack up four straight wins in mid-August. Building on his solid rookie performance, Nieves finished his promising 1987 season with a 14-8 record and 163 strikeouts over 195 innings. Unfortunately, arm troubles developed in 1988, limiting him to just 110 innings pitched; 1988 would be his last year in the majors due to arm injury.

Nieves used his pitching expertise to build an impressive post-playing career as a pitching coach. He was in the New York Yankees organization from 1992 to 1996 and with the Chicago White Sox chain from 1999 to 2007. In 2008, he was named the White Sox bullpen coach, and stayed in that role until the end of the 2012 season. In 2013, he was hired by the Boston Red Sox to be the pitching coach under new manager John Farrell, and he earned a World Series ring as a member of that championship team. He left the Red Sox during the 2015 season and was picked up as pitching coach by the Miami Marlins for the 2016 season, where he stayed until the end of 2018. In 2021, he was named assistant pitching coach of the Detroit Tigers.

The catcher for Nieves' no-hitter was 28-year-old veteran Bill Schroeder. Schroeder had been with the Brewers since 1983, although he had mostly been used in a backup or platoon role. The primary catcher for Milwaukee in 1987 was up-and-coming 22-year-old rookie B.J. Surhoff. Schroeder was often used as the starter against lefties, and with Baltimore's Mike Flanagan on the mound, this was a good time for him to start. Along with that, Surhoff had some dental work earlier in the day and couldn't play. Schroeder played for eight years with Milwaukee and California, compiling a solid .240 batting average and 61 home runs over 376 games. His expertise and patience certainly paid off that night in Baltimore. Schroeder began a highly successful second career in 1995 as a beloved color commentator for Milwaukee Brewer television broadcasts, a position he continues to hold in 2022.

As will be shown in a later chapter, the Nieves/Schroeder battery has one of the lowest combined WAR values of any no-hit battery in major league history. With Nieves at 3.4 WAR and Schroeder at 2.8 (combined total of 6.2), the duo has one of the ten lowest combined WAR values of any pitcher/catcher combination to throw a no-hitter. This low combined total reinforces the perception that this was a highly unlikely no-hitter that day. Of course, this observation is more of a footnote than anything else. The two men have fashioned extraordinary baseball careers that should be celebrated in their entirety.

Below are interviews with both Juan Nieves and Bill Schroeder. I invite you to enjoy them.

Juan Nieves Interview
Conducted by Kevin Hurd on August 31, 2021

Kevin Hurd (KH): Would you consider yourself to be the best player on your Little League, American Legion, Pony, Colt, high school, and minor league teams?

Juan Nieves (JN): Yes. I didn't start pitching until I was 14, until then I played center field and first base. I would also pitch for an AA team in Puerto Rico (ages 15-29) during the off-season when I played high-school ball in Connecticut.

KH: When you were in Little League, Colt, or Pony League, did your league have "outlier" players, players who were always hitting home runs or pitching no-hitters?

JN: Yes, we did. Usually, they were guys that had matured early. I don't recall if any of them made it to the majors.

KH: Did you ever throw a no-hitter in any of these leagues or the minors?

JN: Little League, Pony, Colt, AA? I don't think so. High school, maybe. Minors, no. I had plenty of dominant games, with many strikeouts, allowing one or two hits, but other than possibly in high school, I don't remember any no-hitters.

KH: Did you feel any different (good or bad) on the day of your no-hitter?

JN: No, I felt very normal, like it would be a regular game.

KH: What pitches were working best for you that day?

JN: I was a young pitcher, and I threw mostly fastballs. My other pitches I had a hard time consistently throwing for strikes. So, for this game, the vast majority of pitches I threw were fastballs.

KH: Speaking of young pitchers, you do know that you were the second youngest pitcher, at age 21, to ever throw a no-hitter?

JN: (Laughs) Yes, I have been informed of that.

KH: What was the best defensive play, the closest you came to losing the no-hitter?

JN: There were several very good plays. Early in the game, in the second or third inning, left fielder Jim Paciorek made an unbelievable diving catch on a looper to left. In the fourth and fifth innings, Paul Molitor made a couple of good plays on line shots. And, of course, the great diving catch Robin Yount made on a line drive in center field to end the game.

KH: Do you remember shaking off your catcher's signs much during the game?

JN: No, I was a young pitcher, and I basically threw what was called for.

KH: Do you have any memorabilia/souvenirs, such as a baseball, plaque, uniforms, or something else, from the game in your house?

JN: Yes, I got a video of the game, a jersey, and an undershirt that has stuff written on it. The Hall of Fame kept the baseball and my cap.

KH: Here's a fun question: You were in the movie "For the Love of the Game" in 1999. Have you ever considered doing another movie?

JN: I had a great time being in that movie. Everybody, especially Kevin (Costner) was great to be with. So yes, I would welcome the chance to be in another couple of movies.

KH: Which of your minor league managers, Tim Nordbrook, Mike Pazik, Andy Etchebarren, Terry Bevington, or Tom Trebelhorn, did you like playing for the most?

JN: All of them were helpful. They all knew how to handle me.

KH: You played for two managers in the majors: George Bamburger and Tom Trebelhorn. Did they both help you?

JN: Absolutely. They knew how to handle me, also. In addition, the Brewers GM (Harry Dalton) helped me a lot, too.

KH: Do you think the number of pitches (128) you threw that day led to you getting a sore arm?

JN: No, I didn't get a sore arm until the next year (1988). After the 1987 season, I didn't play winter ball, which led to my arm becoming dormant, which created atrophy. So no, the no-hitter didn't cause my sore arm.

KH: Was your catcher (Bill Schroeder) one you had requested before?

JN: I was 21 years old. I didn't have the pull to request a catcher. (Laughs)

KH: Do you still stay in contact with Bill?

JN: Absolutely. Bill is a broadcaster for Milwaukee and anytime we play them we talk.

KH: Did your team give you a bonus for throwing your no-hitter?

JN: No, they did not. (Laughs)

KH: During the game, when did you think *"I've got a real shot at a no-hitter?"* Was it on the fifth inning, sixth inning, or later?

JN: Through six innings we were ahead 1-0. I was more concerned about winning the game. In the top of the seventh we scored two more runs to go ahead 3-0, and I started thinking more about the no-hitter at that point.

KH: Were you able to get a follow-on job in baseball after your playing days were over in major league baseball, the minors, college, high school, or in the media?

JN: I've had coaching jobs almost continually since 1992.

KH: What do you like most or least about coaching.

JN: I most like helping a player reach his potential. I least like that you can't save them all.

KH: What minor league coaches and managers helped you the most and made a difference in your pursuit of playing in the majors?

JN: I'm probably going to forget some names, but here goes: Mark Newman, Don Cooper, Jim Paul, Herm Starette, in addition to the managers mentioned earlier.

KH: Since you got a job in baseball, do you think having thrown a no-hitter helped you get the job?

JN: No, it probably didn't.

KH: Do you have any kids or grandkids who have or will pursue baseball as a career? Do you encourage them to do so?

JN: No.

KH: Was the no-hitter the highlight of your career? If not, what was?

JN: For my career as a pitcher in the majors, yes, it was the highlight. As far as my professional career, I'd say that in winter ball (1986-1987) when I pitched for Caguas against the Dominican Republic and threw six shutout innings to help with the win was probably my highlight.

KH: Have you been to the section of the baseball Hall of Fame that focuses on no-hitters?

JN: Yes, I have. When my family and I went there, we spent time looking all over the Hall of Fame.

Bill Schroeder Interview
Conducted by Kevin McCaffrey on April 29, 2021

Bill Schroeder: First of all, it was many, many, many years ago, so my memory might be fading a little bit on some of the details so you might want to check on some of the stats or whatever...

Kevin McCaffrey: Yeah, we've done a lot of research into that, so we do have a lot of that information.

KM: (first question) Would you consider yourself to be the best catcher on your Little League, high school, college, or minor league teams?

BS: Well, I don't know about college, I think, yeah, I mean all the way through I felt as though — and everybody in the big leagues — everybody who gets to the minor leagues is always the best. The best of the best. That was always the case. I felt like my minor league career was a good one, (but) it wasn't like resounding. There were a lot of players that I played against in the minor leagues that probably had better talent than me, but I was in the right place at the right time. I worked hard, and I ended up having a seven-year career in the big leagues so a lot of it's being in the right place at the right time. Do they need you? And at the time they did — the Brewers.

KM: Did you feel any different — good or bad — on the day you caught that no-hitter?

BS: Well actually, we were in Baltimore, it was part of a 13-0 streak, you probably know all this.

KM: Yeah, exactly, start of the season, 13-0.

BS: Yeah, that day we won that game, the no-hitter, that was the ninth straight game, and it was cold and rainy in Baltimore. I wasn't even on the lineup card to start that game. B.J. Surhoff, it was his rookie year. He's from the Baltimore area and he had dental work that morning. And he came to the ballpark, his name was in the lineup to start, but he couldn't go. Tom Trebelhorn came up to me during batting practice and says, "You're catching, B.J. can't go." I guess he'd had some molars, or something removed, and he couldn't go, so I caught. My joke to B.J. is: had he not gotten dental work that day there still wouldn't be a no-hitter in Brewer history.

KM: Exactly (hearty laughter).

BS: That's the joke, we have fun with that. Yeah, but you know Juan really had great stuff that day, it was one of those things where whatever he touched turned to gold. There was great defense, Robin's catch at the end, there was a really good play by Dale Sveum at short on a bad hop, Molitor caught a line drive, Jim Paciorek … oh it's coming back to me, isn't it? Jim Paciorek came in, and dove and made a catch in short left, so good defense. The kid, Juan Nieves, just had incredible explosive stuff that day. Basically fastball, curveball, and it was not very hitter-ish weather — it was cold and rainy the whole time.

KM: So, the fastball and the curve were the ones that were working best for him that day?

BS: Oh yeah, that's basically his two pitches. He came up with a little changeup toward the end of his career. He hurt his shoulder and then he turned out to be a pretty good pitching coach with the White Sox and the Marlins. And the Red Sox, too.

KM: You kind of touched on this, what play would you say came the closest to losing the no-hitter?

BS: Well, Jim Paciorek's catch was in the second inning I believe. Molitor speared a line drive down the line — whether it would've been fair or not, I don't know — I forget who hit it, but if it went off his glove it could very well have been called fair. But Robin's catch is the one that gets all the accolades, you know, the ending, the final catch — into right center, two-handing it and all that kind of stuff. A lot of people think "did he have to dive?" He dove, and he two-handed it. He wasn't going to allow that ball to go off the end of his glove for sure. That was probably the best play of the night.

KM: Did Juan shake you off much during the game?

BS: Well once in a while. I'm not gonna say he shook me off a lot, I'm not gonna say he didn't shake me off at all either. It was just typical. He kinda knew what he had going, and I do remember before Eddie Murray flew out to end the game, we got to 2-and-0 on Cal Ripken, and I was kind of setting off the plate a little bit. The game was—we had it pretty much wrapped up, I think it was 7-0 — I kind of set off the outside corner a little bit. I didn't want to lose a no-hitter on a 2-0 pitch or a 3-1 pitch. So, we walked him there. So, in my infinite wisdom we walked Ripken to get to Eddie Murray, one Hall of Famer to another. And then Murray hit the first pitch, and that was the first pitch to Murray that at-bat, ended up being that great catch by Yount.

KM: Do you have any memorabilia or souvenirs from that game?

BS: Well, I had my catcher's mitt. You know back in those days the catcher's mitt, the Rawlings catcher's mitt with the orange around the edges of the glove for the target, I had that glove in my possession. But I gave that glove to the Cape Cod Hall of Fame Museum. I was inducted into the Cape Cod League — it's a great, I don't know if you know anything about the Cape Cod League — it's a great college league (KM: Exactly, I've heard about it). They inducted me into the Hall of Fame there and I gave them that glove. I don't know if it's still there, but I wanted the Cape Cod League Museum Hall of Fame to have the glove because I figured that would be the best place for it. Other than that, no, I don't have anything. I might have kept the jersey, I don't know, from that year. I don't remember. If I did, my kids have it now.

KM: Yeah, well that's cool. And do you stay in touch with Juan Nieves at all?

BS: Oh yeah, I run Brewers fantasy camp. He's been a fantasy coach a couple of times, and you know when he would come in with the Marlins, we'd chit-chat around the batting cage and things like that. It's funny with baseball — out of sight, out of mind — but then when you haven't seen a guy for maybe ten years you pick up right where you left off. It's one of those great relationships that people have and it's one of the things I still cherish most about still being in the game as a broadcaster. This is my 27th year doing Brewers television and I'm able to stay in touch with a lot of the guys, through that and through fantasy camp. These guys come out and coach the fantasy campers down in Arizona. Yeah, I mean, stay in touch as much as you can, but because of those two things I'm able to get in touch with a lot of these guys. And we have nice chats — short, quick, you know "remember the old days" that type of thing, and it's time to move on.

KM: Yeah, one of the things that I've always enjoyed when I hear an interview with a retired player is how much they remember, how many details they remember about individual games, it's so cool.

BS: Yeah, things that really stick into your memory. I haven't thought about the no-hitter, you know, people text me every April 15th, "hey congratulations, happy anniversary" and this year I'm thinking "What do you mean, happy anniversary?" Oh yeah, yeah, yeah — the no-hitter. But it's the only one in Brewer history. There should have been another — C.C. Sabathia should've had one. There was a bad call by the official scorer, I'll stick with that. So, it was the first, hopefully it's not the last, that's for sure. (Author's note: this interview took place five months before Corbin Burnes and Josh Hader combined for Milwaukee's second no-hitter)

KM: Yeah, absolutely. During the game do you remember when you started thinking "He's got a shot at a no-hitter"?

BS: Well, I think once we had the game in hand, I forget the line score, but I think we ended up with a 7-0 lead at one point at the end. Once you get by the sixth inning, I think people started thinking about that. Leave him alone at the end of the dugout, nobody talking to him, he's all by himself — no coaches, no nothin', he's kinda like in the isolation booth. He was there all by himself, but it really hit home at the start of the ninth inning. I remember my father came down from New Jersey for that game. He drove all the way down and saw that game, the no-hitter game, and then drove all the way back after the game. We went back to Milwaukee right after that. Yeah, it's a great memory. You know, for a guy who had a relatively marginal major league career, you can't take that game away from him.

KM: Absolutely, and I believe he was the first player from Puerto Rico to throw a no-hitter.

BS: Oh, I didn't know that.

KM: Yeah, I think I came across that in the research. How about as a broadcaster, when do you start noting that a pitcher has a no-hitter going?

BS: Well, we do the line score, and we talk about it. I think it starts getting interesting when you get through the sixth inning. You know sixth inning, I guess you go through the sixth and all of a sudden, the no-hitter starts to come around. There's always a fine line to walk with that, as a player you don't want to jinx it but as a broadcaster you gotta let people know what's going on.

KM: Yeah, I agree with that.

BS: The whole C.C. Sabathia thing, I don't know if you remember, he had a no-hitter against the Pirates, I think it was the seventh inning if I'm not mistaken, (Author's note: It was the fourth inning), I may be wrong about that but it was a little comebacker to him, he had to bounce off the mound, he bobbled it, lost the handle on it and they gave the guy a hit in Pittsburgh. And that was the only hit. That was, you know, whatever. That's one of those things.

KM: So, would you consider the no-hitter the highlight of your career as a player?

BS: Yeah, I think, as a player that would be the highlight of my career. I had some good games at Yankee Stadium — you know, I'm from New Jersey. We'd always go up there to Yankee Stadium and Shea Stadium and we'd go down to Philly for games. Going to Yankee Stadium was always a special thing, this was before they renovated it. I never played in Yankee Stadium before they renovated it, but I did play afterwards, and I had a couple of good games there. To me, anytime you can do well in a stadium where you sat as a kid, 8, 9, 10 years old, and watch guys like Mickey Mantle, and guys like that, Mel Stottlemyre — you think, "I'm on the same field they were on." That's special.

KM: You mentioned your kids, have any of your kids played baseball?

BS: My son, and I have two girls -- you know softball stuff in school. My son played in college. He went to Grand Canyon University for two years, before that Indian Hills Community College in Iowa. They have a pretty good baseball program. He actually got drafted, I can't remember the year. I know he's been in the Army 11 years so it was probably a couple of years before that, you can do the math if you'd like. If my wife was here, she would know. But yeah, he got drafted, you know like 40-something round. I think Doug Melvin, general manager of the Brewers, did it as a favor for me. He decided that that wasn't the path he wanted to go down. He went back to Arizona where he had an apartment after college and enlisted in the Army.

KM: And he's still in the Army?

BS: He's still in and he's probably going to be getting out soon.

KM: That's great.

BS: Yeah, we're proud of him.

KM: I have just a couple more. Have you been to the Hall of Fame and looked at the section where they focus on the no-hitters?

BS: Yeah, I've been there a couple times. Matter of fact, the Brewers played the Hall of Fame game one year against the Marlins. I think it was the year that

Kirby Puckett was inducted if I'm not mistaken. I went there with my family — my brother and my family when I was probably 10 or 11 years old. And I went back, matter of fact, went into the Hall of Fame and immediately saw the scorecard of the longest game that I played in, the longest game in American League history. White Sox and Brewers, it was 25 innings.

KM: Wow! When was that?

BS: The game that we lost, that was 1985, I think it was. Yeah, Harold Baines won the game in the 25th inning with a three-run homer.

KM: Wow. A couple more — have you done any autograph signings, stuff like that, in spring training or Las Vegas or anything like that?

BS: No, I don't do any of that. That's ... those are for Hall of Famers. I'm far from that. I do a fair amount of that around Milwaukee. When fans send cards to the ballpark for me to sign, I'll sign 'em and send 'em back, things like that. I don't how many people are actually gonna pay for my autograph.

KM: (Laughs) Just one last thing — any other stories you might have regarding any of this — that game or your career?

BS: Well, nothing that would actually jump out on the page. I've been very fortunate, and the Brewers have been good to me. They stuck with me, good times and bad, as a player — I had a couple of arm injuries. I went to the Angels for my last two years. I wouldn't trade my experiences or any of the decisions that I've made for anything. Leaving Clemson University, I went to school there, after my junior year turned out really well. I parlayed a marginal major league catching career into a 27-year broadcasting career.

KM: Yeah, that's great.

BS: I remember an old buddy of mine, he was an old-timer at the time, he told me when I was playing, he says, "You know if you take care of the people in Milwaukee while you're playing, they will take care of you when you're not playing." No truer words have ever been spoken.

KM: Wow, that sounds like that was great advice.

BS: Great advice. I just kinda tend to live by that. Before he died, I think he died a few years ago, I reminded him that he told me that. Good people here in Milwaukee.

KM: I went to Milwaukee one time; I went to a game at County Stadium the second-to-last year before the new park opened.

BS: Yeah, right, 1999. We had some rough years back then, as far as wins and losses. Yeah, great old ballpark.

KM: Hey, thank you so much, Bill, for getting back to me and for talking with me. I'm in Seattle, Kevin Hurd is in Fort Worth, Texas but we're old friends because we both grew up in the Bay Area in California.

BS: Send me text messages on my cell phone that I called you on and let me know where I can pick up a copy of the book.

KM: Absolutely. We're still working on it, we'll definitely let you know. I have the Major League TV package so I'm going to tune into some Brewers games and listen to your broadcast, so that'll be cool.

BS: There you go. We walk down memory lane quite a bit when games get out of hand so you might even hear these stories again.

KM: Oh, I love that, that's great. (Bill laughs) Hey, thank you Bill, thank you so much, this has been great.

BS: You betcha, no problem, thank you.

CHAPTER 3

DAVE STIEB: FIFTH TIME'S A CHARM

September 2, 1990
33-year-old Toronto ace Dave Stieb records his first no-hitter
after four ninth-inning near misses in previous games

"Into right field ... He (Junior Felix) has ... GOT IT! No-hitter for Dave Stieb! The long frustration is finally over! The first in Toronto Blue Jay history, recorded here in Cleveland this afternoon."

Veteran Blue Jays broadcaster Don Chevrier describing the last out in Cleveland. (Adrian Fung, "No-Hitters," published by the Society for American Baseball Research in 2017).

"This Time, Stieb Gets His No-Hitter"
Sports section headline (*New York Times*, September 3, 1990).

"Relief and disbelief. Those are the two things I felt. Then the celebration ensued, and it sank in. Wow, it really did happen. It felt good to get that off my back. I was thinking, now I don't have to concern myself with everybody wishing me a no-hitter."

Dave Stieb recalling his emotions once he finally knew he had pitched his long-elusive no-hitter (as told to columnist Rosie DiManno, *Toronto Star*, September 2, 2015).

"We were doing what we could to break Stieb's concentration. We were yelling at him from the bench, trying to do anything to get him out of his rhythm. The thing that makes him so tough is that he has a hard slider that doesn't break a whole lot, another slider that breaks a foot or more and a curve."

Tom Brookens, Cleveland third baseman (as told to Allan Ryan, "FINALLY! Stieb gets no-hitter after five near-misses and a scary final out," *Toronto Star*, September 3, 1990).

"I didn't have great control. I couldn't find my release point in the early innings. I hung pitches but got away with them. They helped me out a few times by swinging at bad pitches. They hit balls right at people."

Dave Stieb describing his pitching effectiveness that day (Allan Ryan, "FINALLY! Stieb gets no-hitter after five near-misses and a scary final out," *Toronto Star*, September 3, 1990).

"And the seventh is uneventful, the eighth is uneventful. And now I'm like three outs away. And I get the out, I forget what it was, I get Maldonado pinch-hitting — I strike him out — I walk Cole and then I get Browne to fly out and I get it. And it's like, I finally got this albatross off my neck."

Dave Stieb talking about the last few innings in his no-hitter and what it was like to have finally accomplished this goal (Interview with Kevin McCaffrey for this book, May 2, 2021).

After a historic level of frustration, this was the day Dave Stieb and the Toronto baseball world were waiting for. Having four previous no-hit attempts broken up in the ninth inning, Toronto's best pitcher of that era, Dave Stieb, had finally thrown a no-hitter. The only pitcher who has more than three of these near misses is the great Nolan Ryan, with five; however, all of those came after his first of seven no-hitters in 1973.

Each one of Stieb's four close calls has its own story. The first occurred against the White Sox at Comiskey Park in 1985. That no-hitter was broken up when Chicago's Rudy Law hit a home run to deep right field on the first pitch of the ninth inning. For good measure, Chicago's next batter, Bryan Little, hit another home run to right field. By the time that inning started, Stieb had thrown well over 100 pitches, and it was apparent he was spent.

In a later interview, he admitted "My arm was hurting. The only reason I was out there was because I had the no-hitter going. But when I threw those 10 last pitches, it was like throwing BP (batting practice). I had nothing." After the second Chicago homer, manager Bobby Cox pulled Stieb for reliever Gary Lavelle, who promptly gave up Chicago's third consecutive solo home run, this time to future Hall-of-Famer Harold Baines. The White Sox would record two more singles during the inning before tying-run-at-the-plate Ozzie Guillen flew out to left fielder George Bell to end the game with Toronto leading 6-3.

The second and third heartbreaking games occurred in back-to-back starts for Stieb at the very end of the 1988 season, a year in which the Blue Jays finished a mere 2.0 games behind the eventual division winner Boston Red Sox. In the first game against the Cleveland Indians, with two out in the ninth, batter Julio Franco fouled off three consecutive pitches on a 1-2 count. After Stieb threw a ball to make it 2-2, Franco hit a routine grounder to Toronto second baseman Manny Lee. Everyone thinks the game is over and Stieb would have his no-hitter. As Lee settles into position, the grounder hits an infield divot on its second bounce and goes over Lee's head. It's ruled a single and the no-hitter is over.

Six days later, in the bottom of the ninth inning against the worst-in-baseball Baltimore Orioles, with two outs and two strikes on the batter, light-hitting pinch-hitter Jim Traber flares a Stieb curveball over the head of first baseman Fred McGriff for a bloop single. For the second start in a row, one strike away from completing a no-hitter, the game ends in disappointment for Stieb.

The fourth near no-hit game may have been the biggest disappointment of all. Stieb pitched eight and two-thirds perfect innings against a Yankees lineup that included Don Mattingly, Steve Sax, Jesse Barfield, Mel Hall, Luis Polonia, and a very good hitting Bob Geren at catcher. By the time the number nine hitter Roberto Kelly came up in the ninth, Stieb had already struck out pinch-hitters Hal Morris and Ken Phelps to start the inning. Kelly ends up lining a sharp double down the left field line on a 2-0 count. After the game, Stieb remarked "If I haven't gotten a no-hitter after three times, I doubt if I ever will."

Table 3-1. Dave Stieb's No-Hitter Attempts Broken Up in the Ninth Inning

Date	Opposing Team	No-Hitter Broken Up By	Game Situation and Result	Final Score
8/24/1985	Chicago White Sox	Rudy Law	No outs, Bottom of 9th Home run to right field	Tor 6-3
9/24/1988	Cleveland Indians	Julio Franco	Two outs, B-9th, 2-2 count Bad hop single over second base	Tor 1-0
9/30/1988	Baltimore Orioles	Jim Traber	Two outs, B-9th, 2-2 count Bloop single to right field	Tor 4-0
8/4/1989	New York Yankees	Roberto Kelly	Retired first 26 batters in a row, 2-0 count, double down LF line	Tor 2-1

METHODOLOGY: This table lists four no-hitter attempts thrown by Dave Stieb that were broken up in the ninth inning. The games are listed in chronological order. These specific plays were identified from post-game stories and interviews and correlated with game data provided by baseball-reference.com.

LEGEND: LF = left field. The count in balls and strikes to the batter involved was abbreviated 2-0, 2-2, etc. For example, a count of two balls and no strikes to the batter was displayed as a "2-0 count." The term "B-9th" indicates the play took place in the bottom of the ninth inning. Dave Stieb and the Toronto Blue Jays were the visiting team in those first three games.

After this epic level of frustration, it's no wonder the big story of this day was Stieb finally achieving his dream of pitching a no-hitter. He was right to be concerned, too. Even though his 1990 season was outstanding, with Stieb making his seventh All-Star team and setting a Toronto record for wins in a season with 18, it would be the last year he was a mainstay in the Blue Jays rotation. In 1991, he only started nine games due to a series of shoulder and back injuries. He won four of them and lost three others. In 1992 and 1993, his effectiveness waned even more, recording an ERA above 5.00 in both seasons. He did pitch 50 innings for the Blue Jays in 1998 after taking four years off. Once that season ended, he retired at the age of 40.

On that special day in 1990, though, Cleveland couldn't buy a hit against the 33-year-old right-hander. The closest they came was Ken Phelps' deep fly down the right-field line in the eighth inning, which landed just foul. Beyond that, the Cleveland team – featuring Brook Jacoby, Candy Maldonado, Jerry Browne, and

Chris James, along with very talented stars-in-the-making Albert Belle, Sandy Alomar, and Carlos Baerga – mostly hit the ball to the infield or struck out against seven-time American League All-Star Dave Stieb. Specifically, seven balls were hit to the outfield, six were groundouts, and three batters popped out. Two runners were caught stealing, as well. While Stieb walked four that day, he struck out nine Indians, and even though he felt he didn't have his best stuff, Stieb recorded an excellent Game Score (GSc) of 92.

The way Stieb was controlling the game, the outcome wasn't really in doubt after the Blue Jays took a 2-0 lead in the fifth inning. Toronto scoring was due to Fred McGriff's solo home run in the fourth and back-to-back doubles by Ken Williams and Manny Lee to lead off the fifth, which gave the Blue Jays their two-run advantage. McGriff would add another solo shot leading off the top of the ninth inning to make it a 3-0 Toronto lead.

Dave Stieb's batterymate that day was 27-year-old veteran catcher Pat Borders. Borders was in the midst of a breakout offensive season that year, finishing the year hitting .286 with 15 HRs in just 346 at bats. Borders would later become famous as the 1992 World Series MVP when his Blue Jays beat the Atlanta Braves four games to two for the first of Toronto's two consecutive championships. Borders played for 17 seasons – mostly with Toronto – retiring after the 2005 season. Of note, he did not play in the major leagues in 2000, choosing instead to be a part of the gold medal-winning U.S. baseball team at the 2000 Sydney Olympics. By winning both a World Series championship and an Olympic gold medal, he is in a special category with only four other players who have achieved that feat. Borders is the only one who earned his World Series ring before his Olympic medal.

Table 3-2. A World Series Championship and an Olympic Gold Medal

Player	Olympic Team	Position	Gold Medal	World Series Championship(s)
Orlando Hernandez	Cuba	Starting Pitcher	1992 Barcelona	1998-1999-2000 NY Yankees 2005 Chicago White Sox
Jose Contreras	Cuba	Starting Pitcher	1996 Atlanta	2005 Chicago White Sox
Pat Borders	USA	Catcher	2000 Sydney	1992 Toronto Blue Jays

Player	Olympic Team	Position	Gold Medal	World Series Championship(s)
Doug Mientkiewicz	USA	First Baseman	2000 Sydney	2004 Boston Red Sox
Yuli Gurriel	Cuba	First Baseman	2004 Athens	2017 Houston Astros

METHODOLOGY: This table lists all Major League players who have won both a World Series championship and a Gold Medal at the Olympic Games. Players are listed in chronological order associated with their Gold Medal.

Dave Stieb's no-hitter is the only one ever thrown by a Toronto Blue Jay, while they have had six thrown against them since they began as a franchise in 1977. This ties them with five other teams (Colorado Rockies, Milwaukee Brewers, New York Mets, San Diego Padres, and Tampa Bay Rays) who also have only one individual no-hitter.

The Padres were the last franchise to have zero no-hitters. San Diego's 52-year streak of futility was ended in 2021 when Joe Musgrove no-hit the Texas Rangers on April 9 of that year. Interestingly, his catcher for that game (Victor Caratini) became the first catcher in major league history to catch consecutive no-hitters for two different teams. Before Musgrove, the last no-hitter was thrown by Alec Mills of the Chicago Cubs with Caratini behind the plate on September 13, 2020.

Toronto's 30+ year no-hitter drought is currently longer than any other major league team, with the exception of the Cleveland Indians (now known as the Guardians). Cleveland's last no-hitter was a perfect game thrown over 40 years ago by ace Len Barker on May 15, 1981.

Dave Stieb was born in Santa Ana, CA in 1957. He didn't start his baseball career as a pitcher, though. He mostly played outfield at Southern Illinois University, where he only threw 17 innings. Stieb was drafted by the Toronto Blue Jays in the fifth round of the June 1978 Amateur Draft, and the Blue Jays focused on developing him as a hurler. He compiled a 12-2 record in the minors in 1978-1979. He moved quickly through Toronto's farm system, entering the big leagues with the Blue Jays as a 21-year-old early in 1979, and achieving a win-loss record of 8-8. In the 1980s, he had a remarkable record of 140-109. As mentioned previously, Stieb was on the all-star team seven times and was in the Top 10 of Cy Young voting four times.

Despite stiff competition from Hall of Famers and other well-known pitchers, Dave Stieb can arguably be called the greatest pitcher of the 1980s decade. Looking at the chart below, ranked by Wins Above Replacement (WAR) they accumulated in the 1980s, Stieb is nearly 10 WAR above his next closest competitor (Stieb has 48.1 WAR, compared to Bert Blyleven in second place with 38.2 WAR). Stieb also threw the most innings and accumulated the most wins of any pitcher not named Jack Morris. Because of Hall of Famer Morris's prominence in the 1980s, I specifically wanted to include him in this discussion, of course.

As it stands, though, Morris is tied for 11th highest WAR of any pitcher. When this is broken down as a rate using WAR per 200 innings pitched, he's behind everyone on the list, and far behind some of the star pitchers who arrived in the mid-1980s (notably Orel Hershiser, Roger Clemens, Dwight Gooden, and Bret Saberhagen). While Clemens, Gooden, and even Saberhagen had outstanding stretches that started four or more seasons after the beginning of the 1980s, Dave Stieb had the skill and the stamina to perform at an All-Star level for all 10 years of the decade.

Table 3-3. Best Pitchers of the 1980s

Rank	Pitcher (Team(s))	Seasons Pitched	Innings Pitched	WAR (per 200 IP)	Wins (per Season)
1	Dave Stieb (Blue Jays)	1980-1989	2,328.2	48.1 (4.13)	140 (14.0)
2	Bert Blyleven (Pirates, Indians, Twins, Angels)	1980-1989	2,078.1	38.2 (3.68)	123 (12.3)
3	Roger Clemens (Red Sox)	1984-1989	1,284.2	35.5 (5.53)	95 (15.8)
4	Bob Welch (Dodgers, Athletics)	1980-1989	2,082.1	35.3 (3.39)	137 (13.7)
5	Fernando Valenzuela (Dodgers)	1980-1989	2,144.2	33.2 (3.10)	128 (12.8)
6	Orel Hershiser (Dodgers)	1983-1989	1,457.0	32.9 (4.52)	98 (14.0)
7	Bret Saberhagen (Royals)	1984-1989	1,329.0	32.0 (4.82)	92 (15.3)
8	John Tudor (Red Sox, Pirates, Cards, Dodgers)	1980-1989	1,622.2	31.1 (3.83)	104 (10.4)

Rank	Pitcher (Team(s))	Seasons Pitched	Innings Pitched	WAR (per 200 IP)	Wins (per Season)
9	Dwight Gooden (Mets)	1984-1989	1,291.0	30.7 (4.73)	100 (16.7)
10	Nolan Ryan (Astros, Rangers)	1980-1989	2,094.0	30.5 (2.91)	122 (12.2)
11 (tie)	Charlie Hough (Dodgers, Rangers)	1980-1989	2,121.2	30.3 (2.86)	128 (12.8)
11 (tie)	Jack Morris (Tigers)	1980-1989	2,443.2	30.3 (2.48)	162 (16.2)

METHODOLOGY: Pitchers are ranked in order of Wins Above Replacement (WAR) achieved from 1980-1989. WAR measures a player's value in all facets of the game by deciphering how many more wins he's worth than a replacement-level player at his same position. I included the top 12 pitchers so I could incorporate Jack Morris (the decade's wins leader) in the analysis.

LEGEND: Another measure of merit I wanted to include was the number of wins each pitcher accumulated as well. Because a significant number of pitchers were only present for a portion of the decade, I included two rate measures (WAR per 200 innings pitched and wins per season). IP = innings pitched. One-third of an inning is designated as ".1" and two-thirds of an inning is designated as ".2" innings.

Dave Stieb's no-hitter, the only one in Blue Jays history, ranks highly in the best games ever thrown by a Blue Jay pitcher. The table below displays the highest Game Scores ever achieved by a Toronto pitcher. While Stieb's two 1988 and one 1989 near-no-hitters discussed earlier aren't shown in this table, they also achieved high Game Scores of 91, 88, and 90, respectively.

Table 3-4. Blue Jays Highest Game Scores

Rank	Pitcher	Date Score	Opponent	GSc	IP, Hits, Runs, ERs, Walks, Strikeouts
1	Brandon Morrow	8/8/2010 Tor 1-0	Tampa Bay Rays	100	9.0 IP, 1 Hit, 0 Runs, 0 ERs, 2 BBs, 17 Ks
2	Roger Clemens	8/25/1998 Tor 3-0	Kansas City Royals	99	9.0 IP, 3 Hits, 0 Runs, 0 ERs, 0 BBs, 18 Ks

Rank	Pitcher	Date Score	Opponent	GSc	IP, Hits, Runs, ERs, Walks, Strikeouts
3	Roger Clemens	9/7/1997 Tor 4-0	Texas Rangers	97	9.0 IP, 2 Hits, 0 Runs, 0 ERs, 0 BBs, 14 Ks
4 (tie)	Jesse Jefferson	5/16/1980 Tor 1-0 (11 inn)	Oakland Athletics	95	11.0 IP, 4 Hits, 0 Runs, 0 ERs, 4 BBs, 10 Ks
4 (tie)	Pat Hentgen	5/3/1994 Tor 1-0	Kansas City Royals	95	9.0 IP, 2 Hits, 0 Runs, 0 ERs, 2 BBs, 14 Ks
6	Roy Halladay	5/29/2005 Tor 4-0	Minnesota Twins	93	9.0 IP, 2 Hits, 0 Runs, 0 ERs, 0 BBs, 10 Ks
7 (tie)	Jim Clancy	6/19/1982 Tor 3-1 (12 inn)	Oakland Athletics	92	10.0 IP, 3 Hits, 1 Run, 0 ERs, 2 BBs, 10 Ks
7 (tie)	Dave Stieb	9/16/1982 Tor 2-1 (12 inn)	California Angels	92	11.0 IP, 3 Hits, 1 Run, 1 ER, 2 BBs, 7 Ks
7 (tie)	Jimmy Key	6/6/1985 Tor 2-0 (12 inn)	Detroit Tigers	92	10.0 IP, 2 Hits, 0 Runs, 0 ERs, 2 BBs, 6 Ks
7 (tie)	Dave Stieb	9/2/1990 Tor 3-0	Cleveland Indians	92	9.0 IP, 0 Hits, 0 Runs, 0 ERS, 4 BBs, 9 Ks
7 (tie)	Ted Lilly	8/23/2004 Tor 3-0	Boston Red Sox	92	9.0 IP, 3 Hits, 0 Runs, 0 ERs, 2 BBs, 13 Ks

METHODOLOGY: This table includes the highest Game Scores thrown by a pitcher from the Toronto Blue Jays from 1977-2021. Games are ranked by Game Score (GSc) and consider all franchise regular season and postseason games. Game Score measures a pitcher's performance in any given game started. Introduced by baseball writer/statistician Bill James in the 1980s, Game Score is presented as a figure between 0-100 — except for extreme outliers — and usually falls between 40-70.

LEGEND: Dates are shown as month/day/year (for example, June 12, 2018, is shown as 6/12/2018); IP = innings pitched. BB(s) = base(s) on balls. K(s) = strikeout(s). ER(s) = earned run(s). inn = innings (associated with the length of extra-inning games). The Blue Jays joined the American League as an expansion team in 1977, along with the Seattle Mariners. They have been in the East Division the entire time.

NOTE 1: The highest postseason Game Score for a Toronto pitcher was by Dave Stieb in Game 1 of the 1985 ALCS. Stieb registered an 83 GSc in his eight-inning, three-hit, shutout performance against the Royals en route to a 6-1 Blue Jay win in the series opener. Except for giving up a pair of hits to Hall of Famer George Brett, Stieb dominated a powerful Kansas City lineup that included Brett, Steve Balboni, and Jorge Orta. Despite the great start, Toronto would lose the ALCS in seven games, as the Royals rallied from a three-games-to-one deficit to defeat Toronto and face the St. Louis Cardinals in the World Series.

NOTE 2: Brandon Morrow has the highest Game Score for any Blue Jays pitcher, achieving a 100 mark in a one-hit, 17-strikeout effort. While his attempt at a perfect game was gone early with a walk to Dan Johnson of the Rays to lead off the second inning, Morrow still had a no-hitter going with two outs in the top of the ninth inning. On a 1-1 count, Evan Longoria managed to reach first on an infield single to the second baseman. Morrow had thrown 129 pitches to that point in this 1-0 game. Longoria's single moved Ben Zobrist over to third, giving Tampa Bay runners on first and third with two outs in a one-run game. Toronto manager Cito Gaston elected to leave Morrow in the game to face the Rays number four hitter Dan Johnson. Morrow retired Johnson on an eight-pitch swinging strikeout to complete the one-hitter for the win.

NOTE 3: The number two game in this table with a score of 99 was an 18-strikeout, no walks effort by Roger Clemens in 1998. His 18 strikeouts are the most ever achieved by a Toronto pitcher in a single game (Morrow's game is second). Clemens won the Cy Young Award with Toronto in both 1997 and 1998. The number three game in this table was a 1997 two-hitter also thrown by Clemens (with a score of 97).

While other Blue Jay pitchers, such as Cy Young Award winners Roger Clemens and Roy Halladay, have had more dominant stretches than Dave Stieb, Stieb can arguably be described as the most prominent pitcher in Toronto history. The all-time team leader in strikeouts (1,658), wins (175), shutouts (30), complete games (103), and innings pitched (2,895.1), Stieb has accomplished more than any other Toronto pitcher. With seven All-Star selections, Stieb has been chosen to more All-Star teams than any other Toronto player. Inducted in 2005 as a member of the Canadian Baseball Hall of Fame, Dave Stieb's no-hitter is a fitting testament to his excellence as a ballplayer.

Before departing this analysis, though, I'd like to share something of passing interest. Doing the research for this book, I saw that Dave Stieb had gone to San Jose City College (SJCC), a community college located in (logically enough) San Jose, California. Looking further, I discovered the wealth of major leaguers who had attended SJCC. In total, there were 10 pitchers who played at SJCC. Three (Scott Erickson, Dave Righetti, and Dave Stieb) threw no-hitters. That's remarkable. I compared this to the University of Southern California, which counts 58 MLB pitchers as alumni — three of whom also threw no-hitters. While I haven't done exhaustive research on this, I strongly suspect no other school can top that. I am nearly certain that no community college can top the SJCC figure of three pitchers throwing no-hitters.

Below are excerpts from a remarkable interview with Dave Stieb conducted by my associate Kevin McCaffrey. I've only provided light editing for readability that didn't change the tone or content of the material. It's a fascinating view into Dave Stieb and his perspective as a major league star pitcher. Many thanks to Kevin for conducting the interview and, especially, to Dave Stieb for his generous participation. I also had the privilege of conducting a fascinating interview with Pat Borders, Sieb's batterymate that day. Borders's interview follows Stieb's and I encourage the reader to enjoy both of them.

Dave Stieb Interview excerpts
Conducted by Kevin McCaffrey on May 2, 2021

Kevin McCaffrey (KM): The book is the brainchild of Kevin Hurd; his idea was to write a book about no-hitters and take a different approach. He wants to spotlight a number of games and each one has a unique feature about it which is why he chose it. The reason he picked you is because of your history of almost throwing a no-hitter so many times . . .

Dave Stieb (DS): (sarcastically) I love to talk about that, that's just so exciting. (KM laughs) Yeah, the almost.

KM: Would you rather not talk about that; we don't have to if you don't want to.

DS: No, I mean it's history. It's unusual. It's just bad luck. I could've tied Johnny Vander Meer if I didn't get a bad hop and a blooper over Fred McGriff's glove by a foot. Yeah, that's history. That's part of the upsets, and the disappointments, and the almost. Oh yeah, it's a big part of baseball history. It should've happened, so yeah, sure.

KM: So, when you finally got it that had to be a sense of relief, but as you were getting closer were you thinking "Oh no, here we go again"?

DS: Oh, every time. (At that point) it was every time. Here we go again, how'd that happen, how'd that happen, how'd this happen? Why? What I got was the monkey off my back because that was all anybody would talk about for years. So, I was happy to get rid of that.

KM: And one of them was almost a perfect game.

DS: Yeah, there was that one, too, in '89. That was in between the bad hop, the bloop, a couple of others that were really close but yeah, so the perfect game would've really just been the icing on the cake for me as far as just getting that, even before the no-hitter that happened a year later. In the same ballpark that the bad hop happened. Yeah, if I could've secured that perfect game before the no-hitter that would've been like, oh, I wouldn't have cared what happened after that.

DS: I went 2-0 (as I started my professional career at Dunedin in Single A ball) in '78, then I went to instructional ball in Florida in the winter (of that year) and pitched like eight games and did so-so. Then I went back to Single A and I went 5-0. They brought me up to Syracuse because we had no Double A, so I went to Triple A in Syracuse, and I went 5-2. Next thing I know I'm going to Toronto. I'm in the big leagues. They'd said the quickest way to the majors would be pitching. Well, it was true. In less than a year after I'd signed with them, I was in Toronto.

So, I got brought up in late June, I pitched three months there, I went 8-8. The next best pitcher was Tommy Underwood, he was 9-16. And I knew right then, I'm here to stay. This is crazy. So anyway, that was the start of my career with the Blue Jays, and you know as well as I do, I pitched there for 15 years, and had that no-hitter stuff going on, so is that where you want to go with the no-hitter?

KM: Yeah, so did you feel any different — good or bad — on the day of the no-hitter?

DS: No. Oh no. It was just a normal day. I'm warming up, and the only different thing about that day, Kevin, was they had an air show going on. So, they had these jets, these fighter jets flying over the ballpark — during the whole game. And that didn't matter to me, I'd experienced that at Exhibition Stadium with the air show they would have there. Not sure if I pitched during that time or not, but I've seen planes flying over; but this particular day though, they had some air show going because there were a lot of fighter jets flying over the ballpark.

I could just zone that out, that didn't even bother me, it wasn't even an issue. But I remember that, and my bullpen warmup was just probably a normal bullpen warmup. Here I am on Sunday, in Cleveland, and they're not that good but I don't want to put them down because any team can beat you on any given day. So here we are, and I'm warming up, like I said I don't remember anything special. I thought I had great stuff, but I just warmed up. I remember pitching the game, but I remember these jets flying over and I would look up to 'em, "Geez, why the hell is this going on today?"

It was a normal game for me after all the no-hitters I'd taken into the ninth inning, I was just pitching, the thing I will tell you is these guys were swinging aggressively, OK, and they were swinging at a lot of balls that were low or in the dirt, 'cause I don't throw a lot of dirt balls. But I just remember them really being aggressive and I remember striking out the side two times that game and the same three guys. And I know (Tom) Brookens was one of them and I almost want to do my homework and look it up for you and tell you, but you can look that up.

KM: Yeah, we can find that. (Note: it happened in the bottom of the third and sixth innings. Stieb struck out Cory Snyder, Tom Brookens, and Joel Skinner in order both of those innings. Five of the six strikeouts were looking)

DS: I struck out the same three guys twice in that game and that's when I kinda got an inkling, that, and after the 6th-7th inning of striking out the side twice, the same three guys that were just swinging at balls that were balls. My slider was good, you know my fastball was good of course, which it usually is. But my slider, I was throwing it for balls at the right time, they were swinging at 'em and I was getting all these strikeouts; it wasn't a ton like today — you strike out 15-17 guys — just stupid.

But I was true to my form, I walked four guys, OK, (Dave Stieb laughs) I don't think it was just flagrant ball-ball-ball-ball. It was working a guy, then 3-2, walk a guy and the umpire probably wasn't really in my favor so maybe instead of a strikeout it was a walk. So, I walked three guys going to the ninth inning and I got like eight strikeouts. And they'd been swinging at balls in the dirt, my slider, they're just aggressive. And then I remember getting the first out in the ninth, I don't remember who it was. Then the second, I'm not sure the timetable of this, but I know they pinch-hit Candy Maldonado and I struck him out with a high fastball up-and-in. I just blew it by him. It was a ball.

KM: In the ninth inning you blew it by him!

DS: Yeah, he was wanting to break it up, he was swinging, and I struck him out. And then this guy Cole, I don't know his first name, but (Alex) Cole—he's a left-handed hitter, he's a fast guy. And I'll never forget this. I just did one of those brain fart deals and couldn't throw him a strike. I threw him four straight balls. And so, I walked him. And I remember early in the game I walked a guy and they tried to steal, and Pat Borders threw him out. And it was like boom! You're out, you're out! Alright, no threat.

So then up comes Browne, this little lefty hitter and I worked him to the count, I can't remember to this day, but I remember throwing a hanging slider. It was the worst pitch ever to get a no-hitter on (KM laughs). I hang it, but this is a guy that's not gonna hit you out of the ballpark, right? And so I hang it to him, and he hits it and I had to close my eyes, I put my hands over my eyes. I've given up a bad hop in that ballpark. The next game I gave up a blooper over Fred McGriff, and I'm going "What can happen now?"

Did Junior Felix out in right field go blind and it drops? I'd never seen the ball hit and I knew it wasn't going out by any means, but it was a good hit line drive. It was a looping line drive and I just remember looking back and seeing Junior kinda corral it and I put my hand over my eyes saying, "Just let him catch it, God." (Both laugh). And he caught it and that was that.

But it was the worst pitch ever for a no-hitter and I'll tell you this, of all my no-hitters there was never any bullet hit right at people for outs, and this and that, and I've seen some of the no-hitters since then Kevin, that are, during the game I see bullets that are right at the third baseman, they're right at the first baseman, they're at the outfielder; and I'm going, "These guys don't even know how lucky they are to get those no-hitters." 'Cause no ball was hit hard. And that Browne probably hit the hardest ball! But you know what, he probably can't hit the ball that hard, I don't know, I'm sure he's got a home run here and there. But that's how that thing went, and I can't believe I got it.

KM: Yeah, and so you said the fastball and the slider were your best pitches that day?

DS: Oh yeah, that's what I threw then. I threw fastballs, sliders, and then I developed a curve ball. I mean if I ever threw a changeup that was the dumbest thing I'd ever do, 'cause I didn't have a changeup. I was a power pitcher; I didn't throw slow.

KM: Do you remember shaking off Pat Borders much during that game?

DS: Oh my God. Yeah, you know if I did, we'd probably go to the slider. But I think he was on the same page as me. You know, Kevin, it's not a game that really stands out as far as pitch-by-pitch, and him calling the game, 'cause you know I always called my own game. And I think he was on the same page, and he knew the slider was the pitch. He knew they were swinging at sliders in the dirt and outside, or way outside not in the dirt. But they were just swinging, they were really aggressive. And I think he was on the same page, and I know I'm throwing sinkers in and sliders away, and yeah, we were working together well. And that's how that went. He knew it, yeah. Pat Borders, that guy's a great catcher.

KM: I looked at his stats and he caught 125 games that season so did he catch most of your starts?

DS: Oh, he probably caught all of 'em. I mean who was the other catcher that year?

KM: That I don't know (Author's note: It was Greg Myers).

DS: Most of my career I had Ernie Whitt and Buck Martinez. Those were my two catchers and, not to slight them, but they're no Pat Borders. But they did the job, they did good, and I'll tell you, Ernie was a way better hitter than Buck. And you know, as far as throwing guys out they couldn't hold a candle to Pat, so it was an awesome improvement with that guy back there.

KM: Are you still in touch with Pat?

DS: No. You know I saw him at a Blue Jays thing years ago. Otherwise no, I don't talk to Ernie, or Buck, or Pat. I talk to David Wells, I talk to Pat Hentgen, but...Pat Hentgen all the time, David Wells hardly, 'cause he's in a whole different world than I live in. (Dave laughs).

KM: Yeah, I got a few more here. During the no-hitter Dave, when did you think, *"I've got a real shot at a no-hitter"*?

DS: Oh, geez. You know I think it's the same kind of thing with anybody that has one going, you get to the seventh and you're thinking, "OK, I got three more innings." And it might've been the seventh when I struck those guys out again, three in a row. And then it's like in the dugout I go, "Alright man, I got a few innings." And the eighth was really uneventful, I don't remember verbatim as far as the outs, but like I told you, there were no hard-hit balls, there were no great plays. It was just routine outs and then here I am in the ninth going, "OK." I didn't have all those other one-hitters under my belt yet, so it wasn't something to think about. "Here we go again."

But all I could think about was, yeah, "here we go again" was only about the bad hop that happened. Well yeah, I guess it was. It was the bad hop and then the next game in Toronto against the Orioles. But I am kinda thinking, "What can happen here? I got three outs away. What can happen here to mess this up?" So yeah, I'm thinking about it after the sixth inning.

And the seventh is uneventful, the eighth is uneventful. And now I'm like three outs away. And I get the out, I forget what it was, I get Maldonado pinch-hitting — I strike him out — I walk Cole and then I get Browne to fly out and I get it. And it's like, I finally got this albatross off my neck. So that's how that went down. You know what, it's funny, when you look it up on YouTube, they show nobody's sitting around me at all.

KM: Would you say that the no-hitter was the highlight of your career?

DS: No.

KM: What would you say was the highlight?

DS: Geez, if you wanted to break something down to a highlight like that, there's like three or four things that are right there with that. That are very important or unbelievable things that I did in my career, and some pertain to the organization, and some pertain to MLB, you know, a record or something that is in the records. Of course, the no-hitter is one. Winning the first Blue Jay playoff game was another one. To have the opportunity to do that and I won that game, and I kicked the Royals' ass and got that win. 'Cause that was almost like a ... it was an objective that had to be met and I did it. And why I couldn't do that two more times to go to the World Series is ... well it's not unbeknownst to me. It's part of my failure and my team to not back me up. But that is the second most important thing. The other was to represent them in the All-Star Game.

KM: You went to the All-Star Game seven times, right?

DS: Yeah, and to perform well for my organization in that respect and ... I mean I've got one of the most unbelievable records in All-Star history as far as I pitched every damn game that I went to the All-Star Game, too. That's a record. And not only that, but I have an ERA under 1.00. And I pitched over nine innings. I think of doing stuff like that; that's shit that happened I did, and those are things that, when you asked me about that, that's the special things that, yeah, those are the things that I did the most, is the no-hitter, that first playoff victory in their history, All Star Game seven times, pitched in every All-Star Game and had an ERA under 1.00 and it's over nine innings. I mean that's, damn, that's hard to beat.

KM: That's pretty damn good.

DS: Yeah, can you imagine, that's like I started a game, and I gave up less than one run. So, there's that. There are those things, those accolades that I'm very proud of and mind you this though: I don't really even care about those things in the scheme of my life. It's almost like I've got three lives. I got my baseball life, I got my real estate life, my contractor/building houses life -- and those are all three different things that make my life. That's what I did.

KM: Well, it sounds like it's been a good one.

DS: Yeah, but I don't live my life being Dave Stieb the baseball pitcher. I'm not walking around here, holding my head up ... I don't care, I really don't care about that stuff. It was a life, it was a part of my life, it's what it was. I'm thankful for it, but I don't live my life right now because of that. I live my life because of my grandchildren and my kids. That's what makes me and how I live my life.

KM: Well, it can't get any better than that, that's for sure.

DS: Mm hmm.

KM: Hey Dave, this has been great, I thank you so much for getting back to me and for spending so much time. Your stories are just fantastic so thank you, I really appreciate it.

DS: I'll tell you Kevin, anytime somebody comes to me with a book that they want something about my history in, it'd be stupid of me to not want to be a part of that and have it be there, you know. That's why I do this, I don't get paid for it, I don't care. But somebody's doing something like that, yeah, I want that in the archives, I want that in that book, I want that there and I want it to be right. So, I appreciate you guys doing this and thank you for caring that much to do that.

Pat Borders Interview
Conducted by Kevin Hurd on July 1, 2021

Kevin Hurd (KH): Would you consider yourself to be the best catcher on your Little League, American Legion, high school, and minor league teams?

Pat Borders (PB): Actually, up through my fifth year in the minors (in 1987) I played other positions, mostly at third base. I was drafted in the sixth round in 1982 as a third baseman.

KH: Did you have any guys in your Little League that were just incredible — always hit home runs, threw no-hitters, things like that?

PB: I hit pretty well in Little League – I hit five home runs — but there were definitely players better than me who hit 15 home runs or more.

KH: Did you feel any different, good or bad, on the day of (Dave Stieb's) no-hitter?

PB: No, it was pretty much a regular night game.

KH: What pitches — fastball, curve, slider, or change-up — were working best for Dave Stieb that day?

PB: He had a good mix of sliders and fastballs. Good sink.

KH: Did you ever catch a no-hitter in Little League, American Legion, high school, or the minors?

PB: Well, I didn't catch until the minors and didn't catch any (no-hitters) in the minors, so no (laughs).

KH: What was the best defensive play, the closest you came to losing the no-hitter?

PB: I don't remember any real exceptional plays.

KH: What pitcher did you have the hardest time hitting?

PB: That would be Kirk McCaskill. I couldn't hit anything he threw. I either only got one hit off him total, or I only remember getting one hit off of him (Author's note: Pat Borders got one hit in 19 career at bats against Kirk McCaskill. His lone hit was a two-out, two-run triple in the sixth inning of a 1992 game against the White Sox that gave the Blue Jays a 3-0 lead).

KH: Did Dave shake off your signs much during the game?

PB: Not a whole lot, but he did take command at times. When I caught him that night, I'd been a catcher for two or three years and he had been pitching for 12+ years. My knowledge of signs and hitters' strengths and weaknesses was limited, compared to Dave's.

KH: Do you have any memorabilia or souvenirs — such as a baseball, plaque, uniform, or something like that — from the game in your house?

PB: Actually, I've got a ticket stub from the game, signed by Dave Stieb. I'm not a big memorabilia guy. If you walked into my house, you wouldn't know I played major league baseball.

KH: Before you were in the big leagues, you were in the minors from 1982-1988. You played for seven managers. Assuming they were all good, which one or two did you like playing for the most?

PB: That would be Dennis Holmberg, who I played for in 1983-1984. Of all the minor league managers I played for he was the hardest on me, but that helped me, too.

KH: You played in the majors from 1988-2006. You played for many different managers. Again, assuming that they were all good, which one or two did you like playing for the most?

PB: There were two: Cito Gaston and Lou Piniella. Cito Gaston was great at handling people, and Lou impressed me with his ability to chastise and compliment and to motivate people.

KH: Do you think the number of pitchers Dave Stieb threw that day (123) led to him getting a sore arm?

PB: No, I don't think so. I think DNA (genetics) has more of an effect on who gets a sore arm than too many pitches.

KH: Did Dave Stieb request you as his catcher before this game?

PB: Not to my knowledge.

KH: Have you stayed in contact with Dave?

PB: I've seen him a few times but haven't talked to him in a few years.

KH: Did your team (Toronto) give you a bonus for catching the no-hitter?

PB: No, they didn't (laughs).

KH: During the game, when did you think *"he's got a real shot at a no-hitter?"* Fifth inning, sixth inning, or later?

PB: Fourth or fifth inning. Dave had a real wipeout slider that day.

KH: Were you able to get a follow-on job in baseball after your playing days were over? In the majors, minors, college, high school, or media?

PB: I was a minor league coach and manager from 2011-2019. I retired as a player in 2006, and from 2007-2010 I enjoyed my kids.

KH: What kind of work did you do (besides baseball)? Did you enjoy it?

PB: Well, from 2007-2010 I did various things, I wasn't working for anyone else.

KH: Going back to a previous question: Which minor league coaches did you have who helped you the most in your climb to get into the major leagues?

PB: There was a number. Off the top of my head, I would say I got the most help at a key time from Joe Lonnett, who was a scout and roving instructor for Pittsburgh and Toronto from the mid-1980s to the mid-1990s. He was the one who told me to play winter ball in the Dominican Republic at a key time, and that definitely got me noticed and helped on my next step in getting to the majors.

KH: Since you were able to get a job in baseball after your playing career ended, do you think having caught a no-hitter helped you get the job?

PB: No, not really. It didn't hurt, but it's better to have the knowledge and stress of catching to be able to get a coaching job.

KH: Do you have any kids or grandkids who have pursued or will pursue baseball as a career? Do you encourage them to do so?

PB: I've got nine kids. Most, if not all, have gone to college on athletic scholarships, with most of the scholarships being in sports other than baseball or softball. Whatever they are good at I encourage.

KH: Was the no-hitter the highlight of your career? If not, what was?

PB: It wasn't. What were the highlights? Well, several: My dad being at the ballpark for my first major league game and seeing me get my first hit. Being on the 1992-1993 World Series Champions and being World Series MVP in 1992. My biggest thrill, though, was being on the 2000 Olympics Gold Medal-winning baseball team. It was great being on the medal stand and hearing the National

Anthem. As far as our manager (during the Olympics), Tom Lasorda was the right guy in the right job at the right time.

KH: Have you been to the section of the baseball Hall of Fame that focuses on no-hitters?

PB: Yes, but it was a quick visit. I don't recall much of it.

KH: Have you spent time signing autographs in Las Vegas, or in Florida or Arizona during spring training?

PB: Some. Mostly my personal policy for autographs is that I'll try and sign for little kids or anybody who looks to be sincere or humble.

KH: Are there any last things you want to say about the no-hit game?

PB: Dave Stieb's no-hitter was overdue – he lost three no-hitters with two outs in the ninth – and well-earned. He had come close so many times.

Chapter 4

Randy Johnson: A Perfect 40-Year-Old

May 18, 2004
Randy Johnson throws a perfect game for
the very imperfect Arizona Diamondbacks

"A game like this was pretty special. It doesn't come along very often. Not bad for being 40 years old. Everything was locked in."

Randy Johnson reflecting on his accomplishment ("Johnson Simply Perfect at 40," *USA Today*, May 19, 2004).

"This is one of those nights where a superior athlete was on top of his game. There was a tremendous rhythm out there. His focus, his concentration, his stuff, everything was as good as it could possibly be. Everything he's done up to this point pales in comparison."

Arizona Manager Bob Brenly describing his reaction after Randy Johnson's perfect game ("Johnson K's 13 in perfect effort," *ESPN.com*, May 18, 2004).

"I only shook [Hammock] off two or three times ... He called a great game. The thing is he was probably the most excited guy in the clubhouse, and I'm happy for that. He's come a long way."

Randy Johnson giving credit to his batterymate Robby Hammock ("Hammock lives dream, catches gem," *MLB.com*, May 19, 2004).

"Every time you catch [Johnson], you feel that something like this has a chance to happen ... He's so intense, and it's something he has out there on the mound that makes me that much better."

Arizona catcher Robbie Hammock describing what it's like to catch for Randy Johnson ("Hammock lives dream, catches gem," *MLB.com*, May 19, 2004).

"He could smell it at the end. This was a legitimate perfect game, any way you slice it."

Atlanta catcher Johnny Estrada describing Randy Johnson's effort ("May 18, 2004: Randy Johnson pitches a perfect game at age 40," *Society for American Baseball Research (SABR.org)*, 2017).

"Guys that play the game at that level ... do things other people don't dream of doing. They push themselves. That's what he's done. He's been pitching great. I just want to find all those people that were talking about the end of his career last winter."

Former teammate Curt Schilling talking about Randy Johnson's drive for success ("Johnson K's 13 in perfect effort," *ESPN.com*, May 18, 2004).

By the time 2004 arrived, Randy Johnson already had a Hall of Fame career well established. In addition to being named the 2001 World Series MVP for the world champion Diamondbacks, he had accumulated an incredible five Cy Young Awards, one with Seattle in 1995 and four straight with Arizona from 1999-2002. In addition, he had amassed 230 wins and over 3,800 strikeouts as well. He had even thrown a no-hitter previously, shutting down the Tigers in a 1990 game when he was starting out with the Mariners. Randy Johnson was clearly one of the very best pitchers of his generation. He had nothing left to prove.

Yet, on May 18th, Randy Johnson achieved yet another milestone. At 40 years old, he became the oldest pitcher to ever throw a perfect game, surpassing the legendary 37-year-old Boston hurler Cy Young who threw his perfect game 100 years earlier. Johnson's record still stands, as shown in the table below.

Table 4-1. Oldest Perfect Game Pitchers

Rank	Pitcher	Age in years	Team	Date Score	Opponent
1	Randy Johnson	40	Arizona Diamondbacks	5/18/2004 Ari 2-0	Atlanta Braves
2	Cy Young	37	Boston Americans	5/5/1904 Bos 3-0	Philadelphia Athletics
3	David Cone	36 (+198 days)	New York Yankees	7/18/1999 NY 6-0	Montreal Expos
4	Dennis Martinez	36 (+75 days)	Montreal Expos	7/28/1991 Mon 2-0	Los Angeles Dodgers
5	David Wells	34	New York Yankees	5/17/1998 NY 4-0	Minnesota Twins
6	Roy Halladay	33	Philadelphia Phillies	5/29/2010 Phi 1-0	Florida Marlins
7	Jim Bunning	32	Philadelphia Phillies	6/21/1964 (1) Phi 6-0	New York Mets
8	Mark Buehrle	30	Chicago White Sox	7/23/2009 Chi 5-0	Tampa Bay Rays

METHODOLOGY: This table includes all pitchers from 1900-2021 who threw perfect games when they were 30 years old or older. The pitchers are ranked from the oldest to the youngest.

LEGEND: Dates are shown as month/day/year (for example, June 12, 2018, is shown as 6/12/2018). (1) indicates the first game of a doubleheader. "Age" is the pitcher's age in years the day he threw his perfect game. In the case of Dennis Martinez and David Cone, who were both 36 at the time, the number of days above 36 is added to differentiate them. Cy Young's 1904 Boston Americans were renamed the Red Sox in 1908. His opponent that day, the Philadelphia Athletics, moved to Kansas City in 1955 and then to Oakland in 1968. The Montreal Expos became the Washington Nationals in 2005, and the Florida Marlins were renamed the Miami Marlins in 2012.

Randy Johnson was dominating that day against the reigning nine-time National League East Champion Braves (1995-2003). Of the 27 straight outs he recorded against Atlanta batters, 13 were strikeouts. The only other pitchers who recorded more strikeouts during a perfect game were Sandy Koufax in 1965 and Matt Cain in 2012. Both had 14 strikeouts. Johnson was efficient, too, only using 117 pitches in his win.

The Arizona lineup, featuring outfielders Luis Gonzalez, Steve Finley, and Danny Bautista, managed to push across two runs on eight hits to provide enough offense for the victory. In the top of the second inning, Bautista singled to right field with two outs. The next batter, shortstop Alex Cintron, doubled to deep center field, scoring Bautista. Arizona added another run in the top of the seventh when Cintron doubled (again) past the third baseman. Cintron scored on leadoff hitter Chad Tracy's single to center field for Arizona's second run. That was one more than Johnson would need to win the game.

The biggest threat to Johnson's perfect game came in the sixth inning, when Atlanta pitcher Mike Hampton tapped a slow roller that shortstop Cintron scooped up and fired to first base, nipping the runner by a half-step. On another occasion, Shea Hillenbrand made a diving stop of an infield grounder and then had to hurry over to first base to tag the base just in time. The only other time the perfect game was seriously threatened was early in the game. Johnny Estrada had an 11-pitch at bat with one out in the second inning. It was the only time during the game where Johnson went to three balls on a hitter. Near the end of the at-bat, Estrada fouled off three straight 3-2 pitches before going down swinging. Appropriately, Johnson struck out the final batter of the game, pinch-hitter Eddie Perez, with a 98-mph fastball.

The 2004 Atlanta Braves were in the midst of an extremely impressive run when they faced the Diamondbacks. From 1991-2003, the Braves won their division title every year, with the exception of 1994 when the baseball strike forced a premature end to the season in mid-August. At the time the games stopped, the Braves had a very impressive record of 68-46, good enough for second best in the National League. That said, they were a full six games behind the National League East Division leader, the Montreal Expos. While no one can tell what would have happened if the season had played out, it would have been hard for Atlanta to make up that much ground on the other-worldly Expos, led by Hall of Famers Pedro Martinez and Larry Walker, and sporting a .649 winning percentage.

The 2004 version of the Braves divisional dynasty featured a future Hall of Famer in their lineup (Chipper Jones), along with hitting stars Andruw Jones and J.D. Drew. That day, Randy Johnson struck out Chipper Jones three times. He retired perennial All-Star Andruw Jones on two fly outs to Arizona center fielder Steve Finley, and a line out to Luis Gonzalez in left. J.D. Drew, who posted an OPS over 1.000 that year, struck out once, flew out to Danny Bautista in right, and grounded out to Matt Kata at second base.

The disparity in end-of-season records between the division champion Braves and the cellar-dwelling Diamondbacks was historic for two teams involved in a no-hitter. Their game is tied for the greatest negative win differential in history between the team that threw the no-hitter and the team that was no-hit. Based upon their final records, Arizona was a full 45.0 games behind the Atlanta Braves when the 2004 regular season was complete.

Table 4-2. Highest Negative Win Differential Between No-Hitter Teams

Rank	Date	No-hit Pitcher	Pitcher's Team (Season Record)	Opponent (Season Record)	Delta
1 (tie)	8/25/1952	Virgil Trucks	Detroit Tigers (50-104)	New York Yankees (95-59)	-45.0
1 (tie)	5/18/2004	Randy Johnson	Arizona D-backs (51-111)	Atlanta Braves (96-66)	-45.0
3 (tie)	5/5/1917	Ernie Koob	St. Louis Browns (57-97)	Chicago White Sox (100-54)	-43.0
3 (tie)	5/6/1917	Bob Groom	St. Louis Browns (57-97)	Chicago White Sox (100-54)	-43.0
5	8/26/1916	Bullet Joe Bush	Philadelphia Athletics (36-117)	Cleveland Indians (77-77)	-40.5
6	7/30/1973	Jim Bibby	Texas Rangers (57-105)	Oakland Athletics (94-68)	-37.0
7	7/25/2015	Cole Hamels	Philadelphia Phillies (63-99)	Chicago Cubs (97-65)	-34.0
8 (tie)	6/25/2010	Edwin Jackson	Arizona D-backs (65-97)	Tampa Bay Rays (96-66)	-31.0
8 (tie)	9/29/2013	Henderson Alvarez III	Miami Marlins (62-100)	Detroit Tigers (93-69)	-31.0
10	9/9/1945	Dick Fowler	Philadelphia Athletics (52-98)	St. Louis Browns (81-70)	-28.5

METHODOLOGY: This table includes those teams from 1900-2021 who had the greatest negative win differential between their team and the team that was no-hit. Teams are ranked by the highest negative differential ("Delta") between the win-loss record of the team that threw the no-hitter and that of the team that was no-hit. It is calculated by subtracting the end-of-season record of the team that was no-hit from the record of the team that threw the no-hitter. The result is the difference between the two, typically shown as "games behind" (abbreviated as GB) in league or divisional standings.

LEGEND: Dates are shown as month/day/year (for example, June 12, 2018, is shown as 6/12/2018). "Season Record" is the team's final win-loss record for the entire season. The Philadelphia Athletics (mentioned twice) moved to Kansas City in 1955 and then to Oakland in 1968. The St. Louis Browns (also mentioned twice) moved to Baltimore and became the Orioles in 1954.

The 2004 Braves had the second-best record in the National League that season, behind only the Central Division St. Louis Cardinals at 105-57. The Diamondbacks, however, were by far the worst team in the National League, trailing the overall 15th-place "owner-less-and-moving-to-Washington DC-next year" Montreal Expos by a full 16.0 games.

For many reasons, this perfect game was extraordinarily unlikely to occur. First, a perfect game is very rare. As of 2021, there have only been 23 perfect games thrown in the history of baseball. Along with that, Randy Johnson was 40 years old. As outstanding as he was, Johnson was three years older than the oldest perfect-game pitcher in history – the venerable Cy Young. Young had accomplished the feat 100 years earlier.

Finally, the Diamondbacks were one of the 10 worst teams in baseball during the 76 seasons after the end of World War II in 1945 through the 2021 season. For Arizona to even win a game against the Braves was unlikely, as Atlanta took the season series 4-2 that year. Besides Johnson's perfect game, the only other Arizona win against Atlanta was a 6-4, 11-inning victory the day after Johnson's gem. The Braves swept the remaining four games against Arizona by a combined score of 29-9.

Yet, even on a historically bad team, Randy Johnson excelled. This is demonstrated by the fact that he won an extraordinary 31% of all his team's games that season. The table below demonstrates this by showing the winningest pitcher on the 10 worst teams in baseball's post-war period from 1946-2021.

Table 4-3. Winningest Pitchers on the Worst Teams in Baseball

Lowest W-L Pct	Record (W-L Pct)	Team	Best Pitcher (W-L, Pct)	Team Wins	Highest Wins Pct
1	40-120 (.250)	1962 New York Mets	Roger Craig (10-24, .294)	25.0%	4
2	43-119 (.265)	2003 Detroit Tigers	Mike Maroth (9-21, .300)	20.9%	6
3	42-112 (.273)	1952 Pittsburgh Pirates	Murry Dickson (14-21, .400)	33.3%	1
4	47-115 (.290)	2018 Baltimore Orioles	Dylan Bundy (8-16, .333)	17.0%	8
5	47-114 (.292)	2019 Detroit Tigers	Matthew Boyd (9-12, .429)	19.1%	7
6	47-107 (.305)	1961 Philadelphia Phillies	Art Mahaffey (11-19, .367)	23.4%	5
7	50-112 (.309)	1965 New York Mets	Al Jackson (8-20, .286)	16.0%	9
8 (tie)	51-111 (.315)	1963 New York Mets	Al Jackson (13-17, .433)	25.5%	3
8 (tie)	51-111 (.315)	2004 Arizona Diamondbacks	Randy Johnson (16-14, .533)	31.4%	2
8 (tie)	51-111 (.315)	2013 Houston Astros	Jordan Lyles (7-9, .438)	13.7%	10

METHODOLOGY: This table includes the 10 teams with the lowest end-of-season win-loss percentage from 1946-2021. Teams are ranked in order of lowest winning percentage. This ranking is shown on the left side of the table. The ranking on the right side of the table represents the highest percentage of team wins for the pitcher with the most wins on the team identified.

LEGEND: W-L = Win-Loss record for a team or an individual pitcher at the end of the season. Pct = team or pitcher winning percentage where 100% = 1.000.

"Highest Wins Pct" shown in the far right column is the rank order of the 10 pitchers listed based upon that pitcher's percentage of team wins.

NOTE 1: While not listed here, Philadelphia pitcher and Hall of Famer Steve Carlton set the record for the highest percentage of team wins in a single season. In 1972, Carlton went 27-10 on a terrible Phillies team that finished at 59-97. His 27 wins represented 45.8% of last-place Philadelphia's victories. Carlton not only set the record for highest percentage of team wins, he was also the unanimous choice for the National League Cy Young Award that year.

NOTE 2: Mets starter Jack Fisher (8-24) also tied for the 1965 team lead in games won with eight. Al Jackson (8-20) is listed in the table above because his winning percentage was higher than Fisher's (.286 vs. .250).

Randy Johnson had the only winning record of the 10 pitchers listed in the table. The one pitcher who comes remotely close to him in performance is Murry Dickson of the 1952 Pittsburgh Pirates. While Dickson had a greater percentage of his team's wins, he also pitched in eight more games and threw 32 more innings for the Pirates that year than Randy Johnson did with the 2004 Diamondbacks. Of note, Dickson was well regarded as a pitcher throughout his 18-year career. For example, he won 20 games in 1951, was part of the National League All-Star team in 1953, and even received MVP votes in 1952 (the year listed here).

Despite Dickson winning a third of the games on an awful Pirates team, Randy Johnson was clearly more dominant than him or any of the other pitchers listed. With a 2.60 ERA and an incredible 290 strikeouts over 245.2 innings, Randy Johnson was by far the best pitcher on the Diamondbacks that year. Even though he played for such a struggling team and only had a winning percentage of just over .500, Johnson came in second in the National League Cy Young voting, receiving eight first-place votes; finishing right behind Roger Clemens of the Houston Astros. As you might have imagined, Johnson was also Arizona's lone All-Star representative on the 2004 National League team.

This table also demonstrates just how terrible the New York Mets of the early 1960s were. In addition to the 1962 team having the worst record in the post-war era from 1946 on, the Mets also have two other representatives on this "10 Worst" list with their 1963 and 1965 squads. With two more losses, the 53-109 team from 1964 would have also joined the other three to make it four straight teams with 111 or more losses. Things were looking up for New York in 1966, though. That's when the team broke out of 10th place, finishing at 66-95 and just ahead of the 103-loss Chicago Cubs. Not coincidentally, that year a young core of budding stars like Nolan Ryan, Tug McGraw, Ed Kranepool, Cleon Jones, and Ron Swoboda were beginning to emerge. These were some of the players who would lead the Mets to a highly improbable championship just three years later in 1969.

Another remarkable feat Johnson achieved this day was that he threw his second no-hitter, joining an elite group of pitchers. Listed below are those pitchers with a career JAWS of over 50.0 who have thrown more than one no-hitter.

Table 4-4. Top Ten Pitchers with Two or More No-hitters

JAWS	Name	Date	Pitcher's Team	Opposing Team	Score
120.8	Cy Young	9/18/1897 *5/5/1904* 6/30/1908	Cleveland Spiders *Boston Americans* Boston Red Sox	Cincinnati Reds *Phi Athletics* NY Highlanders	6-0 *3-0* 8-0
88.4	Christy Mathewson	7/15/1901 6/13/1905	New York Giants New York Giants	StL Cardinals Chicago Cubs	5-0 1-0
81.3	Randy Johnson	6/2/1990 *5/18/2004*	Seattle Mariners *Arizona D-backs*	Detroit Tigers *Atlanta Braves*	2-0 *2-0*
75.7	Warren Spahn	9/16/1960 4/28/1961	Milwaukee Braves Milwaukee Braves	Phi Phillies SF Giants	4-0 1-0
62.2	Nolan Ryan	5/15/1973 7/15/1973 9/28/1974 6/1/1975 9/26/1981 6/1/1990 5/1/1991	California Angels California Angels California Angels California Angels Houston Astros Texas Rangers Texas Rangers	KC Royals Detroit Tigers Minnesota Twins Baltimore Orioles LA Dodgers Oakland Athletics Toronto Blue Jays	3-0 6-0 4-0 1-0 5-0 5-0 3-0
60.8	Justin Verlander	6/12/2007 5/7/2011 9/1/2019	Detroit Tigers Detroit Tigers Houston Astros	Mil Brewers Toronto Blue Jays Toronto Blue Jays	4-0 9-0 2-0
57.7	Max Scherzer	6/20/2015 10/3/2015	Was Nationals Was Nationals	Pittsburgh Pirates New York Mets	6-0 2-0 (2)
57.5	Bob Feller	4/16/1940 4/30/1946 7/1/1951	Cleveland Indians Cleveland Indians Cleveland Indians	Chi White Sox NY Yankees Detroit Tigers	1-0 1-0 2-1 (1)

JAWS	Name	Date	Pitcher's Team	Opposing Team	Score
57.4	Roy Halladay	5/29/2010 10/6/2010	*Phi Phillies* Phi Phillies	*Florida Marlins* Cincinnati Reds	*1-0* 4-0
54.2	Jim Bunning	7/20/1958 6/21/1964	Detroit Tigers *Phi Phillies*	Boston Red Sox *New York Mets*	3-0 *6-0 (1)*

METHODOLOGY: This table includes the 10 pitchers from 1900-2021 who threw multiple no-hitters and had the highest career Jaffe Wins Above Replacement Score (JAWS). The pitchers are ranked from highest to lowest JAWS. JAWS is a sabermetric baseball statistic developed to evaluate the strength of a player's career and merit for induction into the Baseball Hall of Fame. It is created by averaging a player's career Wins Above Replacement (WAR) with their 7-year peak Wins Above Replacement (WAR). WAR measures a player's value in all facets of the game by deciphering how many more wins he's worth than a replacement-level player at his same position.

LEGEND: Dates are shown as month/day/year (for example, June 12, 2018, is shown as 6/12/2018). (1) or (2) = First or second game of a doubleheader. *The four perfect games are displayed in italics: Cy Young (1904 against the Athletics), Randy Johnson (2004 against the Braves), Roy Halladay (2010 against Florida) and Jim Bunning (1964 against the Mets).*

NOTE 1: All games listed were won by the pitcher's team. All games were in the regular season, except for Roy Halladay's October 2010 no-hitter against Cincinnati. His second no-hitter that season occurred during the first game of Philadelphia's National League Division Series versus the Reds.

NOTE 2: As shown in the table, Nolan Ryan leads all pitchers with seven total no-hit games. Cy Young, Bob Feller, and Justin Verlander are tied for second place with three no-hitters.

NOTE 3: All pitchers on the above list are Hall of Famers, except for Verlander and Scherzer. Those two pitchers are still active and not eligible for the Hall yet. It is entirely possible that both of them will climb in the ranking on this chart as their careers progress.

NOTE 4: There is only one pitcher with a career JAWS above 50.0 who threw more than one no-hitter before 1900. Hall of Famer Pud Galvin (67.6 JAWS) threw no-hitters in 1880 and 1884 for the National League's Buffalo Bisons. I only considered statistics compiled from 1900 and beyond because that's where most baseball analysts agree that the modern era began. Before 1900, the game structure was significantly different. Cy Young's 1897 no-hitter against the Cincinnati Reds is included in this table to give a more complete picture of his no-hitter accomplishments. He would have made this list regardless of whether that game was included because of his two post-1900 no-hitters.

Johnson does indeed hold the record for the longest gap between no-hitters at just under 14 years. This is yet another record he set that day. Johnson is, without question, the best pitcher the Diamondbacks have had in the 25 seasons they have played. With 118 wins for Arizona, he outpaces the next closest player (Brandon Webb with 87) by 31 wins. He is 60 wins ahead of Curt Schilling in third place. He also is far ahead of all other starting pitchers with a career ERA of 2.83 during his time with the Diamondbacks. With a Game Score of 100, Johnson's perfect game is tied with a 2002 Curt Schilling 17-strikeout effort for the highest Game Score in Arizona history. A list of Arizona's highest Game Scores will be explored in greater detail in the chapter on Diamondback pitcher Edwin Jackson's no-hitter.

Johnson's span of excellence covers a long period. He ranks as the fourth best pitcher of the 1990s in terms of WAR achieved. However, it can be argued that his last decade in baseball was his best, as he topped the list of highest WAR achieved by a pitcher in the 2000s.

Table 4-5. Best Pitchers of the 2000s (2000-2009)

WAR Rank	Pitcher (Team(s))	Seasons Pitched	Innings Pitched	WAR (per 200 IP)	Wins (per Season)
1	Randy Johnson (D-backs, Yankees, Giants)	2000-2009	1,885.1	51.3 (5.44)	143 (14.3)
2	Johan Santana (Twins, Mets)	2000-2009	1,709.2	46.3 (5.42)	122 (12.2)
3	Curt Schilling (Phillies, D-backs, Red Sox)	2000-2007	1,569.1	46.2 (5.89)	117 (14.6)
4	Pedro Martinez (Red Sox, Mets, Phillies)	2000-2009	1,468.0	45.6 (6.21)	112 (11.2)

WAR Rank	Pitcher (Team(s))	Seasons Pitched	Innings Pitched	WAR (per 200 IP)	Wins (per Season)
5	Roy Halladay (Blue Jays)	2000-2009	1,883.1	45.4 (4.82)	139 (13.9)
6	Roy Oswalt (Astros)	2001-2009	1,803.1	43.1 (4.78)	137 (15.2)
7	Javier Vazquez (Expos, Yankees, D-backs, White Sox, Braves)	2000-2009	2,163.0	42.3 (3.91)	128 (12.8)
8	Mark Buehrle (White Sox)	2000-2009	2,061.0	41.3 (4.01)	135 (13.5)
9	Mike Mussina (Orioles, Yankees)	2000-2008	1,790.2	40.8 (4.56)	134 (14.9)
10	Tim Hudson (Athletics, Braves)	2000-2009	1,923.1	40.2 (4.18)	137 (13.7)
11	C.C. Sabathia (Indians, Brewers, Yankees)	2001-2009	1,889.1	38.6 (4.09)	136 (15.1)
12	Barry Zito (Athletics, Giants)	2000-2009	1,999.0	35.3 (3.53)	133 (13.3)

METHODOLOGY: Pitchers are ranked in order of Wins Above Replacement (WAR) achieved from 2000-2009. WAR measures a player's value in all facets of the game by deciphering how many more wins he's worth than a replacement-level player at his same position.

LEGEND: Another measure of merit I wanted to include was the number of wins each pitcher accumulated as well. Because a significant number of pitchers were only present for a portion of the decade, I included two rate measures (WAR per 200 innings pitched and wins per season). IP = innings pitched. One-third of an inning is designated as ".1" and two-thirds of an inning is designated as ".2" innings.

Randy Johnson can also make a claim as one of the very best pitchers for another franchise besides the Diamondbacks: the Seattle Mariners. As a Seattle starter for ten seasons from 1989 to 1998, he accumulated 130 wins and over 2,100 strikeouts. While Felix Hernandez led the franchise in both areas, Johnson had the consistently highest Game Scores for the Mariners, as he appeared frequently in the table below. Johnson also threw a 1990 no-hitter for Seattle in his first full year with the team.

Table 4-6. Mariners Highest Game Scores

Rank	Pitcher	Date Score	Opponent	GSc	IP, Hits, Runs, ERs, Walks, Strikeouts
1 (tie)	Erik Hanson	8/1/1990 Oak 1-0 (11 inn)	Oakland Athletics	99	10.0 IP, 2 Hits, 0 Runs, 0 ERs, 0 BBs, 11 Ks
1 *(tie)*	*Felix* *Hernandez*	*8/15/2012* *Sea 1-0*	*Tampa Bay* *Rays*	*99*	*9.0 IP, 0 Hits, 0 Runs,* *0 ERs, 0 BBs, 12 Ks*
3	Randy Johnson	9/16/1992 Cal 2-1 (13 inn)	California Angels	97	9.0 IP, 1 Hit, 1 Run, 0 ERs, 1 BB, 15 Ks
4	Randy Johnson	5/16/1993 Sea 7-0	Oakland Athletics	96	9.0 IP, 1 Hit, 0 Runs, 0 ERs, 3 BBs, 14 Ks
5	Randy Johnson	7/15/1995 Sea 3-0	Toronto Blue Jays	95	9.0 IP, 3 Hits, 0 Runs, 0 ERs, 2 BBs, 16 Ks
6	Randy Johnson	8/14/1991 Sea 4-0	Oakland Athletics	94	9.0 IP, 1 Hit, 0 Runs, 0 ERs, 3 BBs, 12 Ks
7 (tie)	Randy Johnson	8/8/1997 Sea 5-0	Chicago White Sox	93	9.0 IP, 5 Hits, 0 Runs, 0 ERs, 3 BBs, 19 Ks
7 (tie)	Randy Johnson	7/16/1998 Sea 3-0	Minnesota Twins	93	9.0 IP, 1 Hit, 0 Runs, 0 ERs, 3 BBs, 11 Ks
7 (tie)	Felix Hernandez	7/14/2012 Sea 7-0	Texas Rangers	93	9.0 IP, 3 Hits, 0 Runs, 0 ERs, 0 BBs, 12 Ks
7 (tie)	Aaron Harang	6/11/2013 Sea 4-0	Houston Astros	93	9.0 IP, 2 Hits, 0 Runs, 0 ERs, 0 BBs, 10 Ks
15 (tie)	Hisashi Iwakuma	8/12/2015 Sea 3-0	Baltimore Orioles	91	9.0 IP, 0 Hits, 0 Runs, 0 ERs, 3 BBs, 7 Ks
15 (tie)	James Paxton	5/8/2018 Sea 5-0	Toronto Blue Jays	91	9.0 IP, 0 Hits, 0 Runs, 0 ERs, 3 BBs, 7 Ks
30 (tie)	Randy Johnson	6/2/1990 Sea 2-0	Detroit Tigers	89	9.0 IP, 0 Hits, 0 Runs, 0 ERs, 6 BBs, 8 Ks
30 (tie)	Chris Bosio	4/22/1993 Sea 7-0	Boston Red Sox	89	9.0 IP, 0 Hits, 0 Runs, 0 ERs, 2 BBs, 4 Ks
357 (tie)	Kevin Millwood	6/8/2012 Sea 1-0	Los Angeles Dodgers	77	6.0 IP, 0 Hits, 0 Runs, 0 ERs, 1 BB, 6 Ks

METHODOLOGY: This table includes the highest Game Scores thrown by a pitcher from the Seattle Mariners from 1969-2021. Games are ranked by Game Score (GSc) and consider all franchise regular season and postseason games. For comparison purposes, all five Seattle single-pitcher no-hitters are included in this table. Game Score measures a pitcher's performance in any given game started. Introduced by baseball writer/statistician Bill James in the 1980s, Game Score is presented as a figure between 0-100 — except for extreme outliers — and usually falls between 40-70.

LEGEND: Dates are shown as month/day/year (for example, June 12, 2018, is shown as 6/12/2018); IP = innings pitched. BB(s) = base(s) on balls. K(s) = strike-out(s). ER(s) = earned run(s). inn = innings (associated with the length of extra-inning games). The Mariners began operations as an expansion team in 1977, along with the Toronto Blue Jays. They have been in the American League West Division the entire time. *The Mariners only perfect game (thrown by Felix Hernandez on August 15, 2012) is shown in italics.*

NOTE 1: The sixth Mariner no-hitter was a combined effort by six pitchers thrown on June 8, 2012: Kevin Millwood (6 IP), Charlie Furbush (2/3 IP), Stephen Pryor (1/3 IP), Lucas Luetge (1/3 IP), Brandon League (2/3 IP), and Tom Wilhelmsen (1 IP). Seattle won that game 1-0 over the Los Angeles Dodgers. Millwood left the game after six innings due to an injury. With three walks and nine strikeouts, the six pitchers' performance would equate to a Game Score of 93 if their statistics were combined. This game is tied for the Major League record most pitchers used in a no-hitter (six).

NOTE 2: The highest postseason Game Score by a Seattle pitcher was 74 by Freddy Garcia in the opening game of the 2000 ALCS against the Yankees. Garcia threw 6.2 innings of shutout ball, holding New York to three hits and two walks while striking out eight in a 2-0 Mariner victory. While Garcia would emerge victorious in Game 5 as well, Seattle would drop the other four games they played, losing to the Yankees four games to two.

NOTE 3: The top two games in Seattle history with a Game Score of 99 were Felix Hernandez's 2012 perfect game, and a 10-inning gem thrown by Erik Hanson in 1990. During Hanson's effort against the Oakland Athletics, he allowed a single by Carney Lansford with one out in the fourth inning. After that, the next hit he gave up was to Dave Henderson with one out in the 10th inning. He was removed from the game at the end of the 10th inning after throwing 122 pitches. Seattle reliever Mike Schooler allowed three one-out singles in the bottom of the 11th inning, leading to an Oakland run and giving the Athletics a 1-0 win.

NOTE 4: Six of the Top 10 games in Seattle history were thrown by Randy Johnson, who was with the team from mid-season 1989 until mid-season 1998. All those games occurred after his first no-hitter in 1990, and all six had higher Game Scores than his no-hitter (where he achieved a score of 89). Four of the six games were one-hitters.

NOTE 5: In two separate games against the Oakland Athletics, Johnson had no-hit bids broken up in the ninth inning with one out. In his August 1991 game, number eight hitter Mike Gallego hit a line drive single to left field, and in his May 1993 game, number nine hitter Lance Blankenship hit a single down the right field line. In both cases, Johnson was only two outs away from a no-hitter. In Johnson's 1998 no-hit bid against the Twins, he was only five outs away from a no-hitter when Brent Gates hit a grounder through the infield for Minnesota's only hit of the game.

NOTE 6: Johnson's 19-strikeout game against the White Sox in 1997 is the most ever achieved by a Mariner pitcher in a single game. His 16-strikeout game in 1995 is in second place.

Randy Johnson was born in 1963 in Walnut Creek, California. When practicing pitching, he tried to emulate another left-handed pitcher, Oakland's Vida Blue, one of Johnson's boyhood idols. In high school, Johnson excelled in basketball and baseball. He accepted a scholarship to play both sports at the University of Southern California. After three seasons with the Trojans, he was drafted by Montreal in the second round of the 1985 draft. Johnson pitched for Montreal from 1988-1989 and was traded along with two other players to Seattle in May 1989 for pitcher Mark Langston. Johnson pitched for Seattle from 1989-1998, finishing among the top five vote-getters for the Cy Young Award five times, including winning the Cy Young in 1995.

He was traded to Houston at the trade deadline in July 1998 to help the Astros in the pennant race. Johnson excelled in Houston, going 10-1 and helping the Astros run away with the National League Central Division, as they finished 12.5 games ahead of the second-place Cubs. While he pitched well in the NLDS against San Diego in games one and four, the Astros only scored a total of two runs in the games he started.

Johnson signed as a free agent with Arizona in December 1998, where he stayed through the 2004 season. As noted earlier, he led the Diamondbacks to a

World Series championship in 2001 and won the Cy Young Award each season from 1999-2002. The great Greg Maddux is the only other pitcher to ever win four Cy Young Awards in a row. From 2005-2009, Johnson played with the New York Yankees (2005-2006), then back with Arizona (2007-2008), and finally with San Francisco in 2009, where he won his 300th game that year.

In retirement, Johnson spent more time with his family and got involved with photojournalism. He made numerous trips to visit the troops in Afghanistan, and he also aided many charities, including support in fighting cystic fibrosis. In 2015, Johnson was elected to the Baseball Hall of Fame in his first year of eligibility.

Johnson's catcher the day he threw his perfect game was Robby Hammock, who shared catching duties with five other players over the course of the season. Hammock was chosen by Arizona in the 23rd round of the 1998 draft. He played regularly for the Diamondbacks from 2003-2004, along with occasional appearances from 2006-2011. For his career, he had a total of 481 at bats and a JAWS of 0.6. As will be explored further in the chapter on Tom Seaver, the battery of Randy Johnson (81.3 JAWS) and Robby Hammock had the third highest career JAWS differential (80.7) of any pitcher-catcher combination to throw a no-hitter from 1950 on. The second biggest differential (81.5 JAWS) was Randy Johnson (81.3) and Seattle catcher Scott Bradley (minus 0.2) for Johnson's first no-hitter in 1990.

Included below are interviews with both Randy Johnson and Robby Hammock, Johnson's batterymate that day.

Randy Johnson Interview
Conducted by Kevin McCaffrey on August 19, 2021

Kevin McCaffrey (KM): (After opening remarks) Would you consider yourself to have been the best pitcher on your high school team?
Randy Johnson (RJ): Yeah, I guess. There weren't a whole lot of other pitchers on the team other than one of my other best friends and he didn't go and play baseball beyond high school. So, on my team, yes. I would say my team, not in my town, though.
KM: Were there other players in Livermore at the time who made it to the majors?
RJ: I think there were a few. I'm just talking about high school, there were high school players that were more developed with their skills. Better than I was.

KM: I know you were drafted by Atlanta out of high school, but you chose to go to USC (University of Southern California). But when I was looking at your stats at USC it appeared that you were on the roster '83, '84, and '85 but there's only numbers for you in '84.

RJ: I don't know anything. I couldn't help you there, I don't know. I have no idea; I have no idea what's going on there.

KM: Yeah, it said your record was 5-3 in '84 and then there's nothing listed for the other years, and then you were drafted by the Expos in '85.

RJ: Interesting. Have you tried to call the USC Athletic Department?

KM: No, that's a good idea. I'll see if I can find out about that. (Author's note: Johnson went 5-0 with three saves in 15 games – mostly as a reliever – in 1983, and in 1985 he was 6-9 with a 5.32 ERA due to ongoing control issues. Even so, the Expos saw enormous potential in him and drafted Johnson in the second round.) And then, as far as the no-hitter, the perfect game, did you feel any different, good or bad, on that day?

RJ: No. No.

KM: Felt pretty normal?

RJ: Yeah, just another day pitching on a really humid day in Atlanta that I'd been doing for about, up to that point, probably for about 15 years.

KM: And so, what pitches were working for you best that day?

RJ: Slider and fastball, but you know, why were they working that much better on that day, I have no idea. I don't try to overthink those kinds of things. I don't even remember that day. I mean we're talking 16 years ago, 17 years ago. I just don't remember the details.

KM: Do you remember the best defensive play or the closest you came to losing the perfect game that day?

RJ: I think there's a couple ... there's always a couple of plays in no-hitters. There always seems to be a defensive gem. Shea Hillenbrand was the first baseman, and I was late getting over to first base and he did a diving play to stop the ball and then had to hurry and pick himself off the ground and get over to first base to tag the base. That was one and then Mike Hampton, the opposing pitcher, who's also a very good hitting pitcher, hit a high chopper to shortstop and I thought that was going to be a possible hit because he's an extremely fast runner, so yes, there were a couple of different plays.

KM: Do you remember shaking off your catcher Robby Hammock much that day?

RJ: I don't remember (laughs). I don't remember what I had for breakfast yesterday, so I can't remember details of a game over 16 years ago.

KM: My co-writer Kevin Hurd, he actually did interview Robby Hammock and he asked him about that, and he said that Randy Johnson never shook him off, all he did was stare. I thought that was a good one.

RJ: Oh, well. Okay, there you go. Direct from the catcher.

KM: You threw 117 pitches that day but that wasn't really unusual for you. Looking at your career stats you had 100 complete games, you led the National League in innings pitched a couple of times, led the American League in complete games one time, and the NL in complete games three times. But you really were kind of a late bloomer in that you only won 64 games by the time you were 30 and then 239 after that. What do you attribute that to, that you could have such longevity, throw lots of pitches well into your thirties and all the way past 40? What was it about you that allowed you to do that?

RJ: Having my mechanics straightened out in 1992.

KM: And that was when Nolan Ryan helped you with that?

RJ: Exactly, you can look up all that information if you like. I don't need to rehash that. I've been asked about that all the time. I would say that had a great impact on me – that might have happened I was probably around 27-28 years old. And then the next season in '93, that was my first big year in the major leagues winning 18 games after that conversation. My dad had also passed away during the offseason of that year '92, so that had a big impact obviously on me as well. But it took me a while to get my mechanics. There was no other pitcher in the game that was 6 foot 10 who was a starting pitcher, who was throwing 100 miles an hour.

So, for me throwing 100 miles an hour and being at 6 foot 10, there was a lot of inconsistency. Probably 80% of it was because I had inconsistent mechanics and so as soon as I worked out some details and refined things, then I got a little more consistency. And then from that point on I started winning some ballgames after that. From '93 on I started winning a few ballgames then.

KM: Yeah, quite a few. And Robby Hammock was your catcher that day. Is he one that you had requested in the past?

RJ: No, I never requested any catcher. I think at that time, we're talking 2004, the catcher that had caught me, the everyday catcher there, was Damian Miller. He was no longer there I don't think, he was gone (Author's note: Damian

	Miller was Arizona's primary catcher in 2000-2002 and had been an All-Star with Arizona in 2002. In 2004 he was Oakland's primary catcher). So, I think Robby Hammock shared the duties with somebody else at that time, you know.
KM:	Yeah, I was looking at the stats for the catchers that year and it didn't seem like anybody really stood out. Robby Hammock caught the most games with 62 and then there were three other guys who caught 30 to 50 games.
RJ:	Well, that was the year we lost 111 games, so nobody really stood out that year.
KM:	Robby Hammock is now a coach with the Diamondbacks, do you stay in touch with him at all?
RJ:	I see him, I'm almost 60 years old, I have other interests now other than just strictly baseball. I don't coach, I'm not a coach. He is. There's nothing that sends me down there unless they need me for something.
KM:	During the game when did you think, *"I've got a real shot at this"*?
RJ:	I suppose probably when I was going back out maybe for the eighth inning. I've taken a lot of no-hitters I think into the sixth or seventh inning before and have had them lost so I don't think I even was thinking about it until I went out for the eighth inning.
KM:	And did you realize it was a perfect game at that point?
RJ:	I don't remember. I could lie to you and make the story sound interesting. But like I said, I've talked about this, I've talked about hitting that stupid bird, and this year is the twentieth anniversary of our World Series, and I don't have any details of that that I can really talk about. I have a lot of great memories about it, but I don't have any details, you know. It was a long year, and I'm not like a lot of my peers and teammates that are one of just remembering details. I've kind of moved on from my baseball career and have other interests now, and I don't do many interviews anymore, so ….
KM:	I read that you were really into photography, are you doing a lot of that?
RJ:	Well, I studied that at USC, so it's not anything I'm just getting into now. I just have more time for it now.
KM:	And I read that in 2015 you were named a special assistant to the team president Derrick Hall. Do you still have any involvement with the D-Backs?
RJ:	Yes, that's one of the things. I'm not a coach but I go down during spring training, watch the minor league kids throw when they start their spring training. I addressed some of the new draftees this year, so I'm involved in that capacity.

KM: And I've read that you've made 40 trips with the USO (United Services Organization)?

RJ: Extremely. That's why I'm not a coach in baseball. I have other interests. Spending most of my life in baseball and then retiring from it, I felt like there were other important things out there that I wanted to spend some time in and giving my time to the men and women who serve our country is one of those things. So yes, I've travelled however many (trips). I've been doing that since the year I retired. I've been all over the world and I've seen a lot of interesting things. And the men and women of our military have my support.

KM: Oh, that's great, that's really cool. Would you say that the perfect game was the highlight of your career and if not, what was?

RJ: From an individual standpoint, that's an individual performance. The highlight of my career was winning the World Series. But I would say the perfect game was one of the highlights. You know I also struck out 20 batters in a game, so I would say that was another big highlight of my career. But yeah, I'd say the perfect game is right up there but it's not like I think about it every night before I go to bed.

KM: So, have you been to the section of the baseball Hall of Fame that focuses on the no-hitters?

RJ: I have not, I didn't even know they had one. (Laughs)

KM: They do, yeah, so if you make it there again check it out. Do you have any other favorite stories regarding the perfect game or other parts of your career?

RJ: No, I really don't, I'm sorry I'm just a boring interview. (Laughs)

KM: No, you're great, you're great.

RJ: I've been retired for 11 years. I don't even have a baseball at my house. Nothing to play catch with if I wanted to play catch. So, I think that's where I'm at in the game. I don't have a lot of mementos other than my accolades and stuff like that. I've just kinda moved on. I think I'm in the real world now. And when you go to Afghanistan or Iraq or Kuwait, back when I was going and things were still a little crazy in our world – and they're always crazy – and I saw it firsthand, I think that was more important to me.

Baseball people just, at the time when you're playing baseball you're just in a different (world). It's like a little bubble. And I think I'm outside that bubble now and I have been for a while, and I have family and I have other interests. You know, I've moved on from what I did so much of my time. I had so much passion, and I gave so much time and effort to the craft of baseball to be as good as I could be, that now that I'm retired, I've moved on to do other things.

KM: Yeah, well that's great.

RJ: Yeah.

KM: Just a couple more things, how about some of the managers you played for, which ones did you enjoy playing for?

RJ: What does that have to do with the perfect game?

KM: Well not specifically, but just to kind of flesh things out. But if you don't want to answer that, that's okay.

RJ: I'd say probably the most strategic and best manager I ever played for was probably Lou Piniella. That was in Seattle.

KM: Yeah, I'm in Seattle so I'm very familiar with that time. I saw you pitch with the Mariners, so yeah, that was great. How about any managers or coaches in the minor leagues that really helped you a lot to get to the majors?

RJ: None that I can really remember. I'm sure they were all influential on myself and all my teammates. I don't remember many of them anymore because that's probably, you know, from the perfect game going back to the minor leagues – I was in the minor leagues in 1988. So, you're going from '88 to 2004 – which would be 16 years until I threw my perfect game – and then from 2004 until now, that's another 17 years, so you're asking me to remember. I just don't.

KM: (Laughs). Yeah, that's cool. A couple of other quick things – you spent 10 full seasons in the American League, 10 full in the National League, and a couple of years in both. Do you have an opinion about the DH, since you were in both leagues?

RJ: None. Not really.

KM: Do you think it would be a good idea to make it universal, or do you care about that?

RJ: I don't know. I've never been immersed in that conversation before. It's not something I've talked about. I can't remember anytime I ever was asked that question. At least while I've been retired, so that's 11 years. It's not a question I get asked. I'm a pitcher.

KM: Yeah, but it does affect you in that you don't get to hit in the AL. But then in the National League I'm thinking a lot of pitchers like the fact that one out of every nine batters is a pitcher and maybe it's an easier out most of the time.

RJ: I suppose that might be their philosophy, yeah. I probably remain neutral because like you said, I played 10 years in each, so I guess I did okay in both of 'em, pitching against the DH and pitching against pitchers.

KM: Yeah, I'd say you did okay. When you were in the NL did you like to hit?

RJ: At times it took my focus away from pitching, which I didn't like, but every once in a while, I got a hit (Author's note: Randy Johnson collected 78 hits during his career, including 14 doubles and a 2003 home run – a solo blast off of Milwaukee starter Doug Davis).

KM: You mentioned your family, did any of your kids pursue anything in baseball or softball?

RJ: No, they're not playing softball or baseball. No, they just have real lives and jobs and stuff like that.

KM: Well, just on a personal note, I live in Seattle, so I was here in that '95 season, and the Mariners were possibly going to leave for Tampa Bay. But because of you, and Edgar (Martinez), and (Ken) Griffey (Jr.), and (Jay) Buhner and Lou Piniella, etc., the Mariners are still here. So, you certainly left your mark on Seattle. So, baseball fans in Seattle certainly remember you and thank you for that.

RJ: Well, thank you, I appreciate that. I know that Ken Griffey Jr. and Edgar have a nice statue at the ballpark there, so that's nice that they remember them every time they walk in the ballpark there.

KM: Yeah, the Edgar statue just went up about a week or so ago. They just unveiled it.

RJ: I'm familiar with that, yes.

KM: Well, one of these days your statue should be there too, Randy.

RJ: Well don't hold your breath. Thank you very much.

KM: Hey, I really appreciate you doing this, I know you're busy, and it's great — this was really cool – and thank you so much.

RJ: Thank you so much, good luck on the book and the interviews.

Robby Hammock Interview
Conducted by Kevin Hurd on June 19, 2021

Kevin Hurd (KH): Would you consider yourself to be the best catcher on your Little League, American Legion, high school, junior college, college or minor league teams?

Robby Hammock (RH): Yes, I would.

KH: Did you start as a catcher, or did you switch from another position?

RH: I started as a catcher. I wasn't really thrilled with it, but I played catcher because my dad bribed me to play catcher (laughs). He thought being a catcher was a good position to play to progress rapidly in the game. When I was starting out, the league I played in allowed runners to take leads and steal bases (didn't have to wait for the ball to cross the plate to start running) so I got a lot of good experience from that.

KH: I noticed that regarding your minor league years a lot of guys you played with in A and AA didn't make it to MLB but at the AAA level the percentages went way up. Any reason?

RH: It's hard to get to the AAA level. Once you're at that level, if somebody from the parent club gets injured you have a chance to go up for a couple of weeks.

KH: Did you feel any different (good or bad) on the day of your pitcher's (Randy Johnson's) perfect game?

RH: It was a regular game. As far as me (how I felt) I had gotten injured in spring training, had just come back, the night was hot and humid, and I probably shouldn't have been playing. I had not given myself enough time to heal. Our team that year had a lot of problems (Arizona finished with a record of 51-111). A big part of that was we had a lot of injuries that year.

KH: You're from Georgia. The game was played in Atlanta. Did you have family members who attended the game?

RH: Oh, yeah (laughs). I left 40-50 tickets at will-call. It wasn't all family members; a lot of my friends showed up, too.

KH: What pitches (fastball, curve, slider, etc.) were working best for Randy that day?

RH: All of them were working well that day. His location was great. Randy had been having knee and back problems. He was fighting to perform at top condition. On the good side, his velocity was up and on humid nights you can grip the ball better.

KH: Did you ever catch a no-hitter before you caught one in the majors?

RH: No, although I did catch one where we came close but the batter blooped one into center field in the seventh inning.

KH: What was the best defensive play, the closest you came to losing the no-hitter?

RH: There were a couple of good infield plays I should mention. In one of them our shortstop Alex Cintron got a slow roller from Mike Hampton and threw him out at first. The other was when first baseman Shea Hillebrand made a diving tag on the leadoff batter. There were also a couple of line drives to the outfield.

KH: Did Randy shake off your signs much during the game?

RH: There were some, although Randy doesn't do shakes. He stares (laughs). It was a handful of times. Randy threw sliders over the plate, down and in. His fastball command was really good. He had the best slider the game has ever seen. He was 6'10" and he had a later break on his slider which made it very hard to hit.

KH: Do you have any memorabilia/souvenirs, such as a baseball, plaque, uniform, or anything like that, from the game in your house?

RH: Well, I do have some gear. My catcher's mitt is at my dad's house in Georgia. I've got the chest protector and shin guards in my house.

KH: What was going on in your career in the 2003-2004 timeframe?

RH: Well, in 2003 I was a rookie. I had been a utility player in the minors. I continued to play multiple positions for Arizona: catcher, third base, left field, right field, and first base. By the time the season ended I definitely thought I could make the team again, probably as a utility player. The team was making plans for me to be the starting catcher. I got wind of this information and started working out like a madman and wound up with knee and cartilage injuries a couple of weeks before spring training started. That's why I was still rehabbing almost up until the game in May.

KH: Did Randy request you as his catcher before this game?

RH: Well, I was a rookie in 2003, a utility guy. In August 2003, Randy was pitching a day game and I found I was catching him that day. The coaches didn't tell me the previous day because they thought I might not sleep that night (laughs). Randy had asked for me to catch him. Randy felt that it was lucky that the perfect game happened.

KH: Do you still stay in contact with Randy?

RH: No, not really. We both live in Arizona and sometimes we'll see each other around.

KH: Did your team give you a bonus for catching the perfect game?

RH: No, I didn't get anything from the team. However, I did get something from Randy. At the beginning of the next series (in Miami) Randy was transporting a Ferrari and some of the guys on the team jokingly yelled at him to "give Robby one of your Ferraris" (laughs). After the game that night, in the clubhouse Randy said he wanted to give me something. Some of our teammates gathered around, Randy produced a Rolex Box, I opened the box, and inside was a digital face Nike watch. Randy said, "Look at it, it's a new Nike watch." Randy and our teammates laughed, then Randy pulls the real Rolex out. Inscribed on the watch was "Perfect game 5/18/04 from RJ." So yes, I did get a Rolex watch as a bonus.

KH: During the game, when did you think *"He's got a real shot at a perfect game?"* Fifth inning, sixth inning, etc.?

RH: I was mostly focused on winning the game. We won 2-0. A walk and a home run ties it up. If we had been ahead 10-0, I would have thought more about the perfect game.

KH: Were you able to get a follow-on job in baseball after your playing days were over? In the majors, minors, college, high school, or with the media?

RH: Yes. From 2011-2013 I was a hitting coach in the Arizona minors system. I was a minor league manager from 2013-2016 and from 2017 to now I've been a Quality Control and Catching coach with Arizona.

KH: What does the Quality Control job entail?

RH: I'm kind of a jack of all trades. Right now, I'm the first base coach for this upcoming series. I'm in charge of the signs and our running game. I also schedule spring training (30+ games) every year.

KH: Which major league managers did you enjoy playing for the most?

RH: All of them were good, but I'd have to say Bob Brenly and Bob Melvin. Bob Brenly gave me a chance and put me in a spot to succeed. Bob Melvin was a great guy, manager, and communicator.

KH: Which managers and coaches in the minors helped you the most in your pursuit of playing in the majors?

RH: There were many. Off the top of my head, there was Don Wakamatsu (coach), Bob Mariano (hitting instructor/coach), Bill Plummer (catching coach), Joel Youngblood (base-running coach), Rick Schu (hitting coach), and Bobby Dickerson (Manager).

KH: Since you were able to get baseball jobs after your playing career ended, do you think having caught a perfect game helped you get the job?

RH: Yes. At the least, it didn't hurt. The one individual who helped me the most in getting into coaching jobs was Mike Bell.

KH: Do you have any kids who are pursuing baseball or softball as a career? Do you encourage them to do so?

RH: I have a daughter who did softball through high school, then did a different sport in college. I've got two sons of playing age. My oldest was very much into baseball at one time and has now moved away from it. My middle son still enjoys playing baseball at this point in time. My youngest is one and we'll see what he likes when he gets older. I'm not pushing them toward or away from baseball or softball.

KH: Was the perfect game the highlight of your career? If not, what was?

RH: Yes, it was. I wish it wasn't in that I wish I had a longer career and didn't have as many injuries. My best season was 2003 (rookie season) and after that I kept getting injured.

KH: Have you been to the section of the Baseball Hall of Fame that focuses on no-hitters?

RH: No, I haven't.

KH: Have you spent time signing autographs in Las Vegas, or in Florida or Arizona during spring training?

RH: Yes, I have.

KH: Do you have any favorite stories regarding any of these experiences?

RH: Well, I'll tell you a story about something that happened shortly after the perfect game. After the game we continued our road trip, and we were in the locker room, watching Sports Center and drinking champagne. Randy was there and he said, "it was great I had the perfect game, but right now I'm just thinking about my next start." That's how focused Randy was.

KH: Do you have anything further to say about the perfect game?

RH: It was the easiest game I ever caught. 27 up, 27 down, no baserunners, no base-stealing, nothing else to focus on but the hitter at the plate.

KH: Do you have anything additional to say regarding your playing career?

RH: No, I think I have covered it already.

CHAPTER 5

ED HALICKI: HO-HO THROWS A NO-NO

August 24, 1975
Intimidating Giant Ed Halicki throws an unlikely no-hitter
for a struggling franchise.

"Very often I have trouble in the first couple of innings, I don't know exactly why. The last couple of games, I've been getting them out right at the start, and I've been saying to myself, 'Well, maybe this will be my no-hitter.' It's sort of a joke. And I said it again today after I got through the first three innings without anyone getting on base."

Ed Halicki talking about his recent success and how he joked about getting a no-hitter prior to this game (Leonard Koppett, New York Times, August 25, 1975).

"Well, I was pretty much a two-pitch pitcher at that time, and both (my) fastball and slider were working well for me that day. Actually, I had one other game, a 1-0 loss in 11 innings where I thought I pitched better, but I didn't have the extra bit of luck that you sometimes need to get a no-hitter."

Ed Halicki describing what pitches were working best for him that day (interview with the author, August 19, 2021).

"Today I was lucky, you have to be lucky to get a no-hitter. It's something you dream about. Just being in the big leagues is something you dream

about, and it still gets me sometimes when I'm on the field in practice or sitting in the bull pen. Now this."

Ed Halicki on luck and what it's like to be a major leaguer who just threw a no-hitter (Leonard Koppett, New York Times, August 25, 1975).

"You're throwing terrible! Go get 'em!"

Giants bullpen catcher Mike Sadek talking to starting pitcher Ed Halicki just before he took the field in the top of the 1st inning. Sadek didn't want to jinx Halicki. (Scott Ostler, "There are lots of no-nos behind the Giants' no-hitters," NBC Sports Bay Area, June 30, 2010).

"(Ed Halicki talking about the best manager he ever pitched for) They were all good, but I would say Joe Altobelli because he was managing us in 1978, where we had the only winning record (89-73) of the six seasons I was with the Giants. We weren't bad, we were in a division that had the two best teams in baseball, or at least in the National League – the Reds and the Dodgers. We'd play the Reds and Dodgers 36 times a year. We'd usually wind up with 71 to 80 wins a year."

Ed Halicki talking about who was his best manager and what it was like to play in the National League West in the mid-seventies (interview with the author, August 19, 2021)

"Er-ror! Er-ror! Er-ror!" the crowd chanted.

It was the top of the fifth, there were no outs, and Rusty Staub stood on first base, having just hit safely to lead off the inning. There was some question as to whether the play was a single or an error on second baseman Derrel Thomas because he had dropped the ball after it had deflected off the pitcher's leg. Twenty-four-year-old Ed "Ho-Ho" Halicki, in his second season for the Giants, had retired the first 12 batters he faced, striking out five of them. After watching the home team get blown out 9-5 in the first game of the doubleheader, the 24,000 fans recognized they might be seeing something really special, a no-hitter. I have a personal connection with this game, because I was one of those fans that day, along with my older brother Drew and our friend Dan Hillmer.

Chanting for an "error" decision was only partially based on wanting Halicki to pitch a no-hitter. The other part was that it was Derrel Thomas who would be charged with the error. Thomas wasn't popular in San Francisco. For one thing, he had been acquired from the San Diego Padres in the offseason in exchange for fan favorite, all-around character, and long-time Giant Tito Fuentes. More recently, Fuentes has been an announcer and analyst on the Giants' Spanish language network since its inception in 1981. He was inducted in the San Francisco-based Hispanic Heritage Baseball Museum Hall of Fame in 2002. Derrel Thomas arrived as a replacement for Fuentes, and that didn't go over well.

Thomas also established an unfortunate reputation for himself during his tenure with the Giants. During the 1976 season, Thomas was caught washing his car in the parking lot during a game. Admittedly, he was on the Disabled List at the time, so he wasn't eligible to play, and Thomas himself claimed he "was only washing his windshield and teammates John Montefusco and John D'Acquisto were outside, too, but their names weren't mentioned." Still, for a player to be taking care of chores outside the stadium during a game says volumes about the attitudes of the player and the team.

The Giants in the mid-70s were mediocre at best. The 1975 season was in the middle of a stretch from 1974-1977 where San Francisco played below .500 baseball every year and never seriously contended for the division title against the much more talented Dodgers and Reds of that era. This is demonstrated even more dramatically when we expand our perspective to look at the 10-year period from 1972-1981, as shown in the table below.

Table 5-1. San Francisco Giants Season Records from 1972-1981

Win % Rank	Year	Team W-L Record	Winning Percentage	Divisional Finish	Games Behind	GB Rank
8	1972	69-86	.445	5th of 6 in NL West	26.5	7
2	1973	88-74	.543	3rd of 6 in NL West	11.0	2
9	1974	72-90	.444	5th of 6 in NL West	30.0	10
4	1975	80-81	.497	3rd of 6 in NL West	27.5	8
7	1976	74-88	.457	4th of 6 in NL West	28.0	9

Win % Rank	Year	Team W-L Record	Winning Percentage	Divisional Finish	Games Behind	GB Rank
6	1977	75-87	.463	4th of 6 in NL West	16.0	4
1	1978	89-73	.549	3rd of 6 in NL West	6.0	1
10	1979	71-91	.438	4th of 6 in NL West	19.5	6
5	1980	75-86	.466	5th of 6 in NL West	17.0	5
3	1981	56-55	.505	4th of 6 in NL West	11.5	3

METHODOLOGY: The Giants season records from the ten seasons between 1972 and 1981 are listed in chronological order. The seasons are ranked based on winning percentage (left column) and games behind the division champion (right column).

LEGEND: "Win % Rank" is the team's winning percentage ranking compared to the other teams in the table. W-L = the team's Win-Loss record. "Winning Percentage" is the teams winning percentage carried out to the third digit for that season (for example, 44.5% is shown as .445). "Games Behind" is the number of games the Giants finished behind that year's NL West Division champion. "GB Rank" is the ranking of the team based on how many games they finished behind the division champion that season.

NOTE: Both the 1972 and 1981 teams played less than the normally scheduled 162 games due to labor disputes. In 1972, the season started late after an abbreviated Spring Training. In 1981, the players went on strike in the middle of the season, resulting in significantly fewer games being played. As a result, a division winner was named for the first half of the 1981 season and a separate winner was named for the second half of the season. The 1981 Giants finished the first half of the season (before the strike) at 27-32, 10 games behind the Los Angeles Dodgers. The team did much better in the second half (after the strike) at 29-23, only 3.5 games behind the Houston Astros. The record in the table above reflects the team's performance as if their first and second halves were combined. Ironically, the overall best teams in the two National League divisions (the Cardinals and Reds) did not have the best records in their respective divisions for either the first or second half. Consequently, neither of them made the playoffs.

While there have been worse individual teams in the San Francisco era, such as the 100-loss 1985 squad and the nearly as bad teams of 2017 (64-98), 1984 (66-96), and 1996 (68-94), each of those squads preceded playoff teams in following seasons. This proximity to competitiveness and contention was not true of the teams depicted in this 10-year period.

While there were bright points – most notably the 1973 and 1978 teams – none of these 10 teams ever finished closer than third place and mostly they were far behind the division leaders. The worst team during this period – the 1979 team that went 71-91 – was eight years removed from the division champion 1971 squad. The next team that would make the playoffs was in 1987, eight years down the road from the 1979 squad. When Ed Halicki threw his no-hitter in 1975, the Giants were in the middle of arguably the worst era in San Francisco Giants baseball, and things would not get better for many seasons.

With the worst attendance in the San Francisco era during the 1974-1975 seasons, the Giants of that time were operating on a shoestring. They sold or traded iconic stars and promising rookies alike to make ends meet – Tito Fuentes was not alone in this regard. Willie Mays went to the Mets in 1972. Willie McCovey was traded to the Padres and Juan Marichal went to the Red Sox in 1973. Bobby Bonds was traded to the Yankees in 1974, and Dave Kingman went to the Mets in 1975. From my perspective as an 18-year-old Giants fan, it seemed like every day in 1975, the San Francisco Chronicle Sporting Green and the Giants' flagship station KSFO 560 featured stories about the Giants going bust and leaving the Bay Area.

To make things even worse, the team played in Candlestick Park, a windswept, hard-to-get-to stadium that was bitterly cold even on the occasional sunny day. With the combination of a hopeless team, a crumbling stadium replete with stained AstroTurf, and a much better baseball alternative in the reigning three-time World Champion Oakland A's playing just across the Bay, the fans stayed away in droves. The Giants' attendance in 1975 was just a little over 500,000, placing them squarely at the very bottom of the National League in that category. It was at the end of the 1975 season that the Giants' owner, Horace Stoneham, made an agreement with a group representing the Labatt Brewing Company to buy the team and move it to Toronto. Only an injunction filed by San Francisco Mayor George Moscone prevented this from happening.

So, the "Fan Experience" for Giants fans in the 1970s consisted of rooting for an average, no-name team struggling to win half their games each year and watching them play in a miserably cold stadium. It was in this environment that young Ed Halicki found himself pitching a no-hitter against New York. The Mets were the same team that had won the National League pennant two years before and came within one game of winning the World Series against Oakland that season.

As the fans chanted for Thomas to be charged with an error on the play, the ruling from the official scorekeeper came in: "Error." The crowd let loose a cheer. While Halicki and the Giants were pretty much in control throughout the game, Staub's liner that glanced off Halicki was not the only serious threat to the no-hitter. The second batter of the game, Mets second baseman Felix Millan, hit a looping fly ball to right field where Steve Ontiveros made a fine running catch. New York catcher John Stearns hit a line drive leading off the sixth inning that was snagged by Gary Matthews – Halicki called it "the hardest hit ball of the game."

Of course, no one was thinking "no-hitter" in the top of the first inning or even into the sixth. There was too much game left to play. Halicki, by his own admission, didn't really focus on his game being a no-hitter until the eighth, as he described in an interview after the game:

"I thought, I'm this close, I'll probably never get another chance. So, I made up my mind to throw as hard as I could, and if someone was going to break it up, he'd do it off my best stuff, not something trying to be cute. I wasn't particularly rational at that point."

In the end, Halicki pitched an outstanding game, racking up 10 strikeouts against only two walks, which equated to a Game Score of 95. The Giants led for the entire game, eventually winning 6-0 by scoring two runs each in the first, fifth, and seventh innings. The hitting star for the Giants was Gary Thomasson, who had three hits and two runs batted in (RBIs). The Giants also pulled off a rare double steal in the bottom of the fifth with two outs. The aforementioned Derrel Thomas stole home when Mets' catcher John Stearns threw to second trying to get the slow-footed Dave Rader attempting to steal. Both runners were safe, and the Giants went ahead 3-0 on that play.

Like Ed Halicki's no-hitter that day, the Giants have a long history of outstanding pitching performances. As ranked by Game Score, the top pitching performances over the team's 122-year history since 1900 are shown in the table below. All of them, with the notable exception of Matt Cain's unbelievable 14-strikeout perfect game, were very impressive extra inning efforts.

Table 5-2. Giants Highest Game Scores

Rank	Pitcher (Team Home)	Date Score	Opponent	GSc	IP, Hits, Runs, ERs, Walks, Strikeouts
1	Carl Hubbell (NY)	7/2/1933 (1) NY 1-0 (18 inn)	St. Louis Cardinals	132	18.0 IP, 6 Hits, 0 Runs, 0 ERs, 0 BBs, 12 Ks
2	Rube Marquard (NY)	7/17/1914 NY 3-1 (21 inn)	Pittsburgh Pirates	113	21.0 IP, 15 Hits, 1 Run, 1 ER, 2 BBs, 2 Ks
3 (tie)	Johnny Antonelli (NY)	5/1/1955 NY 2-1 (16 inn)	Cincinnati Reds	112	16.0 IP, 6 Hits, 1 Run, 1 ER, 5 BBs, 11 Ks
3 (tie)	Juan Marichal (SF)	7/2/1963 SF 1-0 (16 inn)	Milwaukee Braves	112	16.0 IP, 8 Hits, 0 Runs, 0 ERs, 4 BBs, 10Ks
3 (tie)	Gaylord Perry (SF)	9/1/1967 SF 1-0 (21 inn)	Cincinnati Reds	112	16.0 IP, 10 Hits, 0 Runs, 0 ERs, 2 BBs, 12 Ks
6	Rube Benton (NY)	7/16/1920 NY 7-0 (17 inn)	Pittsburgh Pirates	111	17.0 IP, 9 Hits, 0 Runs, 0 ERs, 2 BBs, 4 Ks
7	Juan Marichal (SF)	5/26/1966 SF 1-0 (14 inn)	Philadelphia Phillies	109	14.0 IP, 6 Hits, 0 Runs, 0 ERs, 1 BB, 10 Ks
8	Juan Marichal (SF)	8/19/1969 NY 1-0 (14 inn)	New York Mets	104	13.1 IP, 6 Hits, 1 Run, 1 ER, 1 BB, 13 Ks
9	Red Ames (NY)	9/2/1907 0-0 Tie (13 inn)	Brooklyn Dodgers	102	13.0 IP, 6 Hits, 0 Runs, 0 ERs, 1 BB, 8 Ks
10 (tie)	John Genewich (NY)	9/23/1928 NY 2-1 (14 inn)	Cincinnati Reds	101	14.0 IP, 5 Hits, 1 Run, 1 ER, 3 BBs, 6 Ks
10 (tie)	*Matt Cain (SF)*	*6/13/2012 SF 10-0*	*Houston Astros*	*101*	*9.0 IP, 0 Hits, 0 Runs, 0 ERs, 0 BBs, 14 Ks*

METHODOLOGY: This table includes the highest Game Scores thrown by a pitcher from the New York/San Francisco Giants from 1900-2021. Games are ranked by Game Score (GSc) and consider all franchise regular season and postseason games. Table 5-3 below limits the eligible games to those pitching performances that were 10 innings or less. Game Score (GSc) measures a pitcher's performance in any given game started. Introduced by baseball writer/statistician Bill James in the 1980s, Game Score is presented as a figure between 0-100 -- except for extreme outliers -- and usually falls between 40-70.

LEGEND: Dates are shown as month/day/year (for example, June 12, 2018, is shown as 6/12/2018). Up through 1957, the Giants franchise played in New York (NY). From 1958 on, they have called San Francisco (SF) home. IP = innings pitched. One-third of an inning pitched has 0.1 added and two-thirds of an inning pitched has 0.2 added (for example, 9 1/3 innings pitched is displayed as 9.1). BB(s) = base(s) on balls; K(s) = strikeout(s); ER(s) = earned run(s); inn = innings (associated with the length of extra-inning games); and (1) or (2) = first or second game of a doubleheader. *The lone Giants perfect game (thrown by Matt Cain) is shown in italics.*

NOTE 1: The three longest pitching performances in Giants history are included in this table – by Rube Marquard (21 innings), Carl Hubbell (18), and Rube Benton (17). While each of them is extraordinary, one stands out among them all: Carl Hubbell's 18-inning shutout of the mighty Cardinals in 1933. With 12 strikeouts and no walks, he achieved an incredible Game Score of 132. This is the third highest score in major league history, only being topped by pitchers Joe Oeschger (153) and Leon Cadore (140) in their epic 1920 Braves-Dodgers pitching duel that ended in a 1-1 tie after 26 innings. Rube Marquard's 21-inning effort is tied with three other pitchers for third place behind Oeschger/Cadore for the most innings ever pitched in a game.

NOTE 2: Hall of Famer Juan Marichal is the only pitcher who appears more than once on this table, and he's listed three times. There are five members of the Hall of Fame on this table: Christy Mathewson, Rube Marquard, Carl Hubbell, Juan Marichal, and Gaylord Perry. Those five represent all the starting pitchers who are wearing Giants caps on their Hall of Fame plaques.

To make this comparison more relatable to the typical game a starting pitcher would throw, the table below shows the highest franchise Game Scores limited to 10 innings or less. Matt Cain and his perfect game, with a score of 101, stands at the top of the list. Ed Halicki's game, with a score of 95, figures prominently too.

Table 5-3. Giants Highest Game Scores of 10 innings or less

Rank	Pitcher (Team Home)	Date Score	Opponent	GSc	IP, Hits, Runs, ERs, Walks, Strikeouts
1	*Matt Cain (SF)*	*6/13/2012 SF 10-0*	*Houston Astros*	*101*	*9.0 IP, 0 Hits, 0 Runs, 0 ERs, 0 BBs, 14 Ks*
2 (tie)	Jonathan Sanchez (SF)	7/10/2009 SF 8-0	SD Padres	98	9.0 IP, 0 Hits, 0 Runs, 0 ERs, 0 BBs, 11 Ks
2 (tie)	Madison Bumgarner (SF)	8/26/2014 SF 3-0	Col Rockies	98	9.0 IP, 1 Hit, 0 Runs, 0 ERs, 0 BBs, 13 Ks
2 (tie)	Chris Heston (SF)	6/9/2015 SF 5-0	NY Mets	98	9.0 IP, 0 Hits, 0 Runs, 0 ERs, 0 BBs, 11 Ks
2 (tie)	Madison Bumgarner (SF)	7/10/2016 SF 4-0	Arizona D-backs	98	9.0 IP, 1 Hit, 0 Runs, 0 ERs, 1 BB, 14 Ks
6 (tie)	Hooks Wiltse (NY)	7/4/1908 (1) NY 1-0 (10 inn)	Phi Phillies	97	10.0 IP, 0 Hits, 0 Run, 0 ERs, 0 BBs, 5 Ks
6 (tie)	Jason Schmidt (SF)	5/18/2004 SF 1-0	Chicago Cubs	97	9.0 IP, 1 Hit, 0 Runs, 0 ERs, 1 BB, 13 Ks
8 (tie)	Juan Marichal (SF)	7/19/1960 SF 2-0	Phi Phillies	96	9.0 IP, 1 Hit, 0 Runs, 0 ERs, 1 BB, 12 Ks
8 (tie)	Tim Lincecum (SF)	10/7/2010 SF 2-0	Atlanta Braves	96	9.0 IP, 2 Hits, 0 Runs, 0 ERs, 1 BB, 14 Ks
8 (tie)	Matt Cain (SF)	4/13/2012 SF 5-0	Pittsburgh Pirates	96	9.0 IP, 1 Hit, 0 Runs, 0 ERs, 0 BBs, 11 Ks
8 (tie)	Tim Lincecum (SF)	7/13/2013 SF 9-0	SD Padres	96	9.0 IP, 0 Hits, 0 Runs, 0 ERs, 4 BBs, 13 Ks
12 (tie)	Ed Halicki (SF)	8/24/1975 (2) SF 6-0	NY Mets	95	9.0 IP, 0 Hits, 0 Runs, 0 ERs, 2 BBs, 10 Ks
14 (tie)	Gaylord Perry (SF)	9/17/1968 SF 1-0	St. Louis Cardinals	94	9.0 IP, 0 Hits, 0 Runs, 0 ERs, 2 BBs, 9 Ks
28 (tie)	Tim Lincecum (SF)	6/25/2014 SF 4-0	SD Padres	92	9.0 IP, 0 Hits, 0 Runs, 0 ERs, 1 BB, 6 Ks
36 (tie)	Jesse Barnes (NY)	5/7/1922 NY 6-0	Phi Phillies	91	9.0 IP, 0 Hits, 0 Runs, 0 ERs, 1 BB, 5 Ks
54 (tie)	Carl Hubbell (NY)	5/8/1929 NY 11-0	Pittsburgh Pirates	90	9.0 IP, 0 Hits, 0 Runs, 0 ERs, 1 BB, 4 Ks

Rank	Pitcher (Team Home)	Date Score	Opponent	GSc	IP, Hits, Runs, ERs, Walks, Strikeouts
54 (tie)	Juan Marichal (SF)	6/15/1963 SF 1-0	Houston Colt .45s	90	9.0 IP, 0 Hits, 0 Runs, 0 ERs, 2 BBs, 5 Ks
54 (tie)	John Montefusco (SF)	9/29/1976 SF 9-0	Atlanta Braves	90	9.0 IP, 0 Hits, 0 Runs, 0 ERs, 1 BB, 4 Ks
71 (tie)	Christy Mathewson (NY)	6/13/1905 NY 1-0	Chicago Cubs	89	9.0 IP, 0 Hits, 0 Runs, 0 ERs, 0 BBs, 2 Ks
130 (tie)	Christy Mathewson (NY)	7/15/1901 NY 5-0	St. Louis Cardinals	87	9.0 IP, 0 Hits, 0 Runs, 0 ERs, 4 BBs, 4 Ks
130 (tie)	Jeff Tesreau (NY)	9/6/1912 (1) NY 3-0	Phi Phillies	87	9.0 IP, 0 Hits, 0 Runs, 0 ERs, 2 BB, 2 Ks
130 (tie)	Rube Marquard (NY)	4/15/1915 NY 2-0	Brooklyn Robins	87	9.0 IP, 0 Hits, 0 Runs, 0 ERs, 2 BBs, 2 Ks
---	Sam Jones (SF)	9/26/1959 SF 4-0 (8 inn)	St. Louis Cardinals	80	7.0 IP, 0 Hits, 0 Runs, 0 ERs, 2 BBs, 5 Ks
---	Red Ames (NY)	9/14/1903 (2) NY 5-0 (5 inn)	St. Louis Cardinals	72	5.0 IP, 0 Hits, 0 Runs, 0 ERs, 2 BBs, 7 Ks
---	Mike McCormick (SF)	6/12/1959 SF 3-0 (5 inn)	Phi Phillies	68	5.0 IP, 0 Hits, 0 Runs, 0 ERs, 1 BB, 2 Ks

METHODOLOGY: This table includes the highest Game Scores of 10 innings or less thrown by a pitcher from the Giants from 1900-2021. Games are ranked by Game Score (GSc) and consider all franchise regular season and postseason games. For comparison purposes, all 16 franchise no-hitters are included in this table. Game Score (GSc) measures a pitcher's performance in any given game started. Introduced by baseball writer/statistician Bill James in the 1980s, Game Score is presented as a figure between 0-100 -- except for extreme outliers -- and usually falls between 40-70.

LEGEND: Dates are shown as month/day/year (for example, June 12, 2018, is shown as 6/12/2018). Up through 1957, the Giants franchise played in New York (NY). From 1958 on, the team has called San Francisco (SF) home. IP = innings pitched. One-third of an inning pitched has 0.1 added and two-thirds of an inning pitched has 0.2 added (for example, 9 1/3 innings pitched is displayed as 9.1). BB(s) = base(s) on balls; K(s) = strikeout(s); ER(s) = earned run(s); inn = innings (associated with the length of extra-inning games); and (1) or (2) = first or second game of a doubleheader. *The lone Giants perfect game (thrown by Matt Cain) is shown in italics.*

NOTE 1: Tim Lincecum's two-hitter in October 2010 was the first game of the NLDS against the Atlanta Braves and is the highest postseason GSc recorded by a Giants pitcher. As Lincecum allowed only two doubles during the game, the Giants took a 1-0 series lead and eventually won the NLDS three games to one on the way to San Francisco's first World Series championship. Lincecum's epic performance on this day was the first playoff win for the Giants after the team collapsed eight years earlier during the final two games of the 2002 World Series in Anaheim.

NOTE 2: Three Giants games are listed that used to be considered no-hitters prior to the 1991 ruling that defined a no-hitter as having to go at least nine innings and be a complete game. The first of these was a 1903 no-hitter thrown by Red Ames against the Cardinals. The 5-0 Giants win was the second game of a doubleheader and was called after five innings due to darkness. The two other games occurred in 1959 and were called after the minimum five innings due to rain. The first one listed was thrown by Sam Jones, who was the first Black pitcher to throw a no-hitter, as he hurled one against the Pirates while a member of the Cubs in 1955. His 1959 effort for the Giants was part of a remarkable season where he won 21 games for San Francisco and represented the team in the August All-Star game. Jones had almost thrown a no-hitter earlier that season when he hurled 7.2 innings of no-hit ball against the Dodgers. Jim Gilliam of Los Angeles hit a chopper to shortstop Andre Rodgers, who clearly booted the play, yet the official scorer ruled it a hit. In his rain-shortened no-hit effort listed in the table, Jones threw seven innings, struck out five Cardinals and walked only two.

NOTE 3: The second shortened no-hitter in 1959 was thrown by 20-year-old Mike McCormick against Philadelphia. Over five innings, McCormick only allowed a lone walk while striking out a pair of Phillies. Starting the bottom of the sixth, McCormick walked two batters and allowed a single, as he loaded the bases with no outs. It was then torrential rains poured down, inundating the field. After 40 minutes the game was called due to rain. Since the sixth inning wasn't complete, only the statistics through the fifth inning counted, as such McCormick was only charged with what he gave up through five innings in San Francisco's 3-0 win.

NOTE 4: Jonathan Sanchez only allowed one baserunner in his 2009 no-hitter against the Padres: a one-out error by the third baseman in the eighth inning. His outstanding performance was the first Giants no-hitter in almost 33 years.

NOTE 5: Madison Bumgarner only allowed one baserunner in his 2014 one-hitter against the Rockies. His attempt at a perfect game was broken up by a leadoff double in the eighth inning. In 2016, his no-hitter against the Diamondbacks was also broken up in the eighth – this time by a one-out single. An Arizona batter had already reached base on an error by this point.

NOTE 6: The only base runners allowed in Chris Heston's 2015 no-hitter were three batters who he hit with pitches. Tied for the second-best Game Score on this table, Heston benefited from the fact that a hit by pitch (unlike a walk) is not counted against a pitcher's GSc. Like Heston, Hooks Wiltse, in his 10-inning no-hitter, only allowed a baserunner due to a hit by pitch. The lone hit in Jason Schmidt's 2004 one-hitter was a two-out infield single in the fifth inning.

NOTE 7: Juan Marichal's 1960 one-hitter was his major league debut. Philadelphia catcher Clay Dalrymple hit a two-out single in the eighth inning. In Matt Cain's 2012 game against Pittsburgh, he allowed a two-out single in the sixth inning to the opposing pitcher (James McDonald) for the only Pirate hit. Two months later, Cain would throw the first perfect game ever for the Giants.

NOTE 8: Tim Lincecum's two no-hitters in 2013 and 2014 were both against the San Diego Padres. He is one of only two pitchers to no-hit the same team twice. The other one is Hall of Famer Addie Joss of the Cleveland Naps. He threw his two no-hitters against the Chicago White Sox in 1908 and 1910.

NOTE 9: The incomparable Christy Mathewson threw no-hitters against the Cardinals (1901) and Cubs (1905). In his 1905 game pitching against future Hall of Famer "Three Finger" Brown, the game was a scoreless tie until the ninth inning when Giants shortstop Bill Dahlen singled home first baseman Dan McGann for the winning run. In that game, Mathewson didn't walk anyone; however, two batters reached base on Giant errors.

With an extremely impressive score of 95, Ed Halicki's no-hitter was one of the best-pitched games in Giants history. Tied for twelfth place among all games of 10 innings or less, Halicki's no-hitter ranks as number six of the 16 no-hitters thrown by Giant pitchers. While this no-hitter is the most prominent highlight of Halicki's baseball career, he threw other nearly as impressive games, also. For example, in 1976, Halicki achieved a Game Score of 94 while throwing 10 innings of shutout ball against the mighty Los Angeles Dodgers at Dodger Stadium.

Halicki only allowed three hits while striking out eight Dodgers and walking none during that game. The Giants won 1-0 in the top of the 11th when Darrell

Evans, pinch-hitting for Halicki, knocked in Gary Thomasson on a one-out sacrifice fly. In addition to his no-hitter, Halicki threw 12 more shutouts for the Giants over the seven seasons he was with the team from 1974-1980. The closest he came to throwing another no-hitter was a one-hit shutout against the Montreal Expos in 1978. Montreal's only hit came early in the game.

Besides joining the elite ranks of no-hit pitchers, Giants starter Ed Halicki was remarkable in other ways, too. Standing at six foot, seven inches tall, Halicki was also an extraordinarily tall player. As shown in the chart below, his height ranks in the top one percent of all players who have ever played in the majors. As a point of interest, the average height of a player in the notoriously tall National Basketball Association is 6'7" – the same height as Ed Halicki.

Table 5-4. Tallest Players in Major League History

Height	Number	Percentage of MLB Players (22,564 total as of 2021)	Comments
6'7"	107	0.4742% (Around 1/2 of 1 percent)	Ed Halicki is in this category
6'8"	38	0.1685% (Around 1/6 of 1 percent)	
6'9"	11	0.0487% (Around 1/20 of 1 percent)	
6'10"	6	0.0266% (Around 1/40 of 1 percent)	Hall of Famer Randy Johnson is in this category
6'11"	1	0.0044% (Ridiculously small percentage)	Jon Rauch, 11-year MLB pitcher from 2002-2013, is only player.
Total	163	0.7223% (Around 3/4 of 1 percent)	

METHODOLGY: This table categorizes the tallest Major League baseball players by height.

LEGEND: Height is listed in feet and inches and abbreviated using (') for feet and (") for inches. For example, a player who is 6 feet, 7 inches is listed as 6'7". Percentages are derived from dividing the total number of players who were listed at a certain height divided by the total number of players who have ever played major league baseball (as of 2021, the total number is listed as 22,564). The resulting (very small) number is calculated to the fourth decimal place of one percent and as a fraction of one percent. For example, there are 107 players who have been listed as 6 feet, 7 inches tall. That number is 107/22,564 or 0.4742%, where 1.0% equals one percent. To make it easier to relate to, the number is also shown as an approximate fraction of one percent. In this example that would be "around 1/2 of 1 percent."

NOTE: There have been two pitchers in the minors (Ryan Doherty and Loek Van Mil) who were both 7'1". They never pitched in the major leagues.

No discussion of great Giants pitchers would be complete without focusing on one of the greatest Dominican pitchers of all-time: Juan Marichal. In a list full of Hall of Famers and perennial All-Stars, Marichal stands out. The Top 10 Dominican pitchers are listed below.

Table 5-5. Best Pitchers Born in the Dominican Republic

Rank	Pitcher (Home)	Team	Season(s)	Career IP	WAR (per 200 IP)	Wins (per season)
1	Pedro Martinez (Mano-guayabo)	LA Dodgers Mon Expos Bos Red Sox NY Mets Phi Phillies	1992-1993 1994-1997 1998-2004 2005-2008 2009	2,827.1	86.1 (6.09)	219 (12.2)
2	Juan Marichal (Laguna Verde)	SF Giants Bos Red Sox LA Dodgers	1960-1973 1974 1975	3,507.0	61.8 (3.52)	243 (15.2)
3	Bartolo Colon (Altamira)	Cle Indians Mon Expos Chi W. Sox LA Angels Bos Red Sox Chi W. Sox NY Yankees Oak Athletics NY Mets Atl Braves Min Twins Tex Rangers	1997-2002 2002 2003 2004-2007 2008 2009 2011 2012-2013 2014-2016 2017 2017 2018	3,461.2	48.1 (2.78)	247 (11.8)
4	Johnny Cueto (San Pedro de Macoris)	Cin Reds KC Royals SF Giants	2008-2015 2015 2016-2021	2,034.1	35.2 (3.46)	135 (9.6)

Rank	Pitcher (Home)	Team	Season(s)	Career IP	WAR (per 200 IP)	Wins (per season)
5	Jose Rijo (San Cristobal)	NY Yankees Oak Athletics Cin Reds	1984 1985-1987 1988-1995 & 2001-02	1,880.0	35.0 (3.72)	116 (8.3)
6	Pedro Astacio (Hato Mayor del Rey)	LA Dodgers Col Rockies Hou Astros NY Mets Bos Red Sox Tex Rangers SD Padres Was Nationals	1992-1997 1997-2001 2001 2002-2003 2004 2005 2005 2006	2,196.2	28.3 (2.58)	129 (8.6)
7	Ervin Santana (La Romana)	LA Angels KC Royals Atl Braves Min Twins Chi W. Sox KC Royals	2005-2012 2013 2014 2015-2018 2019 2021	2,486.2	27.1 (2.18)	151 (9.4)
8	Mario Soto (Bani)	Cin Reds	1977-1988	1,730.1	26.8 (3.10)	100 (8.3)
9	Ramon Martinez (Santo Domingo)	LA Dodgers Bos Red Sox Pit Pirates	1988-1998 1999-2000 2001	1,895.2	25.9 (2.73)	135 (9.6)
10	Juan Guzman (Santo Domingo)	Tor Blue Jays Bal Orioles Cin Reds TB D. Rays	1991-1998 1998-1999 1999 2000	1,483.1	24.5 (3.30)	91 (9.1)

METHODOLOGY: To qualify for inclusion in this table, pitchers had to be of Dominican heritage and born in the Dominican Republic (DR). Pitchers are ranked from 1-10 based upon their career Wins Above Replacement (WAR) between 1900-2021. WAR measures a player's value in all facets of the game by deciphering how many more wins he's worth than a replacement-level player at his same position.

LEGEND: Home = the place a pitcher was born in the DR. Team and season(s) are the teams a pitcher played for and the season(s) they were with each team listed in chronological order. Career IP = career innings pitched. Career WAR = the pitcher's accumulated WAR over his career. Career Wins = the number of wins each pitcher accumulated over his career. Because pitchers had different career lengths, I included two rate measures (WAR per 200 innings pitched and wins per season). Multiple pitchers missed entire seasons for various reasons. Therefore, those missed seasons don't count as part of the wins per season calculation. Specifically, Bartolo Colon missed the 2010 season, and Jose Rijo returned after a five-year break from 1996-2000 to pitch in 2001 and 2002 for the Reds. Johnny Cueto is active beyond 2021.

NOTE 1: Pedro Martinez and Juan Marichal are the most accomplished pitchers on this list. Three-time winner of the Cy Young Award and eight-time All-Star, Martinez helped lead Boston to the 2004 World Championship for their first World Series win since 1918. Ten-time All-Star Juan Marichal was the premier starting pitcher for the great Giants teams of the 1960s. Marichal threw a no-hitter against the Colt .45s in 1963, striking out five and walking only two Houston batters. Both Martinez and Marichal were elected to the Hall of Fame – Martinez on the first ballot in 2015, and Marichal on his third try in 1983.

NOTE 2: Ervin Santana threw a no-hitter against Cleveland in 2011. His Angels won the game 3-1, with the Indians scoring their lone run in the bottom of the first inning on an error by shortstop Erick Aybar, an Ezequiel Carrera stolen base, a fielder's choice, and a Santana wild pitch. Los Angeles tied the game in the fifth inning on a sacrifice fly by 19-year-old rookie Mike Trout. The Angels scored two more runs in the sixth and ninth innings to put the game away.

NOTE 3: Ramon Martinez hurled a no-hitter against the third-year Marlins in 1995, with the Dodgers winning 7-0. Martinez had a perfect game until the eighth inning when Florida right fielder Tommy Gregg drew a full-count walk. He was the only baserunner for the Marlins. Besides being on this esteemed list, Ramon Martinez and Pedro Martinez are connected in a different way: Ramon is Pedro's older brother. Two other pitchers on this list are also related: Jose Rijo is Juan Marichal's son-in-law.

NOTE 4: Besides Pedro Martinez and Juan Marichal, many of the other impressive pitchers on this list were named as All-Stars during their playing career: Bartolo Colon (1998 and 2005 – winning the Cy Young Award with the Angels in 2005, too); Johnny Cueto (2014 and 2016); Jose Rijo (1994); Ervin Santana (2008 and 2017); Mario Soto (1982-1984); Ramon Martinez (1990); and Juan Guzman (1992).

NOTE 5: The Dominican Republic team has fared well in the World Baseball Classic, winning it all in the 2013 games. Undefeated, the team only gave up 14 runs during the entire tournament. No-hit pitcher Edinson Volquez of the San Diego Padres was a member of the 2013 championship team. He was on the Miami Marlins when he threw his no-hitter against the Arizona Diamondbacks in 2017.

When Halicki faced former Giant star Dave Kingman (6'6") their combined height (13'1") had to be one of the tallest combined pitcher-batter matchups of that time. In this game, Kingman, who crushed a grand slam in the first game that afternoon, popped out once against Halicki. The other two times he came to the plate, he struck out. Strikeouts were not unusual for Kingman, with over 1,800 of them during his career. From where I sat in the stands, it looked like he wasn't within two feet of any of Halicki's pitches during those at bats.

Halicki faced two batters that day who have interesting achievements tied to this game. Mike Vail, a pinch-hitter for the Mets in the top of the sixth, received a walk – it was one of only two Halicki issued. Vail is a Bay Area guy who went to high school in San Jose and college at De Anza College in Cupertino (I attended De Anza as well, a few years after Vail). Because of his background, I suspect he grew up as a Giants fan, too. Vail made his major league debut just six days earlier on August 18. He wound up accomplishing a 23-game hitting streak — this was a rookie record at the time. The current rookie hitting streak record of 34 games was achieved in 1987 by Benito Santiago. This game happened in the middle of Vail's hitting streak. Even though Vail never got a hit during the game, the rule states that if all a player's at-bats result in walks, hit by pitch, defensive interference, or a sacrifice bunt, his hitting streak stays intact. Since Vail had only one plate appearance which resulted in a walk, this game didn't count against him. Mike Vail ended up with a solid 10-year major league career playing for seven different teams, including a brief stint with the Giants in 1983.

Leading off the ninth inning, pinch hitter Jesus Alou came close to breaking up Halicki's no-hitter (and shutout) a couple times with long foul balls down the left field line. Alou had played for the Giants for six years, and his appearance in this game gave the three remarkable Alou brothers (Felipe, Matty, and Jesus) a combined total of 5,000 games played. They even played in the same Giants outfield together on September 15, 1963 – another first that hasn't been repeated. Five-thousand games played is an extraordinary milestone, as no other set of brothers has achieved anywhere close to that many. It would have been ironic if Vail during his record-setting hitting streak or Alou during his milestone achievement game had broken up the no-hitter. In the end, Jesus Alou popped up, Del Unser received Halicki's second walk, Felix Milan struck out, and Wayne Garrett grounded out to first base to end the game. Ed Halicki had his no-hitter, and he was in the record books.

Ed Halicki grew up in New Jersey and was a late-round draftee, being picked in the 24th round of the 1972 draft. His first season in 1974 certainly didn't portend a dominant no-hit performance in his future, as he went 1-8 with a 4.24 ERA for the Giants. Even before his no-hit game, Halicki was the number five starter on the Giants in 1975. He was heading into this game with a 7-10 record for a San Francisco team battling to finish over .500, sitting at 21.5 games behind Cincinnati's Big Red Machine in the National League West.

This was also one of the games that had the most closely matched starting pitchers in terms of career JAWS scores. Opposing pitcher Craig Swan (JAWS 14.1) and Ed Halicki (JAWS 12.0) were comparable in terms of what they achieved during their careers. The Giants finished the 1975 season at 80-81, good enough for third place in their division behind the Reds (108-54). The Mets finished at 82-80, which placed them in third place in the National League East behind the Pirates (92-69). Prior to this game, the Giants were 62-66 and the Mets were 66-61. Neither team got into the playoffs for over a decade after this game. The Mets finally returned to the postseason in 1986, and the Giants advanced in 1987.

Ed Halicki, the star of the game, finished the 1975 season with a 9-13 record. He had his best season in 1977, going 16-12, pitching 257 innings, and striking out 168 for the Giants. In June 1980, he went from San Francisco to the California Angels, and was released by the Angels that October. He retired after that season. After his playing career was over, Ed moved to Reno and got into the recreational vehicle and furniture businesses.

Halicki's catcher that day was 26-year-old veteran Dave Rader. Rader had been drafted as the team's number one pick in 1967. He debuted with a bang in 1972, emerging quickly as the primary starter at catcher and coming in second in the National League Rookie of the Year voting, collecting 119 hits, including six home runs. As a left-handed hitter, he remained San Francisco's primary catcher against right-handed pitchers through 1976. His best hitting season was 1975, when he hit .308 with an OPS of .808 against right-handers. Since right-hander Craig Swan was starting for the Mets, it was logical that Rader would be catching Halicki.

Rader was traded to St. Louis after the 1976 season, along with future Cy Young winner Mike Caldwell and solid starter/reliever John D'Acquisto for three players who, except for starter/reliever John Curtis who played with the Giants for three seasons, would be out of baseball within a year or two. Rader would finish out his solid 10-year career playing with the Cardinals, Cubs, Phillies, and Red Sox over the next four seasons.

One final note. Since this was a doubleheader, as a special treat, the Giants had (as between-games entertainment) legendary tight-rope walker Karl Wallenda perform a high wire act. He walked on a tight rope 50 feet above the ground stretching from the third base foul pole to the first base foul pole. Because Candlestick Park had Astro Turf, they couldn't pound stakes into the ground to stabilize the tight rope, so they had several heavy/strong guys pulling on dangling ropes to keep it taut. As a guy behind me in the stands said, "there is NO F*****g way I would trust those guys, especially with the way the wind is swirling." I agreed with that sentiment. The bottom line is that Karl (thankfully) didn't fall.

Ed Halicki Interview
Conducted by Kevin Hurd on August 19, 2021

Kevin Hurd (KH): Would you consider yourself to be the best pitcher on your Little League, Connie Mack, high school, college, and minor league teams?
Ed Halicki (EH): Yes, pretty much at all those levels. In New Jersey back then, Little League started at age nine. I mostly pitched and played shortstop, although I did start as a pitcher.
KH: Did you play any sports in high school besides baseball?
EH: Yes, basketball and football, where I played tight end and defensive end.
KH: Did you pitch any no-hitters at any of those levels you played baseball?
EH: No, I did not.
KH: You were originally drafted in the 38th round by St. Louis in 1968. Why didn't you sign with them?
EH: St. Louis had been scouting me (at Kearny High School in Kearny, New Jersey). They offered me $15,000 as a signing bonus. I decided to go to college instead because the Vietnam War was going on (in 1968) and it would be easier to stay in college than be a minor league pitcher and get cut from the team or injured and be vulnerable to the draft. After college, I signed with the Giants

for $1,000. Teams then weren't giving big signing bonuses to college grads because they thought the college grad would take the money and run.

KH: Did you feel any different, good or bad, on the day of your no-hitter?

EH: No, I pretty much felt the same as always. I've got a couple of funny stories regarding people I knew and how they dealt with the no-hitter. The first involves my dad. The game was televised back to New York, and my dad and other family members were watching the game in northern New Jersey. Around the sixth inning he realized I was pitching a no-hitter but didn't want to leave his chair and go to the bathroom because he didn't want to jinx me. Well, he was able to hold it and made a beeline to the bathroom after the final out. (Laughs)

The other involved a friend of mine from New York who grew up going to a lot of Yankees games – probably over 1,000. He had never seen a no-hitter. He and his girlfriend came to the game and his girlfriend wanted to leave the game in the fourth inning because she was cold, it was the second game of doubleheader, Candlestick Park, etc. They went across the Bay Bridge and drove to her house in the East Bay. They stayed in the car, listening to the game on the radio. After the last out he turned to his girlfriend and said, "Get out of my car, I'm never going to see you again!" (Laughs)

KH: What pitches – fastball, curve, slider, or something else – were working best for you that day?

EH: Well, I was pretty much a two-pitch pitcher at that time, and both (my) fastball and slider were working well for me that day. Actually, I had one other game, a 1-0 loss in 11 innings where I thought I pitched better, but I didn't have the extra bit of luck that you sometimes need to get a no-hitter (Author's note: I highlighted this 1976 game against the Dodgers earlier in this chapter).

KH: What were the best defensive plays, the closest you came to losing the no-hitter?

EH: Three come to mind: Our right fielder Steve Ontiveros made a very nice play on a looper on the right field line in the first inning. (Mets catcher) John Stearns hit a line drive – hardest hit ball of the game – to left field which was caught (by Gary Matthews) in the sixth inning. In the fifth inning, Rusty Staub hit a hard grounder at me, I deflected it, our second baseman (Derrel Thomas) dropped it, threw it to first, and it was too late. It was ruled an error.

KH: Which batters did you have the hardest time getting out?

EH: For me, it was Pete Rose, Bill Madlock, and Ron Cey. With Pete Rose, you had to throw the ball over the plate. If it was anything close, the umpires would give Pete the benefit of the doubt.

KH: Do you remember shaking off (catcher) Dave Rader's signs very much?

EH: No, not much at all. Maybe once or twice – certainly no more than that.

KH: Do you have any memorabilia or souvenirs – such as a baseball, plaque, uniform, or something else – from the game in your house?

EH: I do have a certificate from the Hall of Fame. The Hall has my glove and the ball from the game.

KH: You played in the minors from 1972 to 1975. Of the four managers you played for (Jim McKnight, Dick Wilson, Frank Funk, and Rocky Bridges), which one did you enjoy playing for the most?

EH: Jim McKnight was a stand-up guy, but as far as who I enjoyed playing for the most, that would be Rocky Bridges. I remember a game where I had given up four runs in the first inning, the bases were loaded, and there were two outs. Rocky came walking to the mound and I thought he was going to yank me. When he came to the mound, he told me to look at the scoreboard. There was a bright orange moon just over the top of the scoreboard. Rocky said, "Heckuva orange moon, isn't it?" I took it in for a couple seconds and turned toward Rocky again. He was walking away from the mound. I said, "What did you want to tell me?" Rocky said, "Would you get this last SOB out?" (Laughs). We then went on to score eight runs in the bottom of the inning and went on to win 22-4. (Author's note: Google "Rocky Bridges quotes" and you'll find quite a few funny things Rocky said).

KH: You played in the majors from 1974 to 1980. You played for six different managers: Charlie Fox, Wes Westrum, Bill Rigney, Joe Altobelli, Dave Bristol, and Jim Fregosi. Who did you enjoy playing for the most?

EH: They were all good, but I would say Joe Altobelli because he was managing us in 1978, when we had the only winning record (89-73) of the six seasons I was with the Giants. We weren't bad, we were in a division that had the two best teams in baseball, or at least in the National League – the Reds and the Dodgers. We'd play the Reds and Dodgers 36 times a year. We'd usually wind up with 71 to 80 wins a year.

KH: Did you throw a lot of pitches during your no-hitter? Did you get a sore arm?

EH: No, I didn't have a sore arm that day. We didn't have pitch counts back then. I did have rib injuries a couple times, and I had ulnar nerve damage in my elbow in 1973, so instead of being with the Giants, or AA or AAA teams, I went down to Fresno – which was A-Level at the time – got better and went 14-6 there.

KH: Was your catcher (Dave Rader) one you had requested before?

EH: No, I never requested catchers. All the catchers we had – Rader, Mike Sadek, Marc Hill, and John Boccabella – I liked pitching to.

KH: Do you still stay in contact with Dave Rader?

EH: No, I haven't talked to him in years.

KH: Did the Giants give you a bonus for throwing the no-hitter?

EH: Yes, $2,500. I needed a car badly and $2,500 made the down payment.

KH: During the game, when did you think *"I've got a real shot at a no-hitter?"* Fifth inning, sixth inning, or later?

EH: The way I approached every game was that I at least wanted to pitch five innings because you can get a win with that. After (reaching) that (goal), the seventh inning, because that would be a pretty good job. For this game around the sixth inning, I started thinking "I don't want to screw this up." In the eighth inning I felt like I had to make every pitch count – (throw) good, hard stuff, don't try and be cute. In the ninth inning, Felix Millan – a good contact hitter – struck out on a hanging slider. Then Jesus Alou fouled off six or seven pitches, (and) hit a pop-up down the left field line that third baseman Bruce Miller caught. Then Wayne Garrett grounded out to Willie Montanez. Sometimes you need luck in a no-hitter.

KH: Were you able to get a follow-on job in baseball – in the major leagues, minors, college, high school, or the media after your playing days were over?

EH: No, and I really wasn't looking for baseball jobs. There was too much BS to deal with (in) baseball.

KH: What kind of work did you do?

EH: I was in the Recreational Vehicle (RV) business for a while. I was a commissioned salesman. I did a lot of road shows in the Bay Area and Los Angeles. Usually those were 10-day shows. After that I was in the furniture business, again as a commissioned salesman. It was a small store, and when the owner would leave, I would be in charge – me and another guy. I would also unload trucks, kind of a jack-of-all-trades since we only had two or three workers. I retired in 2008.

KH: Of all the managers, coaches and scouts you dealt with in the minors, who do you feel helped you the most in your climb to the major leagues?

EH: That would be Gordon Maltzberger. He had pitched with the White Sox in the 1940s. He was the one who taught me how to throw the slider. That was my ticket to get to and stay in the majors.

KH: Do you have any kids or grandkids who have or will pursue baseball as a career? Do you encourage them to do so?

EH: We've got one child who's 25. He doesn't do baseball anymore. He's more of an adrenaline junkie, rides around a lot on his mountain bike. I encourage him in whatever he wants to do.

KH: Was the no-hitter the highlight of your career? If not, what was?

EH: It was the highlight, although my first day in the big leagues was pretty good, too.

KH: Have you been to the section of the Hall of Fame that focuses on no-hitters?

EH: Yes, I took my mom and wife there in the late 1990s. Another time we (the Giants) were playing the Hall of Fame game at Abner Doubleday Field, and we visited the Hall after the game.

KH: Did you take any pictures or spend much time there?

EH: No pictures. Yes, we did spend some time looking around.

KH: Have you spent time signing autographs in Las Vegas, or in Florida or Arizona during Spring Training?

EH: No, not comfortable with that scene. I don't like taking money for autographs. I enjoy it more if I'm doing it for a kid. I did one of these autograph shows one year during a Giants Fantasy Camp before spring training.

KH: Do you have any favorite stories regarding any of these experiences?

EH: During the one Fantasy Camp, Dave Kingman and I were walking around, and a fan asked if we were any good (laughs). I said, "Why, between the two of us, we hit 445 home runs." (laughs) (Author's note: Kingman hit 442 home runs. Halicki hit three.)

Also, I had an experience in Houston when I was getting heckled. I was about to say something, and the other players said "The best way to get back at him is to finish the game." When I finished the game – which was a win

– I came off the field and I tossed the heckler the ball and said "Why don't you stick this where the sun don't shine?" (Laughs) The next day the heckler, before the game, came by the dugout and asked me to sign the ball. I refused.

KH: Anything you'd like to add regarding your no-hitter?

EH: I'd rather be lucky than good (Laughs).

KH: Anything you'd like to add regarding your major league career?

EH: Baseball was something I wanted to do since I was five years old, and I fulfilled the dream.

CHAPTER 6

ANDY HAWKINS:
NO-HITTER TAKEN AWAY

July 1, 1990
NY Yankee Andy Hawkins throws an eight-inning no-hitter and loses. An MLB policy change removes his no-hit pitcher designation next year.

"I'm stunned; I really am. This is not even close to the way I envisioned a no-hitter would be. You dream of one, but you never think it's going to be a loss. You think of (Dave) Stewart and Fernando (Valenzuela), coming off the field in jubilation. Not this."

Andy Hawkins reflecting on his accomplishment immediately following the game ("No-Hitter, but With No Glory," *New York Times*, July 2, 1990).

"Their season has been part folly and part frustration, but today the Yankees found a new low to their crazy summer."

Sportswriter Michael Martinez describing the Yankees' frustrating 1990 season ("No-Hitter, but With No Glory," *New York Times*, July 2, 1990).

"He hit it right at me. I made a wrong move to the wrong side, and it got caught in the wind. I didn't think I could catch up to it. When I did, it hit the top of my glove. You get down on yourself because you hate to lose a no-hitter on something like that, but that's baseball. Tomorrow is another day."

Rookie Yankee left fielder Jim Leyritz describing his two-out, three-run error in the bottom of the eighth inning that broke open a 0-0 game and propelled the White Sox to a win ("No-Hitter, but With No Glory," *New York Times,* July 2, 1990).

"(In September 1991) the Committee for Statistical Accuracy, chaired by then MLB Commissioner Fay Vincent, changed the official definition of a no-hitter, declaring it a game of nine innings or more that ends with no hits. The stringent definition eliminated 36 no-hitters from the books that were shortened by rain, darkness or other reasons (and one after the decision), as well as two losing efforts by the away team in which the home team doesn't bat in the bottom of the ninth. (Two such no-nos have been thrown since 1991 that would have qualified under the old rules)."

Committee for Statistical Accuracy 1991 ruling on no-hitters explained ("The true 'no no-hitters': No-hitters not officially recognized by MLB," *nonohitters.com/near-no-hitters*).

"I was very irritated. The thing that bugged me the most was that I had no control over it. At the time, I couldn't have forced the White Sox to bat in the bottom of the ninth. The game was over."

Andy Hawkins describing his reaction when MLB's Committee for Statistical Accuracy took away recognition for his no-hitter because his pitching performance didn't last at least nine full innings (Interview with the author, May 25, 2021).

In the middle of the worst Yankee season since 1913, New York starter Andy Hawkins pitched a game in which the opposing team never got a hit yet won 4-0. The White Sox victory was due to a combination of two walks and three errors in the bottom of the eighth – all with two outs – that allowed Chicago to score four unearned runs. At the time, Hawkins' feat was recognized as a no-hitter since he hadn't allowed a hit when the game ended. The next year, baseball's Committee for Statistical Accuracy removed this recognition as it specifically defined a no-hitter as "a game of nine innings or more that ends with no hits."

This new ruling eliminated no-hitters considered official games that ended earlier than nine innings because of darkness or weather. Along with that, this pronouncement removed from consideration seven-inning no-hitters accomplished under the "seven-inning doubleheader rule" established in 2020. This rule – limiting doubleheader games to just seven innings each – was established during the pandemic when baseball was halted for months. Once play resumed, Major League baseball wanted to complete as many games as they could to make up for lost time, so the doubleheader rule and other measures were taken. Some new rules were made permanent – like the universal designated hitter and a runner starting on second base in extra innings – but the doubleheader rule was dropped after 2021.

Because the two no-hitters thrown during those 2020-2021 doubleheaders – one by Madison Bumgarner of the Diamondbacks and one multi-pitcher game by the Rays –would be complete after seven innings, the 1991 ruling meant they wouldn't officially count as no-hitters. The ruling also applied to games in which a pitcher no-hit the opposing team through nine innings with the score tied where the no-hitter was eventually broken up in the 10th inning or later. Previously, if a pitcher threw nine innings of no-hit ball, even if the game went into extra innings, it was counted as a no-hitter. That wasn't true after 1991.

Finally, the ruling covered the very rare situation where the visiting pitcher threw a no-hitter, but the game ended after 8.5 innings with the home team ahead. In this situation, the bottom of the ninth inning was not played because the home team had won, leaving the no-hit pitcher with only eight innings pitched.

In fact, this last situation, where the losing pitcher(s) threw eight no-hit innings, has happened only four times as the table below displays. Andy Hawkins' no-hitter was one of them. This table lists the four games where this situation applied – one of which was played prior to 1900.

Table 6-1. No-hitters Lost in Games Ended After Eight and a Half Innings.

Date	Pitcher(s)	Inn	Pitcher(s) Team	Score	Winning Team
6/21/1890	Silver King	8.0	Chicago Pirates (Players League)	1-0	Brooklyn Ward's Wonders
7/1/1990	Andy Hawkins	8.0	New York Yankees	4-0	Chicago White Sox
4/12/1992	Matt Young	8.0	Boston Red Sox	2-1	Cleveland Indians
6/28/2008	Jered Weaver Jose Arrendondo	6.0 2.0	Los Angeles Angels	1-0	Los Angeles Dodgers

METHODOLOGY: This table lists the four eight-inning no-hitters which ended after the top of the ninth inning with the team that was no-hit losing the game. The games are listed in chronological order and until 1991, this type of game was counted as a no-hitters.

LEGEND: Dates are shown as month/day/year (for example, June 12, 2018, is shown as 6/12/2018). "Inn" is the number of innings a pitcher threw during the game. For example, Jered Weaver threw six innings and Jose Arrendondo threw two innings during their combined no-hit effort in 2008.

NOTE 1: Silver King's eight-inning no-hitter occurred in the Players' National League of Professional Base Ball Clubs ("Players' League"), a league formed in 1890 and lasting only one season. The Players' League came about because of player dissatisfaction with the reserve clause tying players to the team that originally signed them. Major League Baseball considers the Players' League a major league because of the high caliber of play that season. 22-year-old Silver King was considered the star of the Chicago team, with a WAR of 12.4, a won-loss record of 30-22, and an ERA of 2.69 over 461 innings. King would also pitch for the Kansas City Cowboys (a one-season team in the 1886 National League), St Louis Browns, Pittsburgh Pirates, New York Giants, Cincinnati Reds, and Washington Senators, collecting over 200 wins during his 10 seasons.

During the matchup at Chicago's South Side Park on June 21, 1890, King threw eight innings of no-hit ball against the Brooklyn Ward's Wonders. The Wonders were led by manager John Montgomery Ward, the author of baseball's second perfect game ten years earlier when he pitched for the National League's Providence Grays against the Buffalo Bisons. Baseball's first perfect game had been thrown by Lee Richmond five days earlier than Montgomery's and the next would be thrown by Cy Young in 1904 under modern-day rules.

Technically, on this day in 1890, the Pirates weren't the visiting team, but they did bat first. Chicago, as the home team, elected to lead off the first inning, which was allowed under the rules at that time. The game was tied 0-0, when an errant throw by Pirates' shortstop Dell Darling on an easy seventh-inning grounder off the bat of George Van Haltren allowed Brooklyn's leadoff hitter to reach second base. Van Haltren scored after a Paul Cook sacrifice grounder moved him to third and a Lou Bierbauer sacrifice fly to deep right sent him home. When King's Pirates couldn't score in the top of the ninth inning, the game was over, with King having thrown a no-hitter and taking the loss. Silver King and Andy Hawkins, who threw their eight-inning no-hitters almost exactly 100 years apart, were the only two pitchers in major league baseball history who threw complete game no-hitters that weren't shortened by weather or darkness – recognized as such at the time – that later had this recognition taken away because of the 1991 ruling.

NOTE 2: Boston's Matt Young, in his 2-1 loss to an up-and-coming Cleveland Indians team in early 1992, was the victim of seven walks and a throwing error. Cleveland center fielder Kenny Lofton led off the bottom of the first with a walk. He then stole second and third, scoring on the next play when Hall of Famer Wade Boggs made a throwing error, allowing Lofton to run home. Cleveland scored again in the third inning off consecutive leadoff walks by Young to shortstop Mark Lewis and Lofton, followed by two fielder's choice groundouts, scoring Lewis from third base. Despite nine Red Sox hits and six walks issued by Cleveland pitchers, Boston left 11 runners on base and only scored once, resulting in an Indian victory.

NOTE 3: The Angels' 2008 loss to the Dodgers in Los Angeles featured no-hit efforts by Jered Weaver and Jose Arrendondo. The lone run scored was due to a fifth inning error by Jered Weaver in front of home plate that allowed leadoff Dodger hitter Matt Kemp to reach first base. This was followed by a Kemp steal of second and a throwing error on the play by Angel catcher Jeff Mathis. This allowed Kemp to go to third and score on a sacrifice fly by Dodger third baseman Blake Dewitt for the only run of the game. Both this game and the Matt Young game, though, were never recorded as no-hitters since the commissioner's 1991 ruling occurred before they took place.

Andy Hawkins' game in 1990 was much closer than the 4-0 score indicates. Both Hawkins and opposing pitcher Greg Hibbard of the White Sox were perfect well into the fifth inning, retiring the first 29 batters they faced. It wasn't until there were two outs in the bottom of the fifth when Hawkins finally allowed a baserunner, walking Chicago catcher Ron Karkovice on a 3-2 count. Hawkins would walk five White Sox batters that day while striking out three. Hibbard would give up four hits that day – all singles – during his seven innings of shutout work.

Hawkins deserves a great deal of credit for pitching as well as he did that day. The late afternoon sun and swirling winds at Chicago's Comiskey Park were exceedingly tricky, which contributed to misplayed outfield flies leading to the eighth-inning errors that were the root cause of the four unearned White Sox runs. More problematic than the weather, though, was the caliber of the White Sox lineup that day. Led by All-Star Ozzie Guillen and featuring sluggers Sammy Sosa, Ivan Calderon, Ron Kittle, and Dan Pasqua, the league-leading Chicago lineup was packed. Largely because of their superb hitting, the White Sox boasted the best record in baseball that day at 46-26. They would finish the season with the second-best record in the American League at 94-68, behind only the 103-win, three-time American League champion Oakland Athletics.

Trouble with the wind and sun was a problem for Yankee fielders from the very beginning. Leading off the bottom of the first, White Sox batter Lance Johnson hit what should have been a routine fly ball to Jim Leyritz, but instead required a sliding catch by the left fielder to make the first out of the inning. New York right fielder Jesse Barfield, also battling the sun in right field in addition to the wind, made several nice grabs on violently windblown balls throughout the contest, as did middle infielders Álvaro Espinosa and Steve Sax. Unfortunately, these fielding adventures in the earlier innings would portend the disaster in the eighth that led to four unearned Chicago runs that inning.

Ironically, the weather helped Hawkins, too. The Yankees were beneficiaries of a very strong incoming wind later in the fifth inning. After the walk to Karkovice, Hawkins issued another to Scott Fletcher, which brought budding second-year slugger Sammy Sosa to the plate with two on and two out in a scoreless game. On a 2-1 count, Sosa drove a ball to very deep left field – a ball that Hawkins would say after the game that on any other day would have been "in the upper deck." On this day, the wind knocked it down and kept it in the park, as Leyritz awkwardly corralled it on the warning track.

Hawkins' pitching success was due, in large part, to a good changeup. A Yankee announcer even shook his head at the Yankee pitcher's uncanny effectiveness, noting "he keeps throwing that dead fish up there." After two outs in the eighth, Chicago was still scoreless and hitless, with the first two batters (Karkovice and Fletcher) popping out to start the bottom of the inning. Then Sosa came to the plate.

This time he hit a hard bouncer just to the right of New York third baseman Mike Blowers. Blowers was handcuffed by the grounder and couldn't field the ball cleanly, delaying his throw to first. When Sosa beat the throw with a head-first slide there was a roar from the home crowd celebrating the first White Sox base hit when it was displayed on the scoreboard. However, within a few seconds, the official scorekeeper's call was announced that the play was an error on Blowers, keeping Hawkins' no-hitter intact.

It was then the wheels came off. After Sosa stole second, Ozzie Guillen walked on a 3-2 count, which brought Lance Johnson to the plate. Johnson walked on four straight balls from Hawkins – the Yankee pitcher's fifth walk of the game and the second that inning. By this point Hawkins had thrown 119 pitches in the game, including 30 in the eighth inning alone. By the time it was over, Hawkins would have thrown a whopping 41 pitches in the disastrous eighth inning. If Hawkins wasn't on the verge of a no-hitter, it's entirely likely recently promoted Yankee manager Stump Merrill (replacing Bucky Dent, who had been released in June) would have removed Hawkins after he loaded the bases late in the game by walking Lance Johnson with two outs.

Robin Ventura came to the plate for Chicago in the 0-0 game. On the first pitch, he flied to deep left field. At first, it appeared the ball would stay in the park and be a routine flyout to end the inning. Instead, the ball was buffeted by the winds as Leyritz desperately tried to get a bead on it. He initially turned to his left, and then turned to his right as the ball shifted direction. The ball glanced off the top of the left fielder's glove and fell to the ground for an error. Three runners scored and Ventura ended up on second.

That wasn't the end of it, either. The next batter, Ivan Calderon, reached second base on an error by Yankee right fielder Jesse Barfield when he lost the ball in the sun and misplayed it. Ventura scored on that play to make it 4-0 in favor of the White Sox. The final Chicago batter, Dan Pasqua, popped up for the last out of the inning but the damage was done. The Yankees went down quietly in the ninth with a flyout, a runner safe on an error, and a groundball double play. The game was over and the White Sox, who had been no-hit for eight innings, were the winners in a 4-0 shutout.

In many ways, this game wasn't a surprise for the 1990 Yankees. That season was their worst year in the 108 seasons since pre-Babe Ruth 1913 and one of only ten sub-.500 years since their amazing stretch of baseball dominance began in 1926. Even more remarkably, there appears to be no end in sight to the Yankees' excellence as they routinely compete for the American League pennant. To put this into perspective, there are only ten Yankee losing seasons in the nearly 100 campaigns since 1926:

Table 6-2. New York Yankees Sub-.500 Seasons

Win % Rank	Year	W-L Record	Winning Percentage	Place	Games Behind	GB Rank
4	1965	77-85	.475	6th of 10 teams in American League	25.0	8
8	1966	70-89	.440	10th of 10 teams in American League	26.5	9
7	1967	72-90	.444	9th of 10 teams in American League	20.0	4 (tie)
1	1969	80-81	.497	5th of 6 teams in AL East Division	28.5	10
2	1973	80-82	.494	4th of 6 teams in AL East Division	17.0	3
3	1982	79-83	.488	5th of 7 teams in AL East Division	16.0	2
6	1989	74-87	.460	5th of 7 teams in AL East Division	14.5	1
10	1990	67-95	.414	7th of 7 teams in AL East Division	21.0	7
9	1991	71-91	.438	5th of 7 teams in AL East Division	20.0	4 (tie)
5	1992	76-86	.469	4th of 7 teams in AL East Division	20.0	4 (tie)

METHODOLOGY: The ten losing seasons the New York Yankees endured from 1926-2021 are listed chronologically. The rank order in the far left column represents the highest winning percentages of the ten teams listed (#1 – the 80-81 team in 1969) to the lowest (#10 – the 67-95 team in 1990).

LEGEND: "Win % Rank" is the team's winning percentage ranking compared to the other teams in the table. "W-L Record" = the team's Win-Loss record. "Games Behind" is the number of games the Yankees finished behind that year's American

League or AL East Division champion. "Place" is the finishing place of the team that season in the 10-team American League or the six- or seven-team American League East Division. "GB Rank" is the ranking of the team based on how many games they finished behind the league or division champion that season.

Since the very uncharacteristic losing season of 1925 (when Babe Ruth had a decidedly off year), the Yankees have been extraordinary. Over the next 96 seasons, it can be argued that 1990 was the low point of the New York dynasty. That year, the team ended up in seventh place in the seven-team AL East. They also had the worst winning percentage in the entire 14-team American League and the second-lowest winning percentage in all of baseball, barely beating out the hapless 65-win Atlanta Braves. Along with this, the 1990 New York team had the lowest Yankee winning percentage since the 1913 season. To throw a no-hitter and lose the game seemed to be par for the course in 1990, as New York was in the middle of a four-year stretch of losing seasons.

Between 1965 and 1992 – the 28-season period bounded by the teams in this chart – there were some real high points, too, as the Yankees won the World Series in both 1977 and 1978, beating very talented Dodger teams both times. They also won the American League pennant in 1976 and 1981. The best regular season team in this period, the juggernaut 103-win 1980 Yankee squad, outpaced the 100-win Baltimore Orioles for the AL East title yet were swept by the Kansas City Royals in the ALCS.

Of course, the Yankees have a rich history of pitching excellence. In table 6-3 below, the highest Game Scores ever achieved by Yankees pitchers are shown.

Table 6-3. Yankees Highest Game Scores

Rank	Pitcher (Team)	Date Score	Opponent	GSc	IP, Hits, Runs, ERs, Walks, Strikeouts
1	Herb Pennock (Yankees)	7/4/1925 (1) NY 1-0 (15 inn)	Phil Athletics	114	15.0 IP, 4 Hits, 0 Runs, 0 ERs, 0 BBs, 5 Ks
2 (tie)	Herb Pennock (Yankees)	5/22/1923 NY 3-1 (15 inn)	Chicago White Sox	106	15.0 IP, 4 Hits, 1 Run, 1 ER, 5 BB, 6 Ks
2 (tie)	Whitey Ford (Yankees)	4/22/1959 NY 1-0 (14 inn)	Wash Senators	106	14.0 IP, 7 Hits, 0 Runs, 0 ER, 7 BB, 15 Ks

Rank	Pitcher (Team)	Date Score	Opponent	GSc	IP, Hits, Runs, ERs, Walks, Strikeouts
4	Ray Fisher (Yankees)	5/14/1913 Tie 2-2 (15 inn)	Cleveland Indians	104	15.0 IP, 5 Hits, 2 Runs, 1 ER, 3 BB, 6 Ks
5	Slim Love (Yankees)	5/30/1917 (2) NY 2-0 (15 inn)	Phil Athletics	102	14.0 IP, 6 Hits, 0 Runs, 0 ER, 4 BB, 6 Ks
6	Spud Chandler (Yankees)	9/25/1943 NY 2-1 (14 inn)	Detroit Tigers	99	14.0 IP, 8 Hits, 1 Runs, 1 ER, 1 BB, 8 Ks
7 (tie)	David Wells (Yankees)	5/17/1998 NY 4-0	Minnesota Twins	98	9.0 IP, 0 Hits, 0 Runs, 0 ERs, 0 BBs, 11 Ks
7 (tie)	Roger Clemens (Yankees)	10/14/2000 NY 5-0	Seattle Mariners	98	9.0 IP, 1 Hit, 0 Runs, 0 ERs, 2 BBs, 15 Ks
7 (tie)	Mike Mussina (Yankees)	9/2/2001 NY 1-0	Boston Red Sox	98	9.0 IP, 1 Hit, 0 Runs, 0 ER, 0 BB, 13 Ks
10 (tie)	Jack Powell (Highlanders)	7/15/1904 NY 3-2 (15 inn)	Cleveland Naps	97	15.0 IP, 10 Hits, 2 Runs, 2 ERs, 1 BBs, 9 Ks
10 (tie)	David Cone (Yankees)	7/18/1999 NY 6-0	Montreal Expos	97	9.0 IP, 0 Hits, 0 Runs, 0 ERs, 0 BBs, 10 Ks

METHODOLOGY: This table includes the highest Game Scores thrown by a pitcher from the New York Yankees franchise from the team's inception in 1903 through 2021. Games are ranked by Game Score (GSc) and consider all franchise regular season and postseason games. Table 6-4 below limits the eligible games to those pitching performances that were 10 innings or less. Game Score (GSc) measures a pitcher's performance in any given game started. Introduced by baseball writer/statistician Bill James in the 1980s, Game Score is presented as a figure between 0-100 — except for extreme outliers — and usually falls between 40-70.

LEGEND: Dates are shown as month/day/year (for example, June 12, 2018, is shown as 6/12/2018). IP = innings pitched. One-third of an inning pitched has 0.1 added and two-thirds of an inning pitched has 0.2 added (for example, 9 1/3 innings pitched is displayed as 9.1); BB(s) = base(s) on balls; K(s) = strikeout(s); ER(s) = earned run(s); inn = innings (associated with the length of extra-inning games); and (1) or (2) = first or second game of a doubleheader. While the New

York American League franchise began in 1903, from 1903-1912 the team was known as the Highlanders. From 1913 on, they have been known as the Yankees. *The two Yankees' regular season perfect games (David Wells and David Cone) are in italics. Don Larsen's perfect game in the 1956 World Series is not shown in this table as it achieved a Game Score of 89 and is below the cutoff.*

NOTE 1: Roger Clemens' October 2000 one-hitter was Game 4 of the ALCS against the Seattle Mariners and is the highest postseason Game Score achieved by a Yankee pitcher. The only hit Seattle got was a double by Al Martin to lead off the bottom of the seventh inning. The Yankees won that game to take a 3-1 lead in the series en route to their third consecutive World Series championship.

NOTE 2: Hall of Famer Herb Pennock's amazing 15-inning shutout of the Philadelphia Athletics achieved the highest Game Score (114) in the team's history. He outdueled the legendary Lefty Grove, allowing only four hits and walking no one. The closest any of the Athletics came to scoring was when Jimmy Dykes was thrown out at home plate trying to score on an inside-the-park home run in the top of the 15th inning. The Yankees won the game with two outs in the bottom of the 15th when Steve O'Neil singled in Bobby Veach from second base in a walk-off victory.

NOTE 3: Seven of the 21 longest Yankee pitching performances ever – 14 innings or more – are included in this table, including three of the four longest shutouts: Pennock in 1925, Slim Love's 15-inning shutout in 1917, and Hall of Famer Whitey Ford's 14-inning shutout in 1959. Along with another outstanding Herb Pennock performance in 1923, Ford's Game Score of 106 is tied for second among Yankee greats, as he held the pre-expansion Washington Senators to seven hits while striking out 15 in a 1-0 victory.

NOTE 4: The longest Yankee pitching performance was thrown by Hall of Famer Red Ruffing in 1936, when he went 16 innings in a 5-4 win against Cleveland. Additionally, the one New York shutout of 14 innings or more that isn't already listed in the table was a 14-inning, 10-hit game in 1918 pitched by 21-year-old Herb Thormahlen in a 1-0 win over the White Sox.

The table below displays the highest Game Scores achieved in a game of 10 innings or less. It also includes all franchise no-hitters.

Table 6-4. Yankees Highest Game Scores of 10 innings or less

Rank	Pitcher (Team)	Date Score	Opponent	GSc	IP, Hits, Runs, ERs, Walks, Strikeouts
1 (tie)	David Wells (Yankees)	5/17/1998 NY 4-0	Minn Twins	98	9.0 IP, 0 Hits, 0 Runs, 0 ERs, 0 BBs, 11 Ks
1 (tie)	Roger Clemens (Yankees)	10/14/2000 NY 5-0	Seattle Mariners	98	9.0 IP, 1 Hit, 0 Runs, 0 ERs, 2 BBs, 15 Ks
1 (tie)	Mike Mussina (Yankees)	9/2/2001 NY 1-0	Boston Red Sox	98	9.0 IP, 1 Hit, 0 Runs, 0 ERs, 0 BBs, 13 Ks
4	David Cone (Yankees)	7/18/1999 NY 6-0	Mont Expos	97	9.0 IP, 0 Hits, 0 Runs, 0 ERs, 0 BBs, 10 Ks
5 (tie)	Red Ruffing (Yankees)	8/13/1932 NY 1-0 (10 inn)	Wash Senators	96	10.0 IP, 3 Hits, 0 Runs, 0 ERs, 2 BBs, 12 Ks
5 (tie)	John Candelaria (Yankees)	5/22/1988 NY 2-0	Oakland Athletics	96	9.0 IP, 2 Hits, 0 Runs, 0 ERs, 0 BBs, 13 Ks
5 (tie)	David Wells (Yankees)	9/1/1998 NY 7-0	Oakland Athletics	96	9.0 IP, 2 Hits, 0 Runs, 0 ERs, 0 BBs, 13 Ks
8 (tie)	Johnny Allen (Yankees)	6/4/1933 (2) NY 6-0	Phil Athletics	95	9.0 IP, 1 Hit, 0 Runs, 0 ERs, 1 BB, 11 Ks
8 (tie)	Stan Williams (Yankees)	8/6/1963 (2) NY 1-0	Wash Senators	95	9.0 IP, 1 Hit, 0 Runs, 0 ERs, 1 BB, 11 Ks
8 (tie)	Al Downing (Yankees)	8/25/1963 (1) NY 4-0	Chicago W. Sox	95	9.0 IP, 2 Hits, 0 Runs, 0 ERs, 1 BB, 13 Ks
8 (tie)	Ron Guidry (Yankees)	6/17/1978 NY 4-0	Calif Angels	95	9.0 IP, 4 Hits, 0 Runs, 0 ERs, 2 BBs, 18 Ks
8 (tie)	John Candelaria (Yankees)	7/2/1988 NY 4-0	Chicago W. Sox	95	9.0 IP, 2 Hits, 0 Runs, 0 ERs, 0 BBs, 12 Ks
8 (tie)	Corey Kluber (Yankees)	5/19/2021 NY 2-0	Texas Rangers	95	9.0 IP, 0 Hits, 0 Runs, 0 ERs, 1 BB, 9 Ks
14 (tie)	Don Larsen (Yankees)	10/8/1956 NY 2-0	Brooklyn Dodgers	94	9.0 IP, 0 Hits, 0 Runs, 0 ERs, 0 BBs, 7 Ks
22 (tie)	Monte Pearson (Yankees)	8/27/1938 (2) NY 13-0	Cleve Indians	92	9.0 IP, 0 Hits, 0 Runs, 0 ERs, 2 BBs, 7 Ks
22 (tie)	Allie Reynolds (Yankees)	9/28/1951 (1) NY 8-0	Boston Red Sox	92	9.0 IP, 0 Hits, 0 Runs, 0 ERs, 4 BBs, 9 Ks

Rank	Pitcher (Team)	Date Score	Opponent	GSc	IP, Hits, Runs, ERs, Walks, Strikeouts
22 (tie)	Dave Righetti (Yankees)	7/4/1983 NY 4-0	Boston Red Sox	92	9.0 IP, 0 Hits, 0 Runs, 0 ERs, 4 BBs, 9 Ks
80 (tie)	Allie Reynolds (Yankees)	7/12/1951 NY 1-0	Cleve Indians	88	9.0 IP, 0 Hits, 0 Runs, 0 ERs, 3 BBs, 4 Ks
153 (tie)	Sam Jones (Yankees)	9/4/1923 NY 2-0	Phil Athletics	86	9.0 IP, 0 Hits, 0 Runs, 0 ERs, 1 BB, 0 Ks
153 (tie)	Dwight Gooden (Yankees)	5/14/1996 NY 2-0	Seattle Mariners	86	9.0 IP, 0 Hits, 0 Runs, 0 ERs, 6 BBs, 5 Ks
204 (tie)	G. Mogridge (Yankees)	4/24/1917 NY 2-1	Boston Red Sox	85	9.0 IP, 0 Hits, 1 Run, 0 ERs, 3 BBs, 3 Ks
204 (tie)	Jim Abbott (Yankees)	9/4/1993 NY 4-0	Cleve Indians	85	9.0 IP, 0 Hits, 0 Runs, 0 ERs, 5 BBs, 3 Ks
---	Andy Hawkins (Yankees)	7/1/1990 Chi 4-0	Chicago W. Sox	72	8.0 IP, 0 Hits, 4 Runs, 0 ERs, 5 BBs, 3 Ks

METHODOLOGY: This table lists the highest Game Scores achieved by Yankee pitchers of 10 innings or less from 1903-2021. The rankings include all Yankees postseason games; although only Roger Clemens and Don Larsen achieved high enough Game Scores to be listed individually. For comparison purposes, all team no-hitters from 1903-2021 are included in this table. Game Score (GSc) measures a pitcher's performance in any given game started. Introduced by baseball writer/statistician Bill James in the 1980s, Game Score is presented as a figure between 0-100 — except for extreme outliers — and usually falls between 40-70. For comparison purposes, all 15 no-hitters from 1903-2021 are included in this table.

LEGEND: Dates are shown as month/day/year (for example, June 12, 2018, is shown as 6/12/2018). IP = innings pitched. One-third of an inning pitched has 0.1 added and two-thirds of an inning pitched has 0.2 added (for example, 9 1/3 innings pitched is displayed as 9.1). BB(s) = base(s) on balls; K(s) = strikeout(s); ER(s) = earned run(s); inn = innings (associated with the length of extra-inning games); and (1) or (2) = first or second game of a doubleheader. While the New York American League franchise began in 1903, from 1903-1912 the team was known as the Highlanders. From 1913 on, they have been known as the Yankees. All games in this table were thrown by Yankee pitchers. *The three Yankees' perfect* games *(Don Larsen in the 1956 World Series, and David Wells and David Cone in the regular season) are in italics.*

NOTE 1: Don Larsen's October 1956 perfect game was in Game 5 of the World Series against the Brooklyn Dodgers. This win gave New York a 3-2 advantage en route to a seven-game series victory.

NOTE 2: In 1998, Mike Mussina carried a perfect game against Boston until there were two outs in the bottom of the ninth inning. With a count of one ball and two strikes, Red Sox batter Carl Everett hit a line drive single to left field. Mussina got the next batter (Trot Nixon) to ground out for the third out and preserve the 1-0 win. The game was a scoreless pitcher's duel between Mussina and Boston's David Cone until the Yankees scored an unearned run in the top of the ninth.

NOTE 3: In his 1933 game, Johnny Allen allowed the only two Athletic baserunners on a walk and a single with two outs in the first inning. He then retired the next 25 Philadelphia batters in a row, striking out 11 of them. Stan Williams allowed his only hit during the third inning of his 1963 pitching duel with Washington's Bennie Daniels. The game was won by the Yankees when Tony Kubek scored the only run of the game on a sacrifice fly by Bobby Richardson in the top of the eighth inning.

NOTE 4: Ron Guidry's 18-strikeout performance in his 1978 game against the Angels is the most ever for a Yankees pitcher and tied for twelfth place for the most in a major league game of nine innings or less.

NOTE 5: The only baserunner Corey Kluber allowed in his 2021 no-hitter was a four-pitch walk to the Rangers' Charlie Culberson in the third inning. Apart from that, he was perfect. Sad Sam Jones walked the fifth batter he faced against the Athletics in his 1923 no-hitter, preventing him from achieving a perfect game (although another baserunner reached when the New York shortstop made an error on a groundball in the eighth inning). Jones is also one of only four pitchers to ever throw a no-hitter and not strike out anyone.

If it still counted as an official no-hitter, Andy Hawkins Game Score of 72 for the contest described in this chapter would qualify as the lowest score of any major league no-hitter ever, well behind Ed Lafitte's 1914 Federal League no-hitter at 77. Hypothetically, without the four unearned runs that began with Jim Leyritz's misplaced fly ball in the eighth inning, Hawkins would have achieved a Game Score of 80 headed into the ninth against Chicago. If he had pitched a clean ninth inning with no strikeouts, he would have gained another five points for a score of

85, placing him in the same category as Yankee pitchers George Mogridge and Jim Abbott. This Game Score would have been a much more appropriate measure of the excellent game he threw.

The Yankees had a string of exceptional pitchers in the late 1990s, leading to four World Series championships in 1996 and 1998-2000. The top pitcher of the 1990s (Roger Clemens) played for the champion New Yorkers in 1999. Two other pitchers, David Wells and David Cone, threw perfect games in 1998 and 1999. All three of them are recognized as being among the best pitchers during that decade.

Table 6-5. Best Pitchers of the 1990s

WAR Rank	Pitcher (Team(s))	Seasons Pitched	Innings Pitched	WAR (per 200 IP)	Wins (per Season)
1	Roger Clemens (Red Sox, Blue Jays, Yankees)	1990-1999	2,177.2	68.2 (6.26)	152 (15.2)
2	Greg Maddux (Cubs, Braves)	1990-1999	2,394.2	65.4 (5.46)	176 (17.6)
3	David Cone (Mets, Blue Jays, Royals, Yankees)	1990-1999	2,017.0	52.9 (5.25)	141 (14.1)
4	Randy Johnson (Mariners, Astros, Diamondbacks)	1990-1999	2,063.1	52.1 (5.05)	150 (15.0)
5	Kevin Brown (Rangers, Orioles, Marlins, Padres, Dodgers)	1990-1999	2,211.1	48.1 (4.35)	143 (14.3)
6	Kevin Appier (Royals, Athletics)	1990-1999	1,867.2	47.6 (5.10)	120 (12.0)
7	Tom Glavine (Braves)	1990-1999	2,228.0	45.0 (4.04)	164 (16.4)
8	Chuck Finley (Angels)	1990-1999	2,144.0	44.6 (4.16)	135 (13.5)
9	Mike Mussina (Orioles)	1991-1999	1,772.0	42.0 (4.74)	136 (15.1)
10	Pedro Martinez (Dodgers, Expos, Red Sox)	1992-1999	1,359.1	40.5 (5.96)	107 (13.4)

WAR Rank	Pitcher (Team(s))	Seasons Pitched	Innings Pitched	WAR (per 200 IP)	Wins (per Season)
11	John Smoltz (Braves)	1990-1999	2,142.1	39.8 (3.72)	143 (14.3)
12	Curt Schilling (Orioles, Astros, Phillies)	1990-1999	1,668.1	35.2 (4.22)	99 (9.9)
13	David Wells (Blue Jays, Tigers, Orioles, Yankees)	1990-1999	1,897.0	31.5 (3.32)	127 (12.7)

METHODOLOGY: Pitchers are ranked in order of Wins Above Replacement (WAR) achieved from 2000-2009. WAR measures a player's value in all facets of the game by deciphering how many more wins he's worth than a replacement-level player at his same position.

LEGEND: Another measure of merit I wanted to include was the number of wins each pitcher accumulated as well. Because a significant number of pitchers were only present for a portion of the decade, I included two rate measures (WAR per 200 innings pitched and wins per season). IP = innings pitched. One-third of an inning is designated as ".1" and two-thirds of an inning is designated as ".2" innings.

Of course, no discussion of great Yankee pitchers would be complete without bringing up the greatest closer of all time: Mariano Rivera. A unanimous choice on his first Hall of Fame ballot in 2019, Rivera is the most accomplished pitcher ever to emerge from Panama. For comparison purposes, the top Panamanian pitchers in career Wins Above Replacement (WAR) are listed below.

Table 6-6. Best Pitchers Born in Panama

Rank	Pitcher (Home)	Team	Season(s)	Career IP	WAR (per 200 IP)	Wins (per season)
1	Mariano Rivera (Panama City)	NY Yankees	1995-2013	1,283.2	56.3 (8.77)	82 Wins (4.3) 652 Saves (34.3)
2	Ramiro Mendoza (Los Santos)	NY Yankees Bos Red Sox NY Yankees	1996-2002 2003-2004 2005	797.0	11.8 (2.96)	59 (5.9)

Rank	Pitcher (Home)	Team	Season(s)	Career IP	WAR (per 200 IP)	Wins (per season)
3	Bruce Chen (Panama City)	Atl Braves Phi Phillies NY Mets Mon Expos Cin Reds Hou Astros Bos Red Sox Bal Orioles Tex Rangers KC Royals Cle Indians	1998-2000 2000-2001 2001-2002 2002 2002 2003 2003 2004-2006 2007 2009-2014 2015	1,532.0	10.8 (1.41)	82 (4.8)
4	Juan Berenguer (Agua-dulce)	NY Mets KC Royals Tor B. Jays Det Tigers SF Giants Min Twins Atl Braves KC Royals	1978-1980 1981 1981 1982-1985 1986 1987-1990 1991-1992 1992	1,205.1	10.1 (1.68)	67 (4.5)

METHODOLOGY: To qualify for inclusion in this table, pitchers had to be of Panamanian heritage and born in Panama. Pitchers are ranked based upon their career Wins Above Replacement (WAR) between 1900-2021. WAR measures a player's value in all facets of the game by deciphering how many more wins he's worth than a replacement-level player at his same position. Only WAR achieved in the National and American Leagues count for purposes of this ranking. Pitchers needed to have a Career WAR above 10 to be included in this list.

LEGEND: Home = the place a pitcher was born in Panama. Team and season(s) are the teams they played for and the season(s) they were with each team listed in chronological order. Career IP = career innings pitched. Career WAR = the pitcher's accumulated WAR over his career. Career Wins = the number of wins each pitcher accumulated over his career. Because pitchers had different career lengths, I included two rate measures (WAR per 200 innings pitched and wins per season). Because Mariano Rivera was used exclusively as a reliever after his first season, his career saves and save rate per season are included as well. Bruce Chen missed the entire 2008 season. Therefore, that missed season doesn't count as part of his wins per season calculation.

NOTE 1: Of the players on this list, only Mariano Rivera was named as an All-Star during his playing career – and he was selected 13 times. Mariano was also a legendary postseason pitcher for the Yankees. Throwing 141 innings in relief and earning 42 saves en route to five World Series championships in 1996, 1998-2000, and 2009, Rivera is considered the best postseason closer in baseball. Two other pitchers in this table were World Champions, too. Ramiro Mendoza played for the 1998-1999 Yankees, and Juan Berenguer was part of the 1984 Detroit Tigers and 1987 Minnesota Twins

NOTE 2: While Panama has had limited success at the World Baseball Classic – the national team has never advanced beyond pool play – the 2006, 2009, and 2023 teams have qualified for tournament pool play. Two pitchers on this list have been members of the national team: Bruce Chen was on the inaugural 2006 team and the 2009 team; and Ramiro Mendoza was on the 2009 team.

Thirty-year-old Andy Hawkins was representative of the 1990 New York team, finishing the season at 5-12 with a 5.37 ERA over 157.1 innings. The leader of the Yankees' pitching staff that year, Tim Leary, ended up with 19 losses. Hawkins had a rough season, walking more batters than he struck out in 1990 (82 walks vs.74 strikeouts). Selected out of high school in the first round of the 1978 draft, Hawkins ended up having a successful career that spanned 10 seasons. He was a stalwart of the San Diego Padres pitching staff in the mid-1980s, helping to lead them to the World Series in 1984. His best year was 1985, when he won 18 games and anchored an excellent Padres pitching staff along with Eric Show, Dave Dravecky, and LaMarr Hoyt. Hawkins got off to a stupendous start with San Diego in 1985, winning the first 10 games he started and being named the National League Pitcher of the Month in May when he went 6-0.

Hawkins' success with the Padres propelled him into the free-agent market after the 1988 season. He signed as a 28-year-old free agent with the Yankees in December 1988 and stayed with the team until being released in May 1991. He was soon picked up by Oakland and was subsequently released after three months. He finished his career with a 84-91 record and a 4.22 ERA. After his playing career ended, Hawkins had an extensive follow-on career as a coach in the minors and majors. Of special note, he was the pitching coach for the Rangers from 2008-2015. His stint with Texas included their two American League championships in 2010 and 2011.

Perhaps the perfect post-mortem from Hawkins' no-hitter that got revoked came from former Houston pitcher Ken Johnson. Johnson was the losing pitcher in a nine-inning, 1-0 no-hit loss to the Cincinnati Reds in 1964 due to two ninth-inning errors:

"*I'm sorry to hear he (Hawkins) joined me. I was very happy being the only man to lose a no-hitter.*" Minneapolis Star Tribune, July 2, 1990.

Hawkins' catcher that day was veteran Bob Geren. In 1990, Geren split duties with Matt Nokes and Rick Cerone. While Geren played in parts of five seasons from 1988-93, he was typically a backup or a role player, as he was in 1990. He finished his playing career with a .233 batting average and 22 home runs over 307 games played. After his playing career ended, Geren managed in the Boston Red Sox and Oakland Athletics farm systems. In 1999, he was California League Manager of the Year with the Modesto A's.

Geren became an A's major league coach in 2003. He was bullpen coach until 2005, and bench coach in 2006. Geren was promoted to manager of the Athletics for the 2007 season and stayed in that role until early in the 2011 season. In 2012, he was named bench coach for the New York Mets, staying until their appearance in the 2015 World Series. He then moved on to the Los Angeles Dodgers as bench coach starting in 2016.

I invite you to enjoy my recent interview with Andy Hawkins.

Andy Hawkins Interview
Conducted by Kevin Hurd on May 25, 2021

Kevin Hurd (KH): Would you consider yourself to be the best pitcher on your high school, college, minor league (A-AAA) teams?

Andy Hawkins (AH): For Little League, there was always one guy who was better each year. Same for when I was in high school. I started being the best pitcher on the team starting in the minors. The Hawaii (AAA) team I played on had some very good players, especially Tony Gwynn.

KH: Did you feel any different (good or bad) on the day of your no-hitter?

AH: About the same as I always felt; nothing unusual. It was a day game in Chicago, and I always liked pitching in the daylight.

KH: What pitches (fastball, curve, slider, etc.) were working best for you that day?

AH: My fastball, by far-well over half my pitches. After that, my slider, then my curve.

KH: What was the best defensive play/closest you came to losing that no-hitter?

AH: No real outstanding plays. Most plays were routine. The first five innings went by like a blur; the White Sox pitcher (Greg Hibbard) had a no-hitter until the sixth inning. Like I said, I can't remember any great plays that day.

KH: Did you shake off your catcher's (Bob Geren's) signs much during the game?

AH: Not very much — we were pretty much on the same wavelength. I liked it when Bob was catching, as he had a good arm for throwing out base stealers.

KH: In your career, what batter did you have the hardest time getting out?

AH: Denny Walling (Houston, St. Louis, Texas). No matter what I tried I couldn't get him out. He wasn't an all-star, but he hit like an all-star against me.

KH: Do you have any memorabilia (baseball, plaque, uniform, etc.) from the game in your house?

AH: I have my game glove in a glass case. I gave my hat and shoes to the Hall of Fame.

KH: You played for 10 years in MLB. You played for seven different managers. Who did you like playing for the most?

AH: Without a doubt, Jack McKeon (1988). He handled the pitchers and the veterans very well. He was a real people person.

KH: Do you think the number of pitches you threw that day (131) had any effect on you retiring the next year.

AH: No, not at all. I didn't get a sore arm from the game. At that time, we didn't pay much attention to the pitch count.

KH: Was your catcher (Bob Geren) one you had requested before?

AH: I didn't have enough pull to request my own catcher (laughs).

KH: Do you still stay in contact with Bob Geren?

AH: Not too often. The last time we were in contact was 4 or 5 years ago.

KH: Did the Yankees give you a bonus for throwing your no-hitter?

AH: When we came back to Yankee Stadium after our road trip, I was warming up before the game. Someone came up to me and said I had a call from George Steinbrenner (owner of the Yankees). I went to the clubhouse, picked up the phone and talked with George. He said he wanted to give me a Jeep Wrangler Truck as a bonus for pitching the no-hitter. I told him that he paid me a very good wage to do my job, and I couldn't accept the Wrangler.

KH: During the game, when did you think "I've got a real shot at a no-hitter?" Fifth inning, sixth inning, etc.?

AH: I believe I thought that the first time in the seventh inning.

KH: On September 4, 1991, Major League Baseball, through the Committee for Statistical Accuracy, negated a lot of games that were previously considered no-hitters. Yours was one of them. How did you feel about it?

AH: I was very irritated. The thing that bugged me the most was that I had no control over it. At the time, I couldn't have forced the White Sox to bat in the bottom of the ninth. The game was over. I'm seeing stuff now with Madison Bumgarner pitching a <u>scheduled</u> seven-inning no-hitter and it doesn't count because it wasn't nine innings. I guess if MLB changes their mind and says his seven-inning no-hitter counts, they'll have to look at mine again.

KH: Were you able to get a follow-on job in baseball after your playing days were over, in the majors, minors, college, high school, or media?

AH: I had a lot of coaching jobs (pitching coach mostly) from 2001-2019. Eight years (2008-2015) I was in the majors as a pitching coach for the Texas Rangers. The minor league towns I was a coach at were Savannah (Georgia), Clinton (Iowa), Stockton (California), High Desert (California), Oklahoma, and Omaha (Nebraska).

KH: Post-playing career, besides the coaching jobs, have there been other jobs you have done?

AH: I've worked in real estate, as a construction foreman, and as a ranch manager.

KH: Since you were able to get a job in baseball in your post-playing career, do you think having a no-hitter helped you get the job.?

AH: No, not really. For my first job I interviewed with Reid Nichols of the Texas Rangers, we went to lunch, he looked over my career, liked my baseball knowledge, liked me. That helped me get the job.

KH: Do you have any kids/grandkids who have/will pursue baseball as a career? Did you encourage them to do so?

AH: Actually, none of my kids or grandkids have pursued baseball.

KH: Was the no-hitter the highlight of your career? If not, what was?

AH: No, it wasn't the highlight (laughs). My highlight was playing with the 1984 San Diego Padres, winning the division title, winning the playoff series against the Cubs, and my being the winning pitcher in Game 2 of the World Series.

KH: Have you been to the section of the Baseball Hall of Fame that focuses on no-hitters?
AH: No, I haven't. But like I said in the beginning, I did send them my shoes and my hat from the game.
KH: Have you spent time signing autographs in Las Vegas, or in Florida or Arizona during spring training?
AH: I've been to Arizona to sign some autographs, off the field.
KH: Do you have anything you'd like to say in conclusion?
AH: Baseball was a privilege as a player and as a coach. I was very fortunate; I had 34 years as a player and a coach.

Chapter 7

Bud Smith: Putting on a Show

September 3, 2001
Rookie Bud Smith no-hits the hometown Padres in front of 40 friends and family members as he makes his pitching debut in Southern California

"I didn't start thinking about it until the seventh inning when I started getting a little fatigued. Then I realized I had to finish on adrenaline."
Bud Smith describing when he realized he was throwing a no-hitter (John Maffei, "This Bud makes two," *North County Times*, September 4, 2001.

"I was almost rooting for him to give up a hit so we could get him out of there."
St. Louis pitching coach Dave Duncan describing his anxiety as Smith's pitch count rose throughout the game (Rick Hummel, "No fuss, no muss, no hits," *St. Louis Post-Dispatch*, September 4, 2001).

"That ball was the biggest scare of the night. I thought the only chance I had was if Albert jumped and robbed him."
Bud Smith describing his reaction to Albert Pujols tracking down Bubba Trammell's warning track fly ball in deep left field (Rick Hummel, "Homecoming for Smith turns into one big party," *St. Louis Post-Dispatch*, September 5, 2001).

"His ball has a little movement on it. He has a good changeup. He kept a lot of right-handed batters off balance with it. You have to give him credit. We beat up on him pretty good last time."

San Diego slugger Ryan Klesko admiring Bud Smith's no-hit outing (John Maffei, "This Bud makes two," *North County Times*, September 4, 2001.

"Here goes the no-hitter. He had the crowd behind him. He hit it good, but (St. Louis shortstop) Edgar (Renteria) was in the right spot."

St. Louis catcher Eli Marrero describing what he was thinking in the eighth inning when the Padres sent Hall of Famer Tony Gwynn up to pinch hit ("Rookie Smith pitches improbable no-hitter," *ESPN.com*, September 3, 2001).

Twenty-one-year-old Bud Smith was a young and promising pitcher in the playoff-bound Cardinal rotation in September 2001 as he took the mound. During his last two starts, though, he had real trouble, as he gave up an abysmal 14 runs in 14 innings. His last outing, five days earlier against these very same Padres, he had allowed seven runs over 3.1 innings en route to a 16-14 loss. Yet, on the night of September 3, he felt confident. A Southern California native, he would be the starting pitcher at Qualcomm Stadium in San Diego with 40 friends and family members there to witness the first time he ever started a game in California.

The Cardinals got on the scoreboard even before Smith threw his first pitch, as Albert Pujols hit a two-run home run with two outs in the top of the first inning. They would add to their lead with an unearned run on a catcher's throwing error in the fifth and a two-out, run-scoring double by Placido Polanco in the seventh to give St. Louis a 4-0 lead.

Bud Smith pitched a great game, striking out seven and walking only four for the only San Diego baserunners the entire evening. Smith relied on location with his fastball and curve to keep the Padres off-balance, as his fastball topped out at just 86 miles per hour. San Diego fielded a powerful lineup, too, featuring sluggers Ryan Klesko, Phil Nevin, Bubba Trammell, Ray Lankford, and the ageless Hall of Famer Rickey Henderson batting leadoff. Henderson did get two walks and stole second during the game. The Padres even had one of the best hitters of all time, the incomparable Tony Gwynn, on the bench. He entered the game in the bottom of the 8th inning to pinch hit.

The no-hitter was in jeopardy a few times during the game. In the seventh inning, San Diego right fielder Bubba Trammell hit a very deep fly to left fielder Albert Pujols who snagged it on the warning track, just in front of the fence. In the eighth, pinch-hitter Tony Gwynn hit a sharp groundball right up the middle of the diamond. Because of a perfectly positioned, sharp-fielding shortstop Edgar Renteria, it became the second out of the inning instead of a single. There was also an excellent play in foul territory in the sixth inning, when St. Louis right fielder J.D. Drew crossed over the bullpen mound and reached into the stands to make the out and end the inning with a man on first base.

Of course, this was all new ground for young Bud Smith, as he was one of the youngest pitchers to ever throw a no-hitter, as demonstrated in the table below.

Table 7-1. Youngest Pitchers to Throw a No-Hitter

Rank	Date	Pitcher	Team	Age (years-days)
1	5/1/1906	Johnny Lush	Philadelphia Phillies	20y-205d
2	9/20/1907	Nick Maddox	Pittsburgh Pirates	20y-315d
3	7/15/1901	Christy Mathewson	New York Giants	20y-337d
4	8/30/1912	Earl Hamilton	St. Louis Browns	21y-42d
5	9/21/1970	Vida Blue	Oakland Athletics	21y-55d
6	7/12/1900	Noodles Hahn	Cincinnati Reds	21y-74d
7	8/11/1991	Wilson Alvarez	Chicago White Sox	21y-140d
8	4/16/1940	Bob Feller	Cleveland Indians	21y-165d
9	7/29/1911	Joe Wood	Boston Red Sox	21y-277d
10	9/3/2001	Bud Smith	St. Louis Cardinals	21y-315d

METHODOLOGY: This table includes the youngest pitchers to throw a no-hitter from 1900-2021. Pitchers are ranked by their age when they threw their no-hitter, with the youngest pitcher ranked first.

LEGEND: Dates are shown as month/day/year (for example, June 12, 2018, is shown as 6/12/2018). Age of players is shown in years (y) and days (d) as of the day they threw their no-hitter. For example, Johnny Lush was 20 years and 205 days old when he threw his no-hitter. This is shown in the table as 20y-205d.

As baseball entered the 20th Century in the early 1900s, it's clear teams weren't nearly as concerned with limiting the workload on their young pitchers as they are now. Pitchers were brought up to the majors at a much younger age, which would help explain why there are only four pitchers on this list who threw no-hitters after 1912. Digging deeper, Smith is the only pitcher in the Top 10 who threw his no-hitter in the last 30 years. This speaks not only to Smith's extraordinary ability at a young age, in hindsight it also points to the possibility that Smith was worked too hard, too quickly and that may have contributed to his arm troubles that developed shortly after his no-hitter.

Bud Smith was a trusted stalwart in the Cardinal rotation by the end of the 2001 season. St. Louis Manager Tony La Russa thought so highly of Smith, he named him as the Cardinal starter in the fourth game of the best-of-five 2001 NLDS against Arizona. The Diamondbacks were leading the series at that point two games to one. Smith rewarded the team's confidence in him by holding Arizona to just one run in his five innings on the mound. St. Louis won the game 4-1, evening the series at two games apiece and sending it to a decisive Game 5. Arizona would win the final game 2-1 on a two-out RBI single in the bottom of the ninth inning.

His September no-hitter and subsequent playoff win would be the highlights of Smith's career. He would win two more games after his no-hitter during the final month of the pennant race in 2001. The next season was a disaster for Smith, as he won only one more game and his ERA ballooned to 6.94. His season and major league career would end in July 2002, with him having won only three games after his September 2001 no-hitter. His three wins places him in a tie for fifth place for the fewest career wins after throwing a no-hitter, as depicted in the table below.

Table 7-2. Fewest Wins after Pitching a No-Hitter

Rank	Wins After	Pitcher (Career W-L)	Career Length	Pitcher Team	Date of No-hitter	No-hit Opponent
1	0	Joe Cowley (33-25)	1982-1987	Chicago White Sox	9/19/1986	California Angels
2	1	Weldon Henley (32-43)	1903-1907	Philadelphia Athletics	7/22/1905	St. Louis Browns
3 (tie)	2	Bobo Holloman (3-7)	1953	St. Louis Browns	5/6/1953	Philadelphia Athletics

Rank	Wins After	Pitcher (Career W-L)	Career Length	Pitcher Team	Date of No-hitter	No-hit Opponent
3 (tie)	2	Bob Keegan (40-36)	1953-1958	Chicago White Sox	8/20/1957	Washington Senators
5 (tie)	3	Addie Joss (160-97)	1902-1910	Cleveland Naps	4/20/1910	Chicago White Sox
5 (tie)	3	Alex Main (21-22)	1914-1918	Kansas City Packers	8/16/1915 (Federal)	Buffalo Blues
5 (tie)	3	Bud Smith (7-8)	2001-2002	St. Louis Cardinals	9/3/2001	San Diego Padres
5 (tie)	3	Johan Santana (139-78)	2000-2012	New York Mets	6/1/2012	St. Louis Cardinals
5 (tie)	3	Josh Beckett (138-106)	2001-2014	Los Angeles Dodgers	5/25/2014	Philadelphia Phillies
10 (tie)	4	Tex Carleton (100-76)	1932-1940	Brooklyn Dodgers	4/30/1940	Cincinnati Reds
10 (tie)	4	Mike Warren (9-13)	1983-1985	Oakland Athletics	9/29/1983	Chicago White Sox
10 (tie)	*4*	*Philip Humber (16-23)*	*2006-2013*	*Chicago White Sox*	*4/21/2012*	*Seattle Mariners*
10 (tie)	4	Edinson Volquez (95-89)	2005-2020	Miami Marlins	6/3/2017	Arizona D-backs

METHODOLOGY: This table includes pitchers with the fewest number of wins after throwing a no-hitter from 1900-2021. Pitchers are ranked by the number of wins they accumulated after they threw their no-hitter, with the fewest number of wins at the top of the list.

LEGEND: Dates are shown as month/day/year (for example, June 12, 2018, is shown as 6/12/2018). Career W-L = Career Win-Loss record. Career Length = the period from the season in which the pitcher threw his first major league game and when he threw his last. It does not account for seasons during the period when the pitcher did not play. (Federal) = Federal League game. The Federal League was a major league that spanned two seasons from 1914-1915. *The perfect game listed (Philip Humber in 2012) is in italics.*

While wins are an imperfect way of valuing a pitcher's performance, they do give a general measure of a starting pitcher's effectiveness. To put it simply, pitchers with more wins are typically more effective than those who have fewer. In looking at the 13 pitchers listed on the table above, they primarily fall into three groups.

The first group consists of veteran players who threw a no-hitter towards the end of a long career. This group includes Addie Joss, Johan Santana, Josh Beckett, Tex Carleton, and Edinson Volquez. Hall of Famer Addie Joss, with 160 wins, is something of an exception to this rule since he was in his prime at 30 years old when he threw his second no-hitter. He contracted a bacterial infection later that year and died just after his 31st birthday.

The second group is something of a middle tier who achieved modest success as major league pitchers but didn't stick around for a great length of time. Joe Cowley, Weldon Henley, Bob Keegan, and Alex Main fall into this group. Bob Keegan and Alex Main were rookies in their early 30s and didn't last for many years after they broke into the majors. Weldon Henley, a college graduate when those were much scarcer, left baseball for a career in the business world. Joe Cowley suddenly developed arm and confidence problems, and he didn't win another game after his no- hitter.

Cowley probably fits better in the third group. This group consists of younger pitchers at the beginning of their careers who developed arm problems shortly after stretching themselves and throwing a no-hitter. Cowley belongs here, and I also include Bobo Holloman, Mike Warren, Philip Humber, and Bud Smith in this category. Each of them can make a connection between their arm problems and over usage early in their careers. Often, this overuse resulted in injuries requiring surgery.

This certainly appeared to be the case with Bud Smith. In the middle of a very disappointing 2002 season, it was discovered he had a torn labrum in his throwing shoulder. Even though it was surgically repaired, Smith never regained enough effectiveness to pitch in the majors again. Cowley and Warren are covered in their own chapters. As noted in a later chapter focused on Bo Belinsky, Bud Smith also has one of the lowest career JAWS values (minus 0.3) of any pitcher ever to throw a no-hitter.

The St. Louis catcher that day was veteran Eli Marrero. Marrero played most of his career with the Cardinals (1997-2003), along with playing for the Braves

(2004), Royals (2005), Orioles (2005), Rockies (2006), and Mets (2006). Marrero has the distinction of being one of only two no-hit catchers who played half or more of their careers at other positions. Specifically, of the 4,438 innings he played in the majors, he played roughly half (2,327) of those at catcher. The rest of the time he was in the outfield or at first base. During his early career (1997-2001), he was primarily a backup catcher for the Cardinals. Starting in 2001, he began to transition to playing the outfield and first base. After 2001, he was almost exclusively used in the outfield.

Marrero's situation is rare for a catcher who has caught a no-hit game. Almost all no-hit catchers are career backstops. Besides Marrero, an even bigger exception is Curt Blefary, who played for multiple teams from 1965-1972. The 1965 American League Rookie of the Year with Baltimore, Blefary hardly ever appeared in games as a catcher, as he was primarily a corner outfielder and a first baseman. Specifically, he only caught in 66 of the 834 games he played in throughout his career. In 1968, the "Year of the Pitcher," the Orioles were desperately trying to get some offense in their lineup. That was the year the Orioles experimented with Blefary at catcher, when he appeared in 43 games behind starters Andy Etchebarren and Elrod Hendricks. Yet, on a cloudy and rainy April 27, 1968, experimental catcher Curt Blefary caught Tom Phoebus as he threw a 6-0 no-hitter against the Boston Red Sox.

One of the aspects that is often overlooked during the excitement of a no-hit game is the perspective of the team that got no-hit. As expected, it can be discouraging. If it happens more than once during the same season, it can be absolutely demoralizing. For the Padres, the game highlighted in this chapter was the second time they were no-hit in 2001 – they had been no-hit in May by Florida pitcher A.J. Burnett. While recognizing Smith's accomplishment, it's easy to detect the frustration in San Diego catcher Ben Davis's voice as he said, "It's just unfortunate it has happened to us twice this year, but he did a hell of a job." San Diego manager Bruce Bochy put it more succinctly when he summed it up, "It's not a lot of fun when you get no-hit."

While there have been hundreds of teams that have been no-hit over the years, there have been just 16 teams since 1900 who have had the misfortune of being no-hit twice or more in the same season, like the San Diego Padres were in 2001.

Table 7-3. Teams No-hit Twice in the Same Season

Year	Team	Season Record	Dates	No-hit Pitcher (Team)
1917	Chicago White Sox	100-54	5/5/1917 5/6/1917	Ernie Koob (St. Louis Browns) Bob Groom (St. Louis Browns)
1923	Philadelphia Athletics	69-83	9/4/1923 9/7/1923	Sam Jones (New York Yankees) Howard Ehmke (Boston Red Sox)
1960	Philadelphia Phillies	59-95	8/18/1960 9/16/1960	Lew Burdette (Milwaukee Braves) Warren Spahn (Milwaukee Braves)
1967	Detroit Tigers	91-71	4/30/1967 9/10/1967	Multiple (Baltimore Orioles) Joel Horlen (Chicago White Sox)
1971	Cincinnati Reds	79-83	6/3/1971 6/23/1971	Ken Holtzman (Chicago Cubs) Rick Wise (Philadelphia Phillies)
1973	Detroit Tigers	85-77	4/27/1973 6/15/1973	Steve Busby (Kansas City Royals) Nolan Ryan (California Angels)
1977	California Angels	74-88	6/30/1977 9/22/1977	Dennis Eckersley (Cleveland Indians) Bert Blyleven (Texas Rangers)
1996	Colorado Rockies	83-79	5/11/1996 9/17/1996	Al Leiter (Florida Marlins) Hideo Nomo (Los Angeles Dodgers)
2001	San Diego Padres	79-83	5/12/2001 9/3/2001	AJ Burnett (Florida Marlins) Bud Smith (St. Louis Cardinals)
2010	Tampa Bay Rays	96-66	*5/9/2010* 6/25/2010	*Dallas Braden (Oakland Athletics)* Edwin Jackson (Arizona D-backs)
2015	Los Angeles Dodgers	92-70	8/21/2015 8/30/2015	Mike Fiers (Houston Astros) Jake Arrieta (Chicago Cubs)
2015	New York Mets	90-72	6/9/2015 10/3/2015	Chris Heston (San Francisco Giants) Max Scherzer (Washington Nationals)
2019	Seattle Mariners	68-94	7/12/2019 8/3/2019	Multiple (Los Angeles Angels) Multiple (Houston Astros)
2021	Seattle Mariners	90-72	5/5/2021 5/18/2021	John Means (Baltimore Orioles) Spencer Turnbull (Detroit Tigers)
2021	Texas Rangers	60-102	4/9/2021 5/19/2021	Joe Musgrove (San Diego Padres) Corey Kluber (New York Yankees)
2021	Cleveland Indians	80-82	4/14/2021 5/7/2021 9/11/2021	Carlos Rodon (Chicago White Sox) Wade Miley (Cincinnati Reds) Multiple (Milwaukee Brewers)

METHODOLOGY: This table includes all the teams from 1900-2021 who have had two or more no-hitters thrown against them. Teams are listed in chronological order based upon the date of the last no-hitter thrown.

LEGEND: Dates are shown as month/day/year (for example, June 12, 2018, is shown as 6/12/2018). Season Win-Loss = the no-hit team's win-loss record at the end of the season. No-hit Pitcher (team) = the pitcher who threw the no-hitter and the team they played for on the date of the no-hitter. Multiple = the no-hitter was thrown by two or more pitchers. *The perfect game listed (Dallas Braden in 2010) is in italics.*

NOTE 1: The 1967 Baltimore Orioles threw a no-hitter against the Detroit Tigers on April 30 using two pitchers: Steve Barber (8.2 innings) and Stu Miller (0.1 innings). Detroit won that game 2-1 on three walks, an error, and a wild pitch in the ninth inning.

NOTE 2: Both no-hitters thrown against the Seattle Mariners in 2019 used more than one pitcher. The Angels' July 12 no-hitter wwas thrown by Taylor Cole (2.0 innings) and Felix Pena (7.0 innings). The Astros used four pitchers in their August 3 game: Aaron Sanchez threw the first six innings, with relievers Will Harris, Joe Biagini, and Chris Devenski finishing the game with one inning apiece.

NOTE 3: Milwaukee's 2021 no-hitter against the Cleveland Indians featured Corbin Burnes (8.0 innings) and Josh Hader (1.0 inning). Fifteen of the 16 teams in the table above have been no-hit twice in a single season. The one exception is this same Indians team, who were no-hit three times in 2021.

While it would be easy to jump to the conclusion that a team must be really bad to get no-hit multiple times in a single season, as a blanket statement that would be inaccurate. There have been some excellent teams who have been no-hit more than once in a year, including the division champion 2010 Tampa Bay Rays (96-66), 2015 Los Angeles Dodgers (92-70), and 2015 New York Mets (90-72), along with the American League runner-up 1967 Detroit Tigers (91-71) and the up-and-coming 2021 Seattle Mariners (90-72).

However, the World Series Champion Chicago White Sox (100-54) of 1917 – led by the legendary Shoeless Joe Jackson, and Hall of Famers Ray Schalk and Eddie Collins – was easily the best team to ever be no-hit more than once in a single season. That they were no-hit on consecutive days by the next-to-last place St. Louis Browns (57-97) makes it even more remarkable.

There has been one other team besides the 1917 White Sox which has been no-hit twice by the same team in the same season. The 1960 Phillies, one in a series of awful Philadelphia teams, were no-hit twice by the Milwaukee Braves that season. Being a terrible team doesn't necessarily make it any more likely to get no-hit either. Of the 10 worst teams in baseball since 1946, as displayed in the Randy Johnson chapter, only one was no-hit – the historically bad 1962 New York Mets were no-hit by Hall of Famer Sandy Koufax. Of course, none of them were ever no-hit twice in the same season like the 16 teams on the list above.

Additionally, the outstanding 1917 White Sox team was one of only five teams to be no-hit twice in the same month (May). The 1923 Philadelphia Athletics (September), 1971 Cincinnati Reds (June), 2015 Los Angeles Dodgers (August), and 2021 Seattle Mariners (May) shared the same experience.

Overall, the Dodgers and Phillies have had the most no-hitters pitched against them (20), followed closely by some of the other original 16 teams: Braves (17), Giants (16), and Browns/Orioles (15). Of the expansion era teams, the Padres have been no-hit the most (10).

The Cardinals have thrown 10 no-hitters during the lifetime of their franchise. These included gems by Hall of Famer Bob Gibson in 1971, Daffy Dean (Dizzy's brother) in 1934, and two by ace starter Bob Forsch in 1978 and 1983. Yet, Bud Smith's 2001 no-hitter is the last one thrown by a St. Louis pitcher. Despite having All-Star hurlers like Matt Morris, Chris Carpenter, Lance Lynn, and Adam Wainwright since 2001, the Cardinals currently have a no-hit drought that is longer than all but six major league teams. Considering the success of the Cardinals over the last 20+ years, this is surprising; although the highly successful Boston and Atlanta franchises are both on the list, too.

Table 7-4. Longest Active Franchise No-hit Droughts

Rank	Team	Pitcher	Date Score	Opponent
1	Cleveland Indians	Len Barker	5/15/1981 Cle 3-0	Toronto Blue Jays
2	Toronto Blue Jays	Dave Stieb (Only franchise no-hitter)	9/2/1990 Tor 3-0	Cleveland Indians

Rank	Team	Pitcher	Date Score	Opponent
3	Kansas City Royals	Bret Saberhagen	8/26/1991 KC 7-0	Chicago White Sox
4	Atlanta Braves	Kent Mercker	4/8/1994 Atl 6-0	Los Angeles Dodgers
5	*Texas Rangers*	*Kenny Rogers*	*7/28/1994 Tex 4-0*	*California Angels*
6	Pittsburgh Pirates	Francisco Cordova (9.0) Ricardo Rincon (1.0)	7/12/1997 Pit 3-0 (10 inn)	Houston Astros
7	St. Louis Cardinals	Bud Smith	9/3/2001 StL 4-0	San Diego Padres
8	Boston Red Sox	Jon Lester	5/19/2008 Bos 7-0	Kansas City Royals
9	Colorado Rockies	Ubaldo Jimenez (Only franchise no-hitter)	4/17/2010 Col 4-0	Atlanta Braves
10	Tampa Bay Rays	Matt Garza (Only franchise no-hitter)	7/26/2010 TB 5-0	Detroit Tigers

METHODOLOGY: This table shows the teams with the ten longest droughts between their last no-hitter and the present day. Teams are ranked based on the length of time since the last franchise no-hitter. For example, the #1 ranked team (Cleveland) has the longest period since their last no-hitter.

LEGEND: Dates are shown as month/day/year (for example, June 12, 2018, is shown as 6/12/2018). (9.0) and (1.0) = the number of innings pitched by an individual pitcher in a multiple pitcher no-hitter. (10 inn) = 10-inning game. If the game shown is the only no-hitter in franchise history, it is identified as such. *The two perfect games listed (Len Barker in 1981 and Kenny Rogers in 1994) are in italics.*

NOTE: The Cleveland Indians began playing as the Cleveland Guardians in 2022.

Bud Smith was born in Torrance, California. He played baseball at St. John Bosco High School in Bellflower, California, and at Los Angeles Harbor College. Smith was drafted by St. Louis in the fourth round of the 1998 draft out of Los Angeles Harbor College. He excelled in the minor leagues from 1998-2001, compiling a 36-20 record, and throwing two seven-inning no-hitters with the Arkansas

Travelers of the Texas League (AA) in 2000. He broke in with St. Louis in 2001 and had a 3-2 record coming into his no-hit game.

Eli Marrero, the St. Louis catcher that day, had a successful 10-year major league career, playing mostly with the Cardinals. He was drafted by St. Louis in the third round of the 1993 draft, breaking in with the Cardinals in 1997.

Below are excerpts from a remarkable interview with Bud Smith conducted by my associate Kevin McCaffrey. I've included the interview in its entirety (with only light editing for readability that didn't change the tone or content of the material). I encourage the reader to look at it. It's a fascinating view into Bud Smith and his perspective as a professional pitcher. Many thanks to Kevin for conducting the interview and, especially, to Bud Smith for his generous participation.

Bud Smith interview excerpts
Conducted by Kevin McCaffrey on November 16, 2021

Opening remarks, then interview:

Kevin McCaffrey (KM): Would you consider yourself to have been the best pitcher on your high school team and then later on your college team at Los Angeles Harbor College?

Bud Smith (BS): Okay, so high school I was more of a hitter. I did pitch and was pretty good, probably the best pitcher on my high school team. However, I was drafted (in the) ninth round as a centerfielder by the Detroit Tigers. And then went on to LA Harbor where I did both – hitter and pitcher – and was probably the 1-2 with Chad Qualls. And I was drafted as a pitcher in the fourth round, and he went in the 20th round and did not sign. So he went to Nevada Reno, and he was drafted in I believe the second round. But we were a pretty good 1-2 punch at my junior college. We went all the way to the JUCO World Series in Sacramento.

KM: And how did you do in that series?

BS: We lost both games – it was double elimination in the World Series – and we lost both games. I lost to pitcher Mike Neu who I think the Yankees drafted. (Author note: Mike Neu was drafted by the Reds in the 29th round of the 1999 draft). But it was one of those games – we lost 2-1. I believe he struck out 14 in seven innings, and I struck out 16 in eight innings, and I lost 2-1.

That was kind of the big game, all the scouts were there – they were there throughout the year, but that was the big game that they were there, and I pitched pretty well on a big stage. I had hit throughout that entire year as well and played outfield. I want to say I was the Player of the Year for California junior college. I hit like 16 home runs, and I pitched that year pretty well also. But yeah, I did both, and that was the thing. I still thought I was a hitter even then and after that I had gotten drafted by Chuck Fick of the Cardinals, who's still scouting today. I still run into Chuck, and he has signed a lot of major league players throughout the years to the Cardinals. Junior college was pretty serious 20 years ago.

BS: So, the next year I go to spring training and in my mind I already did Double-A, I went 5-1 in Triple-A, I'm ready, I'm going to spring training thinking I'm gonna make it, I'm still 21. And I remember Tony La Russa calls me in and says "Hey, we're gonna go with these veteran guys that we have. You have some time to grow in Triple-A and we can call you up. Go do your thing in Triple-A." And I was like "Man, all right."

But we had the Benes brothers, Dustin Hermanson, Darryl Kile, Matt Morris, Woody Williams – we literally had all veteran really good starters, so there just wasn't any room for me. And so, I go back to Triple-A, and I think I pitched pretty good, I think I was a Triple-A All Star, and boom, I think right at All Star break I get called in and they asked to call me up. So, I go up to St. Louis and I played that 2001 season – half season – I made 15-16 starts all year and had a great time. I had some success, I had a great time, had the no-hitter, pitched in the playoffs. I mean it was a fun season.

KM: And actually you won Game 4 of the first round of the playoffs.

BS: I was not scheduled to pitch that game. Pretty interesting, we were on the flight, we were down two games to one, and we're flying home with the day off and Tony La Russa and Dave Duncan were talking, and they called me up on the plane and said it was Dustin Hermanson's scheduled start. He was supposed to go that game and I was kinda out, with probably Matt Morris coming back if we had a Game 5. I was out and they called me in and said, "Hey, what do you think, we need you to beat these guys."

And here I'm now on a good 7-8 days of rest. "Oh yeah, I'd like to pitch against these guys, absolutely! Like, get me in there!" It was like, well, here's the thing what we're thinking. They have five left-handed hitters: Steve Finley, Luis Gonzalez, Mark Grace, Craig Counsell and Tony Womack were the Diamondbacks' lefties. And they said, "We want to throw you rather than Dustin in that game, what are your thoughts?" And I was like, "I'm all in, please give me the ball. I felt great this year, let's go." So they go, "OK, you're starting." And I literally had 48 hours to get ready and boom, here we are. I start, I go five innings, I think I gave up a run.

KM: Just one run and four hits.

BS: OK, I think that's what it was, and I thought I was going back out, I probably had 60 or 70 pitches, and I was like "Okay, I'm good." And they literally go, "That's it, you're done, we got Dustin Hermanson warming up." I'm like, "Go ahead." And he comes in and pitches unbelievable, I mean he throws I think four innings, (It was actually three innings – Steve Kline pitched the ninth) and it was like game over. And I was like, "Wow, that's the way to do it right there."

KM: So as far as the no-hitter, did you feel any different, good or bad, on that day: September 3rd, 2001?

BS: Oh yeah, very good. I felt in warmups I was feeling very good. It was the same team, the Padres, who just five days prior shelled me for eight or nine runs at Busch. Ryan Klesko hit a grand slam off his face on the Jumbotron, it was estimated it was like 504 feet. It was one of the longest home runs at Busch by a lefty and I just had one of those unforgettable games that I just didn't pitch good. So now we go out west and my next scheduled start is against the Padres again.

Now being that it's two hours from my hometown, I have about 40 to 50 family and friends on pass-list driving to San Diego to see this start. And that did it for me, that was always a big deal to have family support. Knowing I had a lot of family there was always a big kind of boost for me, let alone some of them for the first time ever seeing me professionally, so that pumped me up. And then I was warming up and I was like, "Man!" Not only was I pretty determined to face these guys again and get 'em, I felt really good warming up and the first three innings went by in a blink, I mean they looked like they had zero interest in me.

They just rocked me five days ago, it was like no big deal, you can tell, they were like "no big deal" on their first at-bats. And I kinda cruised through and I was on and "OK, that was the first time through." So, then the second time through got a little bit challenging and I think we started making a couple of plays and a lineout here and a nice catch right there, and the next thing you know I find myself — I believe it was the seventh – and I was on deck, and I heard the crowd yelling "We're gonna break this up, you rookie!"

And they're yelling at me, and I just remember going, "Man!" I look up at the scoreboard and that's when it just hit me. I just saw all zeroes and I went, "I am almost through this, I have a shot. This is really going on." And that's when it first hit me, it was the sixth or seventh inning – it was the seventh – I might've had nine outs left. But that's when it hit me, and "Man, OK, here we go."

KM: What pitches were working best for you that day?

BS: So, the fastball inside to the righties. The changeup down and away was really working. And as soon as one or the other seemed like they were taking 'em and I was hitting my spots and getting slowly a little more off the plate – an inch here, an inch there. And as soon as you start seeing some of the hitters' reactions, to look back like "man, that's not a strike" — they start questioning that umpire a little bit, and then you start to see them get a little more aggressive.

And I noticed that, that's how focused I was on this day. I was so locked in I could see what was going on. All of a sudden now these guys are pretty much digging in, determined to break this up. And as they were doing that then I started landing my curveball which I hadn't shown very much. I was able to throw that and now it was like, "Wait, he's been showing his fastball (and) changeup, now he's gonna start throwing a third pitch at us?" And that was on. For me having the curveball, all three pitches on was like, "Oh, this is gonna be fun now." Eli Marrero was catching, and he was mixing it up like really well.

And I found myself in the ninth inning, I think I, for the first time I had to step off the mound and they announce Tony Gwynn to pinch hit. I grew up in Long Beach, California where he's from and grew up going to Chris Gwynn and Tony Gwynn baseball camps and the whole thing. I mean, he was the biggest guy out of Long Beach, I mean it was like "Tony Gwynn is...." And this is his final year, off the bench he's batting I think over .340 off the bench that year. The guy has been playing 20 years, and batting titles. They pinch-hit him and I had to take a first step back and kinda regroup.

KM: Yeah, I was just looking at the box score and he was hitting .345 that year, just playing part time when you faced him that day.

BS: Yeah, off the bench he was hitting .345. I mean it was like once they announced him – and we didn't go over him. Before the game Dave Duncan pitching coach, myself and Eli Marrero and Matheny, all the catchers, everybody would go over their entire starting lineup, how we (are) gonna pitch 'em. Dave Duncan had elaborate pitching charts and hitting charts on all these guys, so we knew how we were gonna attack these guys. And on the bench you go over all the right-handed hitters, if they pinch hit they were probably gonna pinch-hit a righty. So, we go over all the right-handed hitters. We did not go over Tony Gwynn, at all. So, when he pinch hit my only thought was *"hit a spot, fastball away and hopefully he hits it at somebody."*

I really thought that, that's all I thought. Eli called fastball away first pitch, I missed. He called fastball away second pitch, I hit my spot down and away and he hit a base hit up the middle, is what I thought. Rocket right by me, and I turned around, and Edgar Renteria is behind second base, one hop and he throws him out. And it's funny to think, oh, they're shifting 20 years ago? But we were, I mean we really were. And that was pretty rare to see where a shortstop was at for that play, but they must have known lefty-on-lefty, he does go up the middle.

I'm sure he does it every time, so I think that's where they meant to play him. Instead of a one hop base hit up the middle (like) I thought, Renteria caught it, no problem, one hop. That was the moment I said, "I think I'm gonna do this. If I can get Tony Gwynn out, I'm gonna be able to do this. I'm doing this right now." Now I was a couple of outs away, it might have been in the eighth, I think, I was about an inning and-a-third away or something like that.

KM: So, on that ball Renteria was positioned perfectly. Were there any really great defensive plays during the game where you actually came close to losing the no-hitter?

BS: There was a line drive to short that Renteria jumped and got early in the fourth. That was a base hit, I thought, off the bat. It was a line drive and he jumped and caught it. There was a foul ball J.D. Drew caught running over the bullpens that were right next to foul territory and he made a great reach out grab. It was foul but it was a great play that got me out of an inning. And then I think there was a chopper in the sixth or seventh that Placido Polanco at third got lost in the lights. It was a high chopper and he had to be quick, and I saw him kind of waiting for it to come down and at the last second he kind of ducks his head and leaves his glove there, and it hit his glove.

    I asked him the next day and he said, "Oh, I lost it in the lights, I was completely lost. I just put my glove where I thought the ball would come out and I felt it hit, I transferred and threw him out by a step." Then, in the ninth inning there was a chopper Ryan Klesko hit with a full count that Renteria backhanded on the run and threw him out. I think that made it two outs in the ninth, that was unbelievable. Everyone asks me, "What was your best pitch?" And I've always said my best pitch was my defense. I wasn't a big strikeout guy. I think I had seven strikeouts that game but that was pretty high for me. I was relying on defense.

KM: And of course, the final out Phil Nevin grounds one back to you, so your defense won it for you.

BS: I knew Phil Nevin from El Dorado High School 10 minutes from me, he goes to Cal State Fullerton, first rounder, all the accolades. He was having a phenomenal year that year, and I was just cross-towning my changeup to him: fastballs in, fastballs in. I fell behind 2-0 and I throw a changeup. Every single time I fell behind I would just keep throwing that changeup and then I finally threw a 2-1 changeup, and he grounded it right back to me.

    And it was kinda funny 'cause right when I fielded it and turned, I don't know why but I just knew I did it, and for some reason I was expecting McGwire to be there, and it wasn't. For some reason it was Pujols, the guy I kinda was close to, and same age and we're in the minor leagues the year before and it was like "What is he doing there?" And we hugged it out and I forgot I'm supposed to hug my catcher. Albert's hugging me and I'm going "I need to hug my catcher." So, I turned, and Eli came running over and then we dogpiled. It was unbelievable.

KM: You mentioned Eli Marrero, you were a rookie, did you shake him off at all during that game?

BS: So, I did not shake him off one time. However, we cross-counted one pitch and I stopped mid-windup because I think he called fastball outside to Ray Lankford, and I said yes and I went windup and as I lifted and looked at my target, he was all the way inside and he had just called outside, and I was already going fastball outside. It was a full count, and I was lifting, and I realized he moved, and I just stopped. I didn't throw the pitch. And I had to reset, and then he called fastball away and he went away, and I actually caught Lankford looking on fastball away which I still wonder if he thought I was going back in, because those guys can kinda feel where these catchers are moving.

He maybe looked back when I stopped, something like that. And then the next pitch I didn't shake off, I went right back to the same call, he might've thought, was going back in. Yeah, I didn't shake very much as a rookie, I trusted those guys. Eli wasn't a full-time catcher, but Matheny was kind of the main guy. Eli was kind of the backup catcher, but he caught a lot, he played a lot of outfield as well, but I mean he was a baseball guy. He knew what he was doing back there.

KM: Was he your catcher frequently or did you ever get to request Matheny being your catcher?

BS: Matheny caught most of my games. Matheny probably caught 10 or 12 of my 15 starts. That was probably Marrero's fourth or fifth start that year for me. Matheny caught the playoff game but the next year, 2002, since he had caught that game (the no-hitter) I think Eli caught every start except maybe one. But that's how you get that rapport, they kind of link you together.

KM: Are you still in touch with Eli?

BS: Not really. Albert was the only one really that I remain, out of all those guys. Jim Edmonds is a local guy. I've run into him since here and there, but for the most part a lot of those guys I haven't remained in contact with.

KM: You threw 134 pitches in that game which is a hell of a lot for a 21-year-old pitcher, and I read that Dave Duncan said he'd hoped someone would get a hit so they could take you out because they were concerned about your pitch count. Do you think that pitch count affected your health at all, your arm or anything?

BS: I really don't. To this day I really don't, because I know coming into my career at Double-A, Triple-A, even some starts earlier, there were games I would go over 100 pitches. Not ever 130, but I went to 110 sometimes in Triple-A or sometimes in Double-A even. I mean it wasn't always back then "at 100 pitches you're gone" type of thing. I know when I did get called up that rookie year La Russa was pretty tight, I mean there were games that I was like, "Oh, I'm good." You know, and he's like "five and two-thirds and you're at 81 pitches. You're done."

I'm going, "Man, I can stay in, what are we doing?" I'd forget, you got major league bullpens and you've got some really good guys, but I always wanted to stay in. So, to me I knew I was fatiguing for sure in that game, once I got over 100, 120. The first thing when it was done, the next day he said you're skipping your next start so there I was gonna have nine days of rest. And then September 11th happened, and I had another three or four days where we were stuck in Milwaukee while all that was going on.

And then the first one back I started in Milwaukee, the first game back to baseball, so I had probably 14 days off. So, I was plenty rested, and I felt better that start than I did. And I felt really good in the no-hitter, but I threw seven shutout (innings) in my next outing in Milwaukee. I don't think I could've pitched better. That was my best two back-to-back outings right there, 16 shutout innings. I mean it was like I was on a nice little roll. Everyone asks that, "Oh, is that how you think you got hurt?" I really don't, I really don't.

KM: So, do you have any memorabilia or souvenirs or anything from the no-hitter?

BS: The cool thing, the trainer with the Cardinals, he used to save all the baseballs after the game, and he would write in calligraphy on the balls. Like "my first major league single, my first major league win." So, I have like six or seven baseballs that he wrote on. He wrote on the no-hitter, the box score, the date, Qualcomm Stadium. He kinda dressed up some balls which is pretty cool that I have, and McGwire gave me a pair of batting gloves – he hit two home runs in one of my starts, and then the Hall of Fame for the no-hitter took my hat and my one cleat which was pretty neat. My son played in the Cooperstown baseball tournament, we got to go to the Hall of Fame, and they displayed it for us. My hat and cleat so my son's team could kinda see it that it was in there.

KM: I was going to ask you about that if you'd been to the Hall of Fame section about the no-hitters, so that's great, that's cool.

BS: Yeah, it was really neat because we got there and I had asked, "You guys have a no-hitter section" and they said "We do but it's not displayed, we rotate different things. He said it's because 70-80% of our items are in a waterproof sealed vault underground. We can only display 20% of our items so the no-hitter thing is not circulating right now." I told him I threw a no-hitter, so he says, "Oh man, come on in." He went and grabbed it for me and brought it out and we were in a little theater room, and he displayed it and welcomed us to take photos of it, so it was cool.

KM: A couple more things, as far as a career highlight, would you say that the no-hitter or pitching in that playoff game – was one a bigger thrill than the other?

BS: That no-hitter was definitely a great game, that kinda changed everything just in terms of I had that under my belt so early it kinda showed that I belonged. It kinda proved that "Yeah, I do belong up here." So, then it was like a lot of the pressure was taken off after that, like if there was any doubt like "He needed to be sent back down" that game kinda stopped that. And that's how I felt, I was like, "All right, I'm good now, I'm here to stay."

The playoff game was a surprise, I wasn't expecting to start, I wasn't scheduled to start, and when they changed it based on the five lefties, I mean it was just like I didn't even have time to really panic or anything. It was just like I gotta get prepared and go. I got a day and a half. So that was fun to get us to Game 5, but I think the no-hitter was just a bigger kind of deal. Just the amount of media I was getting for the next two weeks, everybody was talking about it non-stop.

KM: That just about wraps it up, do you have any other favorite stories you might have, whether about the no-hitter, your time in the big leagues, your time now as a scout, anything else you'd like to talk about?

BS: The one thing, I don't know why, but this story popped up when you asked if I shook off Eli much. My rookie year I had shook off Mike Matheny once and it was against Magglio Ordonez of the White Sox, and I believe he hit over 30 home runs that year. And I remember I struck him out his first at bat with a changeup. Second at bat he came up, two runners on and I was battling, I probably threw 5-6 pitches to him, it was a 2-2 count, and I was blown away. (Matheney) never called a changeup, and I was waiting and waiting, I kept throwing pitches, he kept fouling them off and I'm like, "What are we doing, I struck him out with a changeup, what are we waiting for?"

So, I shook off to the changeup and threw it exactly where I wanted, down and away, and he hit a three-run homer to right-center, 460 feet and luckily that was all I gave up, just three runs. David Wells gave up eight early and I beat them 8-3 and I just remember Matheny calling me over after the game and he goes, "Don't ever shake me off again, rookie. Did you learn anything today?" I say, "He hit it like he knew it was coming." Matheny says, "Well what did you get him out on the first at bat?" "Changeup."

And he goes, "So guess what he's taking away from your arsenal? He will not let you get him out on a changeup, so he's gonna sit on that. So now you have to adjust." I go, "Wait a second, my whole life if I got a guy out with a certain pitch in high school, in college, in the minors, if I got a guy on a curveball the next at bat at some point throw him a curveball and I'll get him out again." He goes, "Not at this level. These guys adjust at bat to at bat." And that's when I was just went mind blown. Like wow, these guys are adjusting that quick. It was like shocking. I mean I never shook Matheny off ever again.

KM: Welcome to the big leagues kid.

BS: Exactly.

KM: Hey Bud, thank you so much, this has been great. I've been doing several of these interviews and this is one of the best. Absolutely, this was great.

BS: Oh, awesome! Yeah, when it's all done send me a little meme or a picture of the book so I can check it out.

KM: Oh yeah definitely, I'll keep you posted. Thank you for taking the time, I really appreciate it. And good luck finding the next Vladimir Guerrero, Jr. for the Blue Jays.
BS: Oh geez, we got a couple of good ones, him and Bichette.
KM: Oh yeah, man, they're a damn good team.
BS: Oh yeah. All right, thanks a lot Kevin.

Chapter 8

Dallas Braden: Mother's Day Perfection

May 9, 2010
Sometimes baseball is absolutely perfect as Oakland journeyman
Dallas Braden pitches baseball's 19th perfect game in
front of his grandmother on Mother's Day 2010

"It was hard to fight 'em (my tears) back. (Braden has) had a lot of things happen to him in his life, and even the last few years has had some unlucky things happen to him in the game of baseball. So that was special to see."

Catcher Landon Powell ("'Grandma Peggy' gets the final word on A's pitcher Dallas Braden, and on A-Rod," *Oakland Tribune*, May 10, 2010).

"... stick it, A-Rod."

Quote from a chuckling Peggy Lindsey, Dallas Braden's grandmother, who was in the stands watching her grandson throw the 19th perfect game in major league history. She was referring to a "don't step on my mound incident" that happened between Braden and Alex Rodriguez a few weeks prior when the Yankees were playing the Athletics in Oakland ("Braden's perfect game 19th ever and second straight against Rays," *ESPN.com*, May 9, 2010).

"The guy had the pitches when he needed them. I didn't see two pitches in the same spot the whole game."

Tampa Bay Rays All-Star third baseman Evan Longoria describing Braden's pitching prowess that day ("Braden throws 19th perfect game," *San Francisco Chronicle*, May 10, 2010).

"I told him he needs to quit stealing my thunder. He makes ridiculous plays."

Dallas Braden describing the outstanding fielding support he received from Oakland third baseman Kevin Kouzmanoff ("Braden's perfect game 19th ever and second straight against Rays," *ESPN.com*, May 9, 2010).

"Mother's Day was not a happy day for me. My Grandmom and I might get dinner, but it was not a celebration. Throwing the perfect game on that day changed everything in that regard."

Dallas Braden describing the feelings he had throwing a perfect game on Mother's Day 2010 in front of his grandmother Peggy, the woman who raised him after his mother died when he was a senior in high school (interview with Rob Adams in conjunction with writing this book, 2021).

Sometimes baseball is simply perfect. On Mother's Day 2010, 24th-round draft pick Dallas Braden threw a perfect game in front of 12,000+ fans at the Oakland Coliseum. Included in the delirious hometown crowd was his beloved grandmother, Peggy Lindsey. Lindsey was the woman who raised Braden after his mother died unexpectedly from cancer nine years earlier. Braden credits his "Grandmom" for setting him on the right path when his life was headed completely in the wrong direction.

Several weeks prior, journeyman pitcher Braden – who had a 3-2 win-loss record so far in this young season and a lifetime record of 17-23 – had gotten into an altercation with Yankee superstar Alex Rodriguez when Rodriguez ran across the mound as he was returning to the dugout between innings. Braden took offense to Rodriguez breaking one of the "unwritten rules of baseball" that it's just the pitchers who have access to the mound. While there was no physical interaction between the two, Braden called out Rodriguez right then and there.

"I don't care if I'm Cy Young or the 25th man on the roster, if I've got the ball in my hand and I'm on that mound, that's my mound," Braden would say after the game.

Because it was a pitcher who was looked at as a bit player for a mediocre team who had called out one of baseball's premier players (and a Yankee at that), the incident blossomed into a full-blown story that sportswriters were following every time Braden took the mound. His outspoken grandmother was happy to let people know what she thought about A-Rod when she told him to "stick it" after Braden's perfect game.

The game itself had quite a few exciting moments, many of which highlighted the glove work of Oakland third baseman Kevin Kouzmanoff, who single-handedly was responsible for several perfect-game-saving plays. It started from the very first hitter, Tampa Bay's leadoff batter Jason Bartlett, who lined an 0-1 fastball right over third base. Kouzmanoff leapt over the bag to snare the potential extra base hit to secure the game's first out.

Leading off the fourth inning, Bartlett again threatened to reach base, this time on a slow dribbler down the third base line. Kouzmanoff raced in, grabbed the ball, and fired to first, barely getting the speedy Bartlett on what looked like a sure infield single. Kouzmanoff also snared three popups in Oakland's expansive foul territory that day.

With one out in the top of the sixth inning, Tampa Bay catcher Dioner Navarro fouled off a 2-1 pitch from Braden. Kouzmanoff sprinted to make a sliding catch in the dirt in front of the Oakland dugout to get the out. The next batter, right fielder Gabe Kapler, fouled out to Kouzmanoff on the twelfth pitch of his at bat. Perhaps the most dramatic foulout of the day came with one out in the eighth inning when Tampa Bay first baseman Carlos Pena fouled the first pitch from Braden that drifted toward the left field stands. Kouzmanoff snared that one as he ran down the Oakland dugout steps. Appreciating Kouzmanoff's glovework, Braden later remarked "(Kouz) was literally everywhere that day."

Even beyond the 12-pitch at bat in the sixth, number nine hitter Gabe Kapler was a tough out that day. In the third inning, he flew out to left fielder Eric Patterson on a ball right down the left field line. In the top of the ninth, Kapler came up as the 27th batter Braden had faced that day. He was the only thing standing between Braden and a perfect game.

With a 2-1 count to Kapler, Braden threw a fastball he described as "painted" on the outside corner, but umpire Jim Wolf disagreed and called it a ball to make the count 3-1. Braden, however, thought it was 2-2. Oakland catcher Landon Powell, knowing the correct count, called for a changeup. Braden, stubbornly thinking the count was two balls and two strikes, shook off Powell. Kapler was likely looking changeup, and Braden's fastball jammed him into grounding to shortstop Cliff Pennington, who threw over to first baseman Daric Barton to complete the perfect game.

Throughout the day, Braden's fastball hovered just above the mid-80s, but he used 68-mph changeups — often on two-strike counts — to induce six Tampa Bay strikeouts. Apart from Kouzmanoff's fielding excellence, there were also hard-hit flies that were snagged by Eric Patterson in left and Rajai Davis in center, though they were caught without too much drama. On this day, the few hard-hit balls always found Oakland gloves. It was a magnificent performance from a pitcher who was seen as a fill-in starter at best, and not anyone to build a rotation around.

This wasn't a cheap victory against a lower division team, either. The Tampa Bay Rays were only one full season removed from being crowned American League pennant winners in 2008. At the time of this game, the Rays had the best record in the American League at 21-9 and they were managed by the legendary Joe Maddon. Tampa Bay would go on to finish the season at the top of the American League with a record of 96-66, good enough to just edge their American League East rivals the New York Yankees for the division title. The team featured All-Star left fielder Carl Crawford and third baseman Evan Longoria, along with sluggers Carlos Pena, Ben Zobrist, Melvin Upton, Jr., and Willie Aybar. Tampa Bay was stacked with strong hitters from the #2 to the #7 positions in the lineup that day. Yet, no one could touch Braden as he struck out six Rays, and scattered three foul outs, five lineouts, six flyouts, and seven groundouts.

Oakland backed up Braden early, scoring runs in the second, third, and fourth innings to give the Athletics a 4-0 lead heading into the top of the fifth. The primary contributors were Kouzmanoff, Powell, first baseman Daric Barton, and right fielder Ryan Sweeney, who managed to cobble together rallies using base hits. Overall, Oakland racked up 12 hits and two walks as they cruised to victory against Tampa Bay's All-Star starting pitcher James Shields.

As expected, Braden's Game Score of 93 is the highest score he ever achieved, although he threw another shutout in August 2010 (Game Score of 80) and an eight-inning, one-hit, scoreless effort in September that earned him a score of 85. The table below shows a comparison of the Game Scores of all 21 perfect games since 1900. Of course, the primary differentiator is how many strikeouts a pitcher achieved as he was retiring all 27 batters he faced. Led by Sandy Koufax and Matt Cain with scores of 101, a case can be made that those are the most dominant games ever thrown by a pitcher.

Table 8-1. Game Scores for Perfect Games

Rank	Pitcher	Team	Date / Score	Opponent	GSc	Innings / Strikeouts
1 (tie)	Sandy Koufax	LA Dodgers	9/9/1965 LA 1-0	Chicago Cubs	101	9.0 IP 14 Ks
1 (tie)	Matt Cain	SF Giants	6/13/2012 SF 10-0	Houston Astros	101	9.0 IP 14 Ks
3	Randy Johnson	Arizona D-backs	5/18/2004 Ari 2-0	Atlanta Braves	100	9.0 IP 13 Ks
4 (tie)	Felix Hernandez	Seattle Mariners	8/15/2012 Sea 1-0	Tampa Bay Rays	99	9.0 IP 12 Ks
5 (tie)	Catfish Hunter	Oakland Athletics	5/8/1968 Oak 4-0	Minnesota Twins	98	9.0 IP 11 Ks
5 (tie)	Len Barker	Cleveland Indians	5/15/1981 Cle 3-0	Toronto Blue Jays	98	9.0 IP 11 Ks
5 (tie)	David Wells	New York Yankees	5/17/1998 NY 4-0	Minnesota Twins	98	9.0 IP 11 Ks
5 (tie)	Roy Halladay	Philadelphia Phillies	5/29/2010 Phi 1-0	Florida Marlins	98	9.0 IP 11 Ks
9 (tie)	Jim Bunning	Philadelphia Phillies	6/21/1964 (1) Phi 6-0	New York Mets	97	9.0 IP 10 Ks
9 (tie)	Mike Witt	California Angels	9/30/1984 Cal 1-0	Texas Rangers	97	9.0 IP 10 Ks
9 (tie)	David Cone	New York Yankees	7/18/1999 NYY 6-0	Montreal Expos	97	9.0 IP 10 Ks
12	Philip Humber	Chicago White Sox	4/21/2012 CHW 4-0	Seattle Mariners	96	9.0 IP 9 Ks

Rank	Pitcher	Team	Date Score	Opponent	GSc	Innings Strikeouts
13 (tie)	Cy Young	Boston Americans	5/5/1904 Bos 3-0	Philadelphia Athletics	95	9.0 IP 8 Ks
13 (tie)	Kenny Rogers	Texas Rangers	7/28/1994 Tex 4-0	California Angels	95	9.0 IP 8 Ks
15 (tie)	Don Larsen	New York Yankees	10/8/1956 NY 2-0	Brooklyn Dodgers	94	9.0 IP 7 Ks
15 (tie)	Tom Browning	Cincinnati Reds	9/16/1988 Cin 1-0	Los Angeles Dodgers	94	9.0 IP 7 Ks
17 (tie)	Charlie Robertson	Chicago White Sox	4/30/1922 Chi 2-0	Detroit Tigers	93	9.0 IP 6 Ks
17 (tie)	Mark Buehrle	Chicago White Sox	7/23/2009 Chi 5-0	Tampa Bay Rays	93	9.0 IP 6 Ks
17 (tie)	Dallas Braden	Oakland Athletics	5/9/2010 Oak 4-0	Tampa Bay Rays	93	9.0 IP 6 Ks
20	Dennis Martinez	Montreal Expos	7/28/1991 Mon 2-0	Los Angeles Dodgers	92	9.0 IP 5 Ks
21	Addie Joss	Cleveland Indians	10/2/1908 Cle 1-0	Chicago White Sox	90	9.0 IP 3 Ks

METHODOLOGY: This table lists the Game Scores for all perfect games from 1900-2021 and includes all regular season and postseason games. Game Score (GSc) measures a pitcher's performance in any given game started. Introduced by baseball writer/statistician Bill James in the 1980s, Game Score is presented as a figure between 0-100 -- except for extreme outliers -- and usually falls between 40-70.

LEGEND: Dates are shown as month/day/year (for example, June 12, 2018, is shown as 6/12/2018). IP = innings pitched; K(s) = strikeout(s); and (1) or (2) = first or second game of a doubleheader.

NOTE 1: Sandy Koufax's 14-strikeout perfect game against the Chicago Cubs is a top contender for the title of "the best-pitched game of all time." It was his fourth no-hitter and came against an excellent hitting Cubs team that included Hall of Famers Billy Williams, Ron Santo, and Ernie Banks as the 3-4-5 hitters in the lineup. This game also was the starting point for the Cubs' remarkable 50-season streak of not being no-hit. Pitcher Bob Hendley of the Cubs was also outstanding, as the Dodgers only managed two baserunners and one hit, setting records for fewest baserunners and hits in a game by both teams combined.

NOTE 2: Matt Cain's perfect game is a statistical match with Sandy Koufax's 1965 game with a 101 Game Score. The Astros were in rebuilding mode in 2012, as they finished the season with 107 losses. Even though they were last in the National League in hitting, they did have budding stars in players like Jose Altuve and J.D. Martinez in their lineup that day. While a Giants victory was assured as the contest went on (the final score was 10-0), the perfect game was saved in the seventh inning when right fielder Gregor Blanco made a legendary diving catch in deep right-center field to prevent an extra-base hit.

NOTE 3: Don Larsen's October 1956 perfect game was in Game 5 of the World Series against the Brooklyn Dodgers. This win gave New York a 3-2 advantage en route to a seven-game series victory. All other perfect games were thrown during the regular season.

NOTE 4: Len Barker's 1981 perfect game was also the last no-hitter thrown by the Indians (now known as the Guardians). Cleveland currently holds the active record for longest no-hitter drought in the majors. Mike Witt's perfect game was on Opening Day of the Angels' 1984 season. Following Tom Browning's perfect game, he would also lose a perfect game in the ninth inning the next season. This is the closest any pitcher has come to throwing two perfect games.

NOTE 5: Cy Young's 1904 perfect game was part of a streak of 25.1 consecutive hitless innings. This is still a Major League record.

NOTE 6: David Wells' perfect game was part of a streak of 38 consecutive batters retired. This was a new American League record at the time. The current American League record is 45, established by Mark Buehrle in 2009 during three starts, the second of which was his perfect game. The Major League record is 46 consecutive batters, set by Yusmeiro Petit of the San Francisco Giants in 2014 through a combination of the final out of one start and six relief appearances.

With Sandy Koufax's game signaling the start of the Chicago Cubs incredible 50-year stretch of not being no-hit, it's interesting to see which other teams have gone for decades without being no-hit. The longest currently active streak is by the Oakland Athletics, as they were last no-hit over 30 years ago in 1991 – they are #10 in the table below.

Table 8-2. Longest Team Streaks Without Being No-Hit

Rank	Team	Last No-Hitter Team	Pitcher	Next No-Hitter Team	Pitcher	Games
1	Chicago Cubs	9/9/1965 LA Dodgers	Sandy Koufax	7/25/2015 Phi Phillies	Cole Hamels	7,920
2	Cincinnati Reds	6/23/1971 Phi Phillies	Rick Wise	4/21/2016 Chi Cubs	Jake Arrieta	7,109
3	New York Yankees	9/20/1958 Bal Orioles	Hoyt Wilhelm	6/11/2003 Hou Astros	Six Pitchers	7,047
4	Pittsburgh Pirates	8/14/1971 StL Cardinals	Bob Gibson	9/28/2012 Cin Reds	Homer Bailey	6,541
5	St. Louis Cardinals	5/11/1919 Cin Reds	Hod Eller	5/15/1960 Chi Cubs	Don Cardwell	6,341
6	Kansas City Royals	5/15/1973 Cal Angels	Nolan Ryan	5/19/2008 Bos Red Sox	Jon Lester	5,550
7	Chicago Cubs	5/2/1917 (10) Cin Reds	Fred Toney	6/19/1952 Bro Dodgers	Carl Erskine	5,413
8	New York Giants	8/31/1915 Chi Cubs	Jimmy Lavender	9/9/1948 Bro Dodgers	Rex Barney	5,053
9	Cincinnati Reds	5/8/1907 Bos Doves	Big Jeff Pfeffer	4/30/1940 Bro Dodgers	Tex Carleton	4,904
10	Oakland Athletics	7/13/1991 Bal Orioles	Four Pitchers	Ongoing	Through 2021	4,767

METHODOLOGY: This table lists the longest team streaks without being no-hit from 1900-2021. Teams are ranked in order of the most games played without being no-hit by an opposing team. No-hit games that were less than nine innings or in other ways did not qualify under major league guidelines as a no-hitter are not included. Postseason games are not included in the tabulation of games in the streak, nor are they included as defining the beginning or end of the streak.

LEGEND: Dates are shown as month/day/year (for example, June 12, 2018, is shown as 6/12/2018). Last No-Hitter = the date and team of the last no-hitter – the streak would start with the next game. Next No-Hitter = the date and team of the next no-hitter thrown against the team in question, thereby ending the streak. The game prior to that date is the last game in the streak. Games = the number of regular season games a team played without having an official no-hitter thrown against them. (10) indicates the game was a 10-inning no-hitter. *The perfect game thrown by Sandy Koufax that became the starting point for Chicago's record streak is in italics.*

NOTE 1: Roy Halladay's 2010 no-hitter against the Cincinnati Reds in the first game of the 2010 NLDS would have ended the Reds' second-longest streak a little more than five seasons earlier. With over 800 less games played, this would have placed Cincinnati in fifth place behind the St. Louis Cardinals if it had counted.

NOTE 2: Oakland's streak is ongoing as of the end of the 2021 season and is the longest current streak in effect. If the Athletics were to continue their streak, they would pass the Chicago Cubs for the Major League record midway through the 2041 season.

NOTE 3: The pitchers who threw the no-hitter for the Astros against the Yankees in 2003 were Roy Oswalt with 1 inning pitched (IP), Pete Munro (2.2 IP), Kirk Saarloos (1.1 IP), Brad Lidge (2 IP), Octavio Dotel (1 IP), and Billy Wagner (1 IP). The fractions (.1 and .2) refer to one-third and two-thirds of an inning pitched. For example, 1.1 refers to one and one-third innings pitched.

NOTE 4: The pitchers who threw the no-hitter for the Orioles against the Athletics in 1991 were Bob Milacki with 6 innings pitched (IP), Mike Flanagan (1 IP), Mark Williamson (1 IP), and Gregg Olson (1 IP).

Dallas Braden was born in Phoenix, Arizona, but grew up in the shadow of the Oakland Coliseum in the nearby community of Stockton, California. He played high school ball, but his senior year was turned upside down when his mother contracted brain cancer and died. It was then that his grandmother Peggy stepped in and took responsibility for Braden's upbringing. By Dallas's own admission, she needed to straighten him out on numerous occasions, for which he is forever grateful.

Braden was selected by the Oakland Athletics out of Texas Tech in the 2004 amateur draft. Developing his skills in the minors from 2004-2006, Braden made his major league debut in April 2007. His first season with Oakland was a disaster, though, as he went 1-8 with a 6.72 ERA. As a result, he bounced back and forth between the majors and Oakland's AA and AAA clubs in Midland, Texas, and nearby Sacramento. Braden improved in 2008 and finally stuck in the Oakland starting rotation in 2009, as he went 8-9 with a 3.89 ERA over 22 starts that year. 2010 – the year of his perfect game – was Braden's best season, when he compiled an 11-14 record with a 3.50 ERA over 30 starts for an 81-81 Oakland club.

His career tailed off after his 109-pitch perfect game, though. Over his next eight starts, Braden went 0-4, with Oakland losing all eight of those games. At the conclusion of that stretch in late June, Braden went on the disabled list with shoulder issues. He would return to the A's starting rotation in late July and continued to be effective, but a shoulder injury and the following surgery effectively ended his major league career in 2011. Since then, Braden has launched a successful career as a baseball color analyst on ESPN Monday Night Baseball and on NBC Sports California broadcasting Oakland games.

Oakland catcher Landon Powell, Braden's batterymate that day, was the Athletics' backup catcher in 2010 season (Kurt Suzuki was the regular starter). A first-round pick for Oakland in the same 2004 draft where they chose Braden, Powell's career was limited to being a backup catcher with Oakland from 2009-2011 due to injuries. One advantage Powell did have that day in 2010 was his familiarity with Dallas Braden. As Powell described in a recent interview with the "Midland Baseball" website, he was very familiar with Dallas Braden's pitching abilities because he had caught him "one hundred times" coming up through the minors.

"In pro-ball, Dallas and I were drafted together, so I had caught him pretty much at every level in the minor leagues, and we were rookies at the major league level together, so I was very familiar with him, having caught him one hundred times before that day. He went out that day, his best pitch was a screwball, he also threw a fastball, slider, but his screwball was working really good that day, and that was something I recognized from the get-go. I think the first inning was three up, three down, second inning there were a couple balls hit hard, but the plays were made. Another fun fact about that day, before I get too far into this, the left fielder that day was Eric Patterson, another former Midland Redskin, so we had two Redskins in the lineup that day for the perfect game," Powell said.

"I didn't really think much of it early in the game, I've been in a lot of games where there was a no-hitter going into the fifth, sixth, seventh innings of a game, but something always would finally happen. Dallas was not an All-Star or a stud by any means for the major league level, he was just a contact left-hander. He had never thrown a complete game at that point in his career, and his ERA was in the 5.00s somewhere, so he wasn't really a guy that anybody thought something like this would happen to. It was about the sixth inning, and I knew he was pitching well, I think we were up like 3-0, pretty much cruising along. Well, I looked up on the scoreboard that inning, and I was like 'man he's got a no-hitter going!' But as I was looking at the scoreboard, I said 'wait a second, I don't think he's walked anybody, and no errors, and that's the first time it dawned on me this isn't a no-hitter, this is a perfect game!' I mean that is a big deal, a perfect game has happened only 18 times, and that was when I got a lump in my throat, and I finally realized the severity of what was happening," Powell added.

Powell, a native North Carolinian, has established a successful post-playing career as head coach for the North Greenville University Crusaders (located in South Carolina) since 2014.

As might be imagined, journeyman starter Dallas Braden and backup catcher Landon Powell combined to form the lowest JAWS of any perfect game battery in baseball history. At 5.2 total career JAWS value, the Braden-Powell duo is #21 out of 21 modern-day perfect game batteries, and it's not even close, as shown in the chart below.

Table 8-3. Perfect Game Pitcher-Catcher JAWS rankings

Rank	Date	Pitcher	JAWS (Rank)	Catcher	JAWS (Rank)	Total JAWS	Team
1	5/5/1904	Cy Young	120.8 (1)	Lou Criger	14.8 (10)	135.6	Boston Americans
2	7/28/1994	Kenny Rogers	42.8 (8)	Ivan Rodriguez	54.2 (1)	97.0	Texas Rangers
3	5/18/2004	Randy Johnson	81.3 (2)	Robby Hammock	0.6 (19)	81.9	Arizona Diamondbacks
4	5/17/1998	David Wells	42.4 (11)	Jorge Posada	37.6 (4)	80.0	New York Yankees
5	5/9/2010	Roy Halladay	57.4 (3)	Carlos Ruiz	21.8 (7)	79.2	Philadelphia Phillies
6	6/13/2012	Matt Cain	29.1 (14)	Buster Posey	40.7 (3)	69.8	San Francisco Giants
7	6/21/1964	Jim Bunning	54.2 (4)	Gus Triandos	14.2 (11-T)	68.4	Philadelphia Phillies
8	10/8/1956	Don Larsen	17.4 (17)	Yogi Berra	48.8 (2)	66.2	New York Yankees

Rank	Date	Pitcher	JAWS (Rank)	Catcher	JAWS (Rank)	Total JAWS	Team
9	7/18/1999	David Cone	52.8 (5)	Joe Girardi	6.3 (16)	59.1	New York Yankees
10	8/15/2012	Felix Hernandez	44.3 (8)	John Jaso	11.1 (14)	55.4	Seattle Mariners
11	7/28/1991	Dennis Martinez	41.0 (12)	Ron Hassey	14.2 (11-T)	55.2	Montreal Expos
12	5/8/1968	Catfish Hunter	37.9 (13)	Jim Pagliaroni	15.2 (9)	53.1	Oakland Athletics
13	10/2/1908	Addie Joss	42.5 (10)	Jay Clarke	9.5 (15)	52.0	Cleveland Naps
14	7/23/2009	Mark Buehrle	47.4 (6-T)	Ramon Castro	3.0 (18)	50.4	Chicago White Sox
15	9/9/1965	Sandy Koufax	47.4 (6-T)	Jeff Torborg	0.4 (20)	47.8	Los Angeles Dodgers
16	9/30/1984	Mike Witt	21.4 (15)	Bob Boone	23.9 (6)	45.3	California Angels
17	4/30/1922	Charlie Robertson	6.8 (19)	Ray Schalk	29.5 (5)	36.3	Chicago White Sox
18	5/15/1981	Len Barker	13.2 (18)	Ron Hassey	14.2 (11-T)	27.4	Cleveland Indians
19	9/16/1988	Tom Browning	18.9 (16)	Jeff Reed	5.7 (17)	24.6	Cincinnati Reds
20	4/21/2012	Phillip Humber	1.7 (21)	A.J. Pierzynski	20.9 (8)	22.6	Chicago White Sox
21	5/9/2010	Dallas Braden	5.0 (20)	Landon Powell	0.2 (21)	5.2	Oakland Athletics

METHODOLOGY: This table lists all the perfect games thrown from 1900-2021. Individual games are ranked from highest to lowest by the combined career Jaffe Wins Above Replacement Score (JAWS) of the pitcher-catcher battery in the perfect game. JAWS is a sabermetric baseball statistic developed to evaluate the strength of a player's career and merit for induction into the Baseball Hall of Fame. It is created by averaging a player's career Wins Above Replacement (WAR) with their 7-year peak WAR. WAR measures a player's value in all facets of the game by deciphering how many more wins he's worth than a replacement-level player at his same position.

LEGEND: Dates are shown as month/day/year (for example, June 12, 2018, is shown as 6/12/2018). Next to each pitcher's and catcher's name is a career JAWS value and a ranking. That number represents where that player ranks when compared to the other 20 players in this table. For example, a ranking of (1) for a pitcher or catcher means that player has the highest JAWS value for all pitchers or catchers included on this table. A ranking with a "-T" affixed to it indicates a tie, as there is more than one player with that JAWS value. For example, (6-T) indicates the player is tied for sixth place in the ranking. Total JAWS is the combined career value of the pitcher and catcher involved in the no-hitter.

NOTE 1: Two perfect games were thrown five days apart in June 1880 by Lee Richmond and John Montgomery Ward. They're not included in this analysis because the rules of baseball were significantly different back then. Before 1893, the pitcher's rubber was 50 feet from home plate. From 1893-present, the pitcher's rubber has been 60 feet 6 inches from home plate. At that time, too, batters could indicate where they wanted the ball thrown, among other differences. It was just a different game, with different levels of competition.

NOTE 2: Ron Hassey caught two perfect games more than ten years apart – one for Len Barker (Cleveland) in May 1981 and one for Dennis Martinez (Montreal) in July 1991. He is the only pitcher or catcher to participate in two perfect games.

NOTE 3: Don Larsen's October 1956 perfect game was in Game 5 of the World Series against the Brooklyn Dodgers. This win gave New York a three-games-to-two advantage en route to a seven-game series victory. All other perfect games were thrown during the regular season.

As shown in the table above, both Braden and Powell had among the lowest JAWS values for any pitcher or catcher to have thrown a perfect game. Specifically, they both were individually the least accomplished players when they produced their perfect game in 2010. Since then, the White Sox' Phillip Humber, with a JAWS value of 1.7, threw a perfect game in 2012. This put him in 21st place and bumped Braden into 20th place among the pitchers. Powell, however, remains firmly in last place at catcher.

As a duo, the next closest battery in competition is Humber and catcher A.J. Pierzynski, who have a combined JAWS value of 22.6 – four times higher than Braden-Powell at 5.2. The pitcher just above Braden in this ranking is Chicago's

Charlie Robertson (6.8), who threw a perfect game for the 1922 White Sox. Landon Powell is immediately behind the Dodgers' Jeff Torborg (0.4), who caught Hall of Famer Sandy Koufax's perfect game in 1965.

For those who want to dig a bit deeper into the perfect game data presented in the table, there are quite a few nuggets. For example, the greatest disparity between pitcher and catcher JAWS values is the whopping difference of 106 points between the legendary Cy Young and his catcher Lou Criger. In more recent times, the greatest disparity is between Hall of Famer Randy Johnson (81.3) and catcher Robby Hammock (0.6) for their perfect game 100 seasons after Cy Young's masterpiece. It's also interesting to note that some extraordinary catchers (Ivan Rodriguez, Yogi Berra, and Buster Posey) have all caught perfect games for "still excellent but less accomplished" pitchers (Kenny Rogers, Don Larsen, and Matt Cain).

Dallas Braden was also the sixth youngest pitcher to ever throw a perfect game, as depicted in Table 8-4 below.

Table 8-4. Youngest Perfect Game Pitchers

Rank	Date	Pitcher	Team	Age (years-days)
1	5/8/1968	Catfish Hunter	Oakland Athletics	22y-30d
2	9/30/1984	Mike Witt	California Angels	24y-72d
3	5/15/1981	Len Barker	Cleveland Indians	25y-312d
4	4/30/1922	Charlie Robertson	Chicago White Sox	26y-89d
5	8/15/2012	Felix Hernandez	Seattle Mariners	26y-129d
6	5/9/2010	Dallas Braden	Oakland Athletics	26y-269d
7	10/8/1956	Don Larsen	New York Yankees	27y-62d
8	6/13/2012	Matt Cain	San Francisco Giants	27y-256d
9	9/16/1988	Tom Browning	Cincinnati Reds	28y-141d
10	10/2/1908	Addie Joss	Cleveland Naps	28y-173d

METHODOLOGY: This table lists the youngest pitchers to throw a perfect game. The pitchers are ranked by their age when they threw their perfect game, with the youngest pitchers ranked first.

LEGEND: Dates are shown as month/day/year (for example, June 12, 2018, is shown as 6/12/2018). The age of players is shown in years (y) and days (d) as of the day they threw their perfect game. For example, Catfish Hunter was 22 years and 30 days old when he threw his perfect game. This is shown in the table as 22y-30d.

NOTE: Hunter, at slightly over 22 years old, was the youngest perfect game pitcher by more than two years over California's Mike Witt. By comparison, Oakland's Dallas Braden was almost 27 when he threw his. It's interesting to note that while both games were at the same Oakland Coliseum, Hunter's 1968 game, 42 years earlier, happened slightly over a month into the Athletics' first season on the West Coast. His gem got the A's off to a roaring start that would soon lead to five division titles and three World Championships over the next eight seasons.

My associate, Rob Adams, conducted a remarkable interview with Dallas Braden. I invite you to enjoy their exchange below.

Dallas Braden Interview
Conducted by Rob Adams in March 2021

What started as an effort by me and Kevin Hurd to interview pitchers and catchers who were part of recent no-hitters turned into an hour I will never forget. Dallas Braden, the author of one of only twenty-three perfect games in Major League history, is so much more than that sunny day at the Oakland Coliseum on May 9, 2010. He is smart, brutally honest, wicked funny, appreciative, 100% comfortable in his own skin (and beard), and extremely humble. If I never talk to another professional athlete, broadcaster, or podcaster again, I'm fine with that because it would likely be a disappointment.

A little background on how Dallas and I connected. It starts with the book Kevin is writing. He has been figuratively carrying around this book for decades. Like me, Kevin loves baseball. We love its history, and the statistics (Kevin was sabermetrics before it was invented!). We became friends in grade school (circa 1962) and spent hours imitating our favorite players' (from the San Francisco Giants, of course) batting stances, pitching motions, and interview style. We would record mock interviews where Kevin might be Lon Simmons (longtime Bay Area announcer), and I might be Willie McCovey. We would switch sports and I might be Bill King or Hank Greenwald, and he would be Rick Barry or Nate Thurmond of the Warriors. Over 50 years later, we interviewed Dallas Braden ... for real! I found Dallas through Facebook and noticed we had one mutual friend. She was one of my six housemates during my senior year at Santa Clara University, and she was from Stockton. Well, Dallas and her son played ball together and are lifetime friends. As Dallas told me, he would do anything for her and her family as they were so supportive of him, his mom, and his amazing grandmother during those years he was growing up (and beyond). She asked if he would talk to me, and he agreed!

I feel this was more of an amazing story than an interview, but I will stick with the question format for now. My goal was to go beyond all the typical questions as much as possible because there are plenty of written sources and video to pick through. We did not record the interview, so answers are from notes.

Rob Adams (RA): Looking back to all the years and games you pitched before the perfect game, do you recall ever throwing a no-hitter?

Dallas Braden (DB): No. I remember some dominating performances like 12-15 strikeouts, but nothing at this level.

RA: It was your fourth season, and you were a solid #2 or #3 starter with Oakland. The A's were notorious for making moves, using 23 pitchers in that 2010 season. What was your mindset in regard to feeling "secure" as an A's player or starting pitcher.

DB: I never felt secure. The A's loved me at that time, but when I pitched, I had the mindset that I was auditioning for the other 29 teams.

RA: We already know you shook off the final pitch of the game, thinking the count was 2-2 and not 3-1. You threw the fastball and Gabe Kapler grounded out. What about the other 26 outs and all the pitches? Did you shake off any pitches your catcher (Landon Powell) or the coaches called?

DB: First off, coaches do not call pitches. They may call for pitch outs or step offs, but not pitches. But the answer is no, no other shake-offs. (Kurt) Suzuki (the primary A's catcher), Powell, and I came up together through the A's system, so we knew each other very well.

RA: The perfecto was thrown against a very good team with a very good manager: Tampa Bay and Joe Maddon. They would go on to win the AL East that year. Their lineup featured (Evan) Longoria, (Carl) Crawford, (Ben) Zobrist, (Carlos) Pena, and other good hitters. At any point in the game did Maddon or anyone else try anything to take you off your game, such as chirping from the dugout, stepping out, or things like that?

DB: I still kid Longo (Longoria) to this day about how funny it was that they had him try to bunt for a base hit. They were actually doing me a favor as he was a great hitter, but (he was) not fast and not a bunter

RA: You had three catchers that year: Suzuki, (Jake) Fox, and Powell. Did you know Powell was going to catch that day? Did you have a preferred catcher of the three?

DB: I did not know and it did not matter because I had come up with these guys. We knew each other very well.

RA: The team did not score a ton of runs in many of your starts. They averaged less than two per game in those you lost. By the fourth inning of this game, the A's were ahead 4-0. Did this change your approach in the game?

DB: No, the mindset was to always attack, be confident in my strengths, move the ball around, and change speeds from (around) 68 to 89 (miles per hour).

RA: It appears that third baseman Kevin Kouzmanoff was your best buddy that day on offense and defense. Other than he and Powell, were there any other players or coaches who stand out that day?

DB: I was a recluse on the days I pitched. I did not want to talk to anyone or be talked to, so nothing was said in the dugout. I joke with Kouz that the two "great' plays he made were not so great. He caught the line drive because he was too lazy to play off the line, and he caught the foul popup because I backed off and let him. But the line drive that Navarro hit at (Eric) Patterson was a top spin liner hit at a guy who had never played that position before at the Coliseum. Patterson went back on the ball, somehow recovered, and made the catch.

RA: Any mementos from that game?

DB: The ball, which I didn't know I had (it was in the back pocket of his game uniform pants!), and the pitching rubber which I didn't know existed until I saw it as part of an A's charity auction. The short version is that I traded my game uniform for it after starting the "give Dallas back his dirty rubber" campaign. And (the A's) have treated my grandmother like royalty ever since. Who could ask for more?

RA: After this game, where you threw 109 pitches – not a heavy workload for you – your next win was not until July 25th, and you went on a winning streak at that point. Had anything changed because of, or due to, the perfect game?

DB: No. The goal was to pitch a perfect game every time out. If not perfect, then a no-hitter, a shutout, or win the game, in that order.

RA: You pitched eight innings of the final game of the season, a win that resulted in the A's finishing the season at 81-81 instead of (a losing record at) 80-82. It was also your 11th win of the season. How satisfying was this win to end the season?

DB: It allowed us to finish on a high note, both the win and record. It matters, as it set us up to feel more confident going into the offseason.

RA. Eleven years have passed since you threw the perfect game. Over 220,000 Major League games have been played in history, but only 23 have been perfect. Even in your busy life of being a husband, parent, and broadcaster, do you think back to that day?

DB: Every day! Everywhere that I go where the A's are playing, I love talking to the fans and hearing their memories of that day. Where they were, how they missed family events because they were not going to turn off the TV or radio, and who they watched or listened with that day. That game is "the gift that keeps on giving" to me and my grandmother. I feel like Willie Wonka and that game is the golden ticket.

RA. Have you ever compared notes on that game with others in your era who threw them, such as Matt Cain, Felix Hernandez, Philip Humber, or the late Roy Halladay?

DB: I don't feel like I am in their league, so no. But I did receive a call from Mark Buehrle (of the White Sox) who had thrown a perfect game the year before. That meant so much to me. When Cainer (Matt Cain) threw his perfect game, I sent him a note suggesting that other than him being right-handed and me being left-handed, him having a monster contract, and him having a World Series ring, we were basically 100% alike.

RA: You faced so many great hitters, too many to mention. Did you ever stand on the mound and see someone like Ichiro come up, and think, "it's Ichiro!" Or was it strictly focus and go with the game plan?

DB: Against the sluggers the goal was "no damage," meaning don't let them hit it out of the park. I didn't want to be a guppy to be swallowed whole.

RA: Any particular batter you felt you could not get out?

DB: Yes, Chone Figgins of the Angels (Figgins was a pesky hitter and a speedy infielder who was an All-Star and regularly got MVP votes). No matter what

RA: I did, it seems like I couldn't get him out. I remember one game where he had two or three hits off me and none of them got out of the infield.

RA: You made a quick transition from playing to broadcasting. Do you think the perfecto gave you street cred beyond your career numbers, and/or was it because you were such a refreshing and interesting interview yourself?

DB: Both, I think. The head of Barstool Sports – David Portnoy – thought I was perfect for what they were doing, but ESPN came calling first. I was out fishing when my agent called and told me ESPN wanted to interview me. I asked, "for what?" For Baseball Tonight, obviously! I remember flying back and interviewing with everyone except Walt Disney. Then came the infamous ESPN layoffs and I went to Barstool Sports and later NBC Sports Bay Area – where he currently works.

RA: You have stated that the perfect game is your second greatest baseball memory or moment behind the game for the hometown Stockton Ports (Stockton is the hometown of Dallas and the famous Ultimate Fighting Championship's Diaz brothers) where your twelfth strikeout meant half price beer for the fans. Is that still true?

DB: Yes, in part because of the beer, and also because I was called up to Double-A after that game. It was a huge moment in my career.

RA: Do you have any kids who have or will pursue baseball as a career? Did you encourage them to do so?

DB: Kids? Two girls who will get to do and play anything they want. No pushing into anything, but (I want them to) enjoy everything!!

RA: Have you been to the section of the Baseball Hall of Fame that focuses on no-hitters?

DB: No. I never have.

RA: Have you spent time signing autographs in Las Vegas, or in Florida or Arizona during spring training?

DB: No. I much prefer just meeting fans and talking baseball.

RA: Are you still in touch with Landon Powell?

DB: Yes, we came up together and are friends. He is the head coach of North Greenville University in South Carolina.

RA: Did the A's pay a bonus or provide any other reward for the perfect game?

DB: No, they offered to create a ring, which I did not want. What they did was treat my grandmother like a queen, and still do to this day.

RA: The game was pitched on Mother's Day. What was that like having lost your mom?

DB: Mother's Day was not a happy day for me. My grandmom and I might get dinner, but it was not a celebration. Throwing the perfect game on that day changed everything in that regard.

RA: Do you have any other favorite memories you'd like to share?

DB: When I was pitching in Stockton, after a game some fans were waiting for me with a gift. They had gone out and bought a yellow A's jersey and put the number 209 on the back (209 is the Area Code for Stockton). We took a picture together and I have the uniform in my closet and the photo in a frame.

Chapter 9

Harvey Haddix:
12 Perfect Innings

May 26, 1959
Pittsburgh starter hurls perhaps the best game ever ... for 12 innings

"13's never lucky so you can guess the rest
Harv gave up a hit and then he lost the whole contest
I wonder how he slept that night knowing how close he came
To a most exclusive club that should include his name"

Lyrics from the song "Harvey Haddix" (from the 2008 album "Volume 1, Frozen Ropes and Dying Quails" by the group The Baseball Project).

"People ask me all the time what the most memorable game I've ever played in was. Half the time I tell them it was Game 7 of the '60 Series. The other half of the time I tell them it was the night Harvey Haddix threw the finest game in the history of baseball. Then they'll look at me and say, 'Harvey who? ... Usually, you have one or two great or spectacular defensive plays in these no-hitters. Not that night. It was the easiest game I ever played in."

Hall of Famer Bill Mazeroski, Pittsburgh's second baseman, reflecting on what it was like to play behind Haddix that night (Albert Chen, "The Greatest Game Ever Pitched," *Sports Illustrated*, June 1, 2009).

"It was an amazing night, just a great baseball night. A game you never forget. It was unbelievable."

Baseball commissioner Bud Selig – a 24-year-old Braves fan sitting in the stands at County Stadium in Milwaukee that night – describing the remarkable pitching performance he witnessed from Harvey Haddix (Mark Miller, "May 26, 1959: Harvey Haddix pitches 12 perfect innings, loses in 13th," *sabr.org*, April 16, 2009).

"It was just another loss, and that is no good."

A dejected Harvey Haddix after the 1-0 loss ("Sweet Smell of Failure," *Sports Illustrated*, June 8, 1959).

"I hit a ball to right field, and I thought it was gone. But a windstorm had started. Aaron went back on it and kind of gave up on it when the wind blew it back and he caught it against the fence. I thought it was gone."

Bob Skinner, Haddix's roommate, describing his long fly ball with one out in the seventh inning, perhaps the closest the Pirates came to scoring a run off Milwaukee ace Lew Burdette (Mark Miller, "May 26, 1959: Harvey Haddix pitches 12 perfect innings, loses in 13th," *sabr.org*, April 16, 2009).

On the night of May 26, 1959, Harvey Haddix threw 12 perfect innings, more than any pitcher has ever thrown before or since. Unfortunately, his Pirate teammates failed to score even one run during the 13 innings they batted, despite compiling 12 singles off Milwaukee starter and National League All-Star Lew Burdette. Ever since the game went into extras, Pittsburgh manager Danny Murtaugh kept asking Haddix if he had one more inning in him each time he was called to go out for another round at the bottom of the 10th, 11th, 12th, and now, the 13th. Haddix always said "yes."

It wasn't that the Pirates weren't good. With powerful hitters like Roberto Clemente, Dick Stuart, Bob Skinner, and Smoky Burgess, the team finished in the top half of the National League in hits, doubles, triples, and batting average in 1959, although, admittedly, Clemente and Stuart weren't in the starting lineup that evening. This Pittsburgh team would go on to win the National League pennant and the World Series against the mighty New York Yankees the very next season.

That night, the Pirates had multiple chances to score. In the third inning, Don Hoak led off with an infield single. After a fielder's choice that left Roman Mejias at first with one out, Haddix hit a shot off Burdette's leg and beat the throw to first. Unfortunately, Mejias made a baserunning error and tried to advance from first to third, where he was thrown out. Dick Schofield followed with a single to right that would have easily scored Mejias from second. With runners at first and third, the next batter, Bill Virdon, flied out to left field to end the inning.

With one out in the seventh, Pittsburgh slugger Bob Skinner hit a long fly he thought was a home run, only to see Hank Aaron catch it against the fence. The Pirates strung together a couple of singles in the top of the ninth, putting runners on first and third with two outs, only to see Skinner ground out to the pitcher for the final out. The Pirates had runners reach first in the 10th, 11th, 12th, and 13th, only to see them stranded there at the end of the inning.

In the other dugout was an extraordinary team, the 1957 World Champion and 1958 National League pennant-winning Milwaukee Braves. The Braves of 1959 were just as intimidating, ending the season in a tie with the Dodgers for the pennant, losing to Los Angeles in the best-of-three playoff series after the conclusion of the 154-game regular season. Led by Hank Aaron, Eddie Mathews, and Joe Adcock, the Braves led the National League in home runs and finished second in runs scored that year.

Yet, by all accounts, this powerful Milwaukee lineup could not do anything until the very end of this game. By the time the 13th inning had started, Haddix had only thrown a remarkably low 104 pitches. He used pinpoint control, as he mixed up his two pitches – his fastball and his breaking ball – to keep the Braves off balance. During the game, the Milwaukee bullpen discovered they could read catcher Smoky Burgess' signals using binoculars, as he wasn't bending down much in the crouch. The relief pitchers would flash signals to the Milwaukee hitters as to whether it was going to be a fastball or a breaking ball. Despite knowing what pitch was coming, Brave batters still couldn't touch Haddix for twelve innings.

The bottom of the 13th had an auspicious start. The first batter, leadoff hitter Felix Mantilla, hit a slow, bouncing chopper to third baseman Don Hoak. His throw to first base was in the dirt and Rocky Nelson couldn't come up with it. Mantilla was safe on a throwing error. The perfect game was over, but the no-hitter was still intact. The next batter, Hall of Famer Eddie Mathews, bunted to Haddix for a sacrifice, moving Mantilla to second base with one out. After Haddix walked the mighty Hank Aaron intentionally to create a double play opportunity, Joe Adcock, Milwaukee's powerful number four hitter, came to the plate.

With a 1-0 count, Haddix hung a slider and Adcock took full advantage of it. Adcock planted the ball in the stands in right center field. The game, and the no-hitter, were over. What happened next resulted in only one of the runs counting, though. Mantilla, who had held at third in case he needed to tag up on a sacrifice fly, ran home and scored. Aaron assumed the game was over, stopped, and cut across the infield, causing Adcock to pass him. Aaron eventually went to third and scored in front of Adcock but was ruled out (the second out of the inning). Adcock was credited with a double instead of a homer. The final score was 1-0 in favor of the Braves.

This game has been described as the greatest game ever pitched. No pitcher has ever thrown 12 perfect innings to start a game. It is also one of only 14 games where a pitcher (or pitchers in some cases) has thrown a no-hitter that went into extra innings and lost the no-hitter after the ninth inning. The entire list is in the table below, shown in chronological order. Of all 14 games, Harvey Haddix has both the highest Game Score at the end of the game (107), and the highest Game Score at the point he lost his no-hitter (114 after 12.1 innings, just before the walk to Hank Aaron).

Table 9-1. No-hitters Broken Up After the Ninth Inning

Pitcher Team	Opponent	Date Score	End of GSc *No-hit GSc*	IP, Hits, Runs, ERs, Walks, Strikeouts
Earl Moore Cleveland Blues	Chi W. Sox	5/9/1901 Chi 4-2 (10 inn)	77 *84@9.0 inn*	10.0 IP, 2 Hits, 4 Runs, 1 ER, 1 BB, 0 Ks
Bob Wicker Chicago Cubs	NY Giants	6/11/1904 Chi 1-0 (12 inn)	107 *? @9.1 inn*	12.0 IP, 2 Hits, 0 Runs, 0 ERs, 1 BB, 10 Ks
Harry McIntire Brook Superbas	Pit Pirates	8/1/1906 Pit 1-0 (13 inn)	102 *? @10.2 inn*	13.0 IP, 4 Hits, 1 Run, 1 ER, 1 BB, 8 Ks
Red Ames NY Giants	Bro Superbas	4/15/1909 Bro 3-0 (13 inn)	89-95 *? @9.1 inn*	13.0 IP, 7 Hits, 3 Runs, 0-3 ERs, 2 BBs, 10 Ks
Tom Hughes NY Highlanders	Cle Naps	8/30/1910 (2) Cle 5-0 (11 inn)	69 *? @9.1 inn*	11.0 IP, 7 Hits, 5 Runs, 5 ERs, 1 BB, 7 Ks
Jim Scott Chicago W. Sox	Was Senators	5/14/1914 Was 1-0 (10 inn)	79 *87@9.0 inn*	9.0 IP, 2 Hits, 1 Run, 1 ER, 2 BBs, 2 Ks

Pitcher Team	Oppo- nent	Date Score	End of GSc *No-hit GSc*	IP, Hits, Runs, ERs, Walks, Strikeouts
Hippo Vaughn Chicago Cubs	Cin Reds	5/2/1917 Cin 1-0 (10 inn)	94 *97@9.1 inn*	10.0 IP, 2 Hits, 1 Run, 0 ERs, 2 BBs, 10 Ks
Bobo Newsom St. Louis Browns	Bos Red Sox	9/18/1934 Bos 2-1 (10 inn)	86 *91@9.2 inn*	10.0 IP, 1 Hit, 2 Runs, 1 ER, 7 BBs, 9 Ks
Three pitchers Cincinnati Reds	Mil Braves	5/26/1956 Mil 2-1 (11 inn)	78 *84@9.2 inn*	10.1 IP, 3 Hits, 2 Runs, 2 ERs, 9 BBs, 5 Ks
Harvey Haddix Pittsburgh Pirates	Mil Braves	5/26/1959 Mil 1-0 (13 inn)	107 *112@12.1*	12.2 IP, 1 Hit, 1 Run, 0 ERs, 1 BB, 8 Ks
Jim Maloney Cincinnati Reds	NY Mets	6/14/1965 NY 1-0 (11 inn)	106 *108@10.0*	11.0 IP, 2 Hits, 1 Run, 1 ER, 1 BB, 18 Ks
Gardner-Fassero Montreal Expos	LA Dodgers	7/26/1991 LA 1-0 (10 inn)	81 *89@9.0 inn*	9.0 IP, 3 Hits, 1 Run, 1 ER, 2 BBs, 4 Ks
Martinez-Rojas Montreal Expos	SD Padres	6/3/1995 Mon 1-0 (10)	101 *96@9.0 inn*	10.0 IP, 1 Hit, 0 Runs, 0 ERs, 0 BBs, 9 Ks
Rich Hill LA Dodgers	Pit Pirates	8/23/2017 Pit 1-0 (10 inn)	91 *95@9.0 inn*	9.0 IP, 1 Hit, 1 Run, 1 ER, 0 BBs, 10 Ks

METHODOLOGY: This table shows all games from 1900-2021 that were no-hitters through nine innings and a hit was allowed in extra innings. The games are listed in chronological order.

LEGEND: Dates are shown as month/day/year (for example, June 12, 2018, is shown as 6/12/2018). IP = innings pitched; BB(s) = base(s) on balls (walks); K(s) = strikeout(s); ER(s) = earned run(s). inn = innings and is used to indicate how many innings a game went. (2) indicates the game was the second game of a doubleheader. "End GSc" shows the pitcher's official Game Score at the end of the game and is related to the statistics posted at the end of the row. *"No-hit GSc" (in italics)* indicates what the pitcher's Game Score would have been at the time immediately before the no-hitter was broken up. It also shows the innings pitched at the point the first hit was given up. For games involving multiple pitchers, the Game Score is for the combined efforts of the pitchers immediately before the first hit was achieved or at the end of the game. This is slightly different from the typical Game Score designation given to an individual pitcher based on his box score performance. All statistics are end-of-game totals.

NOTE 1: For Bob Wicker, Harry McIntire, and Red Ames, play-by-play records aren't available. Because of that, it is uncertain how many strikeouts or walks occurred after they allowed their first hits. Therefore, the no-hit Game Score can't be calculated.

NOTE 2: For Harry McIntire, Red Ames, and Tom Hughes, play-by-play records aren't officially available and there was no differentiation as to whether a run was considered earned or unearned. Because of that, a range of possible high and low Game Scores is provided based upon their pitching line at the end of that day. In other words, their Game Score could fall at either end or in between the extremes. That said, for some of the games, written narratives can effectively determine whether a run was the result of an error or not. For example, in Harry McIntire's game, Brooklyn made the team's only error in the third inning, and Pittsburgh scored its run in the 13th inning. Because of separation of those two events, the Pirates' only run must have been earned. In Tom Hughes's case, his team made an error in the seventh inning and the opposition scored all five runs in the 11th, so all runs were earned. In Red Ames's game, Brooklyn scored all three of the team's runs in 13th inning. The Giants made two errors during the game: one in the fifth inning and one in the 13th. It is likely that two of Brooklyn's three runs were unearned.

NOTE 3: Earl Moore pitched for the Cleveland Blues in 1901 in the first year of the brand-new American League. Cleveland would change its nickname to the Bronchos in 1902, and then the Naps in 1903. In 1915 the team became the Cleveland Indians. The team name was changed to the Cleveland Guardians before the start of the 2022 season. The National League's Brooklyn team was known as the Superbas when New York's Red Ames threw his game against them in 1909. The Superbas changed their name to the Trolley Dodgers in 1911, and then became the Dodgers in 1913 for one season. They were known as the Robins from 1914-1931 and changed back to the Dodgers in 1932. They've kept the Dodger name since then, although, the team moved to Los Angeles in 1958. Tom Hughes played for the New York Highlanders of the American League when he lost to the Cleveland Naps in 11 innings in 1910. New York changed its name to the Yankees in 1913. The Montreal Expos moved to Washington and became the Nationals in 2005. The St. Louis Browns moved to Baltimore and became the Orioles in 1954. The Milwaukee Braves moved to Atlanta in 1966.

NOTE 4: The three pitchers involved in Cincinnati's 11-inning game in 1956 were Johnny Klippstein (7.0 innings), Hersch Freeman (1.0 inning), and Joe Black (1.1 inning). Klippstein, Freeman, and Black held the Braves hitless through 9.2

innings. Black gave up a double with two outs in the 10th and allowed two more hits in the tenth for the loss.

NOTE 5: Mark Gardner (9.0 innings) and Jeff Fassero (0.0 innings) were the two pitchers involved in Montreal's 1991 game against Los Angeles. Gardner allowed two singles to Lenny Harris and Eddie Murray to start the bottom of the 10th inning in a scoreless game, at which point he was relieved by Jeff Fassero. Fassero then gave up the game-winning single on a 2-0 pitch to Darryl Strawberry as the Dodgers won 1-0.

NOTE 6: Pedro Martinez (9.0 innings) and Mel Rojas (1.0 inning) were the two pitchers involved in Montreal's 1995 game against San Diego. Martinez had a perfect game through nine innings; however, the Expos had failed to score, so the 0-0 game went into extra innings. Montreal scored a run in the top of the 10th for a 1-0 lead. In the bottom of the tenth, Martinez gave up a leadoff double to Bip Roberts. Mel Rojas was brought in to relieve Martinez, who had already thrown 96 pitches. After throwing a wild pitch, which allowed Roberts to go to third base, Rojas retired the next three batters for the save, as the Expos won the game 1-0.

With a Game Score of 107, Harvey Haddix also has one of the highest scores of any Pittsburgh pitcher in the team's 122-season history. If his night had ended right after Eddie Mathews' sacrifice bunt in the bottom of the 13th, Haddix's Game Score would have been a remarkable 112 (giving partial credit for one-third of an inning pitched). As shown in the table below, this would rank him in third place for the highest Game Score for a Pirate pitcher, just behind Vern Law's 18-inning effort in 1955 and Babe Adams' 21-inning game in 1914. Both Law and Adams gave up numerous hits during their time on the mound.

Table 9-2. Pirates Highest Game Scores

Rank	Pitcher	Date Score	Opponent	GSc	IP, Hits, Runs, ERs, Walks, Strikeouts
1	Vern Law	7/19/1955 Pit 4-3 (19 inn)	Milwaukee Braves	118	18.0 IP, 9 Hits, 2 Runs, 1 ER, 2 BBs, 12 Ks
2	Babe Adams	7/17/1914 NY 3-1 (21 inn)	New York Giants	117	21.0 IP, 12 Hits, 3 Runs, 3 ERs, 0 BBs, 6 Ks
3	Irv Young	8/22/1908 Pit 1-0 (17 inn)	Brooklyn Superbas	109	17.0 IP, 9 Hits, 0 Runs, 0 ERs, 3 BBs, 3 Ks

Rank	Pitcher	Date Score	Opponent	GSc	IP, Hits, Runs, ERs, Walks, Strikeouts
4	Harvey Haddix	5/26/1959 Mil 1-0 (13 inn)	Milwaukee Braves	107	12.2 IP, 1 Hit, 1 Run, 0 ERs, 1 BB, 8 Ks
5	Deacon Phillipe	6/22/1902 Chi 3-2 (19 inn)	Chicago Orphans	99	18.2 IP, 14 Hits, 3 Runs, 2 ERs, 3 BBs, 6 Ks
6 (tie)	Jack Hallett	9/21/1946 Pit 2-1 (13 inn)	Cincinnati Reds	97	13.0 IP, 7 Hits, 1 Run, 0 ERs, 3 BBs, 9 Ks
6 (tie)	Bob Veale	9/30/1964 Pit 1-0 (16 inn)	Cincinnati Reds	97	12.1 IP, 7 Hits, 0 Runs, 0 ERs, 8 BBs, 16 Ks
6 (tie)	Bob Veale	9/19/1965 Pit 1-0 (10 inn)	Philadelphia Phillies	97	10.0 IP, 1 Hit, 0 Runs, 0 ERs, 5 BBs, 12 Ks
9	Vic Willis	7/28/1908 2-2 Tie (16 inn)	New York Giants	95-99	16.0 IP, 12 Hits, 2 Runs, ? ERs, 2 BBs, 7 Ks
10 (tie)	Bob Veale	4/12/1965 Pit 1-0 (10 inn)	San Francisco Giants	95	10.0 IP, 3 Hits, 0 Runs, 0 ERs, 1 BB, 10 Ks
10 (tie)	Woodie Fryman	9/1/1967 Pit 3-0	Philadelphia Phillies	95	9.0 IP, 3 Hits, 0 Runs, 0 ERs, 1 BB, 15 Ks
10 (tie)	Francisco Cordova	7/12/1997 Pit 3-0 (10 inn)	Houston Astros	95	9.0 IP, 0 Hits, 0 Runs, 0 ERs, 2 BBs, 10 Ks

METHODOLOGY: This table lists the highest Game Scores for Pirate pitchers from 1900-2021. Games are ranked by Game Score (GSc) and consider all franchise regular season and postseason games. Game Score measures a pitcher's performance in any given game started. Introduced by baseball writer/statistician Bill James in the 1980s, Game Score is presented as a figure between 0-100 -- except for extreme outliers -- and usually falls between 40-70.

LEGEND: Dates are shown as month/day/year (for example, June 12, 2018, is shown as 6/12/2018). IP = innings pitched; BB(s) = base(s) on balls; K(s) = strikeout(s); ER(s) = earned run(s). inn = innings and is used to indicate how many innings a game went if it was other than a standard nine-inning game. (1) = first game of a doubleheader

NOTE 1: The highest postseason Game Score ever achieved by a Pirate pitcher was 83. It happened twice within two days in the 1971 World Series against the Orioles. The first pitcher with an 83 GSc was Steve Blass, who threw a three-hit,

5-1 victory against Baltimore's Mike Cuellar in Game 3. His win gave Pittsburgh a much-needed win after the team fell behind two games to none to start the World Series. Things were looking bleak as Game 3 started, as Pittsburgh only had a 20 percent World Series win probability at that point. The only scoring against Blass in that game was a solo home run by Hall of Famer Frank Robinson to lead off the seventh inning. The second 83 GSc was two days later in Game 5 when Nellie Briles threw a two-hit, 4-0 shutout versus Baltimore's Dave McNally. Briles' win gave the Pirates a three-games-to-two lead, and the World Series moved back to Baltimore for the final two games. After losing Game 6 in 10 innings, the Pirates would win Game 7 and the World Series by the score of 2-1 behind Blass's four-hit performance for his second win of the World Series.

NOTE 2: Vern Law threw an extraordinary 18 innings against the mighty Milwaukee Braves in 1955. Roman Mejias pinch-hit for Law in the bottom of the 18th inning. Milwaukee scored in the top of the 19th when future Pittsburgh manager Chuck Tanner singled and knocked in Eddie Mathews from second base. Pittsburgh scored two runs in the bottom of the 19th when hits from Gene Freese, Dale Long, and Frank Thomas combined for a 4-3 win.

NOTE 3: Pittsburgh ace Babe Adams only allowed one run to the New York Giants over 20 innings. In the top of the 21st, he allowed two runs on a two-out, two-run home run by New York's Larry Doyle. The Giants won the game 3-1, as the Pirates failed to score against future Hall of Famer Rube Marquard.

NOTE 4: If Harvey Haddix's 1959 game had ended after his last complete inning in the 12th, his Game Score would have been 110, placing him in third place on Pittsburgh's highest all-time Game Scores table.

NOTE 5: Deacon Phillippe threw his epic game against the National League's Chicago Orphans in 1902. The team changed its name to the Chicago Cubs in 1903. The game was tied 2-2 after nine innings. Pittsburgh lost in the bottom of the 19th inning when Chicago pushed across a run. Both pitchers in this game (Deacon Phillipe and Chicago's Jack Taylor) allowed 14 hits and struck out six opposing batters.

NOTE 6: Bob Veale's 1964 game was #159 in a 162-game season. By helping to defeat the Reds 1-0 as he threw 12.1 shutout innings, he pushed them out of a tie with the first-place Cardinals. The Reds would end up one game behind St. Louis for the National League pennant. In Bob Veale's 1965 one-hitter, the only hit he allowed during his 10 shutout innings was a single to Tony Taylor with one out in the sixth inning. If that game had ended after nine innings, Veale would have achieved a Game Score of 94, placing him tied for third place in Pittsburgh's best nine-inning performances (fourth place if Harvey Haddix's performance is included). Veale's Game Score for his 10-inning 3-hit shutout against the Giants in 1965 would have been 88 after nine innings.

NOTE 7: Vic Willis's 16-inning effort in 1908 occurred before the earned run statistic had been created, so he doesn't have an official Game Score because it's unclear whether the two runs he allowed were earned or unearned. After analyzing the game, his score could only be in the range of 95-99, which places him within the team's top Game Scores. It's not clear why the game stopped after 16 innings – most likely it was due to bad weather or darkness.

Just as impressive, if Harvey Haddix's game had ended after nine innings, he would have thrown the only perfect game in Pittsburgh history. Up until 1991, Haddix's game was counted as a no-hitter. That year, Major League Baseball's Committee for Statistical Accuracy announced that a no-hitter would be redefined as "a game in which a pitcher or pitchers complete a game of nine innings or more without allowing a hit." Because the Braves had a hit by the time the game ended in the 13th inning, Haddix's game no longer qualified and it was removed from the list.

Regardless of whether it is officially listed as a no-hitter, Haddix's pitching excellence is there for the record. With a Game Score of 95 after nine innings (and 100 after 10 innings), Haddix would have tied the highest nine-inning Game Score of any pitcher in Pirates' history. The top Pittsburgh Game Scores for a game of 10 innings or less are shown in Table 17-3 below. Haddix would rank as the number one nine-inning score along with Woodie Fryman's 15-strikeout effort in 1967 and Francisco Cordova's 1997 combined no-hitter. His 10-inning score would beat Bob Veale's one-hitter by three points.

Table 9-3. Pirates Highest Game Scores of 10 Innings or Less

Rank	Pitcher	Date / Score	Opponent	GSc	IP, Hits, Runs, ERs, Walks, Strikeouts
1	Bob Veale	9/19/1965 Pit 1-0 (10 inn)	Philadelphia Phillies	97	10.0 IP, 1 Hit, 0 Runs, 0 ERs, 5 BBs, 12 Ks
2 (tie)	Bob Veale	4/12/1965 Pit 1-0 (10 inn)	San Francisco Giants	95	10.0 IP, 3 Hits, 0 Runs, 0 ERs, 1 BB, 10 Ks
2 (tie)	Woodie Fryman	9/1/1967 Pit 3-0	Philadelphia Phillies	95	9.0 IP, 3 Hits, 0 Runs, 0 ERs, 1 BB, 15 Ks

Rank	Pitcher	Date Score	Opponent	GSc	IP, Hits, Runs, ERs, Walks, Strikeouts
2 (tie)	Francisco Cordova	7/12/1997 Pit 3-0 (10 inn)	Houston Astros	95	9.0 IP, 0 Hits, 0 Runs, 0 ERs, 2 BBs, 10 Ks
5 (tie)	Bert Blyleven	8/16/1980 Pit 5-0	Montreal Expos	94	9.0 IP, 2 Hits, 0 Runs, 0 ERs, 1 BB, 12 Ks
5 (tie)	Larry McWilliams	9/20/1983 Pit 4-0	New York Mets	94	9.0 IP, 2 Hits, 0 Runs, 0 ERs, 0 BBs, 11 Ks
7 (tie)	Bob Friend	9/7/1955 Pit 2-0	Chicago Cubs	93	9.0 IP, 1 Hit, 0 Runs, 0 ERs, 0 BBs, 8 Ks
7 (tie)	Earl Francis	9/26/1962 Pit 1-0 (11 inn)	Cincinnati Reds	93	10.0 IP, 2 Hits, 0 Runs, 0 ERs, 1 BB, 6 Ks
7 (tie)	Woody Fryman	7/1/1966 Pit 12-0	New York Mets	93	9.0 IP, 1 Hit, 0 Runs, 0 ERs, 0 BBs, 8 Ks
7 (tie)	John Candelaria	8/9/1976 Pit 2-0	Los Angeles Dodgers	93	9.0 IP, 0 Hits, 0 Runs, 0 ERs, 1 BB, 7 Ks
7 (tie)	Jose DeLeon	7/31/1983 (2) NY 1-0 (12 inn)	New York Mets	93	9.0 IP, 1 Hit, 0 Runs, 0 ERs, 3 BBs, 11 Ks
7 (tie)	Jose DeLeon	8/20/1983 Pit 4-0	Cincinnati Reds	93	9.0 IP, 2 Hits, 0 Runs, 0 ERs, 0 BBs, 11 Ks
7 (tie)	Paul Wagner	8/29/1995 Pit 4-0	Colorado Rockies	93	9.0 IP, 1 Hits, 0 Runs, 0 ERs, 3 BBs, 11 Ks
27 (tie)	Bob Moose	9/20/1969 Pit 4-0	New York Mets	90	9.0 IP, 0 Hits, 0 Runs, 0 ERs, 3 BBs, 6 Ks
40 (tie)	Nick Maddox	9/20/1907 Pit 2-1	Brooklyn Superbas	89	9.0 IP, 0 Hits, 1 Run, 0 ERs, 3 BBs, 5 Ks
148 (tie)	Dock Ellis	6/12/1970 (1) Pit 2-0	San Diego Padres	85	9.0 IP, 0 Hits, 0 Runs, 0 ERs, 8 BBs, 6 Ks
269 (tie)	Cliff Chambers	5/6/1951 (2) Pit 3-0	Boston Braves	83	9.0 IP, 0 Hits, 0 Runs, 0 ERs, 8 BBs, 4 Ks
1135 (tie)	Lefty Leifield	9/26/1906 (2) Pit 8-0 (6 inn)	Philadelphia Phillies	76	6.0 IP, 0 Hits, 0 Runs, 0 ERs, 2 BBs, 6 Ks
---	Howie Camnitz	8/23/1907 (2) Pit 1-0 (5 inn)	New York Giants	64	5.0 IP, 0 Hits, 0 Runs, 0 ERs, 5 BBs, 2 Ks

METHODOLOGY: This table lists the highest Game Scores of 10 innings or less for Pirate pitchers from 1900-2021. Games are ranked by Game Score (GSc) and consider all franchise regular season and postseason games. For comparison purposes, all six franchise no-hitters from 1900-2021 are included in this table. Game Score measures a pitcher's performance in any given game started. Introduced by baseball writer/statistician Bill James in the 1980s, Game Score is presented as a figure between 0-100 — except for extreme outliers — and usually falls between 40-70.

LEGEND: Dates are shown as month/day/year (for example, June 12, 2018, is shown as 6/12/2018). IP = innings pitched; BB(s) = base(s) on balls; K(s) = strikeout(s); ER(s) = earned run(s). inn = innings and is used to indicate how many innings a game went if it was other than a standard nine-inning game. (1) or (2) = first or second game of a doubleheader

NOTE 1: Those six Pirate no-hitters represent the fewest total thrown by a non-expansion franchise, meaning a team that was in existence in 1901. The next closest franchises with the fewest no-hitters are the original Washington Senators/Minnesota Twins with seven, and the Detroit Tigers with eight. Every other non-expansion franchise has at least ten no-hitters to its credit. Five of the expansion teams have six or more no-hitters, too, with the Colts/Astros (established 1962) leading the pack with 13 and the Angels (1961) at 11. All totals are through the end of the 2021 season.

NOTE 2: If Harvey Haddix's 1959 game had ended after nine innings, his Game Score would have been 95, placing him at the top of Pittsburgh's best nine-inning performances, along with Woodie Fryman and Francisco Cordova. His 10-inning Game Score would have been the best Pirate Game Score of 10 innings or less. Bob Veale's top performances are covered in more detail in Table 9-2 Notes.

NOTE 3: In his 1997 game, Francisco Cordova threw nine innings of no-hit baseball. Unfortunately, Pittsburgh had failed to score up to that point. Ricardo Rincon replaced Cordova to start the top of the ninth inning, as Cordova had already thrown 121 pitches by that point and there was no end in sight. Rincon threw a scoreless 10th inning, thereby preserving the no-hitter. Pittsburgh won the game in the bottom of the 10th when pinch-hitter Mark Smith hit a two-out, three-run home run off Houston reliever John Hudek for a 3-0 Pirate victory.

NOTE 4: In his 1907 game, Nick Maddox gave up what clearly was an unearned run against Brooklyn in the fourth inning due to back-to-back throwing errors by Maddox and Honus Wagner. While this game does not have an official Game Score because unearned runs were not counted as a statistic at that time, it would have been 89 based on the story accompanying the game.

NOTE 5: Bob Friend gave up his lone hit to Frank Baumholtz of the Cubs with two outs in the fourth inning. Ron Hunt of the Mets led off the second inning with a single in Woody Fryman's 1966 one-hitter.

NOTE 6: In July 1983, Jose DeLeon gave up the lone hit of his stretch against the Mets to Hubie Brooks with one out in the ninth inning of a scoreless game. After Brooks' single, Keith Hernandez grounded into a double play to end the inning. Lee Mazzilli pinch-hit for DeLeon in the top of the 10th. The Mets would win the game in the bottom of the 12th when Mookie Wilson scored on a George Foster fielder's choice. Three weeks later, DeLeon would have another no-hitter broken up late in the game when Dan Driessen of the Reds hit a two-out double in the seventh inning. Both of these games earned identical Game Scores of 93.

NOTE 7: Dock Ellis' no-hitter in 1970 is remarkable for many reasons. With eight walks and a hit batter, it has one of the lowest Game Scores of any no-hitter ever pitched (85). Far more amazing, Ellis was, by his own admission, on LSD at the time he pitched. He took the drug earlier in the day when he thought he was not scheduled to start. His story is told in the critically acclaimed 2014 film *No No: A Dockumentary*, currently available to watch on Amazon.

NOTE 8: Two games that were originally included as no-hitters but had their designation revoked in 1991 with the policy change are included in this table: Lefty Leifield's six-inning shutout against the Phillies in 1906 and Howie Camnitz's five-inning shutout of the Giants in 1907. Both of these games were the second games of doubleheaders, and both were called before nine innings were played because of darkness. Leifield and Camnitz were well into their games when they ended. Hall of Famer Honus Wagner is credited with preserving the no-hit efforts with his exceptional fielding in both contests.

Harvey Haddix became an instant celebrity after his near-perfect game. He was featured in Life and Sports Illustrated articles. Haddix was also invited to go on To Tell the Truth and the Ed Sullivan Show, but he declined. He felt it was more important to stay with the team. Looking at the 1959 Pirates schedule after May 26, they still had two games in Milwaukee, then four games in Cincinnati (May 29-31, with May 30-31 being on the weekend). Haddix pitched again on Tuesday, June 2, beating St. Louis 3-0.

In 1959 there were no National League teams in New York City (both the Giants and Dodgers left after 1957 season, and the expansion Mets wouldn't make their appearance until 1962). Live television shows usually liked to showcase the athletes shortly after their accomplishment. There was nothing that seemed convenient for this to happen with the Pirates' schedule. Haddix threw his "almost perfect game" on a Tuesday. Based on the Pittsburgh rotation, he likely would have pitched on Sunday, May 31. The Ed Sullivan Show was on Sunday nights. Based on scheduling and traveling difficulties, it's easy to see where Haddix would just say "thanks, but no thanks."

Haddix had an impressive career apart from this one extraordinary game, too. In 1947, he started his professional career in Winston-Salem (North Carolina) playing Class C ball. From 1948-1950, he threw for Columbus (Ohio) in AAA ball. In 1951-1952, Haddix was in the Army (during the Korean War) and was an athletic director at Fort Dix, New Jersey where he pitched for the camp baseball team. In August 1952, he made his major league debut with the Cardinals.

From 1953-1955 with St. Louis, he had his greatest success as a major league pitcher, as he made the National League All-Star team each year. He had his best year in 1953 when he led the National League in shutouts with six, as he achieved a 20-9 won-loss record and a 3.06 ERA as a 27-year-old. He was traded to the Phillies in 1956 and then to Cincinnati in 1958, when he earned his first of three consecutive Gold Glove Awards. The Reds then traded him to Pittsburgh before the 1959 season along with Smoky Burgess and Don Hoak.

Harvey Haddix was one of the best pitchers of the 1950s. Breaking in with the Cardinals at the end of the 1952 season, Haddix quickly established himself as a star, finishing second to Brooklyn's Jim Gilliam in the 1953 Rookie of the Year voting. He compares favorably to all the 1950s pitching stars, ranking 15th in WAR achieved during the decade.

Table 9-4. Best Pitchers of the 1950s

WAR Rank	Pitcher (Team(s))	Seasons Pitched	Innings Pitched	WAR (per 200 IP)	Wins (per Season)
1	Robin Roberts (Phillies)	1950-1959	3,011.2	60.4 (4.01)	199 (19.9)
2	Warren Spahn (Braves)	1950-1959	2,822.2	57.1 (4.05)	202 (20.2)
3	Billy Pierce (White Sox)	1950-1959	2,383.0	43.7 (3.67)	155 (15.5)

WAR Rank	Pitcher (Team(s))	Seasons Pitched	Innings Pitched	WAR (per 200 IP)	Wins (per Season)
4	Early Wynn (Indians, White Sox)	1950-1959	2,562.0	37.4 (2.92)	188 (18.8)
5	Bob Rush (Cubs, Braves)	1950-1959	2,047.0	33.5 (3.27)	110 (11.0)
6	Sal Maglie (Giants, Indians, Dodgers, Yankees, Cardinals)	1950-1958	1,638.2	31.2 (3.81)	114 (12.7)
7	Johnny Antonelli (Dodgers, Braves, Giants)	1950 1953-1959	1,721.1	31.1 (3.61)	116 (14.5)
8	Ned Garver (Browns, Tigers, Athletics)	1950-1959	1,904.1	28.0 (2.94)	106 (10.6)
9	Mike Garcia (Indians)	1950-1959	1,960.1	26.5 (2.70)	128 (12.8)
10	Whitey Ford (Yankees)	1950-1959	1,561.2	26.3 (3.37)	121 (12.1)
11	Bob Lemon (Indians)	1950-1958	2,015.1	25.5 (2.53)	150 (16.7)
12	Murry Dickson (Pirates, Cardinals, A's, Yankees)	1950-1959	1,918.0	25.0 (2.61)	106 (10.6)
13 (tie)	Don Newcombe (Dodgers, Reds)	1950-1959	1,773.2	24.0 (2.71)	126 (12.6)
13 (tie)	Curt Simmons (Phillies)	1950 1952-1959	1,625.1	24.0 (2.95)	103 (11.4)
15	Harvey Haddix (Cardinals, Phillies, Reds, Pirates)	1952-1959	1,572.0	23.8 (3.03)	95 (10.6)

METHODOLOGY: Pitchers are ranked in order of Wins Above Replacement (WAR) achieved from 1950-1959. WAR measures a player's value in all facets of the game by deciphering how many more wins he's worth than a replacement-level player at his same position. I included the top 15 pitchers so I could incorporate Harvey Haddix into the analysis.

LEGEND: Another measure of merit I wanted to include was the number of wins each pitcher accumulated as well. Because a significant number of pitchers were only present for a portion of the decade, I included two rate measures (WAR per 200 innings pitched and wins per season). IP = innings pitched. One-third of an inning is designated as ".1" and two-thirds of an inning is designated as ".2" innings.

Haddix was a key member of the 1960 World Champion Pirates, winning two games in the World Series, including the decisive seventh game against the Yankees. He stayed with Pittsburgh through the 1963 season. At that point, he was traded to Baltimore, where he was used primarily as a relief pitcher. He finished his career with the Orioles at the end of the 1965 season. For his career, he compiled a 136-113 record with a 3.63 ERA over 14 seasons.

After his playing career ended, Haddix joined the ranks of major league pitching coaches, working with the New York Mets, Cincinnati Reds, Boston Red Sox, Cleveland Indians, and the Pirates. He got his second World Series Championship ring as a member of the Pirates' staff in 1979.

Haddix's batterymate on the day he threw his extraordinary near-perfect game, Smoky Burgess, was also a very accomplished player. A left-handed hitter and nine-time All-Star, Burgess had an impressive 18-year career starting in 1949 with the Cubs. He also played with the Phillies, Reds, Pirates, and White Sox and was a member of the Pittsburgh World Champion team in 1960. With a career record of over 1,300 hits and 126 home runs, Burgess was known as a hitting threat. In 1959, when he caught Haddix's game, Burgess was in his prime. As Pittsburgh's primary starting catcher and a Pirate representative on the All-Star team that year, he batted .297 with 11 home runs and an OPS of .834 that season.

During the last several years of his career, Burgess became almost exclusively used as a pinch-hitter, setting the Major League record for career pinch-hits with 145. His record was broken by Manny Mota in 1979, who collected 150 pinch-hits over his career. When Burgess's playing career ended, he spent many years with the Atlanta Braves as a scout and a minor league batting coach with the Pulaski (Virginia) Braves in the Appalachian League.

CHAPTER 10

NOLAN RYAN: BEST FOR LAST

May 1, 1991
Nolan Ryan is the oldest pitcher to throw a no-hitter,
throwing his best game ever at 44

"I had the best command of all three pitches. This is the best. This is my most overpowering night."

Nolan Ryan giving an assessment of his pitching performance that game ("Unhittable, Unbelievable: Ryan Fires No. 7," *New York Times*, May 2, 1991).

"My back hurts, my heel hurts and I've been pounding Advil all day. I don't feel good. I feel old today. Watch me."

Ryan speaking to Texas Rangers pitching coach Tom House prior to the game ("Officiating in History: Nolan Ryan's 7th No-Hitter – May 1, 1991," *Referee*, April 27, 2022).

"So now Ryan has as many no-hitters as there are seas, heavens, wonders of the world, days of the week, sacraments, deadly sins, and innings before you stretch."

Sportswriter Steve Wulf describing Nolan Ryan's achievement ("Heaven for Seven: Nolan Ryan's No-hitters Have Rescued a Septet of Appreciative Catchers from Obscurity," *Sports Illustrated*, May 13, 1991).

"As each inning went on, you could see it in his eyes. You could hear him talking to himself. You could see that he really sensed it and knew what to do with it."

Texas catcher Mike Stanley describing the increasing intensity and determination of Nolan Ryan that night (*Sports Illustrated*, May 13, 1991).

"There is always somebody who defies the odds. For baseball, it is him (Ryan)."

Toronto All-Star Joe Carter giving his post-game assessment of Nolan Ryan's historic achievement ("This Day in History, May 1: Nolan Ryan," *bleacherreport.com*, May 1, 2008).

On June 11, 1990, Nolan Ryan threw a 5-0 no-hit shutout for the Texas Rangers against the Oakland Athletics. He set several records that day. He broke his own record for most no-hitters by a single pitcher by throwing his sixth. He also broke the record for throwing a no-hitter for his third team (he had thrown no-hitters for the California Angels and Houston Astros prior to this). Finally, and perhaps most impressively, at 43 years old, he became the oldest pitcher ever to throw a no-hitter. It was a remarkable feat for a man who was already a certainty for the Hall of Fame by that point in his career.

Less than one year later, he did it again at the age of 44. On May 1, 1991, Nolan Ryan threw his seventh no-hitter, blanking the Toronto Blue Jays 3-0. The game itself wasn't overly dramatic. Texas scored all three of its runs in the third inning, highlighted by a two-run Ruben Sierra home run to deep left field. That's all Ryan would need.

Ryan dominated a hard-hitting Toronto lineup – leading the majors at the time with a .276 batting average – that featured All-Stars Devon White, Roberto Alomar, Kelly Gruber, Joe Carter, and John Olerud. Striking out 16 batters, Ryan allowed just a pair of two-out walks – one in the first and one in the seventh. No Blue Jay runner ever made it past first base. The other 11 outs were similarly non-threatening: five popouts, two flyouts, one lineout, and three groundouts. Only four balls even made it to the outfield.

As the *New York Times* observed, the Blue Jays did not hit a single ball hard as they flailed helplessly at Ryan's assortment of fastballs, sharp curves and changeups.

The closest Toronto came to a hit was in the sixth when Manny Lee hit a blooper to center field, which Gary Pettis caught on the run at his shoe tops. That's it.

In 1990, Ryan was two years older than Cy Young had been when he claimed the crown of oldest no-hit pitcher 82 years earlier. In 1991, Ryan broke his own record. The table below displays the five oldest pitchers to throw a no-hitter. Ryan would be #1 and #2 on the list if both of his record-breaking games were included.

Table 10-1. Oldest Pitchers to Throw a No-hitter

Rank	Date Score	Pitcher	Age	Team	Opponent
1	5/1/1991 Tex 3-0	Nolan Ryan	Over 44 years old	Texas Rangers	Toronto Blue Jays
2	6/30/1908 Bos 8-0	Cy Young	Over 41 years old	Boston Red Sox	New York Highlanders
3	5/18/2004 Ari 2-0	*Randy Johnson*	*Almost 41 years old*	*Arizona Diamondbacks*	*Atlanta Braves*
4	4/28/1961 Mil 1-0	Warren Spahn	Over 40 years old	Milwaukee Braves	San Francisco Giants
5	9/25/1956 Bro 5-0	Sal Maglie	Over 39 years old	Brooklyn Dodgers	Philadelphia Phillies

METHODOLOGY: This table depicts the five oldest pitchers to throw a no-hitter between 1900-2021. Pitchers are ranked by age with the oldest pitchers listed first.

LEGEND: Dates are shown as month/day/year (for example, June 12, 2018, is shown as 6/12/2018). Score = the winner and score of the game. Age = the age of the pitcher when he threw his no-hitter. Team = the team the pitcher played for when he threw his no-hitter. Opponent = the opposing team the pitcher no-hit. *Italicized game (Randy Johnson in 2004) was a perfect game.*

Ryan not only extended his record that day as the oldest pitcher – now at the age of 44 -- to throw a no-hitter, he also broke his record for the number of no-hitters thrown by a single pitcher (now seven). In addition to Ryan setting these almost certainly unbreakable records, he threw one of the greatest games of his career and arguably the best game in Texas Ranger history. Ranked by Game Score, it is also the best-pitched no-hitter of his career, and arguably the best game he ever threw.

Table 10-2. Nolan Ryan's Seven No-hitters

Rank	Date	Team	Opponent	Score	GSc	Strike-outs	Walks
1	5/1/1991	Texas Rangers	Toronto Blue Jays	Tex 3-0	101	16	2
2	7/15/1973	California Angels	Detroit Tigers	Cal 6-0	100	17	4
3	6/11/1990	Texas Rangers	Oakland Athletics	Tex 5-0	99	14	2
4	5/15/1973	California Angels	Kansas City Royals	Cal 3-0	96	12	3
5	9/26/1981	Houston Astros	Los Angeles Dodgers	Hou 5-0	95	11	3
6	9/28/1974	California Angels	Minnesota Twins	Cal 4-0	94	15	8
7	6/1/1975	California Angels	Baltimore Orioles	Cal 1-0	92	9	4

METHODOLOGY: All seven Nolan Ryan no-hitters are ranked by Game Score (GSc) in descending order. Game Score measures a pitcher's performance in any given game started. Introduced by baseball writer/statistician Bill James in the 1980s, Game Score is presented as a figure between 0-100 — except for extreme outliers — and usually falls between 40-70. For comparison purposes, all five franchise no-hitters are included in this table.

LEGEND: Dates are shown as month/day/year (for example, June 12, 2018, is shown as 6/12/2018). Team = the team Ryan played for when he threw his no-hitter. Opponent = the opposing team Ryan no-hit. Outcome = the winner and score of the game. Strikeouts and Walks are the number of each he threw during the game.

NOTE 1: All games in the table are complete game, nine-inning shutouts. Ryan also threw 13 games of nine or more innings where he allowed only one-hit.

NOTE 2: Ryan threw two other non-no-hit games where he registered a Game Score of 100 or more:

1) On August 17, 1990, he pitched ten shutout innings for the Texas Rangers in the first game of a doubleheader against the Chicago White Sox. He allowed

three singles, struck out 15 batters, and walked no one for a game score of 101. When Ryan was relieved, the game was tied 0-0. Texas won when the Rangers scored on a triple and single in the bottom of the 13th inning.

2) On July 9, 1972, he threw a complete game 3-0 shutout for the California Angels against the Boston Red Sox. He only allowed a walk and a single in the first inning while striking out 16 for a game score of 100.

Ryan's first no-hitter was in 1973 with the California Angels. His seventh was in 1991 with the Rangers. The nearly 18-year spread is the longest gap between a pitcher's first no-hitter and last no-hitter. Only five pitchers have ever had a gap of 10 years or more between first and last no-hitters, as shown in the table below. Four of the five were easy selections for the Hall of Fame. The fifth, Justin Verlander, is a first ballot lock for election to the Hall.

Table 10-3. Longest Time Between First and Last No-hitters

Rank	Pitcher	Date	Team	Opponent	Score	Time Between
1	Nolan Ryan	5/15/1973 5/1/1991	Cal Angels Tex Rangers	KC Royals Tor Blue Jays	Cal 3-0 Tex 3-0	Almost 18 years
2	Randy Johnson	6/2/1990 *5/18/2004*	Seattle M's *Ari D-backs*	Det Tigers *Atl Braves*	Sea 2-0 *Ari 2-0*	Almost 14 years
3	Justin Verlander	6/12/2007 9/1/2019	Det Tigers Hou Astros	Mil Brewers Tor Blue Jays	Det 4-0 Hou 2-0	Over 12 years
4	Bob Feller	4/16/1940 7/1/1951	Cle Indians Cle Indians	Chi White Sox Detroit Tigers	Cle 1-0 Cle 2-1	Over 11 years
5	Cy Young	9/18/1897 6/30/1908	Cle Spiders Bos Red Sox	Cin Reds NY Highlanders	Cle 6-0 NY 8-0	Almost 11 years

METHODOLOGY: The table lists the five pitchers who had gaps of 10 years or more between their first no-hitter and last no-hitter. Pitchers are listed in order of the longest time between the two events.

LEGEND: Each row in the table represents a separate no-hitter thrown by the no-hit pitcher listed on the left. Dates show when the no-hitter was thrown and are written as month/day/year (for example, June 12, 2018, is shown as 6/12/2018). The "Team" is the team the pitcher was on when he threw the no-hitter. "Opponent" is the opponent on the day of the no-hitter. "Score" is the final score of the game. "Time Between" is the number of years between the pitcher's first no-hitter and last no-hitter. For Nolan Ryan, Bob Feller, Cy Young, and Justin Verlander, each of them threw one or more no-hitters in between the dates listed. *Italicized game (Randy Johnson in 2004) was a perfect game.*

NOTE: Cy Young's Cleveland Spiders were a National League franchise from 1887-1899. They were known as the Cleveland Blues their first two years and changed their name to the Spiders in 1889. The National League contracted in 1900 from 12 teams to eight. After a horrendous 20-134 season, the Spiders were one of the four teams that were eliminated, along with the Baltimore Orioles, Louisville Colonels, and Washington Senators. The Orioles and Senators are separate from teams that bore the same names in later years. The New York Highlanders joined the American League in 1903 as a replacement for the defunct Baltimore Orioles. The team changed its name to the New York Yankees in 1913.

Of the five pitchers listed in the table above, four achieved their first and last no-hitters with different teams. Only six pitchers have thrown no-hitters for two or more teams since 1900. Nolan Ryan is the only pitcher to throw no-hitters for three separate teams. The complete list is in the table below.

Table 10-4. Pitchers with No-hitters for Two or More Teams

Pitcher	Team	Date	Opponent	Score
Nolan Ryan	California Angels	5/15/1973	Kansas City Royals	Cal 3-0
	California Angels	7/15/1973	Detroit Tigers	Cal 6-0
	California Angels	9/28/1974	Minnesota Twins	Cal 4-0
	California Angels	6/1/1975	Baltimore Orioles	Cal 1-0
	Houston Astros	9/26/1981	Los Angeles Dodgers	Hou 5-0
	Texas Rangers	6/11/1990	Oakland Athletics	Tex 5-0
	Texas Rangers	5/1/1991	Toronto Blue Jays	Tex 3-0
Justin Verlander	Detroit Tigers	6/12/2007	Milwaukee Brewers	Det 4-0
	Detroit Tigers	5/7/2011	Toronto Blue Jays	Det 9-0
	Houston Astros	9/1/2019	Toronto Blue Jays	Hou 2-0
Jim Bunning	Detroit Tigers	7/20/1958 (1)	Boston Red Sox	Det 3-0
	Philadelphia Phillies	*6/21/1964 (1)*	*New York Mets*	*Phi 6-0*
Randy Johnson	Seattle Mariners	6/2/1990	Detroit Tigers	Sea 2-0
	Arizona D-backs	*5/18/2004*	*Atlanta Braves*	*Ari 2-0*

Pitcher	Team	Date	Opponent	Score
Hideo Nomo	Los Angeles Dodgers Boston Red Sox	6/17/1996 4/4/2001	Colorado Rockies Baltimore Orioles	LA 9-0 Bos 3-0
Mike Fiers	Houston Astros Oakland Athletics	8/21/2015 5/7/2019	Los Angeles Dodgers Cincinnati Reds	Hou 3-0 Oak 2-0

METHODOLOGY: This table lists all pitchers who threw complete game no-hitters for more than one team between 1900-2021. Pitchers are ranked in this table based on the number of no-hitters they threw. For the four pitchers who threw two no-hitters for different teams, they are listed in chronological order based upon the date they threw their first no-hitter. A team is defined as a major league franchise – simply changing a team's name or a franchise moving from one city to another doesn't qualify them as being on different teams. For example, Cy Young threw three no-hitters: two with Boston in the American League (1904 and 1908), and one with Cleveland in the National League (1897). Boston changed its name from the Americans to the Red Sox during this period – while they had a different name, they're still the same franchise. Also, since Young's no-hitter with the Cleveland Spiders was prior to 1900, it doesn't count for purposes of this table.

LEGEND: Each row in the table represents a separate no-hitter thrown by the no-hit pitcher listed to the left. The "Team" is the team the pitcher was on when he threw the no-hitter. Dates show when the no-hitter was thrown and are written as month/day/year (for example, June 12, 2018, is shown as 6/12/2018). (1) = first game of a doubleheader. "Opponent" is the opponent on the day of the no-hitter. "Score" is the final score of the game. *Italicized games (Jim Bunning in 1964 and Randy Johnson in 2004) were perfect games.*

NOTE: Kevin Millwood participated in two no-hitters for different teams. One was a complete game no-hitter against the Giants while he was with the Phillies in 2003. The other was the first six innings of a six-pitcher no-hitter for the Mariners versus the Dodgers in 2012. Since the second game was not a complete game, it doesn't count for purposes of this table.

In addition to being one of Ryan's best games ever, this game is also tied for the highest Game Score of any game ever thrown by a franchise pitcher in the team's 60+ seasons of baseball. Ryan's 101 game score was the highest for any franchise pitcher in a nine-inning game.

Table 10-5. Senators and Rangers Highest Game Scores

Rank	Pitcher (Team)	Date Score	Opponent	GSc	IP, Hits, Runs, ERs, Walks, Strikeouts
1	Tom Cheney (Washington)	9/12/1962 Was 2-1 (16 inn)	Baltimore Orioles	115	16.0 IP, 10 Hits, 1 Run, 1 ER, 4 BBs, 21 Ks
2 (tie)	Mike Paul (Texas)	7/14/1972 Cle 2-0 (14 inn)	Cleveland Indians	101	11.0 IP, 3 Hits, 0 Runs, 0 ERs, 0 BBs, 10 Ks
2 (tie)	Nolan Ryan (Texas)	8/17/1990 (1) Tex 1-0 (13 inn)	Chicago White Sox	101	10.0 IP, 3 Hits, 0 Runs, 0 ERs, 0 BBs, 15 Ks
2 (tie)	Nolan Ryan (Texas)	5/1/1991 Tex 3-0	Toronto Blue Jays	101	9.0 IP, 0 Hits, 0 Runs, 0 ERs, 2 BBs, 16 Ks
5 (tie)	Nolan Ryan (Texas)	4/26/1990 Tex 1-0	Chicago White Sox	99	9.0 IP, 1 Hit, 0 Runs, 0 ERs, 2 BBs, 16 Ks
5 (tie)	Nolan Ryan (Texas)	6/11/1990 Tex 5-0	Oakland Athletics	99	9.0 IP, 0 Hits, 0 Runs, 0 ERs, 2 BBs, 14 Ks
7	Frank Bertaina (Washington)	8/26/1968 (2) Was 1-0 (13 inn)	Minnesota Twins	98	11.0 IP, 2 Hits, 0 Runs, 0 ERs, 4 BBs, 9 Ks
8	Yu Darvish (Texas)	4/2/2013 Tex 7-0	Houston Astros	96	8.2 IP, 1 Hit, 0 Runs, 0 ERs, 0 BBs, 14 Ks
9 (tie)	Gaylord Perry (Texas)	7/22/1975 Tex 4-0	Cleveland Indians	95	9.0 IP, 2 Hits, 0 Runs, 0 ERs, 1 BB, 13 Ks
9 (tie)	*Kenny Rogers (Texas)*	*7/28/1994 Tex 4-0*	*California Angels*	95	*9.0 IP, 0 Hits, 0 Runs, 0 ERs, 0 BBs, 8 Ks*
11 (tie)	Jim Bibby (Texas)	7/30/1973 Tex 6-0	Oakland Athletics	94	9.0 IP, 0 Hits, 0 Runs, 0 ERs, 6 BBs, 13 Ks
16 (tie)	Bert Blyleven (Texas)	9/22/1977 Tex 6-0	California Angels	93	9.0 IP, 0 Hits, 0 Runs, 0 ERs, 1 BB, 7 Ks

METHODOLOGY: This table lists the highest Game Scores for expansion Washington Senators and Texas Rangers pitchers from 1961-2021. Games are ranked by Game Score (GSc) and consider all franchise regular season and postseason games. For comparison purposes, all five franchise no-hitters from 1961-2021 are included in this table. Game Score measures a pitcher's performance in any given game started. Introduced by baseball writer/statistician Bill James in the 1980s,

Game Score is presented as a figure between 0-100 — except for extreme outliers — and usually falls between 40-70.

LEGEND: Dates are shown as month/day/year (for example, June 12, 2018, is shown as 6/12/2018); IP = innings pitched. BB(s) = base(s) on balls. K(s) = strikeout(s). ER(s) = earned run(s). inn = innings (associated with the length of games that were more or less than nine innings). One-third of an inning pitched has 0.1 added and two-thirds of an inning pitched has 0.2 added (for example, 9 1/3 innings pitched is displayed as 9.1). BB(s) = base(s) on balls; K(s) = strikeout(s). (1) or (2) indicates the game is the first or second game of a doubleheader. This franchise established itself as the Washington Senators expansion team in 1961. Prior to 1961, the original Washington Senators played as part of the American League from its inception in 1901 until 1960. That team moved to Minnesota and became the Twins in 1961. The new Senators expansion team played in Washington from 1961 until it moved to Arlington and became the Texas Rangers prior to the 1972 season. The team's home city for each of the games in the table is indicated in the "Team" entry underneath the pitcher's name. *Kenny Rogers' perfect game in 1994 is italicized.*

NOTE 1: The highest postseason Game Score for a franchise pitcher was a 90 achieved by Cliff Lee in the third game of the 2010 ALCS against the Yankees. Lee struck out 13 and only allowed two hits and one walk over eight shutout innings. After the Rangers scored six runs in the top of the ninth inning to take a commanding 8-0 lead, manager Ron Washington elected to pull Lee in favor of relief pitcher Neftali Feliz. Lee had thrown 122 pitches by that point, and Washington wanted to reduce the fatigue on Lee's arm in case the series went to seven games. As it turned out, Texas won the ALCS over New York in six games.

NOTE 2: Tom Cheney achieved a game score of 115 for a 16-inning complete game win against the Baltimore Orioles in 1962. Over the course of the game, he allowed one run on 10 hits – including four doubles -- and four walks, while striking out 21 batters. The Senators went ahead 2-1 in the 16th when Bud Zipfel hit a home run in the top of the inning. Cheney came out for the bottom of the 16th and shut down Baltimore for the win. Cheney's 21 strikeouts are the most ever achieved by a pitcher in a single game. Nolan Ryan's two 16-strikeout performances – tied for second (101) and fifth (99) place on the team's Game Score ranking – are second place on the franchise strikeout list and the most achieved by a Senator/Ranger pitcher in a nine-inning contest.

Cheney's 16-inning effort may not have been his best game, though. He achieved a Game Score of 94 on April 11, 1963, when he threw a nine-inning, one-hit shutout against the Boston Red Sox. Cheney only allowed a single in the fourth inning and a walk in the sixth, while striking out 10 Red Sox batters. The final score was 8-0.

NOTE 3: Mike Paul pitched 11 shutout innings against Cleveland in his 1972 game. When Paul was relieved, the score was tied 0-0. Cleveland won when the Indians scored two unearned runs in the top of the 14th inning. Nolan Ryan pitched 10 shutout innings and struck out 15 batters in an August 1990 contest versus the White Sox. When Brad Arnsberg came in to pitch the 11th, the game was tied 0-0. Texas won when the Rangers scored on a Gary Pettis leadoff triple and Ruben Sierra single in the bottom of the 13th inning.

NOTE 4: Yu Darvish retired the first 26 Astros he faced in his April 2013 game against the Astros. No Houston batter reached base until shortstop Marwin Gonzalez hit a single up the middle with two outs in the bottom of the ninth inning. The Rangers were leading 7-0 at the time, Darvish had already thrown 111 pitches, and it was only the third contest in a long 162-game season. Manager Ron Washington didn't want to overstress the arm of his star pitcher, so he brought in reliever Michael Kirkman to finish the game.

NOTE 5: Jim Bibby's no-hitter was especially notable since it came against the reigning World Champion Oakland Athletics right in the middle of their three-season championship run. Bert Blyleven allowed only two baserunners in his 1977 no-hitter against the Angels. The first one was in the fifth inning on an error by the shortstop to the leadoff hitter. The second was on a walk to pinch-hitter Carlos May with two outs in the ninth inning of a 6-0 game.

NOTE 6: Kenny Rogers' 1994 perfect game was just that: 27 batters, eight strikeouts, seven groundouts, 12 flyouts (including one very close lineout to end the game). Nobody reached base.

Nolan Ryan was with the Texas Rangers for only five seasons from 1989 to 1993. He was between the ages of 42 to 46 during those years. While still effective during his last two years, he was not as imposing as he had been, as he compiled a win-loss record of 10-14 in 1992-1993. Yet, it can be argued that Ryan was the most dominant pitcher in Ranger history. Even though he was only with Texas for a relatively short period, Ryan recorded four of the six highest Game Scores of any Ranger pitcher ever. No one else appears more than once in the top 10 list for the franchise.

Of course, Nolan Ryan features prominently on other teams' lists of highest Game Scores. His tenure with the Angels, including his four no-hitters for California, will be discussed at length in this chapter and Chapter 13 in Volume II (Bo Belinsky). He also threw a no-hitter and made his mark for Houston, as shown in the table below.

Table 10-6. Colt .45s and Astros Highest Game Scores

Rank	Pitcher (Team/Lg)	Date Score	Oppo-nent	GSc	IP, Hits, Runs, ERs, Walks, Strikeouts
1	Mike Cuellar (Astros/NL)	7/24/1967 Hou 2-1 (11 inn)	Phi Phillies	101	11.0 IP, 2 Hits, 1 Run, 0 ERs, 2 BBs, 12 Ks
2 (tie)	Gerrit Cole (Astros/AL)	5/4/2018 Hou 8-0	Ari D-backs	100	9.0 IP, 1 Hit, 0 Runs, 0 ERs, 1 BB, 16 Ks
2 (tie)	Justin Verlander (Astros/AL)	9/1/2019 Hou 2-0	Tor B. Jays	100	9.0 IP, 0 Hits, 0 Runs, 0 ERs, 1 BB, 14 Ks
4 (tie)	Turk Farrell (Colt .45s/NL)	4/12/1963 Hou 2-1 (12 inn)	LA Dodgers	99	12.0 IP, 4 Hits, 1 Run, 1 ER, 2 BBs, 11 Ks
4 (tie)	Don Wilson (Astros/NL)	6/18/1967 Hou 2-0	Atl Braves	99	9.0 IP, 0 Hits, 0 Runs, 0 ERs, 3 BBs, 15 Ks
6 (tie)	Turk Farrell (Colt .45s/NL)	8/6/1962 Cin 1-0 (13 inn)	Cin Reds	98	12.0 IP, 6 Hits, 0 Runs, 0 ERs, 1 BB, 9 Ks
6 (tie)	Ken Forsch (Astros/NL)	9/24/1971 (1) Hou 2-1 (21 inn)	SD Padres	98	13.0 IP, 6 Hits, 1 Run, 1 ER, 1 BB, 8 Ks
6 (tie)	Mike Scott (Astros/NL)	9/25/1986 Hou 2-0	SF Giants	98	9.0 IP, 0 Hits, 0 Runs, 0 ERs, 2 BBs, 13 Ks
9	Mike Cuellar (Astros/NL)	7/1/1966 Hou 2-1 (12 inn)	Cin Reds	97	11.0 IP, 3 Hits, 1 Run, 1 ER, 0 BBs, 10 Ks
10 (tie)	Bob Bruce (Colt .45s/NL)	9/27/1964 Hou 1-0 (12 inn)	LA Dodgers	96	12.0 IP, 5 Hits, 0 Runs, 0 ERs, 2 BBs, 6 Ks
10 (tie)	Nolan Ryan (Astros/NL)	7/22/1986 Hou 1-0 (10 inn)	Mon Expos	96	9.1 IP, 1 Hit, 0 Runs, 0 ERs, 4 BBs, 14 Ks
10 (tie)	Mike Scott (Astros/NL)	6/8/1990 Hou 3-1 (10 inn)	Cin Reds	96	10.0 IP, 3 Hits, 1 Run, 1 ER, 1 BB, 15 Ks
13 (tie)	Nolan Ryan (Astros/NL)	9/26/1981 Hou 5-0	LA Dodgers	95	9.0 IP, 0 Hits, 0 Runs, 0 ERs, 3 BBs, 11 Ks

Rank	Pitcher (Team/Lg)	Date Score	Opponent	GSc	IP, Hits, Runs, ERs, Walks, Strikeouts
15 (tie)	Don Wilson (Astros/NL)	5/1/1969 Hou 4-0	Cin Reds	94	9.0 IP, 0 Hits, 0 Runs, 0 ERs, 6 BBs, 13 Ks
15 (tie)	Mike Fiers (Astros/AL)	8/21/2015 Hou 3-0	LA Dodgers	94	9.0 IP, 0 Hits, 0 Runs, 0 ERs, 3 BBs, 10 Ks
21 (tie)	Darryl Kile (Astros/NL)	9/8/1993 Hou 7-1	NY Mets	93	9.0 IP, 0 Hits, 1 Run, 0 ERs, 1 BB, 9 Ks
25 (tie)	Ken Johnson (Colt .45s/NL)	4/23/1964 Cin 1-0	Cin Reds	92	9.0 IP, 0 Hits, 1 Run, 0 ERs, 2 BBs, 9 Ks
31 (tie)	Larry Dierker (Astros/NL)	7/9/1976 Hou 4-0	Mon Expos	91	9.0 IP, 0 Hits, 0 Runs, 0 ERs, 4 BBs, 8 Ks
40 (tie)	Don Nottebart (Colt .45s/NL)	5/17/1963 Hou 4-1	Phi Phillies	90	9.0 IP, 0 Hits, 1 Runs, 0 ERs, 3 BBs, 8 Ks
71 (tie)	Ken Forsch (Astros/NL)	4/7/1979 Hou 6-0	Atl Braves	88	9.0 IP, 0 Hits, 0 Runs, 0 ERs, 2 BBs, 3 Ks
---	Aaron Sanchez +3 (Astros/AL)	8/3/2019 Hou 9-0	Sea Mariners	76	6.0 IP, 0 Hits, 0 Runs, 0 ERs, 2 BBs, 6 Ks

METHODOLOGY: This table lists the highest Game Scores for Houston pitchers from 1962-2021. Games are ranked by Game Score (GSc) and consider all franchise regular season and postseason games. For comparison purposes, all 11 Houston no-hitters are included in this table. Game Score measures a pitcher's performance in any given game started. Introduced by baseball writer/statistician Bill James in the 1980s, Game Score is presented as a figure between 0-100 — except for extreme outliers — and usually falls between 40-70.

LEGEND: Dates are shown as month/day/year (for example, June 12, 2018, is shown as 6/12/2018); IP = innings pitched. BB(s) = base(s) on balls. K(s) = strikeout(s). ER(s) = earned run(s). inn = innings (associated with the length of games that were more or less than nine innings). One-third of an inning pitched has 0.1 added and two-thirds of an inning pitched has 0.2 added (for example, 9 1/3 innings pitched is displayed as 9.1). BB(s) = base(s) on balls; K(s) = strikeout(s). (2) indicates the game is the second game of a doubleheader. The Houston franchise has been known by different names and played in both the National and American Leagues since it burst onto the scene in 1962 as a National League expansion team. It began as the

Colt .45s (often shortened to just "Colts"). With the move to the Astrodome in 1965, the team changed its name to the Astros. With the 1969 expansion to 12 teams in each league and the split of the two leagues into east and west divisions, Houston became a part of the National League West Division. With further expansion in 1994, Houston was moved to the newly created National League Central Division, where they stayed until 2013. That year, Major League Baseball decided that rather than having imbalanced league structures, they would move one team from the 16-team National League to the 14-team American League. This way, both leagues would consist of 15 teams. As a result, Houston moved from the National League to the American League West Division. The team name and the league Houston played in for each of the games in the table is indicated in the "Team/Lg" entry underneath the pitcher's name.

NOTE 1: The highest Houston postseason Game Score was a 90 achieved by two Astro pitchers in the 1986 NLCS against the Mets. In Game 1, Mike Scott shut out New York 1-0 on five hits. The only run scored in that Mike Scott/Dwight Gooden pitching duel was a leadoff home run by first baseman Glenn Davis in the bottom of the second. In the pivotal Game 5 with the series tied at two games each, Nolan Ryan also recorded a Game Score of 90 as he threw nine innings of two-hit ball. Unfortunately, one of those hits was a one-out solo home run to Darryl Strawberry in the fifth inning, which tied the game at 1-1. Ryan was relieved by Charlie Kerfeld in the 10th, and the game remained tied through the bottom of the 12th until Gary Carter knocked in Wally Backman for the winning run. The Mets would go on to win Game 6 and the series the next evening by the score of 7-6, in a back-and-forth, 16-inning marathon game.

NOTE 2: Aaron Sanchez was the starting pitcher for a combined four-pitcher no-hitter in August 2019. Sanchez pitched six innings and earned a Game Score of 76 in a 9-0 no-hitter against the Mariners. Will Harris, Joe Biagini, and Chris Devenski finished the game, each pitching one inning of no-hit ball. With a total of eight strikeouts and four walks, the combined performance of the four pitchers would have earned a Game Score of 91 if the game had been thrown by a single pitcher.

NOTE 3: In his 11-inning 1967 win (Game Score 101), Mike Cuellar had a perfect game until Phillies second baseman Cookie Rojas hit a double to left field with two outs in the fifth inning. After that, the only other hit Cuellar allowed was a one-out single to first baseman Bill White in the top of the 11th en route to a 2-1 win over Philadelphia. The one run Cuellar gave up was unearned as the result of a walk and a two-out throwing error by Houston's third baseman in the top of the ninth.

NOTE 4: The only hit allowed by Gerrit Cole in his 16-strikeout performance in 2018 was a one-out double in the bottom of the fifth inning to Arizona second baseman Chris Owings. Prior to that, he had only allowed a full count walk to lead-off hitter David Peralta in the fourth inning. Those were the only Arizona hitters to reach base. Cole's 16 strikeouts is tied for the second-most ever by a Houston pitcher in a single game. Don Wilson (1968), Nolan Ryan (1987), and Randy Johnson (1998) achieved 16 as well. Ryan's 16 strikeouts as an Astro were achieved during an eight-inning performance in a 4-2 win against the Giants in 1987. The most strikeouts he ever had in a game was 19 in four different games for the California Angels from 1974-1977. Overall, he notched 16 or more strikeouts 16 different times for the Angels, Rangers, Mets, and Astros.

NOTE 5: The most strikeouts ever achieved by a Houston pitcher was 18, when Don Wilson won the second game of a July 1968 doubleheader against the Reds by the score of 6-1 behind his five-hit, two-walk performance. Don Wilson was a standout for the Astros from when he burst on the scene in 1967 as a 22-year-old rookie after a one-game cup-of-coffee late in 1966. Wilson threw his 15-strikeout no-hitter against the Braves as a rookie. This is the most strikeouts a Houston pitcher has ever thrown in a no-hitter, earning him a 99 Game Score. Don Wilson threw his second no-hitter in 1969 against the Reds, striking out 13 in that contest. His 1969 no-hitter was the second game of a two-game series between the teams, both of which were no-hitters – Cincinnati's Jim Maloney had thrown his second career no-hitter the day before. During his nine seasons with a decidedly middle-of-the-road Astros team from 1966-1974, Wilson compiled 104 wins and was named to the NL All-Star team in 1971. Sadly, Don Wilson died at his home from carbon monoxide poisoning in January 1975. The coroner's office ruled it an accident.

NOTE 6: Justin Verlander threw his lone no-hitter for the Astros in 2019 against an out-of-contention Blue Jays team. Houston was riding high at the time, leading the American League West Division by 9.5 games with the second-best record in baseball. This no-hitter made him only the sixth pitcher to have three no-hitters to his credit. The game was a 0-0 tie until the top of the ninth, when third baseman Abraham Toro hit a two-out, two-run home run to give Houston a 2-0 edge. There was some question how far Verlander would go in the game, as he had already thrown

108 pitches prior to the start of the bottom of the ninth. He ended up finishing the game at 120 pitches.

NOTE 7: Ken Forsch's 1979 no-hitter against the Braves placed him and his brother Bob in a unique category: they are the only two brothers who have thrown no-hitters. Bob Forsch threw two no-hitters: one in 1978 against the Phillies and his second in 1983 versus the Expos. Ken Forsch's catcher that day, longtime Astro Alan Ashby, caught the first of three no-hitters for the Astros. The other two no-hitters Ashby caught were thrown by Nolan Ryan in 1981 and Mike Scott in 1986.

Ashby and Ryan's no-hitter was against the division rival Dodgers as the two teams battled it out for a playoff spot in the 1981 division series created because of the players' strike in the middle of the season. Behind Ryan's 11-strikeout no-hitter, the Astros would win by the score of 5-0 and would eventually win the second-half division title by 1.5 games over the Reds. The Dodgers would beat Houston in the NLDS in a thrilling five-game set. Los Angeles would prevail over the Expos in an exciting five-game NLCS. then defeat the Yankees four games to two in the World Series.

Ashby and Scott's no-hitter against the Giants in 1986 clinched the division title for the Astros that year. The Astros would fall to the 108-win Mets in an exciting six-game NLCS. Going beyond five games in the NLDS was relatively new, as Major League Baseball changed the league championship series format from best-of-five to best-of-seven games in 1985. The Mets would go on to beat the Red Sox in a legendary seven-game World Series.

NOTE 8: In Nolan Ryan's 9.1-inning one-hit performance in 1986, the only hit he allowed was a double to Montreal's Mike Fitzgerald with one out in the fifth inning. He was relieved by Dave Smith with one out in the top of the 10th inning after he walked two of the first three batters he faced in a scoreless tie. Houston would win the game in the bottom of the inning when first baseman Glenn Davis hit a solo home run off Expo starter Floyd Youmans.

NOTE 9: Mike Fiers no-hitter in 2015 was the first by an Astros pitcher since the team's move to the American League in 2013. Interestingly, his opponent that day was the National League Dodgers in an inter-league game. His second of two no-hitters would also be an inter-league game, as he held the Reds hitless in 2019 when he was pitching for the Oakland Athletics. Darryl Kile only allowed one baserunner in his 1993 no-hitter – a one-out walk to Mets shortstop Jeff McKnight in the fourth inning. Unfortunately for Houston and Kile, McKnight would score all the way from first on a two-strike wild pitch. Kile's catcher, Scott Servais, thought the ball hit McKnight. Consequently, Servais didn't chase the ball and McKnight kept going past second on his way to third base. First baseman Ken Caminiti saw what was happening, ran in, picked up the ball, and threw to third base. Caminiti's throw was wild and McKnight scored on a wild pitch and a throwing error. Houston's offense more than overcame the error as they tallied seven runs in the 7-1 victory.

NOTE 10: Ken Johnson's no-hitter against Cincinnati in 1964 is the only time a pitcher has thrown a nine-inning complete game no-hitter and lost. The Reds recorded the only run of the game with two outs in the top of the ninth when Pete Rose scored from third on a fielding error by Houston second baseman Nellie Fox. Rose had reached second base with one out when Johnson made a throwing error trying to get him at first base on a groundball hit back to the pitcher. Rose had advanced to third on a fielder's choice.

Drafted by the NY Mets in the 12th round of the 1965 amateur draft, Nolan Ryan pitched in the minors from 1965-66, where he compiled a 23-13 record. He debuted with the Mets in late 1966 and threw regularly for New York from 1968-71 where he compiled a 29-37 record, including 487 strikeouts over 507 innings.

In what is one of the most lopsided deals of all time, Ryan was traded with starting outfielder Leroy Stanton and two minor leaguers to the California Angels for shortstop Jim Fregosi in December 1971. Ryan pitched for the Angels from 1972-1979, making the all-star team five times, winning 20 games twice, winning 19 games two other times, and finishing in the Top 10 for the Cy Young Award four times.

Ryan signed as a free agent with Houston in 1980, where he pitched for the Astros from 1980-1988. During that time, he led the league in ERA once, and strikeouts twice. He signed as a free agent with Texas in 1989, where he led the league in strikeouts in 1989 and 1990. An eight-time All-Star in both leagues, Ryan's postseason success included being on the champion New York Mets team in 1969 and starting postseason games with the Angels and the Astros.

The all-time major league leader in strikeouts (along with 50 other categories), Ryan was elected to the Hall of Fame in 1999 with 98.8% of the vote. Of course, this begs the question, "who were the 1.2% who didn't vote for Ryan?! What possible reason could they have had?!"

After his playing career, Ryan led several business ventures and held numerous positions of responsibility, including Texas Rangers president and CEO (2008–2013) and Houston Astros special assistant (2014–2019).

Mike Stanley, Ryan's batterymate that day Nolan threw his seventh and final no-hitter, is a long-time veteran of the major leagues, playing for the Texas Rangers, New York Yankees, Boston Red Sox, Toronto Blue Jays, and Oakland Athletics from 1986 to 2000. In 1995, he represented the New York Yankees on the American League All-Star team. He also won the Silver Slugger Award as a catcher with the Yankees in 1993. Primarily a catcher during his early years, he played first base and designated hitter as he got older. Stanley currently serves as an assistant baseball coach for the Lake Highland Preparatory School in Orlando, Florida.

While Mike Stanley was the most accomplished catcher to partner with Nolan Ryan on a no-hitter, no catcher ever caught more than one of the seven he threw. The list of catchers runs from the accomplished (Stanley, Ellie Rodriguez, and Alan Ashby) to the relatively obscure (Jeff Torborg, Art Kusnyer, John Russell, and Tom Egan). Of course, simply playing in the major leagues for any length of time, especially having caught a no-hit game, is a wonderful accomplishment by itself.

CHAPTER 11

MAX SCHERZER: BEST NO-HITTER OF ALL TIME?

October 3, 2015
Max Scherzer dominates the Mets,
while striking out 17 in an unparalleled performance

"Guys, I'm speechless about that. I don't know what to say. You go out there and try to have as much success as possible. You try to accomplish as much as you can and do everything you can .... To have that happen twice in a season, it's special. And when you start talking about the history of the game, you can't even really think about that. That's why I'm speechless."

Max Scherzer talking to reporters as he reflects on his performance that night ("Max Scherzer strikes out 9 straight en route to 2nd no-hitter of season," *espn.com*, October 3, 2015).

"You don't get to see that every day. We're fortunate to have the pitching staff that we do, especially with a guy like Max. He can do that any time he goes out and makes a start."

Washington veteran second baseman Dan Uggla reflecting on Max Scherzer's pitching dominance (Adam Rubin, "Max Scherzer joins rare company with second no-hitter of 2015," *espn.com*, October 3., 2015).

"It's almost like playing a game of H-O-R-S-E. He makes a shot, you got to make a shot. For me, that's what it felt like tonight. If I can just go out there and keep executing my pitches, I'm going to give my best effort to try and match him."

Scherzer describing the pitching duel he had with Mets' ace Matt Harvey through six innings (Seth Berkman, "Max Scherzer's No-Hitter Will Cost the Mets," *New York Times*, October 3, 2015)

"He was great, we were bad. So when you pitch as good as he does, it's tough to take good swings. He made all the pitches he had to make. He was very, very good."

Mets' manager Terry Collins describing the game ("Max Scherzer strikes out 9 straight en route to 2nd no-hitter of season," *espn.com*, October 3, 2015).

"You always go back when you don't accomplish your goals. You always reflect on how you can be better. And there's ways I can be a better pitcher. I do think I was a better pitcher in 2015 than I was in 2014. I feel like I'm able to do more things with the baseball and sequence guys different. I just feel like all of my pitches are better. But I still have room for improvement. I gave up a bunch of home runs there in the second half. That's something I have to improve upon in 2016."

Scherzer talking about how he's always trying to become a better pitcher (Adam Rubin, "Max Scherzer joins rare company with second no-hitter of 2015," *espn.com*, October 3., 2015).

In what is ranked as the highest no-hitter Game Score ever thrown, Washington Nationals pitcher Max Scherzer pitched an utterly dominating game, striking out 17 New York Mets while walking no one. The only Mets batter to reach base was catcher Kevin Plawecki when he was safe at first on a throwing error by Washington third baseman Yunel Escobar to lead off the sixth inning.

That was a terrible day for the Mets overall, as they dropped a doubleheader to the Nationals, having lost the first game at Citi Field 3-1. In Scherzer's no-hitter, there were just three balls hit with authority by New York. Two were flyouts to left fielder Tyler Moore hit by Michael Cuddyer (second inning) and Michael Conforto (fourth inning). Also, Curtis Granderson lined out to second baseman Dan Uggla in the fourth. None of those outs were difficult plays.

Scherzer baffled Mets batters all night long as he seemed to get better as the game went on. Sixteen of his 17 strikeouts were on swinging strikes, including nine straight swinging strikeouts from the sixth to the ninth inning. This Mets team wasn't a pushover either. While they had clinched the division title just prior to the two games that day, they were still playing for home field advantage in the playoffs. New York had an impressive lineup, which included strong hitters such as All-Star Curtis Granderson, Michael Conforto, and Michael Cuddyer. All-Stars Yoenis Cespedes and Daniel Murphy were also inserted as pinch-hitters late in the game (they both struck out).

The Mets definitely wanted to win this game, as they started their ace Matt Harvey in the second-to-the-last game of the season. While they would lose this game, the Mets would beat both the Dodgers and the Cubs to become National League champions. They would go on to lose to the Kansas City Royals in the World Series four games to one.

The Nationals managed to collect five hits this game while striking out 18 times against Matt Harvey and the Mets relievers. Their first run was scored in the sixth on a New York error, a Clint Robinson single, and a Wilson Ramos sacrifice fly. Their second, and last, run came on a solo home run to deep left field by Dan Uggla in the seventh. That's all Scherzer would need.

Scherzer's game stands out for many reasons. In a career where the three-time Cy Young winner and eight-time All-Star has excelled, this no-hit, 17-strikeout game represents his best performance. With a game score of 104, it is the second highest nine-inning game score of all time, and the highest score of any no-hitter. The table below shows all nine-inning games where a pitcher earned a game score of 100 or more.

Table 11-1. Major League Baseball's Highest Nine-Inning Game Scores

Rank	Pitcher	Team	Date Score	Opponent	GSc	IP, Hits, Runs, ERs, Walks, Strikeouts
1	Kerry Wood	Chicago Cubs	5/6/1998 Chi 2-0	Houston Astros	105	9.0 IP, 1 Hit, 0 Runs, 0 ERs, 0 BBs, 20 Ks
2	Max Scherzer	Wash Nationals	10/3/2015 (2) Was 2-0	NY Mets	104	9.0 IP, 0 Hits, 0 Runs, 0 ERs, 0 BBs, 17 Ks

Rank	Pitcher	Team	Date Score	Opponent	GSc	IP, Hits, Runs, ERs, Walks, Strikeouts
3	Clayton Kershaw	LA Dodgers	6/18/2014 LA 8-0	Colorado Rockies	102	9.0 IP, 0 Hits, 0 Runs, 0 ERs, 0 BBs, 15 Ks
4 (tie)	Nap Rucker	Brooklyn Superbas	9/5/1908 (2) Bro 6-0	Boston Doves	101	9.0 IP, 0 Hits, 0 Runs, 0 ERs, 0 BBs, 14 Ks
4 (tie)	*Sandy Koufax*	*LA Dodgers*	*9/9/1965 LA 1-0*	*Chicago Cubs*	*101*	*9.0 IP, 0 Hits, 0 Runs, 0 ERs, 0 BBs, 14 Ks*
4 (tie)	Nolan Ryan	Texas Rangers	5/1/1991 Tex 3-0	Toronto B. Jays	101	9.0 IP, 0 Hits, 0 Runs, 0 ERs, 2 BBs, 16 Ks
4 (tie)	*Matt Cain*	*SF Giants*	*6/13/2012 SF 10-0*	*Houston Astros*	*101*	*9.0 IP, 0 Hits, 0 Runs, 0 ERs, 0 BBs, 14 Ks*
8 (tie)	Warren Spahn	Milw Braves	9/16/1960 Mil 4-0	Phil Phillies	100	9.0 IP, 0 Hits, 0 Runs, 0 ERs, 2 BBs, 15 Ks
8 (tie)	Nolan Ryan	Calif Angels	7/9/1972 Cal 3-0	Boston Red Sox	100	9.0 IP, 1 Hit, 0 Runs, 0 ERs, 1 BB, 16 Ks
8 (tie)	Nolan Ryan	Calif Angels	7/15/1973 Det 6-0	Detroit Tigers	100	9.0 IP, 0 Hits, 0 Runs, 0 ERs, 4 BBs, 17 Ks
8 (tie)	Curt Schilling	Arizona D-backs	4/7/2002 Ari 2-0	Milw Brewers	100	9.0 IP, 1 Hit, 0 Runs, 0 ERs, 2 BBs, 17 Ks
8 (tie)	*Randy Johnson*	*Arizona D-backs*	*5/18/2004 Ari 2-0*	*Atlanta Braves*	*100*	*9.0 IP, 0 Hits, 0 Runs, 0 ERs, 0 BBs, 13 Ks*
8 (tie)	Brandon Morrow	Toronto Blue Jays	8/8/2010 Tor 1-0	TB Rays	100	9.0 IP, 1 Hit, 0 Runs, 0 ERs, 2 BBs, 17 Ks
8 (tie)	Max Scherzer	Wash Nationals	6/14/2015 Was 4-0	Milw Brewers	100	9.0 IP, 1 Hit, 0 Runs, 0 ERs, 1 BB, 16 Ks
8 (tie)	Gerrit Cole	Houston Astros	5/4/2018 Hou 8-0	Arizona D-backs	100	9.0 IP, 1 Hit, 0 Runs, 0 ERs, 1 BB, 16 Ks
8 (tie)	Justin Verlander	Houston Astros	9/1/2019 Hou 2-0	Toronto B. Jays	100	9.0 IP, 0 Hits, 0 Runs, 0 ERs, 1 BB, 14 Ks

METHODOLOGY: This table lists the highest nine-inning Game Scores in any game from 1900-2021. Games are ranked by pitcher Game Score (GSc) in descending order. This table includes considered all regular season and postseason games. Game Score measures a pitcher's performance in a game start. Introduced by baseball writer/statistician Bill James in the 1980s, Game Score is presented as a figure between 0-100 — except for extreme outliers like in this table — and usually falls between 40-70.

LEGEND: Dates are shown as month/day/year (for example, June 12, 2018, is shown as 6/12/2018); IP = innings pitched. BB(s) = base(s) on balls. K(s) = strikeout(s). ER(s) = earned run(s). (2) indicates the game is the second game of a doubleheader. *Sandy Koufax's, Randy Johnson's, and Matt Cain's perfect games in 1965, 2004, and 2012 are italicized.*

NOTE 1: The highest postseason GSc ever achieved was a 98 by Roger Clemens of the New York Yankees in Game 4 of the 2000 ALCS against the Mariners. Clemens only gave up one hit – a double by Seattle left fielder Al Martin leading off the seventh inning – while walking two batters and striking out 15. New York won the game 5-0, giving them a three-games-to-one advantage in a series they eventually won in six games. The Yankees would go on to defeat the Mets in an all-New York "Subway Series" in five games for the team's third consecutive championship.

NOTE 2: Kerry Wood only allowed a single to Houston shortstop Ricky Gutierrez to lead off the third inning in his remarkable 20-strikeout, zero walks game. He also hit Craig Biggio with a pitch in the sixth inning (which doesn't count against Game Score). His 20 strikeouts in nine innings of work is tied for the record with Roger Clemens (1986 and 1996), Max Scherzer (in a May 2016 game), and Randy Johnson (for the first nine innings of an 11-inning game in 2001).

NOTE 3: The only baserunner Clayton Kershaw allowed in his dominating, 15-strikeout no-hitter against the Rockies in 2014 was on a throwing error by shortstop Hanley Ramirez in the top of the seventh inning. Nap Rucker allowed three baserunners during his 1908 no-hitter – all on errors by Brooklyn defenders. Rucker's opponents that day, the Boston Doves, were renamed the Rustlers in 1911, and then the Braves in 1912. Eventually, the Braves would move to Milwaukee in 1953 and Atlanta in 1966. Rucker's Brooklyn Superbas became the Dodgers in 1911 and 1912 before reverting back to the Superbas for the 1913 season. In 1914, they renamed themselves the Brooklyn Robins and stayed that way until 1932, when they once again became the Dodgers. The Dodgers moved to Los Angeles in 1958.

NOTE 4: Warren Spahn's no-hitter against the Phillies in 1960 was the second time the Braves no-hit the Phillies that year – Lew Burdette had done it one month before. This was the first time a team no-hit an opponent twice in the same season since Ernie Koob and Bob Groom of the St. Louis Browns no-hit the Chicago White Sox on consecutive days in 1917.

NOTE 5: Nolan Ryan appears three times in this table, more than any other pitcher. In his 1972 one-hitter, he gave up a first inning walk and single. He then retired Boston's final 26 batters. Curt Schilling's 2002 no-hit attempt was broken up on a one-out single by Milwaukee's Raul Casanova in the third inning. Gerrit Cole gave up a double to Arizona's Chris Owings with one out in the fifth inning in his 2018 game.

NOTE 6: After allowing a leadoff walk in the second inning and a one-out walk in the ninth, Brandon Morrow's no-hitter was broken up with two outs in the ninth when Tampa Bay's Evan Longoria hit an infield single on a 1-1 count. With runners on first and third, Morrow got Dan Johnson to strikeout swinging for the final out in a 1-0 win. In Justin Verlander's 2019 no-hitter against the Blue Jays, the only baserunner he allowed was a one-out walk to Toronto second baseman Cavan Biggio in the first inning. Verlander retired the next 26 batters in the 2-0 win. It was Verlander's third no-hitter, and the second time he had no-hit the Blue Jays – the first time was in 2011.

Apart from Nolan Ryan (three appearances), Max Scherzer is the only pitcher who appears more than once on this list, with his one-hit, 16 strikeout performance on June 14 earlier in the year earning a score of 100. He had a no-hitter going in June 2015 until he allowed a single to Milwaukee's Carlos Gomez to lead off the seventh inning.

There have been numerous extra-inning Game Scores higher than Kerry Wood's 105 score. The highest two Game Scores ever recorded were in the same 26-inning game in 1920. Both starting pitchers (Joe Oeschger and Leon Cadore) went the distance in a game that was called because of darkness as a 1-1 tie.

Table 11-2. Highest Game Scores Ever Recorded

Rank	Pitcher	Date Score	Team	Opponent	GSc	IP, Hits, Runs, ERs, Walks, Strikeouts
1	Joe Oeschger	5/1/1920 1-1 tie (26)	Boston Braves	Brooklyn Robins	153	26.0 IP, 9 Hits, 1 Run, 1 ER, 4 BBs, 7 Ks
2	Leon Cadore	5/1/1920 1-1 tie (26)	Brooklyn Robins	Boston Braves	140	26.0 IP, 15 Hits, 1 Run, 1 ER, 5 BBs, 7 Ks

METHODOLOGY: This table lists the two highest Game Scores ever recorded. The two performances – from the same game – are ranked by pitcher Game Score

(GSc) in descending order. This table considered all regular season and postseason games. Game Score measures a pitcher's performance in any given game started. Introduced by baseball writer/statistician Bill James in the 1980s, Game Score is presented as a figure between 0-100 — except for extreme outliers as shown in this table — and usually falls between 40-70.

LEGEND: Dates are shown as month/day/year (May 1, 1920, is shown as 5/1/1920); IP = innings pitched. BB(s) = base(s) on balls. K(s) = strikeout(s). ER(s) = earned run(s). (26) = the number of innings the game went; in this case it was 26.

Of course, Scherzer's game has the highest Game Score among all pitchers in Montreal/Washington franchise history.

Table 11-3. Expos and Nationals Highest Game Scores

Rank	Pitcher (Team)	Date Score	Opponent	GSc	IP, Hits, Runs, ERs, Walks, Strikeouts
1	Max Scherzer (Washington)	10/3/2015 (2) Was 2-0	NY Mets	104	9.0 IP, 0 Hits, 0 Runs, 0 ERs, 0 BBs, 17 Ks
2	Max Scherzer (Washington)	6/14/2015 Was 4-0	Mil Brewers	100	9.0 IP, 1 Hit, 0 Runs, 0 ERs, 1 BB, 16 Ks
3	Bill Stoneman (Montreal)	6/16/1971 Mon 2-0	SD Padres	98	9.0 IP, 1 Hit, 0 Runs, 0 ERs, 1 BB, 14 Ks
4	Max Scherzer (Washington)	6/20/2015 Was 2-0	Pit Pirates	97	9.0 IP, 0 Hits, 0 Runs, 0 ERs, 0 BBs, 10 Ks
5	J. Zimmermann (Washington)	9/28/2014 Was 1-0	Miami Marlins	96	9.0 IP, 0 Hits, 0 Runs, 0 ERs, 1 BB, 10 Ks
6	J. Zimmermann (Washington)	6/8/2014 Was 6-0	SD Padres	95	9.0 IP, 2 Hits, 0 Runs, 0 ERs, 0 BBs, 12 Ks
7 (tie)	Dan Schatzeder (Montreal)	8/9/1984 Mon 1-0 (10 inn)	Chicago Cubs	94	10.0 IP, 4 Hits, 0 Runs, 0 ERs, 1 BB, 11 Ks
7 (tie)	Pedro Martinez (Montreal)	6/3/1995 Mon 1-0 (10 inn)	SD Padres	94	9.0 IP, 1 Hit, 0 Runs, 0 ERs, 0 BBs, 9 Ks
7 (tie)	Jeff Fassero (Montreal)	6/29/1996 Mon 1-0	Phi Phillies	94	9.0 IP, 2 Hits, 0 Runs, 0 ERs, 0 BBs, 11 Ks
7 (tie)	Javier Vazquez (Montreal)	9/14/1999 Mon 3-0	LA Dodgers	94	9.0 IP, 1 Hit, 0 Runs, 0 ERs, 1 BB, 10 Ks
17 (tie)	*D. Martinez* *(Montreal)*	*7/28/1991* *Mon 2-0*	*LA* *Dodgers*	*92*	*9.0 IP, 0 Hits, 0 Runs,* *0 ERs, 0 BBs, 5 Ks*

Rank	Pitcher (Team)	Date Score	Opponent	GSc	IP, Hits, Runs, ERs, Walks, Strikeouts
22 (tie)	Charlie Lea (Montreal)	5/10/1981 (2) Mon 4-0	SF Giants	91	9.0 IP, 0 Hits, 0 Runs, 0 ERs, 4 BBs, 8 Ks
32 (tie)	Bill Stoneman (Montreal)	4/17/1969 Mon 7-0	Phi Phillies	90	9.0 IP, 0 Hits, 0 Runs, 0 ERs, 5 BBs, 8 Ks
38 (tie)	Bill Stoneman (Montreal)	10/2/1972 (1) Mon 7-0	NY Mets	89	9.0 IP, 0 Hits, 0 Runs, 0 ERs, 7 BBs, 9 Ks
---	Pascual Perez (Montreal)	9/24/1988 Mon 1-0 (6 inn)	Phi Phillies	74	5.0 IP, 0 Hits, 0 Runs, 0 ERs, 1 BB, 8 Ks
---	David Palmer (Montreal)	4/21/1984 (2) Mon 4-0 (5 inn)	St. Louis Cardinals	69	5.0 IP, 0 Hits, 0 Runs, 0 ERs, 0 BBs, 2 Ks

METHODOLOGY: This table includes the highest Game Scores thrown by a pitcher from the Expos and Nationals from 1969-2021. Games are ranked by Game Score (GSc) and consider all franchise regular season and postseason games. For comparison purposes, all seven franchise no-hitters are included in this table. Game Score measures a pitcher's performance in any given game started. Introduced by baseball writer/statistician Bill James in the 1980s, Game Score is presented as a figure between 0-100 — except for extreme outliers — and usually falls between 40-70.

LEGEND: Dates are shown as month/day/year (for example, June 12, 2018, is shown as 6/12/2018); IP = innings pitched. BB(s) = base(s) on balls. K(s) = strikeout(s). ER(s) = earned run(s). inn = innings (associated with the length of games that were more or less than nine innings). One-third of an inning pitched has 0.1 added and two-thirds of an inning pitched has 0.2 added (for example, 9 1/3 innings pitched is displayed as 9.1). BB(s) = base(s) on balls; K(s) = strikeout(s). (1) or (2) indicates the game is the first or second game of a doubleheader. The Montreal Expos joined the National League East Division in 1969 as an expansion team. In 2005, the team moved to Washington, DC and became the Nationals. The team's home city for each of the games in the table is indicated in the "Team" entry underneath the pitcher's name. *Italicized game (Dennis Martinez in 1991) was a perfect game. Los Angeles pitcher Mike Morgan also took a perfect game into the sixth inning during this contest.*

NOTE 1: The highest postseason Game Score thrown by a franchise pitcher was an 84 by Max Scherzer in Game 2 of the 2019 NLCS against the Cardinals.

Scherzer threw seven innings of one-hit, shutout ball. He was pulled for a pinch-hitter in the top of the eighth inning with the Nationals leading 1-0. By that point in the game, Scherzer had already thrown over 100 pitches. Washington would go on to win the game 3-1, and the series in a four-game sweep of St. Louis. They would continue their success in an exciting seven-game victory over the Houston Astros in the World Series for the franchise's first-ever championship and the first title for a Washington-based team since the original Senators beat the New York Giants in 1924.

NOTE 2: Third baseman Yunel Escobar made a throwing error in the sixth inning for the only baserunner allowed by Max Scherzer in his October 3, 2015, no-hitter – the second-to-last game of the season. Max Scherzer hit Pittsburgh batter Jose Tabata on a 2-2 pitch with two outs in the ninth inning for the only baserunner allowed during his June 20, 2015, no-hitter.

NOTE 3: Pedro Martinez threw a perfect game for nine innings on July 3, 1995. Unfortunately for him, his team failed to score, so, the game was tied 0-0 at the end of nine innings. The Expos scored in the top of the 10th, and Martinez came out to pitch in the bottom of the inning. San Diego's leadoff hitter, Bip Roberts, stroked a 2-0 pitch to right field for a line drive double to break up the perfect game. Montreal's closer Mel Rojas retired the next three hitters to save the win.

NOTE 4: Bill Stoneman was a bright and shining star for the expansion Expos right from the beginning. His no-hitter in April 1969 was only the ninth game the team ever played. It was also rookie Stoneman's first complete game. His last complete game was his second no-hitter in October 1972. In between, he became an All-Star in 1971 and that same year threw the team's best-pitched game until Max Scherzer appeared in 2015. In Stoneman's 1971 one-hitter against the Padres, the only hit he allowed was a single to center fielder Cito Gaston with one out in the seventh inning, while striking out 14 Padres en route to a 2-0 win.

NOTE 5: While not officially recognized as a no-hitter, Pascual Perez threw five innings of no-hit ball against the Phillies before the game was stopped due to rain. It was near the end of the season, and both teams were well out of the 1988 pennant race. The Expos were ahead 1-0 and the game was considered official. In his April 1984 game, David Palmer was perfect for five innings as the Expos defeated a good St. Louis team by the score of 4-0. Palmer retired 15 Cardinals in a row and was prepared to come out in the bottom of the sixth when the game was called due to rain. While Palmer didn't get credit for a no-hitter, because the minimum five innings were played and the Expos were ahead, the game was considered complete.

With three of the top four scores in franchise history – including two no-hitters, and with all three occurring in 2015 – Scherzer is tops among the highest team Game Scores with three appearances. This accomplishment is even more remarkable given the impressive company on a list that includes Hall-of-Famer Pedro Martinez, Dennis Martinez (only franchise perfect game), and Bill Stoneman (two franchise no-hitters, including the first one just nine games into Montreal's inaugural season). Incredibly, Scherzer only played seven seasons for Washington.

Scherzer's span of excellence for the Tigers and the Nationals during the 2010s is extraordinary. Along with Clayton Kershaw and Justin Verlander, he ranks in the top tier of that decade in terms of WAR achieved. With three Cy Young Awards for each of them – all occurring in the 2010s with the exception of Verlander's 2022 award – these three certain Hall of Famers stand head and shoulders above the decade's outstanding pitchers.

Table 11-4. Best Pitchers of the 2010s

WAR Rank	Pitcher (Team(s))	Seasons Pitched	Innings Pitched	WAR (per 200 IP)	Wins (per Season)
1	Clayton Kershaw (Dodgers)	2010-2019	1,996.0	59.3 (5.94)	156 (15.6)
2	Justin Verlander (Tigers, Astros)	2010-2019	2,142.0	56.8 (5.30)	160 (16.0)
3	Max Scherzer (Tigers, Nationals)	2010-2019	2,063.2	54.8 (5.31)	161 (16.1)
4	Cole Hamels (Phillies, Rangers, Cubs)	2010-2019	1,958.0	45.5 (4.65)	115 (11.5)
5	Chris Sale (White Sox, Red Sox)	2010-2019	1,629.2	44.6 (5.47)	109 (10.9)
6	Zack Greinke (Royals, Brewers, Angels, Dodgers, Diamondbacks, Astros)	2010-2019	1,984.0	43.9 (4.43)	155 (15.5)
7	David Price (Rays, Tigers, Blue Jays, Red Sox)	2010-2019	1,887.1	37.6 (3.98)	140 (14.0)
8 (tie)	Madison Bumgarner (Giants)	2010-2019	1,836.0	32.6 (3.55)	119 (11.9)
8 (tie)	Jacob DeGrom (Mets)	2014-2019	1,101.2	32.6 (5.92)	66 (11.0)

WAR Rank	Pitcher (Team(s))	Seasons Pitched	Innings Pitched	WAR (per 200 IP)	Wins (per Season)
10	Corey Kluber (Indians)	2011-2019	1,341.2	32.5 (4.84)	98 (10.9)
11 (tie)	Johnny Cueto (Reds, Royals, Giants)	2010-2019	1,511.0	32.0 (4.24)	106 (10.6)
11 (tie)	Felix Hernandez (Mariners)	2010-2019	1,999.0	32.0 (3.51)	111 (11.1)

METHODOLOGY: Pitchers are ranked in order of Wins Above Replacement (WAR) achieved from 2010-2019. WAR measures a player's value in all facets of the game by deciphering how many more wins he's worth than a replacement-level player at his same position.

LEGEND: Another measure of merit I wanted to include was the number of wins each pitcher accumulated as well. Because a significant number of pitchers were only present for a portion of the decade, I included two rate measures (WAR per 200 innings pitched and wins per season). IP = innings pitched. One-third of an inning is designated as ".1" and two-thirds of an inning is designated as ".2" innings.

While statistically not his most overwhelming season, Scherzer's 2015 campaign was nonetheless extremely impressive. With three remarkable games that included two no-hitters, he is also among the most accomplished pitchers when measuring the time between no-hitters. With only 91 games between his two no-hitters, he is in the top 10 pitchers in that category, led by Johnny Vander Meer's other-worldly achievement of throwing no-hitters in consecutive starts in 1938.

Table 11-5. Pitchers with Fewest Games Between No-hitters

Rank	Pitcher	Date	Team	Opponent	Results	Games Between
1	Johnny Vander Meer	6/11/1938 6/15/1938	Cincinnati Reds	Boston Bees Brook Dodgers	Cin 3-0 Cin 6-0	2 Games
2	Warren Spahn	9/16/1960 4/28/1961	Milwaukee Braves	Phil Phillies SF Giants	Mil 4-0 Mil 1-0	21 Games
3	Jake Arrieta	8/30/2015 4/21/2016	Chicago Cubs	LA Dodgers Cin Reds	Chi 2-0 Chi 16-0	48 Games

Rank	Pitcher	Date	Team	Opponent	Results	Games Between
4	Nolan Ryan	9/28/1974 6/1/1975	California Angels	Minn Twins Balt Orioles	Cal 4-0 Cal 1-0	51 Games
5	Nolan Ryan	5/15/1973 7/15/1973	California Angels	KC Royals Detroit Tigers	Cal 3-0 Cal 6-0	58 Games
6	Allie Reynolds	6/12/1951 9/28/1951	New York Yankees	Cleve Indians Bos Red Sox	NY 1-0 NY 8-0	76 Games
7	Homer Bailey	9/28/2012 7/2/2013	Cincinnati Reds	Pitt Pirates SF Giants	Cin 1-0 Cin 3-0	88 Games
8	Max Scherzer	6/20/2015 10/3/2015	Washington Nationals	Pitt Pirates NY Mets	Was 6-0 Was 2-0	91 Games
9	Virgil Trucks	5/15/1952 8/25/1952	Detroit Tigers	Wash Senators NY Yankees	Det 1-0 Det 1-0	99 Games
10	Roy Halladay	*5/29/2010* 10/6/2010	Philadelphia Phillies	*Fla Marlins* Cin Reds	*Phi 1-0* Phi 4-0	114 Games

METHODOLOGY: This table lists pitchers who have thrown multiple no-hitters with the least amount of games between two of them during the period 1900-2021. The pitchers are ranked in ascending order determined by the number of games their team played in between their no-hitters. For example, the Cincinnati Reds only played two games between Johnny Vander Meer's consecutive no-hitters.

LEGEND: Dates are shown as month/day/year (for example, June 12, 2018, is shown as 6/12/2018). "Games Between" indicates the number of games a team played in between no-hitters. *Italicized game (Roy Halladay in May 2010) was a perfect game.*

NOTE 1: The Boston Bees were known as the Boston Braves from 1912-1935. They changed their name to the Bees in 1936, and then changed back to the Braves in 1941. The Braves moved from Boston to Milwaukee in 1953 and then to Atlanta in 1966.

NOTE 2: Max Scherzer's second no-hitter (on October 3, 2015) was the second game of a doubleheader and the second-to-last game of the 2015 regular season. Allie Reynolds' second no-hitter (on September 28, 1951) was the first game of a doubleheader and the victory ensured at least a tie for the American League pennant that year. The Yankees won the second game against the Red Sox 11-3 and clinched the pennant outright.

NOTE 3: Jake Arrieta's 2015 no-hitter against Los Angeles was the second time the Dodgers were no-hit in nine days. That's the shortest interval since the 1923 Philadelphia Athletics were no-hit twice in three days. Virgil Trucks' no-hitters in 1952 represented two of his five wins over the course of the season (he went 5-19 that year) and two of the last-place Tigers' 50 total wins.

NOTE 4: Roy Halladay's second no-hitter (on October 6, 2010) was the first game of the 2010 NLDS against the Cincinnati Reds.

Besides the legendary Steve Rogers, who spent his entire 13-year career from 1973-1985 pitching for the Expos, no other pitcher has had as much success for Montreal as Dennis Martinez. He was the last Expo to throw a no-hitter and the only franchise pitcher to throw a perfect game in the 53 seasons the team has been in existence. Martinez is also, by far, the most accomplished Nicaraguan pitcher to play in the major leagues. The only two Nicaraguan pitchers who achieved a career WAR above 10 are listed below.

Table 11-6. Best Pitchers Born in Nicaragua

Rank	Pitcher (Home)	Team	Season(s)	Career IP	WAR (per 200 IP)	Wins (per season)
1	Dennis Martinez (Granada)	Bal Orioles Mon Expos Cle Indians Sea Mariners Atl Braves	1976-1986 1986-1993 1994-1996 1997 1998	3,999.2	49.3 (2.47)	245 (10.7)
2	Vicente Padilla (Chinandega)	Ari D-backs Phi Phillies Tex Rangers LA Dodgers Bos Red Sox	1999-2000 2000-2005 2006-2009 2009-2011 2012	1,571.1	12.0 (1.53)	108 (7.7)

METHODOLOGY: To qualify for inclusion in this table, pitchers had to be of Nicaraguan heritage and born in Nicaragua. Pitchers are ranked from highest to lowest based upon their career Wins Above Replacement (WAR) between 1900-2021. WAR measures a player's value in all facets of the game by deciphering how many more wins he's worth than a replacement-level player at his same position.

LEGEND: Home = the place a pitcher was born in Nicaragua. Team and season(s) are the teams a pitcher played for and the season(s) they were with each team listed in chronological order. Career IP = career innings pitched. Career WAR = the pitcher's accumulated WAR over his career. Career Wins = the number of wins each pitcher accumulated over his career. Because pitchers had different career lengths, I included two rate measures (WAR per 200 innings pitched and wins per season).

NOTE 1: Dennis Martinez is easily the most accomplished pitcher on this list. A four-time All-Star, Martinez notched double-digit wins for each of the eight years he was with Montreal. His best year was his stellar 1991 season in Montreal when he threw a perfect game, led the league in Earned Run Average (ERA), and received Cy Young and MVP votes.

NOTE 2: In addition to Dennis Martinez, Vicente Padilla also received All-Star recognition. Padilla was named to the National League All-Star team as a member of the Phillies in 2002. A baseball-loving country, Nicaragua qualified for the World Baseball Classic for the first time in 2023.

Max Scherzer was a first-round draft pick for the Diamondbacks out of the University of Missouri in the 2006 draft. After being developed in Arizona's minor league system, he premiered for the team in 2008. He was traded as part of a three-team deal to the Detroit Tigers after the 2009 season. He excelled with the Tigers, winning his first Cy Young Award in 2013, and being named to both the 2013 and 2014 American League All-Star teams.

Prior to the 2015 season, Scherzer signed with the Washington Nationals. Named to six All-Star teams and winning the Cy Young Award two more times, Scherzer led the Nationals to three playoff appearances, including the franchise's only world championship in 2019. He was traded to the Dodgers at the deadline in 2021. Scherzer is currently playing for the New York Mets, having signed with them as a free agent prior to the 2022 season.

Veteran catcher Wilson Ramos, Scherzer's batterymate in this game, has played for 12 seasons. Signed by the Minnesota Twins as a 16-year-old amateur free agent from Venezuela in 2004, Ramos debuted with the Twins in 2010. The Twins traded him that year to the Washington Nationals, where he soon blossomed into the team's starting catcher.

Named as an All-Star with Washington in 2016, Ramos signed as a free agent with the Tampa Bay Rays after the season. Since then, he has played with the Philadelphia Phillies, New York Mets, Detroit Tigers, and Cleveland Indians. Ramos was named as an All-Star again in 2018 while playing with the Rays. As of 2022, Ramos is a free agent after being released by Cleveland after the 2021 season.

Wilson Ramos has caught three no-hitters during his career, including both of Scherzer's no-hitters and Jordan Zimmermann's 2014 no-hitter.

Chapter 12

Hideo Nomo:
Rocky Mountain High

September 17, 1996
Japanese pitcher Hideo Nomo throws the first (and only) no-hitter at Coors Field

> *"Throwing a no-hitter at this place, he should be canonized on the spot."*

Dodgers catcher Mike Piazza reflecting on what a huge accomplishment it is for Hideo Nomo to throw a no-hitter at Coors Field. (Bob Nightengale, "NoooooooMo," *The Los Angeles Times*, September 18, 1996).

> *"That was huge, especially to do it in Colorado. With the hitters they have over there and for Nomo to throw a no-hitter ... is a tremendous effort."*

Dodgers manager Bill Russell not only bringing up the extremely hitter-friendly environment at Coors Field, but also what a great-hitting team the Rockies had that year ("Dodgers Nomo pulled no-hitter right out of thin air at Coors Field," *Spokesman.com*, September 19, 1996).

> *"(Nomo) probably doesn't realize how unbelievable that accomplishment is. People in Japan probably don't know Coors Field, but I'm betting it won't be done again."*

Dodgers' teammate Eric Karros reflecting on Nomo's accomplishment ("Dodgers Nomo pulled no-hitter right out of thin air at Coors Field", *Spokesman.com*, September 19, 1996).

> *"(Nomo's no-hitter) is arguably the greatest regular season pitching performance in baseball history."*

Sportswriter Jack Moore arguing that Nomo's no-hitter — as the first and only no-hitter ever thrown at Coors Field, and against one of the best-hitting teams of all time — was a historic accomplishment ("Throwback Thursday: Hideo Nomo Defies the Odds for a Coors Field No-No," *Vice Sports*, September 17, 2015).

> *"You may not believe me, but I'm glad we picked up the win at this time rather than I accomplished a no-hitter. We're battling for the division title, so this is a big win."*

Hideo Nomo, speaking through a translator, downplaying the significance of his remarkable achievement ("Dodgers Nomo pulled no-hitter right out of thin air at Coors Field," *Spokesman.com*, September 19, 1996).

As Los Angeles pitcher Hideo Nomo came to bat in the top of the ninth with two outs and two runners on base with the Dodgers leading the Rockies 9-0, the outcome of the game had long been decided. Yet, despite the thumping Los Angeles had given the hometown team, Colorado fans recognized the enormous accomplishment that was happening right before their eyes, and they stood and gave Nomo a standing ovation. They knew Nomo was on the verge of accomplishing something that would be unlikely to happen ever again. He was about to no-hit the Colorado Rockies at the notoriously hitter-friendly Coors Field.

In early 1995, Hideo Nomo came to the United States as the first star Japanese player to be signed by a Major League baseball team. While reliever Masanori Murakami led the way in 1964 as the first Japanese baseball player to sign with an American team when he joined the San Francisco Giants, he only stayed with them a couple of seasons before returning to Japan because of contract obligations. Nomo was the first player to be signed by an American team on a permanent basis. Since then, Japanese stars Yu Darvish, Kenta Maeda, Masahiro Tanaka, Hiroki Kuroda, Hideki Matsui, the great Ichiro Suzuki, and the other-worldly two-way player Shohei Ohtani all followed in Nomo's path.

By the time Nomo started against the Colorado Rockies in September 1996, he had already faced the team five times in the two years he had been a Dodger. The three times he started in Los Angeles, Nomo was dominant, as the Dodgers cruised to victory in all three games by a combined score of 18-5. Pitching in the thin air of Coors Field, Nomo was a disaster, allowing 12 earned runs in just over nine innings during the two games he started. Colorado pitchers had a difficult time, too, as they finished the season last in the National League with a team ERA of 5.59, almost a full run behind the next closest team, the San Francisco Giants at 4.71.

Nomo wasn't the only opposing pitcher who was victimized by Rockies' batters, either. In 1996, Colorado led the league by substantial margins in batting average (.287), on-base percentage (.355), slugging percentage (.472), and OPS (.827), as the team scored an astounding 961 runs – almost 200 more than the next closest team (the Reds at 778). The Rockies boasted a starting lineup that featured five starters who hit over .300: left fielder Ellis Burks (.344, 40 HRs), second baseman Eric Young (.324, .393 OBP), right fielder Dante Bichette (.313, 31 HRs), first baseman Andres Galarraga (.304, 47 HRs), and third baseman Vinny Castilla (.304, 40 HRs). In addition, Colorado featured future Hall of Famer Larry Walker (.276, .912 OPS), who missed two months in the middle of the 1996 season due to a broken collarbone. All the players listed above, except for Walker, were in the starting lineup against Nomo the day he threw his no-hitter.

As powerful as the Rockies lineup was that year, they were Supermen at Coors Field and well below average on the road. The team batting average at Coors was a herculean .343, and on the road the Rockies hit a paltry .228. To put this in perspective, the National League batting leader in 1996 was Hall of Famer Tony Gwynn at .353, and Colorado's Ellis Burks was second at .344. The Rockies as a team batting at Coors Field were just behind Ellis Burks. As a result of the extraordinary advantage the Rockies had at home, Coors Field had an extremely high park factor (PF) of 129, meaning that batters had roughly a 29% advantage hitting at Coors Field when compared to an average park. By comparison, the next closest park in the National League that season was Olympic Stadium, home of the Montreal Expos, which had a PF of 106.

When the strength of the Colorado lineup combined with the extreme advantage hitters had at Coors Field, a strong argument can be made that Hideo Nomo's no-hitter was the most impressive no-hitter ever pitched. In support of this, the top 10 no-hitters ranked by highest opponent Composite Batting Average (BAc) are shown below. BAc is a statistic created by baseball analyst Gary Belleville that combines park factor and each player's batting average weighted by the number of plate appearances the player had in the game. The result of these calculations is the composite batting average for the opposing lineup a pitcher faced at a specific park on a given day. Given the conditions he faced in Colorado, Nomo's 1996 no-hitter stands out as the most difficult no-hitter ever pitched – as measured by BAc – and it's not even close.

Table 12-1. Top Nine-Inning No-Hitters by Composite Batting Average (BAc)

Rank	Pitcher	Team	Date Score	Opponent	Ballpark (Park Factor)	BAc
1	Hideo Nomo	LA Dodgers	9/17/1996 LA 9-0	Colorado Rockies	Coors Field (129)	.302
2	Ken Holtzman	Chicago Cubs	8/19/1969 Chi 3-0	Atlanta Braves	Wrigley Field (106)	.289
3	Clay Buchholz	Boston Red Sox	9/1/2007 Bos 10-0	Baltimore Orioles	Fenway Park (112)	.288
4 (tie)	Babe Ruth Ernie Shore	Boston Red Sox	6/23/1917 (1) Bos 4-0	Wash Senators	Fenway Park (105)	.284
4 (tie)	Nolan Ryan	Calif Angels	5/15/1973 Cal 3-0	KC Royals	Royals Stadium (107)	.284
6 (tie)	Miles Main	KC Packers	8/16/1915 KC 5-0	Buffalo Blues	Intl Fair Assoc Grounds (104)	.282
6 (tie)	Jim Colborn	KC Royals	5/14/1977 KC 6-0	Texas Rangers	Royals Stadium (105)	.282
6 (tie)	Kent Mercker +2	Atlanta Braves	9/11/1991 Atl 1-0	SD Padres	Atl-Ful County Stadium (111)	.282
9	Ray Caldwell	Cleve Indians	9/10/1919 (1) Cle 3-0	NY Yankees	Polo Grounds (100)	.281
10 (tie)	Nick Maddox	Pitt Pirates	9/20/1907 Pit 2-1	Brooklyn Superbas	Exposition Park (108)	.280
10 (tie)	Vern Kennedy	Chicago W. Sox	8/31/1935 Chi 5-0	Cleve Indians	Comiskey Park (104)	.280

METHODOLOGY: This table lists the top 10 no-hitters based upon the highest Composite Batting Average (BAc) a no-hit pitcher faced from the opposing team between 1900-2021. The list is ranked in descending order from highest to lowest BAc. The author of this innovative analysis and creator of the BAc statistic is retired

IT professor, baseball analyst, and Montreal Expos fan Gary Belleville. For this analysis, he calculated the "weighted neutralized batting average" for each no-hitter by using a combination of park neutral batting averages for each hitter in the no-hit lineup multiplied by the number of times a hitter batted that day. He then multiplied that by the Park Factor for the field where the game was played to determine the BAc. I stand in awe of this guy!! The result of his calculations (BAc) is a direct reflection of the degree of difficulty faced by the pitcher who threw the no-hitter. Park Factor indicates the difference between runs scored in a team's home and road games and is helpful in assessing how much a specific ballpark contributes to the offensive production of a team or player. A Park Factor over 100 indicates a park that is more favorable to hitters, and the higher the number, the greater the impact. Conversely, a Park Factor lower than 100 is more favorable to pitchers.

LEGEND: Dates are shown as month/day/year (for example, June 12, 2018, is shown as 6/12/2018). (1) or (2) indicates the game is the first or second game of a doubleheader. BAc = Composite Batting Average. "Ballpark" is the location where the game was played.

NOTE 1: The no-hitter thrown by Boston's Babe Ruth and Ernie Shore was completely accomplished by Ernie Shore. Babe Ruth started the game and walked the first batter, second baseman Ray Morgan of the Washington Senators. Ruth disagreed with two balls he thought were strikes. He was so upset that he punched home plate umpire Brick Owens and was thrown out of the game. Ernie Shore entered to relieve Ruth and Morgan was promptly thrown out trying to steal second base. Shore then retired 26 batters in a row, completing the no-hitter in what would have been a perfect game except for the walk Ruth allowed.

NOTE 2: Kent Mercker's 1991 no-hitter with the Braves was a multi-pitcher effort. Hall of Fame manager Bobby Cox pulled Mercker after six innings with Atlanta leading 1-0 against a very good Padres club. The Braves were in the middle of a tight pennant race with the Dodgers, and Cox didn't want to take any chances. Mark Wohlers pitched the seventh and eighth innings, getting all six San Diego hitters to ground out or fly out. Closer Alejandro Pena came in to pitch the ninth and retired the first two hitters. The next batter, Darrin Jackson, reached first base on an error by third baseman Terry Pendleton. The game ended with the tying run on first and the winning run at the plate when Hall of Famer Tony Gwynn flew out to Otis Nixon in deep left field.

NOTE 3: The game between the Kansas City Packers and the Buffalo Blues was a Federal League contest played in Buffalo at the International Fair Association Grounds. The Federal League was a major league in existence from 1914 to 1915.

Unlike many other no-hitters, Nomo's effort did not feature any fielding plays that stood out as being particularly challenging. The closest the Rockies came to getting a hit was in the fourth inning when Andres Galarraga hit a difficult fielder's-choice grounder to shortstop Greg Gagne for the second out. In the seventh, Galarraga hit a line drive to right fielder Raul Mondesi, and Vinny Castilla hit a high fly to Wayne Kirby in center field. Despite the thin air, the ball didn't seem to be traveling as far that night because of high humidity. The start of the game had been delayed two hours due to rain. On any other night those fly balls might have left the ballpark in Denver.

The game's final inning was remarkable in many ways. Not only did everyone involved realize what an extraordinary event they were witnessing, Japanese television networks picked up the broadcast feed and began showing it live on monitors throughout Tokyo during rush hour. Hideo Nomo was a legend in Japan, and he was on the verge of throwing the first no-hitter by a Japanese pitcher in American baseball. Japanese fans didn't want to miss a minute, as play-by-play announcer and first-ever Japanese player to play in the United States Masanori Murakami described the action on the field.

The Dodger franchise has a rich history of pitching excellence, from Nap Rucker with the Brooklyn Superbas in the early 1900s to Hall of Famer Burleigh Grimes of the Brooklyn Robins in the teens and twenties to the nearly unbeatable duo of Sandy Koufax and Don Drysdale in the 1960s to the present-day ace Clayton Kershaw. Below is a list of the best games by a franchise pitcher since 1900.

Table 12-2. Dodgers Highest Game Scores

Rank	Pitcher (Team)	Date Score	Opponent	GSc	IP, Hits, Runs, ERs, Walks, Strikeouts
1	Leon Cadore (Brook Robins)	5/1/1920 1-1 Tie (26 inn)	Bos Braves	140	26.0 IP, 15 Hits, 1 Run, 1 ER, 5 BBs, 7 Ks
2	Phil Douglas (Brook Robins)	7/7/1915 (2) 0-0 Tie (16 inn)	Bos Braves	119	16.0 IP, 4 Hits, 0 Runs, 0 ERs, 3 BBs, 8 Ks

Rank	Pitcher (Team)	Date Score	Opponent	GSc	IP, Hits, Runs, ERs, Walks, Strikeouts
3	Jeff Pfeffer (Brook Robins)	9/4/1917 0-0 Tie (14 inn)	Phi Phillies	114	14.0 IP, 3 Hits, 0 Runs, 0 ERs, 1 BB, 9 Ks
4 (tie)	Burleigh Grimes (Brook Robins)	7/18/1918 Bro 3-2 (16 inn)	Chi Cubs	104	16.0 IP, 7 Hits, 2 Runs, 0 ERs, 4 BBs, 4 Ks
4 (tie)	Johnny Allen (Brook Dodgers)	9/15/1941 Bro 5-1 (17 inn)	Cin Reds	104	15.0 IP, 6 Hits, 0 Runs, 0 ERs, 4 BBs, 3 Ks
6 (tie)	Burleigh Grimes (Brook Robins)	5/14/1920 Bro 5-1 (14 inn)	StL Cards	102	14.0 IP, 7 Hits, 1 Runs, 1 ERs, 1 BBs, 9 Ks
6 (tie)	Clayton Kershaw (LA Dodgers)	6/18/2014 LA 8-0	Col Rockies	102	9.0 IP, 0 Hits, 0 Runs, 0 ERs, 0 BBs, 15 Ks
8 (tie)	Nap Rucker (Brook Superbas)	9/5/1908 (2) Bro 6-0	Bos Doves	101	9.0 IP, 0 Hits, 0 Runs, 0 ERs, 0 BBs, 14 Ks
8 (tie)	*Sandy Koufax (LA Dodgers)*	*9/9/1965 LA 1-0*	*Chi Cubs*	*101*	*9.0 IP, 0 Hits, 0 Runs, 0 ERs, 0 BBs, 14 Ks*
10 (tie)	Doc Scanlan (Brook Dodgers)	6/21/1911 Phi 2-1 (15 inn)	Phi Phillies	100-104	15.0 IP, 6 Hits, 2 Runs, ? ERs, 6 BBs, 9 Ks
10 (tie)	Eddie Stack (Brook Dodgers)	9/4/1912 Bro 2-1 (13 inn)	Bos Braves	100	13.0 IP, 3 Hits, 1 Run, 1 ER, 3 BBs, 6 Ks
10 (tie)	Don Drysdale (LA Dodgers)	5/22/1959 LA 2-1 (13 inn)	SF Giants	100	13.0 IP, 6 Hits, 1 Run, 1 ER, 2 BBs, 11 Ks

METHODOLOGY: This table includes the highest Game Scores thrown by a pitcher from the Brooklyn/Los Angeles franchise from 1900-2021. Games are ranked by Game Score (GSc) and consider all franchise regular season and post-season games. For comparison purposes, all 16 franchise no-hitters are included in this table. Game Score measures a pitcher's performance in any given game started. Introduced by baseball writer/statistician Bill James in the 1980s, Game Score is presented as a figure between 0-100 — except for extreme outliers — and usually falls between 40-70.

LEGEND: Dates are shown as month/day/year (for example, June 12, 2018, is shown as 6/12/2018); IP = innings pitched. BB(s) = base(s) on balls. K(s) = strike-out(s). ER(s) = earned run(s). inn = innings (associated with the length of games that were more or less than nine innings). One-third of an inning pitched has 0.1

added and two-thirds of an inning pitched has 0.2 added (for example, 9 1/3 innings pitched is displayed as 9.1). BB(s) = base(s) on balls; K(s) = strikeout(s). (1) or (2) indicates the game is the first or second game of a doubleheader. The Dodgers were based in Brooklyn when they started in the American Association in 1884. The team joined the National League in 1890 as the Brooklyn Bridegrooms. As the turn of the century arrived in 1900, the team was called the Superbas. The team was known as the Dodgers from 1911-1912 before changing back to the Superbas in 1913. In 1914, the team became the Robins and stayed that way until they settled on the Dodgers for good in 1932. In 1958, the team moved from Brooklyn to Los Angeles. The team's home city and name for each of the games in the table is indicated in the "Team" entry underneath the pitcher's name. *Italicized game (Sandy Koufax in 1965) was a perfect game, and the last of four no-hitters the ace threw from 1962-1965.*

NOTE 1: The highest postseason Game Score thrown by a franchise pitcher was an 89 by Don Drysdale in Game 3 of the 1963 World Series against the Yankees. Drysdale threw nine innings of three-hit, shutout ball en route to a 1-0 win. Los Angeles would go on to sweep the 104-win New York team in four games. The Yankees finished over 10 games ahead of the second-place White Sox and were in the midst of a five-season stretch from 1960-1964 where they won the American League pennant every season. The powerful 1963 team featured sluggers like Hall of Famer Mickey Mantle, all-time single-season home run leader Roger Maris, MVP Elston Howard, All-Star Joe Pepitone, and others. Drysdale allowed only two singles to leadoff hitter Tony Kubek and one to Mantle that day for a critical win that put the Dodgers ahead by three games and within one win of the Series victory.

NOTE 2: Leon "Caddy" Cadore's 140 Game Score accumulated over a 26-inning marathon is the second highest score in Major League history. The highest score ever recorded was a 153 by Cadore's opponent that day, Joe Oeschger of the Boston Braves. With 26 innings in the books, Cadore and Oeschger together set the record for the most innings thrown by a pitcher in a single game. After 26 innings, with the two starting pitchers still in the game, the contest was declared a 1-1 tie and called due to darkness. Cadore faced an astounding 96 batters that day – a record for the most batters faced by a pitcher in a single game – 18 more than the minimum for a 26-inning contest. Cadore was in trouble numerous times, especially in the first nine innings, though the Braves only scored a single sixth-inning run despite having 21 baserunners throughout the game. After struggling early, Cadore settled down, retiring 15 straight batters, allowing a single in the 20th, and then setting down 19 more. Leon Cadore was a solid pitcher for Brooklyn throughout the 1917-1922 seasons, with the exception of 1918. Before Opening Day 1918, Cadore joined the Army and was sent to France to help lead the all-Black 369th Infantry Regiment – the legendary "Harlem Hellfighters" – on the Western Front in World War I. Lieutenant Cadore returned home in one piece and picked up where he left off with Brooklyn in 1919, although he later admitted that the 26-inning game took a lot out of him and he never fully recovered from that herculean event.

NOTE 3: After being purchased from the Cincinnati Reds in June 1915, "Shufflin' Phil" Douglas promptly threw one of the greatest games in Brooklyn history – a 16-inning, four-hit shutout against the Boston Braves. Unfortunately for Douglas, the Robins couldn't score a run either. Being the second game of a doubleheader, it was almost certainly called because of darkness (though the reason for stopping the game was not confirmed) and declared a 0-0 tie. Douglas had a nine-season career with mixed results, playing for five different teams. He could be an amazingly good pitcher but was extremely unreliable due to his alcoholism. Despite his magnificent performance that day, Douglas was only with Brooklyn for a few months. The team decided they needed to part ways and sold him to the Cubs before the 1915 season ended.

NOTE 4: Jeff Pfeffer threw a great game on September 4, 1917, allowing only three hits and one walk over 14 innings. The game was called for unknown reasons after 14 innings as a scoreless tie. Pfeffer's opponent from the Phillies that day was Joe Oeschger, the same pitcher who would set the record with Leon Cadore for most innings pitched in a game (26) and compile the highest Game Score (153) ever achieved. Combined with his previous start on August 31 when he threw a one-run, five-hit game, Pfeffer's pitching achievements rank among the most impressive back-to-back pitching performances in baseball history.

NOTE 5: Hall of Famer Burleigh "Ol' Stubblebeard" Grimes is the only pitcher listed twice in this table. With 270 career wins over a 19-year career, Grimes was known for his competitiveness. He was also the last pitcher in baseball who was allowed to throw the spitball, since he was an established thrower of the pitch before it became outlawed in 1920.

NOTE 6: Doc Scanlan pitched an exceptional game on June 21, 1911, holding the Philadelphia Phillies to just two runs over 16 innings. Unfortunately, the Dodgers only scored one run and lost the game. The earned-run statistic came into being the next year, so a Game Score can't be determined without having a contemporary news report or looking at a play-by-play description of the game (neither of which were available). Because Brooklyn made two errors, it isn't clear whether the two runs were earned or unearned. In reviewing the box score it appears the runs were earned, but that can't be determined with certainty. Regardless, the only possible range of outcomes is between 100 (if both runs were earned) to 104 (if both runs were unearned). Choosing the low end of the possible outcomes places Scanlan in a tie for 10th place on the franchise's best Game Score list.

The Dodger franchise has also thrown 22 no-hitters since 1900, the most for a team during that period. In second place is the Chicago White Sox with 20. The top Game Scores for games of 10 innings or less are shown below. The list includes all no-hit games, with Hideo Nomo's effort in Colorado in a tie at 47th place with a score of 91.

Table 12-3. Dodgers Highest Game Scores of 10 innings or less

Rank	Pitcher (Team)	Date Score	Opponent	GSc	IP, Hits, Runs, ERs, Walks, Strikeouts
1	Clayton Kershaw (LA Dodgers)	6/18/2014 LA 8-0	Colorado Rockies	102	9.0 IP, 0 Hits, 0 Runs, 0 ERs, 0 BBs, 15 Ks
2 (tie)	Nap Rucker (Brook Superbas)	9/5/1908 (2) Bro 6-0	Boston Doves	101	9.0 IP, 0 Hits, 0 Runs, 0 ERs, 0 BBs, 14 Ks
2 (tie)	*Sandy Koufax (LA Dodgers)*	*9/9/1965 LA 1-0*	*Chicago Cubs*	*101*	*9.0 IP, 0 Hits, 0 Runs, 0 ERs, 0 BBs, 14 Ks*
4 (tie)	Van Mungo (Brook Dodgers)	9/29/1935 (1) Bro 2-0	Philadelphia Phillies	98	9.0 IP, 2 Hits, 0 Runs, 0 ERs, 0 BBs, 15 Ks
4 (tie)	Sandy Koufax (LA Dodgers)	6/4/1964 LA 3-0	Philadelphia Phillies	98	9.0 IP, 0 Hits, 0 Runs, 0 ERs, 1 BB, 12 Ks
4 (tie)	Ramon Martinez (LA Dodgers)	6/4/1990 LA 6-0	Atlanta Braves	98	9.0 IP, 3 Hits, 0 Runs, 0 ERs, 1 BBs, 18 Ks
7 (tie)	Bill Singer (LA Dodgers)	7/20/1970 LA 5-0	Philadelphia Phillies	97	9.0 IP, 0 Hits, 0 Runs, 0 ERs, 0 BBs, 10 Ks
7 (tie)	Clayton Kershaw (LA Dodgers)	9/29/2015 LA 8-0	SF Giants	97	9.0 IP, 1 Hit, 0 Runs, 0 ERs, 1 BB, 13 Ks
9	Nap Rucker (Brook Superbas)	7/24/1909 (2) Bro 1-0	St. Louis Cardinals	96	9.0 IP, 2 Hits, 0 Runs, 0 ERs, 3 BBs, 16 Ks

Rank	Pitcher (Team)	Date Score	Opponent	GSc	IP, Hits, Runs, ERs, Walks, Strikeouts
10 (tie)	Sandy Koufax (LA Dodgers)	8/11/1960 LA 3-0	Cincinnati Reds	95	9.0 IP, 2 Hits, 0 Runs, 0 ERs, 1 BB, 13 Ks
10 (tie)	Sandy Koufax (LA Dodgers)	6/20/1961 LA 3-0	Chicago Cubs	95	9.0 IP, 2 Hits, 0 Runs, 0 ERs, 2 BBs, 14 Ks
10 (tie)	Sandy Koufax (LA Dodgers)	6/30/1962 LA 5-0	New York Mets	95	9.0 IP, 0 Hits, 0 Runs, 0 ERs, 5 BBs, 13 Ks
10 (tie)	Sandy Koufax (LA Dodgers)	4/19/1963 LA 2-0	Houston Colt .45s	95	9.0 IP, 2 Hits, 0 Runs, 0 ERs, 2 BBs, 14 Ks
10 (tie)	Sandy Koufax (LA Dodgers)	9/29/1965 LA 5-0	Cincinnati Reds	95	9.0 IP, 2 Hits, 0 Runs, 0 ERs, 1 BB, 13 Ks
10 (tie)	Chan Ho Park (LA Dodgers)	9/29/2000 LA 3-0	San Diego Padres	95	9.0 IP, 2 Hits, 0 Runs, 0 ERs, 1 BB, 13 Ks
10 (tie)	Clayton Kershaw (LA Dodgers)	5/1/2016 LA 1-0	San Diego Padres	95	9.0 IP, 3 Hits, 0 Runs, 0 ERs, 0 BBs, 14 Ks
17 (tie)	Ramon Martinez (LA Dodgers)	7/14/1995 LA 7-0	Florida Marlins	94	9.0 IP, 0 Hits, 0 Runs, 0 ERs, 1 BB, 8 Ks
26 (tie)	Dazzy Vance (Brook Robins)	9/13/1925 (1) Bro 10-1	Philadelphia Phillies	93	9.0 IP, 0 Hits, 1 Run, 0 ERs, 1 BB, 9 Ks
47 (tie)	F. Valenzuela (LA Dodgers)	6/29/1990 LA 6-0	St. Louis Cardinals	91	9.0 IP, 0 Hits, 0 Runs, 0 ERs, 3 BBs, 7 Ks
47 (tie)	Kevin Gross (LA Dodgers)	8/17/1992 LA 2-0	SF Giants	91	9.0 IP, 0 Hits, 0 Runs, 0 ERs, 2 BBs, 6 Ks
47 (tie)	Hideo Nomo (LA Dodgers)	9/17/1996 LA 9-0	Colorado Rockies	91	9.0 IP, 0 Hits, 0 Runs, 0 ERs, 4 BBs, 8 Ks
74 (tie)	Josh Beckett (LA Dodgers)	5/25/2014 LA 6-0	Philadelphia Phillies	90	9.0 IP, 0 Hits, 0 Runs, 0 ERs, 3 BBs, 6 Ks
99 (tie)	Mal Eason (Bro Superbas)	7/20/1906 Bro 2-0	St. Louis Cardinals	89	9.0 IP, 0 Hits, 0 Runs, 0 ERs, 3 BBs, 5 Ks
99 (tie)	Tex Carleton (Brook Dodgers)	4/30/1940 Bro 3-0	Cincinnati Reds	89	9.0 IP, 0 Hits, 0 Runs, 0 ERs, 2 BBs, 4 Ks
99 (tie)	Rex Barney (Brook Dodgers)	9/9/1948 Bro 2-0	New York Giants	89	9.0 IP, 0 Hits, 0 Runs, 0 ERs, 2 BBs, 4 Ks
99 (tie)	Sandy Koufax (LA Dodgers)	5/11/1963 LA 8-0	SF Giants	89	9.0 IP, 0 Hits, 0 Runs, 0 ERs, 2 BBs, 4 Ks

Rank	Pitcher (Team)	Date Score	Opponent	GSc	IP, Hits, Runs, ERs, Walks, Strikeouts
99 (tie)	Jerry Reuss (LA Dodgers)	6/27/1980 LA 8-0	SF Giants	89	9.0 IP, 0 Hits, 0 Runs, 0 ERs, 0 BBs, 2 Ks
142 (tie)	Carl Erskine (Brook Dodgers)	5/12/1956 Bro 3-0	New York Giants	88	9.0 IP, 0 Hits, 0 Runs, 0 ERs, 2 BBs, 3 Ks
142 (tie)	Sal Maglie (Brook Dodgers)	9/25/1956 Bro 5-0	Philadelphia Philles	88	9.0 IP, 0 Hits, 0 Runs, 0 ERs, 2 BBs, 3 Ks
191 (tie)	Carl Erskine (Brook Dodgers)	6/19/1952 Bro 5-0	Chicago Cubs	87	9.0 IP, 0 Hits, 0 Runs, 0 ERs, 1 BB, 1 K
249 (tie)	Ed Head (Brook Dodgers)	4/23/1946 Bro 5-0	Boston Braves	86	9.0 IP, 0 Hits, 0 Runs, 0 ERs, 3 BBs, 2 Ks
249 (tie)	Rich Hill (LA Dodgers)	9/10/2016 LA 5-0	Miami Marlins	86	7.0 IP, 0 Hits, 0 Runs, 0 ERs, 0 BBs, 9 Ks
1524 (tie)	Walker Buehler (LA Dodgers)	5/4/2018 LA 4-0	San Diego Padres	77	6.0 IP, 0 Hits, 0 Runs, 0 ERs, 3 BBs, 8 Ks
1736 (tie)	Fred Frankhouse (Brook Dodgers)	8/27/1937 LA 5-0 (8 inn)	Cincinnati Reds	76	7.2 IP, 0 Hits, 0 Runs, 0 ERs, 6 BBs, 3 Ks

METHODOLOGY: This table includes the highest Game Scores of 10 innings or less thrown by a pitcher from the Brooklyn/Los Angeles franchise from 1900-2021. Games are ranked by Game Score (GSc) and consider all franchise regular season and postseason games. For comparison purposes, all 22 franchise no-hitters are included in this table – this is more than any other team in baseball. Game Score measures a pitcher's performance in any given game started. Introduced by baseball writer/statistician Bill James in the 1980s, Game Score is presented as a figure between 0-100 — except for extreme outliers — and usually falls between 40-70.

LEGEND: Dates are shown as month/day/year (for example, June 12, 2018, is shown as 6/12/2018); IP = innings pitched. BB(s) = base(s) on balls. K(s) = strikeout(s). ER(s) = earned run(s). inn = innings (associated with the length of games that were more or less than nine innings). One-third of an inning pitched has 0.1 added and two-thirds of an inning pitched has 0.2 added (for example, 9 1/3 innings pitched is displayed as 9.1). BB(s) = base(s) on balls; K(s) = strikeout(s). (1) or (2) indicates the game is the first or second game of a doubleheader. The Dodgers were based in Brooklyn when they started the American Association in 1884. The team joined the

National League in 1890 as the Brooklyn Bridegrooms. As the turn of the century arrived in 1900, the team was known as the Superbas. The team was known as the Dodgers from 1911-1912 before changing back to the Superbas in 1913. In 1914, the team became the Robins in 1914 and stayed that way until they settled on the Dodgers for good in 1932. In 1958, the team moved from Brooklyn to Los Angeles. The team's home city and name for each of the games in the table is indicated in the "Team" entry underneath the pitcher's name. For comparison purposes, all franchise no-hitters are included in this table. *Italicized game (Sandy Koufax in 1965) was a perfect game, and the last of four no-hitters the ace threw from 1962-1965.*

NOTE 1: Clayton Kershaw's 15-strikeout no-hitter is the third highest Game Score ever achieved in a nine-inning game. It is eclipsed only by Kerry Woods' 20-strikeout performance in 1998 and Max Scherzer's 17-strikeout no-hitter in 2015. Kershaw only allowed one baserunner during his performance, when Corey Dickerson of the Rockies was safe on a throwing error by Dodger shortstop Hanley Ramirez leading off the seventh inning. Kershaw was dominant throughout this game, as he induced 12 swinging strikeouts, including Dickerson to end the contest.

NOTE 2: 23-year-old, second-year pitcher Nap Rucker was a stalwart for the Superbas in 1908, earning 17 wins (and losing 19) for the 101-loss Brooklyn team. The 14 strikeouts he recorded in his no-hitter against the Boston Doves were the most by a Brooklyn pitcher until he struck out 16 in the second game of a double-header against the Cardinals in 1909. His team record would be broken by Hall of Famer Dazzy Vance with 17 strikeouts in a 10-inning contest in 1925. The current team record of 18 was set by Sandy Koufax in a 1959 game against the Giants and achieved by him again in a 1962 contest versus the Cubs. Most recently, Ramon Martinez struck out 18 Braves in his 1990 three-hitter – tied for fourth place with a Game Score of 98. The Boston Doves – the team Rucker faced that day of his no-hitter – became the Boston Rustlers in 1911 and then the Boston Braves in 1912. The Braves moved to Milwaukee in 1953 and to Atlanta in 1966.

NOTE 3: Dodger great Sandy Koufax is all over this chart. He appears seven times in the top sixteen scores, far more than the next closest pitcher – Clayton Kershaw with three appearances. The only other pitcher in the top 16 who appears more than once is Nap Rucker, who is listed twice. Ramon Martinez just missed this distinction, as he is tied for 17th with his 1995 no-hitter versus the Marlins, a game in which he only allowed a full count walk to Tommy Gregg with two outs in the eighth inning. In his 1964 no-hitter against the Phillies, Koufax faced the minimum 27 batters. The only baserunner he allowed was a two-out, full-count walk to slugger Dick Allen in the fourth inning of a scoreless game. Allen was caught stealing during the next at bat.

NOTE 4: Bill Singer was responsible for both baserunners in his 1970 no-hitter against the Phillies, although they didn't count against his Game Score. He hit Oscar Gamble, the second batter of the game, and he made a throwing error in the seventh inning on a Don Money grounder back to the mound. Apart from that, he gave up no walks and didn't allow a hit.

NOTE 5: Hall of Famer Dazzy Vance allowed a walk to Philadelphia's Heinie Sand, the first batter of the game during his no-hitter against the Phillies in 1925. Sand was left stranded at first when Vance retired the next three batters in a row – two by strikeout. Vance would not allow another hit or walk for the rest of the game, yet the Phillies scored a run in the top of the second inning. Leadoff hitter Nelson "Chicken" Hawks reached second base courtesy of two errors on the same play by Brooklyn left fielder Jimmy Johnston. Hawks advanced to third base on a passed ball and scored on a sacrifice fly. While it wasn't a shutout, Vance retired the next 22 batters he faced, got his no-hitter, and Brooklyn won the game 10-1. Vance had thrown a one-hit shutout against the Phillies just five days earlier.

NOTE 6: Jerry Reuss did not allow a walk or hit during his 1980 no-hitter against the Giants. The only San Francisco runner reached base when Jack Clark was safe on a throwing error by shortstop Bill Russell. Carl Erskine nearly threw a perfect game in his 1952 no-hitter against the Cubs. The only Chicago baserunner reached first when Erskine walked relief pitcher Willie Ramsdell with two outs in the third inning. Erskine threw his second no-hitter in 1956 against the New York Giants, Brooklyn's National League rivals. Hall of Fame catcher Roy Campanella caught both games.

NOTE 7: Rich Hill pitched seven perfect innings and was cruising against the Marlins when a blister reappeared on his finger. Manager Dave Roberts decided to pull Hill since this was a recurring issue with him and Los Angeles was in the midst of a pennant race late in the season. Reliever Joe Blanton allowed a single with two outs in the eighth to stop any chance of a no-hitter, but the Dodgers beat the Marlins 5-0.

NOTE 8: Walker Buehler was the starting pitcher and went six innings in a combined no-hitter against the Padres on May 4, 2018. The no-hitter was then completed by three pitchers who each threw one full inning: Tony Cingrani, Yimi Garcia, and Adam Liberatore. The Dodgers won by the score of 4-0. With the combined statistics of 9.0 innings pitched, 0 hits, 0 runs, 5 walks, and 13 strikeouts, the four pitchers together would have earned a Game Score of 95, making it tied for 10th place among the best games ever thrown by a Dodger pitcher. This was also Buehler's third career start, and the game was played in Monterrey, Mexico, as part of Major League Baseball's international outreach program.

NOTE 9: Fred Frankhouse threw 7.2 innings of no-hit ball against the Reds in August 1937. The game was called due to heavy rain in the eighth inning with Frankhouse on the mound. Since the Dodgers were leading 5-0, Brooklyn was awarded the win and the game counted as a no-hitter until baseball changed the policy in 1991 when no-hit games had to consist of at least nine innings pitched.

One of the keys to Dodger success has been the team's ability to attract and cultivate talented players from Japan, Mexico, and South Korea. Hideo Nomo was one of the first foreign-born pitchers to come on board. In addition to being the first Japanese star to play in the American major leagues, Nomo ranks highly among the top Japanese pitchers to play baseball in the United States. Nomo is also the only Japanese pitcher to throw a no-hitter – he has two – and he leads the pack with 123 career wins. The top five Japanese pitchers in career Wins Above Replacement (WAR) are listed below.

Table 12-4. Best Pitchers Born in Japan

Rank	Pitcher (Home)	Team	Season(s)	Career IP	WAR (per 200 IP)	Wins (per season)
1	Yu Darvish (Habikino)	Tex Rangers LA Dodgers Chi Cubs SD Padres	2014-2017 2017 2018-2020 2021	1,293.1	26.2 (4.05)	79 (9.9)
2	Hideo Nomo (Osaka)	LA Dodgers NY Mets Mil Brewers Det Tigers Bos Red Sox LA Dodgers TB D-Rays KC Royals	1995-1998 1998 1999 2000 2001 2002-2004 2005 2008	1,976.1	21.8 (2.21)	123 (10.3)
3	Hiroki Kuroda (Osaka)	LA Dodgers NY Yankees	2008-2011 2012-2014	1,319.0	21.6 (3.28)	79 (11.3)

Rank	Pitcher (Home)	Team	Season(s)	Career IP	WAR (per 200 IP)	Wins (per season)
4	Masahiro Tanaka (Itami)	NY Yankees	2014-2020	1,054.1	17.5 (3.32)	78 (11.1)
5	Hisashi Iwakuma (Higashi)	Sea Mariners	2012-2017	883.2	17.0 (3.84)	63 (10.1)

METHODOLOGY: To qualify for inclusion in this table, pitchers had to be of Japanese heritage and born in Japan. Pitchers are ranked from 1-5 based upon their career Wins Above Replacement (WAR) between 1900-2021. WAR measures a player's value in all facets of the game by deciphering how many more wins he's worth than a replacement-level player at his same position. Only WAR achieved in the National and American Leagues count for purposes of this ranking. Pitchers needed to have a Career WAR above 10 to be included in this list.

LEGEND: Home = the place a pitcher was born in Japan. Team and season(s) are the teams they played for and the season(s) they were with each team listed in chronological order. Career IP = career innings pitched. Career WAR = the pitcher's accumulated WAR over his career. Career Wins = the number of wins each pitcher accumulated over his career. Because pitchers had different career lengths, I included two rate measures (WAR per 200 innings pitched and wins per season). Yu Darvish and Hideo Nomo missed entire seasons during their careers. Therefore, those missed seasons don't count as part of the wins per season calculation. Specifically, Yu Darvish missed the 2015 season, and Hideo Nomo missed 2006 and 2007.

NOTE 1: Many of the impressive pitchers on this list were named as All-Stars during their playing career: Yu Darvish (2012-2014, 2017, and 2021), Hideo Nomo (1995), Masahiro Tanaka (2014 and 2019), and Hisashi Iwakuma (2013). No other pitcher on this list besides Nomo threw a no-hitter, and Nomo threw two of them. His second one was for the Boston Red Sox against the Orioles in the second game of the season in April 2001.

NOTE 2: While the players listed have achieved a great deal playing in the Major Leagues, many of them got their starts in Japanese professional baseball. Yu Darvish racked up 93 wins and had a 1.99 ERA in seven seasons in Japan. Hideo Nomo accumulated 78 wins with a 3.15 over five seasons. Hiroki Kuroda registered

124 wins and a 3.55 ERA in 13 seasons. Masahiro Tanaka recorded 103 wins over eight seasons in Japan (through 2021). He continues to play there.

NOTE 3: Using statistics accumulated through 2021, the legendary Shohei Ohtani does not yet qualify for this "Top Five" pitchers list, as his 2018 season was abbreviated, and he missed 2019 and 2020 due to injury. His 2021 season was extraordinary, though, as he was named an All-Star pitcher and won the American League MVP Award. It's very possible he will eventually surpass all the outstanding pitchers on this list.

NOTE 4: Japan has dominated the World Baseball Classic, winning it all in 2006, 2009, and 2023. Yu Darvish starred as part of the 2009 and 2023 teams, and Shohei Ohtani was a member of the 2023 champions, who beat the United States in a 3-2 thriller.

No discussion of great Dodger pitchers would be complete without mentioning the sensational Mexican-born Fernando Valenzuela, who burst on the scene as a full-time starter in 1981, winning the Rookie of the Year and Cy Young Awards, as he helped lead the Dodgers to the 1981 World Series championship. Among many outstanding Mexican pitchers to play in the major leagues, Valenzuela leads them all in career WAR and wins. He is also the only Mexican pitcher to throw a no-hitter, although Francisco Cordova threw nine innings of no-hit ball for the Pirates in his 10-inning multi-pitcher no-hitter against the Astros in 1997. The Top 10 Mexican pitchers are listed below.

Table 12-5. Best Pitchers Born in Mexico

Rank	Pitcher (Home)	Team	Season(s)	Career IP	WAR (per 200 IP)	Wins (per season)
1	Fernando Valenzuela (Navojoa)	LA Dodgers Cal Angels Bal Orioles Phi Phillies SD Padres StL Cardinals	1980-1990 1991 1993 1994 1995-1997 1997	2,930.0	37.4 (2.55)	173 (10.2)
2	Teddy Higuera (Los Mochis)	Mil Brewers	1985-1994	1,380.0	30.3 (4.39)	94 (10.4)

Rank	Pitcher (Home)	Team	Season(s)	Career IP	WAR (per 200 IP)	Wins (per season)
3	Ismael Valdez (Ciudad Victoria)	LA Dodgers Chi Cubs Ana Angels Sea Mariners Tex Rangers SD Padres Fla Marlins	1994-2000 2000 2001 2002-2003 2003 2004 2004-2005	1,827.1	24.5 (2.68)	104 (8.7)
4	Esteban Loaiza (Tijuana)	Pit Pirates Tex Rangers Tor Blue Jays Chi White Sox NY Yankees Was Nationals Oak Athletics LA Dodgers Chi White Sox	1995-1998 1998-2000 2000-2002 2003-2004 2004 2005 2006-2007 2007-2008 2008	2,099.0	23.0 (2.19)	126 (9.0)
5	Yovani Gallardo (Penjamillo)	Mil Brewers Tex Rangers Bal Orioles Sea Mariners Cin Reds Tex Rangers	2007-2014 2015 2016 2017 2018 2018	1,816.2	19.2 (1.60)	121 (10.1)
6	Joakim Soria (Monclova)	KC Royals Tex Rangers Det Tigers Pit Pirates KC Royals Chi White Sox Mil Brewers Oak Athletics Ari D-backs Tor Blue Jays	2007-2011 2013-2014 2014-2015 2015 2016-2017 2018 2018 2019-2020 2021 2021	763.0	18.6 (4.88)	36 Wins (2.6) 229 Saves (16.4)
7	Jorge De La Rosa (Monterrey)	Mil Brewers KC Royals Col Rockies Ari D-backs Chi Cubs	2004-2006 2006-2007 2008-2016 2017-2018 2018	1,522.2	14.9 (1.96)	104 (6.9)
8	Francisco Cordova (Cerro Azul)	Pit Pirates	1996-2000	753.2	14.1 (3.75)	42 (8.4)
9	Jesse Flores (Guadalajara)	Chi Cubs Phi Athletics Cle Indians	1942 1943-1947 1950	973.0	13.7 (2.82)	44 (6.3)

Rank	Pitcher (Home)	Team	Season(s)	Career IP	WAR (per 200 IP)	Wins (per season)
10	Armando Reynoso (San Luis Potosi)	Atl Braves Col Rockies NY Mets Ari D-backs	1991-1992 1993-1996 1997-1998 1999-2002	1,079.2	12.3 (2.28)	68 (5.7)

METHODOLOGY: To qualify for inclusion in this table, pitchers had to be of Mexican heritage and born in Mexico. Pitchers are ranked from 1-10 based upon their career Wins Above Replacement (WAR) between 1900-2021. WAR measures a player's value in all facets of the game by deciphering how many more wins he's worth than a replacement-level player at his same position.

LEGEND: Home = the place a pitcher was born in Mexico. Team and season(s) are the teams a pitcher played for and the season(s) they were with each team listed in chronological order. Career IP = career innings pitched. Career WAR = the pitcher's accumulated WAR over his career. Career Wins = the number of wins each pitcher accumulated over his career. Because pitchers had different career lengths, I included two rate measures (WAR per 200 innings pitched and wins per season). Because Joakim Soria was a career reliever, his career saves and save rate per season are included as well. Multiple pitchers missed entire seasons for various reasons. Therefore, those missed seasons don't count as part of the wins per season calculation. Specifically, Fernando Valenzuela missed the 1992 season, Teddy Higuera in 1992, Joakim Soria in 2012, Jesse Flores in 1948 and 1949.

NOTE 1: Fernando Valenzuela is the most accomplished pitcher on this list. Winner of the 1981 Cy Young and Rookie of the Year Awards, he helped lead Los Angeles to the World Championship, beating the Astros, Expos, and Yankees in the postseason. He played a key role in the team's championship run that year, winning a game in each of the three postseason series, including the must-win Game 3 of the World Series when they trailed New York two games to none. Valenzuela was a stalwart in the Dodger rotation throughout the 1980s, as he was named to the NL All-Star team six years in a row from 1981-1986. He capped off his time with Los Angeles by throwing a no-hitter against the Cardinals on June 29, 1990. Dave Stewart of the Oakland Athletics threw one against the Blue Jays the same day – the only time no-hitters were thrown on the same day.

NOTE 2: Francisco Cordova is the other no-hit pitcher listed. On July 12, 1997, he threw a no-hitter against the Astros for the first nine innings of the game, striking out 10 and walking only two for a Game Score of 95. Unfortunately, the Pirates were unable to score, and the game went into extra innings. Cordova had already thrown 121 pitches, so Bucs manager Gene Lamont brought in reliever Ricardo Rincon in the top of the 10th. Rincon kept the no-hitter intact, and the Pirates won in the bottom of the inning on a two-out, three-run homerun by pinch-hitter Mark Smith.

NOTE 3: Many of the impressive pitchers on this list were named as All-Stars during their playing career: Fernando Valenzuela (1981-1986), Teddy Higuera (1986), Esteban Loaiza (2003-2004), Yovani Gallardo (2010), and Joakim Soria (2008 and 2010).

NOTE 4: Mexico has been highly competitive during the World Baseball Classic, reaching the second round in 2013 and 2017, while advancing to the semifinals in 2023. Yovani Gallardo (2013 & 2017), Joakim Soria (2009 & 2017), Esteban Loaiza (2006), and Jorge De La Rosa (2006) were all chosen to be part of the national team during the WBC Tournament.

The Dodgers have been especially adept at courting Korean baseball stars as well. The top two Korean pitchers to play in the major leagues broke in with the Dodgers: The top three Korean pitchers in career Wins Above Replacement (WAR) are listed below.

Table 12-6. Best Pitchers Born in South Korea

Rank	Pitcher (Home)	Team	Season(s)	Career IP	WAR (per 200 IP)	Wins (per season)
1	Hyun Jin Ryu (Incheon)	LA Dodgers " " Tor B. Jays	2013-2014 2016-2019 2020-2021	976.1	18.7 (3.83)	73 (9.1)
2	Chan Ho Park (Gongju)	LA Dodgers Tex Rangers SD Padres NY Mets LA Dodgers Phi Phillies NY Yankees Pit Pirates	1994-2001 2002-2005 2005-2006 2007 2008 2009 2010 2010	1,993.0	18.1 (1.82)	124 (7.3)

Rank	Pitcher (Home)	Team	Season(s)	Career IP	WAR (per 200 IP)	Wins (per season)
3	Byung-Hyun Kim (Gwangju)	Ari D-backs Bos R. Sox Col Rockies Ari D-backs Fla Marlins	1999-2003 2003-2004 2005-2007 2007 2007	841.0	11.1 (2.64)	54 Wins (6.0) 86 Saves (9.6)

METHODOLOGY: To qualify for inclusion in this table, pitchers had to be of Korean heritage and born in South Korea. Pitchers are ranked based upon their career Wins Above Replacement (WAR) between 1900-2021. WAR measures a player's value in all facets of the game by deciphering how many more wins he's worth than a replacement-level player at his same position. Only WAR achieved in the National and American Leagues count for purposes of this ranking. Pitchers needed to have a Career WAR above 10 to be included in this list.

LEGEND: Home = the place a pitcher was born in South Korea. Team and season(s) are the teams they played for and the season(s) they were with each team listed in chronological order. Career IP = career innings pitched. Career WAR = the pitcher's accumulated WAR over his career. Career Wins = the number of wins each pitcher accumulated over his career. Because pitchers had different career lengths, I included two rate measures (WAR per 200 innings pitched and wins per season). Of note, Byung-Hyun Kim was a closer for the first half of his career and was selected to the National League All-Star team in that capacity. Because of this, his career saves and save rate per season are included as well. Hyun Jin Ryu missed the entire 2015 season and only appeared briefly in one game during the 2016 season. Therefore, those missed seasons don't count as part of his wins per season calculation. Ryu is still an active pitcher beyond the 2021 season.

NOTE 1: All three of the impressive pitchers on this list were named as All-Stars during their playing career: Hyun Jin Ryu (2019), Chan Ho Park (2001), and Byung-Hyun Kim (2002). No one on this list threw a no-hitter; however, all three were considered elite pitchers at their peaks. Ryu even finished in second and third place for the Cy Young Award in 2019 and 2020.

NOTE 2: While the players listed have achieved a great deal playing in the Major Leagues, Hyun Jin Ryu got his start in Korean professional baseball playing with the Hanwha Eagles. Ryu racked up 98 wins and had a 2.80 ERA in six seasons in Korea.

NOTE 3: South Korea has had success at the World Baseball Classic, advancing to the semifinal round in 2006 and the final in 2009 before losing to Japan both times. Most recently, the South Korean team has been eliminated during pool play in 2013, 2017, and 2023. All three pitchers have been part of the South Korean team during the World Baseball Classic: Chan Ho Park (2006), Byung-Hyun Kim (2006), and Hyun Jin Ryu (2009).

Hideo Nomo was born in 1968 into a working-class family in Osaka, Japan. When he graduated from high school in 1987, he failed to catch the attention of college and pro scouts in Japan. He wound up pitching for a company-sponsored semi-pro team, where he perfected his corkscrew motion and forkball. He started playing for the Osaka Kintetsu Buffaloes in the Japan Pacific League in 1990 at the age of 21. In his first season he won Rookie of the Year, accumulated 287 strikeouts, achieved a win-loss record of 18-8, and won the league's Most Valuable Player Award. He wound up signing with the Dodgers in February 1995.

Nomo's first game for the Dodgers was May 2, 1995. He pitched five scoreless innings but the Giants wound up winning 4-3 in 15 innings. Nomo also pitched in the 1995 All-Star Game. At the end of his rookie season, Nomo had a 13-6 record, 236 strikeouts and won the Rookie of the Year award. After 12 seasons in the majors, Nomo had a win-loss record of 123-109, an ERA of 4.24, and had struck out 1,918 batters over 1,976 innings, just shy of one per inning on average. He also played a key role in helping Los Angeles qualify for the playoffs in 1995 and 1996 as either the division champion or a wild card entrant.

With a record of 78-46 in the Japan League, Nomo's combined lifetime win-loss record in both Japan and America was 201-155. He was inducted into the Japanese Baseball Hall of Fame in 2014. Since his retirement from baseball, he has mostly been a coach and mentor, mainly with Japan League teams.

The catcher for Hideo's 1996 no-hitter was Mike Piazza, who wound up with 2,127 hits and 427 home runs over his extraordinary 16-season career. Piazza was catcher for two no-hitters during his career – his first was in 1995, when he caught Ramon Martinez's no-hitter with the Dodgers. A Rookie of the Year Award winner and 12-time All-Star, Piazza was inducted into the Hall of Fame in 2016. The New York Mets retired his uniform number, 31, in a ceremony that same year. Piazza has been involved in various endeavors since retirement. He is a mentor and coach for Italian players and is currently serving as the manager of the Italian national baseball team. Piazza is also an owner of an Italian soccer team: A.C. Reggiana, in Italy's third division.

Conclusion

By this point in my book, you have gotten to know me, and have probably discovered far more about no-hitters than you knew before. Through the interviews and analysis I have presented, you have also seen how extraordinarily difficult it is to throw a no-hitter and the overwhelming joy felt by the pitchers and catchers who achieved this rare feat. You have seen it described in their own words, from Hall of Famer Randy Johnson and perennial All-Star Dave Stieb to rookie stars Juan Nieves and Bud Smith. I hope you have enjoyed the stories I presented, as well as learning from my analysis and insights. Like every no-hit game, each chapter is special, and the players involved have their own, unique stories to tell. Every player's remarkable story could fill a book, and I attempted to present their experiences in a concise way, as I extracted the most compelling aspects of their performance, their team, and their individual careers.

The scope of the book expanded significantly as I did my research. For example, as I began my research on Cincinnati pitcher Jim Maloney's no-hitter, I found myself questioning how does that game, and every other no-hitter by a Reds pitcher, rank among the greatest games thrown. I was amazed and pleased to see familiar names and not-so-familiar names among the team's most successful one-game pitchers. I decided to do this for all teams, as the questions surrounding which pitchers threw the best games for each franchise resulted in my doing a statistical analysis for every team.

Because pitchers have stopped staying in games until the bitter end of horrendously long extra-inning games, for those teams who have been around since 1900 or 1901, I created two tables: one which includes all a team's games, and one which limits the number of innings a starting pitcher accumulated to 10 or less. The 10-inning limit was chosen because the longest no-hitters (like Jim Maloney's) were 10 innings. I found the results fascinating, as I was reminded how some team's pitchers dominated their franchise's record books. Much like no-hitters, I also discovered how relatively unknown pitchers have had extraordinary single-game performances that top their team's record books. For those who may be disappointed their favorite team isn't included in Volume I, those teams will all be covered in Volume II.

One other aspect I found interesting as I wrote Jim Maloney's chapter, was that a gentleman named Dolf Luque was tied for the highest Game Score of 10-innings or less by a Reds pitcher. Luque was a big star in the U.S. when he threw his 10-inning shutout against the Braves in 1925. In Cuba, where Luque was born, he had a delirious following. The reason Luque was so wildly popular was that he was Cuban. Again, I was intrigued. As a result, I researched and created a table displaying the 10 best pitchers born in Cuba – Luque comes in at number two, just behind the legendary Luis Tiant. I also created tables for pitchers from Japan, the Dominican Republic, Mexico, and many other nations. Those tables are included in appropriate chapters in both volumes.

I also had a question as I researched Dave Steib's chapter. I wondered how he ranked among the other great pitchers of the 1980s. I was surprised to find that he was ranked at the top of the list of Wins Above Replacement achieved from 1980-1989. I was inspired to research this from every decade from the 1900s to the 2020s. As a result, I created tables identifying the top 12-15 pitchers from each decade. Because the rankings were based on career excellence, there weren't many surprises in those tables; however, they were a great reminder of who the dominant pitchers were during each decade. Some pitchers, like Randy Johnson and Nolan Ryan, were among the top pitchers in more than one decade.

Along the way, individual and team performances caused me to research some specific topics for each no-hitter I wrote about. Which teams have the longest winning streaks to start a season (Juan Nieves' chapter)? Which players have both a World Series Championship and an Olympic Gold Medal (Dave Stieb's chapter)? Who were the winningest pitchers on the worst teams in baseball (Randy Johnson's chapter)? ... And so on. Every chapter has one or more of these "deep dives" into fascinating topics that are unique to the chapter.

Of course, the most important aspect of each of these no-hitters is the story behind them. Most of the chapters in both volumes feature interviews with the no-hit pitchers and catchers. This is what I am most proud of – that I was able to draw upon their generous participation to craft a story that tells not only what happened that day, but what it was like. I also drew upon the wealth of knowledge available in contemporary newspaper reports, extraordinary stories from the Society for Advanced Baseball Research (SABR), and the completely invaluable resources that are baseball-reference.com and stathead.com.

And, as I close this volume, I want to address a burning question that inspired me to begin this book years ago: which no-hitter was the greatest game ever thrown? In this volume, I have explored what I feel are the five most likely candidates:

Was it Max Scherzer's October 2015 no-hitter against the pennant-winning New York Mets where he achieved 17 strikeouts and had the highest Game Score ever achieved in a no-hitter (104)?

Was it Hideo Nomo's September 1996 game against the Colorado Rockies at Coors Field – the best-hitting team ever to be no-hit?

Was it 40-year-old Randy Johnson's May 2004 perfect game against the dominant Atlanta Braves; a game in which he pitched for one of the worst teams in baseball history – the 51-111 Diamondbacks?

Was it Harvey Haddix's 12 innings of perfect ball in May 1959 against the reigning champion Milwaukee Braves – a game which he lost when the Braves scored in the bottom of the 13th inning?

Was it Sandy Koufax's September 1965 perfect game against the Chicago Cubs – a game where he faced down three future Hall of Famers (Ernie Banks, Billy Williams, and Ron Santo)?

Every one of the games rightfully has its own adherents. All of the games, except Koufax's, are covered in detail in Volume 1.

This is why I love baseball so much. While there are so many illuminating statistics, there are also a nearly infinite number of questions that have no definitive answer. Every one of those five no-hitters (and others, too) can rightfully be called "the best ever." Which one is your choice?

I encourage you to continue reading this book in Volume II. The big question for that volume is "which no-hitter is the most unlikely one ever thrown?"

For the record – and while it's extremely close – I believe that Scherzer's 17-strikeout gem just noses out the others as the best ever. I look forward to debating this with you!

Play ball!

Appendix I

Career Ranking of All No-hit Pitchers

Table A-1. No-hit Pitcher Career JAWS Ranking (1900-2021)

Rank	Pitcher	Career JAWS	Team	No-hitter Date	Opponent
1	Walter Johnson	127.0	Washington Senators	7/1/1920	Boston Red Sox
2	Cy Young	120.8	Cleveland Spiders Boston Americans *Boston Red Sox*	9/18/1897 5/5/1904 *6/30/1908*	Cincinnati Reds Phi Athletics *NY Highlanders*
3	Christy Mathewson	88.4	New York Giants New York Giants	7/15/1901 6/13/1905	St Louis Cards Chicago Cubs
4	Tom Seaver	84.7	Cincinnati Reds	6/16/1978	St Louis Cards
5	Randy Johnson	81.3	Seattle Mariners *Arizona D-backs*	6/2/1990 5/18/2004	Detroit Tigers *Atlanta Braves*
6	Warren Spahn	75.8	Milwaukee Braves	9/16/1960 4/28/1961	Phi Phillies SF Giants
7	Bob Gibson	75.2	St Louis Cardinals	8/14/1971	Pit Pirates
8	Phil Niekro	75.1	Atlanta Braves	8/5/1973	SD Padres
9	Bert Blyleven	72.4	Texas Rangers	9/22/1977	Cal Angels
10	Gaylord Perry	71.2	San Francisco Giants	9/17/1968	St. Louis Cards

Rank	Pitcher	Career JAWS	Team	No-hitter Date	Opponent
11	Justin Verlander*	65.6	Detroit Tigers Detroit Tigers Houston Astros	6/12/2007 5/7/2011 9/1/2019	Mil Brewers Tor Blue Jays Tor Blue Jays
12	Ed Walsh	64.1	Chicago White Sox	8/27/1911	Boston Red Sox
13	Nolan Ryan	62.2	California Angels California Angels California Angels California Angels Houston Astros Texas Rangers Texas Rangers	5/15/1973 7/15/1973 9/28/1974 6/1/1975 9/26/1981 6/11/1990 5/1/1991	KC Royals Detroit Tigers Minnesota Twins Bal Orioles LA Dodgers Oak Athletics Tor Blue Jays
14	Clayton Kershaw*	61.1	Los Angeles Dodgers	6/18/2014	Col Rockies
15	Jim Palmer	58.0	Baltimore Orioles	8/13/1969	Oak Athletics
16	Carl Hubbell	57.9	New York Giants	5/8/1929	Pit Pirates
17	Bob Feller	57.5	Cleveland Indians Cleveland Indians Cleveland Indians	4/16/1940 4/30/1946 7/1/1951	Chi White Sox NY Yankees Detroit Tigers
18 (tie)	Roy Halladay	57.4	Philadelphia Phillies *Philadelphia Phillies*	5/29/2010 *10/6/2010*	Florida Marlins *Cincinnati Reds*
18 (tie)	Juan Marichal	57.4	San Francisco Giants	6/15/1963	Houston Astros
20	Kevin Brown	56.5	Florida Marlins	6/10/1997	SF Giants
21	Ted Lyons	55.5	Chicago White Sox	8/21/1926	Boston Red Sox
22	Dazzy Vance	54.8	Brooklyn Dodgers	9/13/1925	Phi Phillies
23 (tie)	Jim Bunning	54.2	Detroit Tigers *Philadelphia Phillies*	7/20/1958 *6/21/1964*	Boston Red Sox *New York Mets*
23 (tie)	Max Scherzer*	54.2	Was Nationals Was Nationals	6/20/2015 10/3/2015	Pit Pirates New York Mets
25	David Cone	52.8	*New York Yankees*	*7/18/1999*	*Montreal Expos*

Rank	Pitcher	Career JAWS	Team	No-hitter Date	Opponent
26	Eddie Cicotte	51.5	Chicago White Sox	4/14/1917	St. Louis Browns
27	Brett Saberhagen	51.0	Kansas City Royals	8/26/1991	Chi White Sox
28	Dave Stieb	50.4	Toronto Blue Jays	9/2/1990	Cle Indians
29	Dennis Eckersley	49.9	Cleveland Indians	5/30/1977	Cal Angels
30	Johan Santanna	48.3	New York Mets	6/1/2012	St. Louis Cards
31	Cole Hamels	48.2	Philadelphia Phillies	7/25/2015	Chicago Cubs
32 (tie)	Sandy Koufax	47.4	Los Angeles Dodgers Los Angeles Dodgers Los Angeles Dodgers *Los Angeles Dodgers*	6/30/1962 5/11/1963 6/4/1964 *9/9/1965*	NY Mets SF Giants Phi Phillies *Chicago Cubs*
32 (tie)	Mark Buehrle	47.4	Chicago White Sox *Chicago White Sox*	4/18/2007 *7/23/2009*	Texas Rangers *Tampa Bay Rays*
34	Dwight Gooden	46.0	New York Yankees	5/14/1996	Seattle Mariners
35	Nap Rucker	45.9	Brooklyn Dodgers	9/5/1908	Boston Braves
36 (tie)	Noodles Hahn	44.3	Cincinnati Reds	7/12/1900	Phi Phillies
36 (tie)	Felix Hernandez	44.3	*Seattle Mariners*	8/15/2012	*Tampa Bay Rays*
38	Jesse Tannehill	44.1	Boston Red Sox	8/17/1904	Chi White Sox
39	Bob Lemon	43.5	Cleveland Indians	6/30/1948	Detroit Tigers
40	Kenny Rogers	42.8	*Texas Rangers*	*7/28/1994*	*Cal Angels*
41	Addie Joss	42.7	Cleveland Indians Cleveland Indians	10/2/1908 4/20/1910	*Chi White Sox* Chi White Sox
42	David Wells	42.4	*New York Yankees*	*5/17/1998*	*Minnesota Twins*

Rank	Pitcher	Career JAWS	Team	No-hitter Date	Opponent
43	George Mullin	41.9	Detroit Tigers	7/4/1912	St. Louis Browns
44	Vida Blue	41.7	Oakland Athletics	9/21/1970	Minnesota Twins
45	Carlos Zambrano	41.1	Chicago Cubs	9/14/2008	Houston Astros
46	Dennis Martinez	41.0	*Montreal Expos*	*7/28/1991*	*LA Dodgers*
47	Charles Bender	40.9	Philadelphia A's	5/12/1910	Cle Indians
48	Lon Warneke	40.2	St. Louis Cardinals	8/30/1941	Cincinnati Reds
49	Jon Lester	39.7	Boston Red Sox	5/19/2008	KC Royals
50	Jack Morris	38.0	Detroit Tigers	4/7/1984	Chi White Sox
51	Catfish Hunter	37.9	*Oakland Athletics*	*5/8/1968*	*Minnesota Twins*
52	Bill Dinneen	37.7	Boston Red Sox	9/27/1905	Chi White Sox
53 (tie)	Jim Maloney	37.5	Cincinnati Reds Cincinnati Reds	8/19/1965 4/30/1969	Chicago Cubs Houston Astros
53 (tie)	Fernando Valenzuela	37.5	Los Angeles Dodgers	6/29/1990	St. Louis Cards
55	Smokey Joe Wood	37.2	Boston Red Sox	7/29/1911	St. Louis Browns
56	Hoyt Wilhelm	36.7	Baltimore Orioles	9/20/1958	NY Yankees
57	John Candelaria	36.4	Pittsburgh Pirates	8/9/1976	LA Dodgers
58	Al Leiter	36.3	Florida Marlins	5/11/1996	Col Rockies
59	Milt Pappas	36.1	Chicago Cubs	9/2/1972	SD Padres
60	Virgil Trucks	35.9	Detroit Tigers Detroit Tigers	5/15/1952 8/25/1952	Was Senators NY Yankees

Rank	Pitcher	Career JAWS	Team	No-hitter Date	Opponent
61	Howard Ehmke	35.8	Boston Red Sox	9/7/1923	Phi Athletics
62 (tie)	Joe Bush	35.5	Philadelphia A's	8/26/1916	Cle Indians
62 (tie)	Dutch Leonard	35.5	Boston Red Sox Boston Red Sox	8/30/1916 6/3/1918	St. Louis Browns Detroit Tigers
64	Sam Jones	35.2	New York Yankees	9/4/1923	Phi Athletics
65	Corey Kluber*	34.4	New York Yankees	5/19/2021	Texas Rangers
66	Ray Caldwell	33.8	Cleveland Indians	9/10/1919	NY Yankees
67	Josh Beckett	33.4	Los Angeles Dodgers	5/25/2014	Phi Phillies
68	Jered Weaver	32.9	Los Angeles Angels	5/2/2012	Minnesota Twins
69	Burt Hooton	32.7	Chicago Cubs	4/16/1972	Phi Phillies
70 (tie)	Rick Wise	32.3	Philadelphia Phillies	6/23/1971	Cincinnati Reds
70 (tie)	Jerry Reuss	32.3	Los Angeles Dodgers	6/27/1980	SF Giants
72 (tie)	Rube Marquard	31.3	New York Giants	4/15/1915	Bro Dodgers
72 (tie)	Sonny Siebert	31.3	Cleveland Indians	6/10/1966	Was Senators
72 (tie)	Derek Lowe	31.3	Boston Red Sox	4/27/2002	TB Devil Rays
75	Larry Dierker	30.1	Houston Astros	7/9/1976	Montreal Expos
76	Claude Hendrix	29.9	Chicago Whales (Federal League)	5/15/1915	Pit Rebels
77	Dean Chance	29.2	Minnesota Twins	8/25/1967	Cle Indians
78	Matt Cain	29.1	*San Francisco Giants*	*6/13/2012*	*Houston Astros*

Rank	Pitcher	Career JAWS	Team	No-hitter Date	Opponent
79	Sal Maglie	28.9	Brooklyn Dodgers	9/25/1956	Phi Phillies
80	Mel Parnell	28.8	Boston Red Sox	7/14/1956	Chi White Sox
81	Hooks Wiltse	28.3	New York Giants	7/4/1908	Phi Phillies
82 (tie)	Jesse Haines	27.3	St. Louis Cardinals	7/17/1924	Boston Braves
82 (tie)	Kevin Millwood	27.3	Philadelphia Phillies	4/27/2003	SF Giants
84	Don Wilson	27.1	Houston Astros Houston Astros	6/18/1967 5/1/1969	Atlanta Braves Cincinnati Reds
85	Ewell Blackwell	26.8	Cincinnati Reds	6/18/1947	Boston Braves
86	Earl Wilson	26.4	Boston Red Sox	6/26/1962	LA Angels
87	Lew Burdette	26.3	Milwaukee Braves	8/18/1960	Phi Phillies
88	George Mogridge	26.2	New York Yankees	4/24/1917	Boston Red Sox
89 (tie)	Fred Toney	26.1	Cincinnati Reds	5/2/1917	Chicago Cubs
89 (tie)	Anibal Sanchez*	26.1	Florida Marlins	9/6/2006	Arizona D-backs
89 (tie)	Ervin Santana	26.1	Los Angeles Angels	7/27/2011	Cle Indians
92	Ken Holtzman	25.8	Chicago Cubs Chicago Cubs	8/19/1969 6/3/1971	Atlanta Braves Cincinnati Reds
93 (tie)	Johnny Vander Meer	25.3	Cincinnati Reds Cincinnati Reds	6/11/1938 6/15/1938	Boston Braves Bro Dodgers
93 (tie)	A.J. Burnett	25.3	Florida Marlins	5/12/2001	SD Padres
95	Dave Stewart	25.2	Oakland Athletics	6/29/1990	Tor Blue Jays
96	Kevin Gross	25.1	Los Angeles Dodgers	8/17/1992	SF Giants

Rank	Pitcher	Career JAWS	Team	No-hitter Date	Opponent
97	Jim Tobin	24.8	Boston Braves	4/27/1944	Bro Dodgers
98 (tie)	Jeff Tesreau	24.4	New York Giants	9/6/1912	Phi Phillies
98 (tie)	Mike Scott	24.4	Houston Astros	9/25/1986	SF Giants
98 (tie)	Scott Erickson	24.4	Minnesota Twins	4/27/1994	Mil Brewers
101 (tie)	Wilson Alvarez	24.2	Chicago White Sox	8/11/1991	Bal Orioles
101 (tie)	Ramon Martinez	24.2	Los Angeles Dodgers	7/14/1995	Florida Marlins
103	Jake Arrieta*	23.8	Chicago Cubs Chicago Cubs	8/30/2015 4/21/2016	LA Dodgers Cincinnati Reds
104	Ken Forsch	23.5	Houston Astros	4/7/1979	Atlanta Braves
105	Chris Bosio	23.4	Seattle Mariners	4/22/1993	Boston Red Sox
106	Bob Forsch	23.3	St. Louis Cardinals St. Louis Cardinals	4/16/1978 9/26/1983	Phi Phillies Montreal Expos
107 (tie)	Frank Smith	23.2	Chicago White Sox Chicago White Sox	9/6/1905 9/20/1908	Detroit Tigers Phi Athletics
107 (tie)	Allie Reynolds	23.2	New York Yankees New York Yankees	7/12/1951 9/28/1951	Cle Indians Boston Red Sox
109	Joel Horlen	23.0	Chicago White Sox	9/10/1967	Detroit Tigers
110	Earl Hamilton	22.9	St. Louis Browns	8/30/1912	Detroit Tigers
111	Hideo Nomo	21.8	Los Angeles Dodgers Boston Red Sox	9/17/1996 4/4/2001	Col Rockies Bal Orioles
112 (tie)	Bill Monbouquette	21.7	Boston Red Sox	8/1/1962	Chi White Sox
112 (tie)	Tim Lincecum	21.7	San Francisco Giants San Francisco Giants	7/13/2013 6/25/2014	SD Padres SD Padres
114 (tie)	Ubaldo Jimenez	21.6	Colorado Rockies	4/17/2010	Atlanta Braves

Rank	Pitcher	Career JAWS	Team	No-hitter Date	Opponent
114 (tie)	Jesse Barnes	21.6	New York Giants	5/7/1922	Phi Phillies
116	Mike Witt	21.5	*California Angels*	*9/30/1984*	*Texas Rangers*
117	Jordan Zimmerman	21.3	Washington Nationals	9/28/2014	Miami Marlins
118 (tie)	Dave Righetti	21.1	New York Yankees	7/4/1983	Boston Red Sox
118 (tie)	Jim Abbott	21.1	New York Yankees	9/4/1993	Cle Indians
120	Darryl Kile	20.6	Houston Astros	9/8/1993	New York Mets
121	Monte Pearson	20.5	New York Yankees	8/27/1938	Cle Indians
122	Bill Singer	20.2	Los Angeles Dodgers	7/20/1970	Phi Phillies
123	John Montefusco	19.8	San Francisco Giants	9/29/1976	Atlanta Braves
124	Jim Bibby	19.6	Texas Rangers	7/30/1973	Oak Athletics
125	Sam Jones	19.2	Chicago Cubs	5/12/1955	Pit Pirates
126 (tie)	Jack Kralick	18.9	Minnesota Twins	8/26/1962	KC Athletics
126 (tie)	Tom Browning	18.9	*Cincinnati Reds*	*9/16/1988*	*LA Dodgers*
128	Clay Buchholz	18.2	Boston Red Sox	9/1/2007	Bal Orioles
129	Francisco Liriano	17.8	Minnesota Twins	5/3/2011	Chi White Sox
130	Ken Johnson	17.6	Houston Colt .45s	4/23/1964	Cincinnati Reds
131	Don Larsen	17.4	*New York Yankees*	*10/8/1956*	*Bro Dodgers*
132	Tex Carleton	17.1	Brooklyn Dodgers	4/30/1940	Cincinnati Reds

Rank	Pitcher	Career JAWS	Team	No-hitter Date	Opponent
133	Eric Milton	17.0	Minnesota Twins	9/11/1999	Anaheim Angels
134	Hisashi Iwakuma	16.9	Seattle Mariners	8/12/2015	Bal Orioles
135 (tie)	Joe Benz	16.4	Chicago White Sox	5/31/1914	Cle Indians
135 (tie)	Steve Busby	16.4	Kansas City Royals Kansas City Royals	4/27/1973 6/19/1974	Detroit Tigers Mil Brewers
135 (tie)	Wade Miley*	16.4	Cincinnati Reds	5/7/2021	Cle Indians
138	Jim Colborn	16.2	Kansas City Royals	5/14/1977	Texas Rangers
139	Don Cardwell	15.9	Chicago Cubs	5/15/1960	St. Louis Cards
140 (tie)	Jimmy Callahan	15.8	Chicago White Sox	9/20/1902	Detroit Tigers
140 (tie)	Chick Fraser	15.8	Philadelphia Phillies	9/18/1903	Chicago Cubs
142	Carl Erskine	14.5	Brooklyn Dodgers Brooklyn Dodgers	6/19/1952 5/12/1956	Chicago Cubs NY Giants
143	Dock Ellis	14.3	Pittsburgh Pirates	6/12/1970	SD Padres
144	Clyde Wright	13.6	California Angels	7/3/11970	Oak Athletics
145	Matt Garza	13.5	Tampa Bay Rays	7/26/2010	Detroit Tigers
146	Len Barker	13.2	*Cleveland Indians*	*5/15/1981*	*Tor Blue Jays*
147 (tie)	Terry Mulholland	12.8	Philadelphia Phillies	8/15/1990	SF Giants
147 (tie)	James Paxton*	12.8	Seattle Mariners	5/8/2018	Tor Blue Jays
149	Dick Bosman	12.7	Cleveland Indians	7/19/1974	Oak Athletics
150	Vern Kennedy	12.6	Chicago White Sox	8/31/1935	Cle Indians

Rank	Pitcher	Career JAWS	Team	No-hitter Date	Opponent
151 (tie)	Rube Foster	12.5	Boston Red Sox	6/21/1916	NY Yankees
151 (tie)	Sean Manaea*	12.5	Oakland Athletics	4/21/2018	Boston Red Sox
153 (tie)	Bob Rhoads	12.3	Cleveland Naps	9/18/1908	Boston Red Sox
153 (tie)	Edwin Jackson	12.3	Arizona Diamondbacks	6/25/2010	Tampa Bay Rays
155	Jim Wilson	12.2	Milwaukee Braves	6/12/1954	Phi Phillies
157	Bob Groom	12.1	St. Louis Browns	5/6/1917	Chi White Sox
157 (tie)	Ed Halicki	12.0	San Francisco Giants	8/24/1975	New York Mets
157 (tie)	Mike Fiers*	12.0	Houston Astros Oakland Athletics	8/21/2015 5/7/2019	LA Dodgers Cincinnati Reds
159 (tie)	Vern Bickford	11.7	Boston Braves	8/11/1950	Bro Dodgers
159 (tie)	Kent Mercker	11.7	Atlanta Braves	4/8/1994	LA Dodgers
161	Dave Davenport	11.6	St. Louis Terriers (Federal League)	9/7/1915	Chicago Whales
162	Carlos Rodon*	11.3	Chicago White Sox	4/14/2021	Cle Indians
163	Paul Dean	11.1	St. Louis Cardinals	9/21/1934	Bro Dodgers
164	Tom Hughes	10.6	Boston Braves	6/16/1916	Pit Pirates
165	Lucas Giolito*	10.3	Chicago White Sox	8/25/2020	Pit Pirates
166	Clyde Shoun	10.0	Cincinnati Reds	5/15/1944	Boston Braves
167	Don Nottebart	9.8	Houston Colt .45s	5/17/1963	Phi Phillies
168	Hod Eller	9.6	Cincinnati Reds	5/11/1919	St. Louis Cards

Rank	Pitcher	Career JAWS	Team	No-hitter Date	Opponent
169	Dick Fowler	9.1	Philadelphia A's	9/9/1945	St. Louis Browns
170	Nick Maddox	9.0	Pittsburgh Pirates	9/20/1907	Bro Superbas
171 (tie)	Edinson Volquez	8.8	Miami Marlins	6/3/2017	Arizona D-backs
171 (tie)	John Means*	8.8	Baltimore Orioles	5/5/2021	Seattle Mariners
173	Bob Moose	8.6	Pittsburgh Pirates	9/20/1969	New York Mets
174	Henderson Alvarez III	8.5	Miami Marlins	9/29/2013	Detroit Tigers
175	Ray Washburn	8.3	St. Louis Cardinals	9/18/1968	SF Giants
176	Cliff Chambers	8.2	Pittsburgh Pirates	5/6/1951	Boston Braves
177 (tie)	Bobby Burke	7.7	Washington Senators	8/8/1931	Boston Red Sox
177 (tie)	Tommy Greene	7.7	Philadelphia Phillies	5/23/1991	Montreal Expos
177 (tie)	Joe Musgrove*	7.7	San Diego Padres	4/9/2021	Texas Rangers
180	Homer Bailey	7.5	Cincinnati Reds Cincinnati Reds	9/28/2012 7/2/2013	Pit Pirates SF Giants
181	Charlie Lea	7.4	Montreal Expos	5/10/1981	SF Giants
182	Bill Dietrich	7.3	Chicago White Sox	6/1/1937	St. Louis Browns
183	Frank Allen	7.2	Pittsburgh Rebels (Federal League)	4/24/1915	StL Terriers
184 (tie)	Charlie Robertson	6.8	*Chicago White Sox*	*4/30/1922*	*Detroit Tigers*
184 (tie)	Tom Phoebus	6.8	Baltimore Orioles	4/27/1968	Boston Red Sox
186	Pete Dowling	5.9	Cleveland Blues	6/30/1901	Mil Brewers

Rank	Pitcher	Career JAWS	Team	No-hitter Date	Opponent
187	Bill Stoneman	5.8	Montreal Expos Montreal Expos	4/17/1969 10/2/1972	Phi Phillies New York Mets
188	Jimmy Lavender	5.4	Chicago Cubs	8/31/1915	NY Giants
189	George Culver	5.2	Cincinnati Reds	7/29/1968	Phi Phillies
190 (tie)	Ed Head	5.0	Brooklyn Dodgers	4/23/1946	Boston Braves
190 (tie)	Dallas Braden	5.0	*Oakland Athletics*	*5/9/2010*	*Tampa Bay Rays*
192	Spencer Turnbull*	4.8	Detroit Tigers	5/18/2021	Seattle Mariners
193	Joe Cowley	4.3	Chicago White Sox	9/19/1986	Cal Angels
194	Weldon Henley	3.9	Philadelphia A's	7/22/1905	St. Louis Browns
195	Juan Nieves	3.4	Milwaukee Brewers	4/15/1987	Bal Orioles
196 (tie)	Bob Keegan	3.2	Chicago White Sox	8/20/1957	Was Senators
196 (tie)	Jonathan Sanchez	3.2	San Francisco Giants	7/10/2009	SD Padres
198	Dave Morehead	3.1	Boston Red Sox	9/16/1965	Cle Indians
199	Alex Main	3.0	Kansas City Packers (Federal League)	8/16/1915	Buffalo Blues
200	Ernie Koob	2.8	St. Louis Browns	5/5/1917	Chi White Sox
201 (tie)	Jeff Pfeffer	2.4	Boston Braves	5/8/1907	Cincinnati Reds
201 (tie)	Ed Lafitte	2.4	Brooklyn Tip-Tops (Federal League)	9/19/1914	KC Packers
203	Jose Jimenez	2.3	St. Louis Cardinals	6/25/1999	Arizona D-backs
204	Bill McCahan	2.1	Philadelphia A's	9/3/1947	Was Senators

Rank	Pitcher	Career JAWS	Team	No-hitter Date	Opponent
205	Philip Humber	1.7	*Chicago White Sox*	*4/21/2012*	*Seattle Mariners*
206	Bo Belinsky	1.4	Los Angeles Angels	5/5/1962	Bal Orioles
207	Tyler Gilbert*	1.1	Arizona Diamondbacks	8/14/2021	SD Padres
208 (tie)	Rex Barney	0.8	Brooklyn Dodgers	9/9/1948	NY Giants
208 (tie)	Chris Heston	0.8	San Francisco Giants	6/9/2015	New York Mets
208 (tie)	Alec Mills*	0.8	Chicago Cubs	9/13/2020	Mil Brewers
211	Bobo Holloman	0.0	St. Louis Browns	5/6/1953	Phi Athletics
212	Bud Smith	-0.3	St. Louis Cardinals	9/3/2001	SD Padres
213	Mike Warren	-0.9	Oakland Athletics	9/29/1983	Chi White Sox
214	Mal Eason	-1.5	Brooklyn Dodgers	7/20/1906	St. Louis Cards
215	Iron Davis	-1.7	Boston Braves	9/9/1914	Phi Phillies
216	Don Black	-1.9	Cleveland Indians	7/10/1947	Phi Athletics

METHODOLOGY: All pitchers who threw a single-pitcher no-hitter between 1900-2021 are listed in order of their Jaffe Wins Above Replacement Score (JAWS). JAWS is a sabermetric baseball statistic developed to evaluate the strength of a player's career and merit for induction into the Baseball Hall of Fame. It is created by averaging a player's career Wins Above Replacement (WAR) with their 7-year peak WAR. WAR measures a player's value in all facets of the game by deciphering how many more wins he's worth than a replacement-level player at his same position. WAR7 = The WAR value of a player's best seven seasons. In the event of a tie, the player who threw the earlier no-hitter is listed first.

LEGEND: Dates are shown as month/day/year (for example, June 12, 2018, is shown as 6/12/2018). Career JAWS represents a player's JAWS for his entire career, including any games played before 1900. An asterisk (*) next to a player's name indicates the player was active in 2022, with a strong probability his JAWS will increase further. *Italicized no-hitters are perfect games.* Team names or home cities are occasionally abbreviated to conserve space:

Bal = Baltimore
Bro = Brooklyn
Cal = California
Cards = Cardinals
Chi = Chicago
Cle = Cleveland
Col = Colorado
D-backs = Diamondbacks
KC = Kansas City
LA = Los Angeles
Mil = Milwaukee
NY = New York
Oak = Oakland
Phi = Philadelphia
Pit = Pittsburgh
SD = San Diego
SF = San Francisco
StL = St. Louis
TB = Tampa Bay
Tor = Toronto
Was = Washington

About the Author

Kevin Hurd grew up in the town of Los Altos, California, a suburb of San Francisco in an area now known as "Silicon Valley." Kevin is a 1975 graduate of Homestead High School in Cupertino. He attended nearby De Anza Community College from 1975-1977 and then transferred to California Polytechnic State University in San Luis Obispo, where he graduated in 1979 with a bachelor's degree in business administration. While working full-time as an Air Force Reserve officer, he earned his master's in business administration degree with a specialization in aviation from Embry-Riddle Aeronautical University in 2000.

Kevin has been an avid San Francisco Giants fan since 1965, and he estimates he attended around 20 games from 1965-1982. While he enjoyed every one of them, two games stood out in his memory. As a nine-year-old fan in 1966, he saw legendary Giant Willie McCovey hit three home runs – including a walk-off blast in the bottom of the 10th inning – in a 6-4 win versus the New York Mets. His other favorite game was witnessing Ed Halicki's 1975 no-hitter at Candlestick Park.

That game, in part, inspired him later in life to research and write about no-hitters. Halicki's unforgettable no-hitter is featured in Chapter 5 of Volume I. Included in that chapter is Kevin's interview with Halicki himself. Understandably, the Giants seasons he has enjoyed the most have been the Word Series championship years of 2010, 2012, and 2014.

Sports have always been a big part of Kevin's life. He was a standout defensive middle guard on the Homestead High School football team, achieving Honorable Mention All-League status in the highly competitive Santa Clara Valley Athletic League. He also excelled at track and field as a high school discus thrower, being voted the Most Valuable Player on his team during his junior year. Additionally, Kevin was an accomplished javelin thrower in college. During his sophomore year at De Anza, he finished in fifth place in the Northern California Junior College Track and Field Finals.

Apart from his athletic success and his lifelong interest in baseball, Kevin crafted a very successful and personally rewarding 30-year Air Force career. After graduating from Officer Training School at Lackland Air Force Base, Texas, in 1984, he attended Undergraduate Navigator Training, followed by Advanced Navigator Training in the KC-135, where he was the top graduate in his class. Throughout his career, Kevin served with distinction as a KC-135 (air refueling tanker) and RC-135 (strategic reconnaissance aircraft) navigator and staff officer, retiring at the rank of lieutenant colonel in 2014.

During his Air Force career, Kevin was called upon to fly combat and combat support missions while deployed to Saudi Arabia during the 1991 Gulf War and to the Mediterranean in support of the 1999 Kosovo War. Kevin was awarded numerous medals during his career, including the Air Force Meritorious Service Medal for meritorious service to the United States, and the Air Medal on eight separate occasions for acts of heroism or meritorious achievement while participating in aerial flight. While he admits his wartime service was demanding, the mission he recalls as being the most stressful was while he and his crew were en route to Italy as they deployed in support of Kosovo operations. His aircraft stalled over the North Atlantic Ocean and rapidly fell 23,000 feet before the crew recovered control. This necessitated an emergency return and landing at a Canadian air base and a subsequent ground evacuation for the crew and all 50 passengers onboard. Kevin received an Aerial Achievement Medal for his actions that day.

Kevin had a post-Air Force stint working six years in security operations at the Western Currency Facility in Fort Worth, Texas, before deciding to devote his time and energy to writing. More specifically, he was inspired to write about baseball, a topic he has been passionate about his entire life. "From Randy Johnson to Dallas Braden" is Kevin's first book of what he hopes will be many more.

Kevin lives near Fort Worth with his lovely wife Doris. They have been married for 34 years and have two wonderful adult daughters, Christine and Catherine.